MARSILIUS OF INGHEN

STUDIES IN THE HISTORY OF CHRISTIAN THOUGHT

EDITED BY

HEIKO A. OBERMAN, Tucson, Arizona

IN COOPERATION WITH
HENRY CHADWICK, Cambridge
JAROSLAV PELIKAN, New Haven, Conn.
BRIAN TIERNEY, Ithaca, N.Y.
ARJO VANDERJAGT, Groningen

VOLUME L

M. J. F. M. HOENEN

MARSILIUS OF INGHEN

MARSILIUS OF INGHEN

DIVINE KNOWLEDGE IN LATE MEDIEVAL THOUGHT

BY

M. J. F. M. HOENEN

E.J. BRILL
LEIDEN • NEW YORK • KÖLN
1993

This book has been published with financial support from the Netherlands organization for scientific research (NWO) and from the Royal Netherlands Academy of Arts and Sciences (KNAW).

The paper in this book meets the guidelines for permanence and durability of the Committee on Production Guidelines for Book Longevity of the Council on Library Resources.

B
765
.M3436
1992

Library of Congress Cataloging-in-Publication Data

Hoenen, M.J.F.M., 1957-
    Marsilius of Inghen : divine knowledge in late medieval thought / by M.J.F.M. Hoenen.
       p.   cm. — (Studies in the history of Christian thought, ISSN 0081-8607 ; v. 50)
    Includes bibliographical references and index.
    ISBN 9004095632 (acid-free paper)
    1. Marsilius, of Inghen, d. 1396—Contributions in concept of divine knowledge. 2. God—Omniscience—History of doctrines—Middle Ages, 600-1500. I. Marsilius, of Inghen, d. 1396. Selections. English. 1992. II. Title. III. Series.
B765.M3436 1992
231'.4—dc20
                                                                            92-29893
                                                                            CIP

ISSN 0081-8607
ISBN 90 04 09563 2

© Copyright 1993 by E.J. Brill, Leiden, The Netherlands

All rights reserved. No part of this publication may be reproduced, translated, stored in a retrieval system, or transmitted in any form or by any means, electronic, mechanical, photocopying, recording or otherwise, without prior written permission of the publisher.

Authorization to photocopy items for internal or personal use is granted by E.J. Brill provided that the appropriate fees are paid directly to Copyright Clearance Center, 27 Congress Street, SALEM MA 01970, USA. Fees are subject to change.

PRINTED IN THE NETHERLANDS

TABLE OF CONTENTS

Preface XI
List of abbreviations XIV

1. INTRODUCTION 1
   A pivotal problem in Western thinking 1
      Divine knowledge 2
      The obviousness of God's knowledge 3
      Divine knowledge before and after the Middle Ages 4
   The life of Marsilius 7
   Marsilius and late medieval thinking
   1. Nominalism 11
      Fifteenth- and sixteenth-century sources 11
      Nominalism and the developments in the
      fourteenth century 13
      Marsilius and the *moderni* 14
   2. *Commentator Aristotelis* 16
      The influence of Buridan 16
      Aristotle and natural reason 17
   3. The commentary on the Sentences and its sources 19
   Some methodological remarks 22

2. ARGUMENTS FOR DIVINE KNOWLEDGE 25
   The argument from immateriality 25
   The argument from perfection 26
   The argument from causality 27
   Marsilius of Inghen 29
      The argument from perfection 29
      God's knowledge as perfection 30
      The argument from causality 31
      God's causality 31
      God's modes of knowledge 32
      The relation between God's knowledge and God's essence 33

3. DIVINE ATTRIBUTES 35
   Introduction: Thomas Aquinas 35
   Knowledge as an attribute: positions in the period 1280-1310
   1. Unity vs. plurality 39
      Henry of Ghent 40
      Godfrey of Fontaines 41

    2. Duns Scotus 42
        The formal distinction between the attributes 43
        Infinity leaves the formal distinction intact 44
        The distinction precedes knowledge, and is not constituted
        by it 44
        The formal distinction and God's unity 45
    3. Thomistic criticism 45
  William of Ockham 46
        Criticism of Scotus's formal distinction 47
        Criticism of Henry of Ghent 49
        The position of Ockham 50
        The attribute as (real) perfection 50
        The attribute as (conceptual) predicate in the human mind 51
        The criticism by John Lutterell 52
        The criticism by the papal committee 53
        Robert Holcot 54
  Marsilius of Inghen 56
        Attributional *ratio* vs. attributional perfection 57
        The attributional perfections in God 57
        The attributional *rationes* in the human mind 60

4. GOD'S KNOWLEDGE OF CREATION 63
  Introduction 63
  Aristotle 65
  Arabian philosophy 66
    Avicenna 66
    Averroes 71
  Duns Scotus 75
    Criticism of the argument from causality 76
    God's knowledge is non-reflective 78
    Criticism of other views 79
    The relation between God and the thing known 80
  Some controversial issues 84
    1. Stages in God 84
    2. God can know things without ideas 85
    3. The object of God's knowledge 86
    4. The production of the thing as intelligible being 88
  William of Ockham 89
    Ockham on Averroes 90
    Ockham on Thomas Aquinas 91
    Ockham on Duns Scotus 94

Ockham's alternative	95
How does God know the creatures?	96
Peter Aureoli: the arguments from infinity	98
Gregory of Rimini	102
Ways of knowledge	105
Marsilius of Inghen	107
Marsilius's interpretation of Aristotle and Averroes	108
Arguments for God's knowledge of the creatures	109
Two problems	112
1. God's knowledge of evil	112
2. Provability of God's infinite power	114
2.1 The unprovable infinite effective power of God	114
2.2 The provable infinite intrinsic power of God	116
Marsilius's response to Peter Aureoli	117
The distinction between primary and secondary object	117
The argument from infinity	118

5. DIVINE IDEAS 121
    Thomas Aquinas 121
        1. The relation between thing and idea 123
        2. Ideas of matter and accidents 124
        3. Ideas of particulars 124
    Duns Scotus 125
        The function of the ideas 126
        Which things are correlated with ideas? 128
        Ontological status of the known in God 130
        Criticism of Henry of Ghent 131
    The influence of Scotus: followers and critics 132
    William of Ockham 135
        Which things are correlated with ideas? 138
        The ontological status of the ideas 138
        John Lutterell and the papal committee 139
        Robert Holcot and Adam Wodeham 140
    Marsilius of Inghen 141
        Introduction 141
        Properties of the divine ideas 145
        1. What ideas are not 147
        2. What ideas are 148
        Reaction to the views of some other theologians 151
        Marsilius's criticism of Ockham 153
        The position of Marsilius 154

The ideas are neither really nor formally distinct 155
The ideas are *extrinsece et obiectivaliter* distinct 156

6. DIVINE FOREKNOWLEDGE AND FUTURE CONTINGENTS.
FIRST PART: THE PERIOD 1250-1330 157
The main sources 159
    Aristotle 159
    Augustine 162
    Boethius 162
    Anselm 164
    The literature on the fallacies 165
Thomas Aquinas 166
Semantic aspects 172
    The necessity of God's knowledge 172
    The immutability of God's knowledge 173
Duns Scotus 175
    God does not know future contingents by means of ideas 175
    God does not know the contingent through his eternity 176
    The position of Scotus 177
    First interpretation 177
    Second interpretation 178
    The two interpretations and the first Scotists 178
    The mixed position of Antonius Andreas and
    Robert Cowton 179
    The contingency of God's knowledge according to Scotus ... 181
    Contingency and certainty 182
    Contingency and immutability 183
William of Ockham 184
    Setting the problem 184
    Ockham's criticism of other views 185
    Veritas determinata in contingent propositions
    about the future 187
    Contingency and (im)mutability of God's knowledge 189
    Rules on the (im)mutability of God's knowledge in
    the strict sense 192

7. DIVINE FOREKNOWLEDGE AND FUTURE CONTINGENTS.
SECOND PART: THE PERIOD 1330-1400 195
Gregory of Rimini 196
    Criticism of other positions 198
    The position of Gregory of Rimini 201

Certainty and contingency 202
The logico-semantic approach 202
    Criticism of Thomas Aquinas 204
The influence of man on divine knowledge 208
    The (im)mutability of divine knowledge 212
Marsilius of Inghen 215
    Introduction 215
    Definition of God's foreknowledge 216
    The object of God's foreknowledge 217
    The contingency of the future 218
    The commentaries on Aristotle: Marsilius's criticism
    of Plato and Bradwardine 218
    The commentary on the Sentences: contingency
    and God as the cause of sin 221
    Veritas (in)determinata in propositions about the future 223
    How does God know future contingents? 224
    Contingency and certainty: the semantic approach 227
Modality and (im)mutability of God's foreknowledge 228
    Propositions about the (im)mutability of knower and known 230
Man's influence on divine knowledge 231
    The causality of human will: response to Adam Wodeham ... 232

8. SYNTHESIS AND EVALUATION 235
Theological and philosophical framework 236
Developments between 1250 and 1400 237
    1. Does God know creation? Reaction to Aristotle and
    Averroes, ca. 1255-1290. 239
    2. Unity vs. plurality. Influence of Henry of Ghent,
    ca. 1280-1332/43 241
    3. Renewed reflection on the status of science
    from ca. 1298 242
    4. Logico-semantic approach, from ca. 1317 (England)
    and ca. 1343 (Paris) 244
Marsilius and the development of the main views
on divine knowledge 246
    Thomas Aquinas and Marsilius of Inghen 247
    Duns Scotus and Marsilius of Inghen 249
    William of Ockham and Marsilius of Inghen 250
    Other influences 252
    Marsilius as *modernus* 253

Bibliography 255
    Reference works 255
    Primary sources 255
        1. Manuscripts 255
        2. Printed sources 256
    Secondary literature 260

Index of manuscripts 271
Index of names 272
    Ancient, medieval, and early modern authors 272
    Modern authors 275
Index of subjects and places 279

PREFACE

The idea for an extensive study on Marsilius of Inghen, on whose work no monograph had been published since 1949, was conceived in 1983-1984, during my stay at the Tübingen *Institut für Spätmittelalter und Reformation*, then under the direction of Professor Heiko Oberman. My colleague Manuel Santos-Noya and I had started preparations for a new critical edition of Marsilius's most monumental work, his commentary on the *Sentences*. I felt that this edition needed to be complemented by a thorough study of the historical and philosophical background of Marsilius's thought, based on the wealth of new evidence on fourteenth-century developments that has become available in recent years. One of the aims of this study, as I saw it, should be to situate Marsilius in the philosophy and theology of his days. As for my particular approach, it did not take me long to choose the problem of divine knowledge, partly because this subject had always had a special attraction for me, but also and in particular because it touches on so many aspects of theology and philosophy in the Middle Ages.

This book would not have been possible without the support of several persons and institutions. In the past couple of years, the *Royal Netherlands Academy of Arts and Sciences* (KNAW) has generously provided me with financial support as a Research Fellow. The *Netherlands Organisation for Scientific Research* (NWO) kindly took care of the expenses required for translating the manuscript. To these institutions I express my sincere thanks. I also want to thank the members of the *Institut für philosophische Grundfragen* at the University of Tübingen, with whom I have been collaborating on the edition of Marsilius's commentary on the *Sentences* since 1989. In particular I am grateful to the Director, Professor Georg Wieland. The Institute provided the setting for a year of fruitful research and writing. The final draft of this book was conducted during my stay at the *Institute for Research in the Humanities* at the University of Wisconsin. I thank all members, and in particular Professor William Courtenay, Professor David Lindberg, and Loretta Freiling, for their unfailing helpfulness, and for all they did to make my stay so pleasant and memorable in every respect.

Of the many people with whom, over the years, I had the pleasure to engage in stimulating philosophical discussions, and whose kind hospitality I have enjoyed on countless occasions, I mention in particular Zenon Kaluza, Olaf Pluta, Manuel Santos-Noya, Manfred Schulze, and Josef Schneider. Blake Billings, Mathew Kramer, Steven Nadler, and Pieter Seuren read parts of the manuscript and made many helpful comments. I am indebted to them for the many improvements they made possible. Finally, I owe a particular word of thanks to my colleague and friend from Leiden University, Jan Sleutels, who took it upon him to translate the entire manuscript. Without his tireless support, his ingenuity, and his flexibility, this book would never have been finished in time.

I would also like to thank Professor Heiko A. Oberman, editor of *Studies in the History of Christian Thought*, for accepting this volume as part of the series.

Nijmegen, August 1992

LIST OF ABBREVIATIONS

AHDLMA	*Archives d'Histoire Doctrinale et Littéraire du Moyen Age*
BFSMA	Bibliotheca Franciscana Scholastica Medii Aevi
BGPhThMA	Beiträge zur Geschichte der Philosophie und Theologie des Mittelalters
BPhM	*Bulletin de Philosophie Médiévale*
CCSL	Corpus Christianorum Series Latina
CoSPhR	Cornell Studies in the Philosophy of Religion
CUP	*Chartularium Universitatis Parisiensis*
DS	*Dictionnaire de spiritualité*
ed. Leon.	Editio Leonina (Thomas Aquinas)
ed. Vat.	Editio Vaticana (John Duns Scotus)
FcS	*Franciscan Studies*
FZPhTh	*Freiburger Zeitschrift für Philosophie und Theologie*
FzS	*Franziskanische Studien*
HWdPh	*Historisches Wörterbuch der Philosophie*
JHI	*Journal of the History of Ideas*
LThK	*Lexikon für Theologie und Kirche*
Med. Stud.	*Mediaeval Studies*
MM	Miscellanea Mediaevalia
MPhP	*Mediaevalia Philosophica Polonorum*
OPh	Opera Philosophica (William of Ockham)
OTh	Opera Theologica (William of Ockham)
RThAM	*Recherches de Théologie Ancienne et Médiévale*
ScG	*Summa contra gentiles (Thomas Aquinas)*
SPhHPh	Studies in Philosophy and the History of Philosophy
STGM	Studien und Texte zur Geistesgeschichte des Mittelalters
STheol	*Summa theologiae (Thomas Aquinas)*
ThWzNT	*Theologisches Wörterbuch zum Neuen Testament*
VKHUTMG	Veröffentlichungen der Kommission für die Herausgabe ungedruckter Texte aus der mittelalterlichen Geisteswelt

Throughout the book, passages which Marsilius borrowed *verbatim* from other authors are indicated by *italics*.

CHAPTER ONE

INTRODUCTION

A PIVOTAL PROBLEM IN WESTERN THINKING

Marsilius of Inghen († 1396) is attracting the attention of a rapidly growing number of researchers today. Prepared by the important studies of Ritter, Maier, and Möhler, and more recently developed in the works of Markowski and Bos, Marsilius's position in the philosophical and theological climate of the later Middle Ages is now becoming fairly well delineated.[1] The picture of Marsilius which emerges from the literature is that of a universal scholar and prolific writer whose works addressed virtually all topics occupying the thought of his time. His writings constitute a compendium of late medieval intellectual life. He assimilated both thirteenth-century and fourteenth-century views, working them into a characteristic blend that became known after his death as the *via marsiliana*. Although Marsilius's theology is generally reckoned to belong to nominalism, his theology and metaphysics were in several respects 'pre-Ockhamite', as noted by Ritter. This observation has been confirmed by the work of Möhler and several recent studies.[2]

The present study will address in particular Marsilius's view of divine knowledge, placing it in the historical and systematical context of the thirteenth and fourteenth centuries. This study will in fact be the first in the literature on Marsilius to examine the present topic from this perspective. Our aim is to assess the extent to which Marsilius belonged to the line of so-called 'modern' thinkers that included Ockham († 1347), Adam Wodeham († 1358), and Gregory of Rimini († 1358), and in what manner and degree he distanced himself from this line. Our second aim will be to inquire which aspects of divine knowledge Marsilius handled philosophico-*metaphysically*, and which he handled philosophico-*semantically*.

A careful examination of the problem of divine knowledge is particularly well suited for gaining new insight into Marsilius's position in the scientific world of the late Middle Ages. Three areas of interest stand out in this context. First, divine knowledge constitutes a classical problem that had already been posed by philosophers as early as the fifth century B.C. Important Western theologians such as Augustine and Anselm († 1109) wrote treatises on the

---

[1] These studies are listed in the bibliography below. For a complete inventory of works on Marsilius, see my 'Marsilius von Inghen, Bibliographie. Appendix zu der geplanten Edition der wichtigsten Werke des Marsilius von Inghen', *BPhM* 31 (1989), 150-167; 32 (1990), 191-195.

[2] We shall come back to this point in the final chapter.

subject. As the reading of Peter Lombard's († 1160) *Sentences* became institutionalized at the universities, which in Paris and Oxford happened in the first half of the thirteenth century, divine knowledge was discussed by virtually every theologian in his commentary on this work. This means we have an exceptionally rich stock of material, ideally suited for historically situating a fourteenth-century thinker in the context of his own time as well as in that of the older traditions.

Secondly, the topic of divine knowledge finds itself at the crossroads of various questions in metaphysics and theology, as well as in ethics, logic, and semantics. This means that it opens up a broad field of investigation that is especially fruitful for classifying and determining a thinker's position.

Finally, important to the historical context was the influence of the three major views which had emerged by the turn of the fourteenth century, viz., that of Thomas Aquinas († 1274), that of Scotus († 1308), and that of Ockham, each of which was to become characteristic of a certain school of thought, and was acknowledged as such by contemporary theologians. This means that Marsilius, as a fourteenth-century theologian, had three different theoretical solutions to reckon with: whether he ignored them or based his own position on one of them, it was impossible to remain neutral. It may reasonably be presumed that Marsilius carefully worked out his own stand on the issue in this manner. This makes the historian's task of classifying Marsilius's position much easier.

Divine knowledge

Divine knowledge was understood as the knowledge God has of himself and of his creatures — to which we must add, however, that it was sometimes denied that God has knowledge of things other than himself. The reasons that are usually mentioned for attributing knowledge to God are his immateriality, his perfection, and his position and status as the first, ordering principle of reality. In subsequent chapters, this third aspect will prove to be of special importance. The principle that gives order and dynamism to reality must have knowledge of what is so structured. This already suggests that God's knowledge is not an isolated property; rather, it is related to his will and to his power of creation, be it *ex nihilo* or otherwise. Reality is arranged according to a rational scheme originating in the mind of the first principle. Foreknowledge and providence are therefore related issues: the latter is a concrete and practical expression of the first.

It should be clear that this view raises questions about a number of *metaphysical* assumptions: what is the relation between immateriality and intellect, and how can a perfect principle have knowledge of something other than itself without being dependent upon the object of knowledge? If God's knowledge of created being includes the free acts of man, then specifically *ethical* questions arise. Is it possible for man to act differently from the way foreseen by God? Are we still responsible for our actions even if God has foreknowledge of them? Questions like these become particularly pressing if it is further assumed that God's knowledge is eternal and unchangeable. Here we feel that our conception of man as freely disposing of himself and of reality clashes, or at least sits uncomfortably, with the idea that reality is eternally and immutably given to the mind of God.

Finally, questions like the above also have their *logical* and *semantic* counterparts. What to think of assertions about contingent events being true before the events have actually happened? Is an assertion such as 'Peter will sin' true even before Peter actually commits a sin, and if so, can Peter still be said to sin freely? If, on the other hand, the assertion is not true before he commits a sin, then how can God know that Peter will sin? Is there only *one* meaning to hypothetical expressions such as, 'If God knows that Peter will sin, then Peter will necessarily sin', or can they be construed in more than one way?

The obviousness of God's knowledge

In the period with which we are concerned here, the received view among theologians was that God has perfect knowledge of his creatures, including perfect knowledge of their future free acts. To the medieval mind the idea was so evident that it was simply part of the commonsense, and was doubted by virtually no one. Its obviousness ultimately derived from the Scripture, self-evident as it was taken to be, where divine omniscience is expressed in the Creator-God's personal, caring relation to his creation, and his care for man in particular.[3] The biblical vision is continued in the works of the Fathers, where providence is associated in particular with the notion of creation. Interesting in this connection are Origen's († ca. 254) attempts to give a decisive proof of God's immateriality and intellectuality.[4]

The degree to which the biblical notion of God as Creator was entrenched in the work of the theologians we shall examine can hardly be overestimated. This entrenchment is perfectly understandable, given that the composition of a commentary on the Scripture was a requirement within the theological curriculum of the day. Moreover, the duality of cause and care entered deeply into their private lives as well, which does indeed seem to be a precondition

---

[3] On divine providence in the Scripture, see *ThWzNT*, s.v. 'προνοέω, πρόνοια' (Behm, Würthwein); *LThK*, 2th ed., s.v. 'Vorsehung' (J. Schmid). See also G. von Rad, *Weisheit in Israel*, Neukirchen-Vluyn ³1985, 189-228.

[4] For a discussion of the patristic notion of providence, see L. Scheffczyk, *Schöpfung und Vorsehung*, ed. M. Schmaus and A. Grillmeier, Freiburg-Basel-Wien 1963 (Handbuch der Dogmengeschichte, 2/2a), 30-70 (contains bibliographical references). For Origen, see the text quoted in Ph. Böhner and E. Gilson, *Christliche Philosophie von ihren Anfängen bis Nikolaus von Cues*, Paderborn ³1954, 61-63.

for a theological idea to become self-evident. It was a personal duty for the ordained to observe the *breviarium*, whose prayers included psalm texts voicing the Creator's care for his creatures, assuring the creatures that they may trust him.[5] This personal prayer, which bore the character of an objective value and obligation, surely contributed to the fact that the biblical image of God became firmly rooted in the commonsense and spontaneous experience of the theologian. It can thus be assumed that the *sententiarius*, who according to custom invoked the Holy Spirit's inspiration before starting his lectures (the so-called 'divini nominis invocatio'), lived in the awareness that God was able to grant him this mercy, and thus, we may surmise, that God has knowledge.

Although God's knowledge is also mentioned in the secular philosophical literature of the time, it is clear from the above that it was omniscience as a *religious conviction* that was the *self-evident starting point* of reflection. The underpinning of this religious evidence, however, was usually sought by means of philosophical argument. As we shall see later, the disagreements which came to the fore were located precisely at the philosophical level, and not at that of theology. Faith taught that God was omniscient, thus providing both the starting point and the goal of philosophical reflection.

Divine knowledge before and after the Middle Ages

The notion of an omniscient God was not restricted to the Scripture and the works of the Fathers. Both before the Middle Ages, in the non-Christian culture of Antiquity, and after medieval times, the deity's knowledge was a subject of constant speculation, as indeed it still is. We shall briefly review some examples.

One of the first to hold that the principle of reality is intelligent was the Greek thinker Diogenes of Apollonia (second half of the fifth century B.C.). He believed that the air is divine, that it has knowledge, gives order to all things, and that it rules over everything.[6]

A more differentiated view of great historical moment is found in Plato († 348/7 B.C.). In the *Timaeus*, he distinguished between the ways the demiurge, a transcendent spirit, takes care of the superlunar and sublunar spheres. Although the deity rules all things by a single divine law, only the superlunar is created immediately by him. The production of (mutable) sublunar things is delegated to the creatures of the superlunar sphere.[7]

---

[5] On the medieval breviary, see P. Salmon, *L'office divin. Histoire de la formation du bréviaire*, Paris 1959 (Lex orandi, 27); id., *L'office divin au Moyen Age. Histoire de la formation du bréviaire du IXe au XVIe siècle*, Paris 1967 (Lex orandi, 43); *Lexikon des Mittelalters*, s.v. 'Brevier' (Th.A. Schnitker and D. v. Huebner; with bibliography).

[6] A. Laks, *Diogène d'Apollonie. La dernière cosmologie présocratique*, Villeneuve d'Ascq 1983 (Cahiers de philologie, 9), 33-55, and 102-105.

[7] A.P. Bos, *Providentia divina. The Theme of Divine 'pronoia' in Plato and Aristotle*,

A similar distinction between levels of providence recurred in the (pseudo-?) Aristotelian treatise *De mundo* and in the work of Alexander of Aphrodisias (ca. 200 after Christ). According to the author of *De mundo*, divine providence is also active in the sublunar sphere, but much more inefficiently than in the superlunar sphere. The closer to the deity, the more intensive is the structuring effect of divine providence. Alexander of Aphrodisias also endorsed the view that divine care extends to the sublunar level, but only as far as the level of kinds. He thus sought to evade the problem of how the deity can simultaneously take care of an infinity of individuals, and how to account for the fact that some individuals are wronged.[8]

A different and more radical line of development is found in the Stoics (ca. 300 B.C. - 250 A.D.). Here divine providence is connected with universal causality: providence now oozes through into even the smallest detail. The entire universe is structured by the immanent divine *logos*. Chance in the sense of an indeterminate event is simply ruled out.[9]

Arguably the most interesting opinion in Antiquity was that of Proclus († 485). In more than one respect, his characterization of divine knowledge matches descriptions found in the late Middle Ages. Proclus sought to steer a middle course between, on the one hand, the peripatetic view of Alexander of Aphrodisias and others that the deity does not know the contingent and the individual, a view which was unacceptable to him, and on the other hand, the Stoics' claim that the deity knows everything, and that all things happen of necessity. According to Proclus, the deity has knowledge of everything, including contingent events, but without annihilating contingency as such. Nor does this affect the deity's necessity. The contingent is not known through the contingent itself, but through the deity's own nature. The deity thus knows the contingent in a necessary manner, and the mutable in an immutable manner. Arguing along these lines, Proclus attempted to hold on to perfect divine providence, as well as to the contingency of the world. In this respect his starting point is comparable to that of medieval Christian writers, who were also looking for a happy medium between the all-pervasive

---

Assen-Amsterdam 1976, 19f.

[8] On the notion of providence in *De mundo*, see P. Moraux, *d'Aristote à Bessarion. Trois exposés sur l'histoire et la transmission de l'Aristotélisme Grec*, Les Presses de l'Université Laval 1970 (Les conférences Charles de Koninck), 56-57. The authenticity of *De mundo* has been discussed most recently by A.P. Bos, 'Greek Philosophical Theology and the *De mundo*', *On and Off the Beaten Track. Studies in the History of Platonism*, ed. T.G. Sinnige, Nijmegen 1985, 1-30. For the opinion advocated by Alexander of Aphrodisias, see R.W. Sharples, 'Alexander of Aphrodisias on Divine Providence: Two Problems', *The Classical Quarterly* 32 (1982), 198-211; id., 'Alexander of Aphrodisias: Scholasticism and Innovation', *Aufstieg und Niedergang der römischen Welt*, Teil II Bd. 36/2, ed. W. Haase, Berlin 1987, S. 1176-1243, esp. 1216-1218 (with bibliography on pp. 1226-1243).

[9] H. Dörrie, 'Der Begriff 'Pronoia' in Stoa und Platonismus', *FZPhTh* 24 (1977), 60-87; M.L. Colish, *The Stoic Tradition from Antiquity to the Early Middle Ages. I: Stoicism in Classical Latin Literature*, Leiden ²1990, 31-35 (with bibliographical references).

providence of God and the freedom and responsibility of the individual person.[10]

After the Middle Ages, the problem of divine knowledge recurred frequently, as in the exchanges on human freedom and divine providence between Erasmus († 1536) and Luther († 1546), and between the Dominican Bañez († 1604) and the Jesuit De Molina († 1600).[11] Other well-known examples are the discussions on the subject by Spinoza († 1677) in his *Korte verhandeling* and by Leibniz († 1716) in his *Theodicy*. Also, a separate part in Baumgarten's († 1762) *Metaphysics* was devoted to the attributes of the divine intellect.[12]

In our time, the problem of divine knowledge is discussed most frequently in its logical dimensions, particularly in the English literature.[13] It is worth noting that some of the modern opinions correspond quite closely to positions discussed in the Middle Ages. In an influential paper from 1962 by Arthur N. Prior, for instance, the suggestion is put forward that it is impossible for an omniscient God to know a future contingent fact, as there is nothing in (present) reality to justify his knowledge of the fact. Prior is here endorsing a view that was attributed by Ockham to Aristotle.[14] Nelson Pike (1970), on

---

[10] Proclus Diadochus, *Tria opuscula*, ed. H. Boese, Berlin 1960 (Quellen und Studien zur Geschichte der Philosophie, 1), *De decem dubitationes circa providentiam*, q. 2 par. 8, 14-17. This treatise was translated into Latin in 1280 by William of Moerbeke, see ibid., XI. On Proclus, see F.P. Hager, 'Proklos und Alexander von Aprodisias über ein Problem der Lehre von der Vorsehung', *Kephalaion. Studies in Greek Philosophy and its Continuation*, ed. J. Mansfeld and L.M. de Rijk, Assen 1975, 171-182; W. Beierwaltes, 'Pronoia und Freiheit in der Philosophie des Proklos', *FZPhTH* 24 (1977), 88-111. A recent study on the influence of Proclus in the Middle Ages is E.P Bos and P.A. Meijer, eds., *On Proclus and His Influence in Medieval Philosophy*, Leiden 1992 (Philosophia antiqua, 53).

[11] On the debate between Erasmus and Luther, see E. Iserloh, 'Luthers Absage an den Humanismus. Der späte Erasmus', *Reformation, katholische Reform und Gegenreformation*, ed. H. Jedin, Freiburg 1967 (Handbuch der Kirchengeschichte, 4), 146-157; G.B. Winkler, 'Das Psalmenargument des Erasmus im Streit um den freien Willen', *Histoire de l'exégèse au XVIe siècle. Textes du colloque international tenu a Genève en 1976*, comp. O. Fatio and P. Fraenkel, Genève 1978 (Etudes de philologie et d'histoire, 34), 95-117. The exchange between Banez and De Molina is discussed in H. Jedin, 'Die erneuerte Scholastik: Michael Bajus und der Gnadenstreit', *Reformation, katholische Reform und Gegenreformation*, 561-573, esp. 570-573. See also F. Stegmüller, *Geschichte des Molinismus I: Neue Molinaschriften*, Münster 1935 (BGPhThMA, 32), 1*-80*.

[12] Spinoza, *Korte verhandeling van God, de mensch en des zelfswelstand*, ed. C. Gebhardt, Heidelberg 1925, repr. 1972 (Opera, 1), Part I c. 2 and 5-6, respectively 19-27 and 40-43; Leibniz, *Essais de Théodicée*, ed. C.I. Gerhardt, Berlin 1885, repr. Hildesheim 1961 (Die philosophischen Schriften, 1), Première partie par. 2, 102-103; A.G. Baumgarten, *Metaphysica*, editio VII, Halle 1779, repr. Hildesheim 1963, Prol. IV, c. 1 sectio 2 par. 863ff.

[13] A helpful overview is given by W.J. Wainwright, *Philosophy of Religion. An Annotated Bibliography of Twentieth-Century Writings in English*, New York-London 1978, 85-117 (items 111-158); and M. Ravizza, 'Bibliography', *God, Foreknowledge, and Freedom*, ed. J.M. Fischer, Stanford, California 1989 (Stanford Series in Philosophy), 329-338.

[14] A.N. Prior, 'The Formalities of Omniscience', *Philosophy* 37 (1962), 114-129 (reprinted in *Papers on Time and Tense*, Oxford 1968); cf. William of Ockham, *Expositio in librum Perihermenias Aristotelis*, ed. A. Gambatese and S. Brown, St. Bonaventure, New York 1978

the other hand, holds that God *can* have knowledge of a future contingent event, but that because of his timelessness God cannot know the event's aspect of time. This was the position Thomas Aquinas attributed to the *antiqui nominales*.[15] Finally, this very position is challenged by Norman Kretzmann and Eleonore Stump (1981), who claim that it is possible for a timeless and eternal being to have knowledge of the sequence of events in time. This was also the view of the majority of medieval theologians.[16]

Contemporary interest in divine knowledge is by no means limited to its systematic philosophical aspects. In recent years the more purely historical dimensions have attracted attention, as is testified for instance by the *Cambridge History of Later Medieval Philosophy* (1982), as well as by several other publications on the subject.[17]

THE LIFE OF MARSILIUS

Having briefly introduced the problem of divine knowledge, we now turn to the historical record of our central character, Marsilius of Inghen.[18] Marsilius probably came from the town of Nijmegen in the East of the Low Countries (Netherlands). In the literature it is often said that he stemmed rather from one of the villages in the vicinity, but this view is most probably wrong.[19] The year of his birth, which must have been around 1340, cannot be given with absolute certainty.

(OPh, 2), I c. 6, 423.

[15] N. Pike, *God and Timelessness*, London 1970, 53-96; cf. Thomas Aquinas, *Summa theologiae*, Rome 1888 (ed. Leonina, 4), I q. 14 a. 15 ad 3, 195b.

[16] N. Kretzmann and E. Stump, 'Eternity', *The Journal of Philosophy* 78 (1981), 429-458, esp. 457. Other systematic monographs on divine knowledge include P. Helm, *Eternal God. A Study of God without Time*, Oxford 1988; W. Hasker, *God, Time, and Knowledge*, Ithaca-London 1989 (CoSPhR); E.R. Wierenga, *The Nature of God. An Inquiry into Divine Attributes*, Ithaca-London 1989 (CoSPhR); L. Trinkaus Zagzebski, *The Dilemma of Freedom and Foreknowledge*, New York-Oxford 1991 (contains bibliographical references).

[17] C. Normore, 'Future Contingents', *The Cambridge History of Later Medieval Philosophy from the Rediscovery of Aristotle to the Disintegration of Scholasticism 1100-1600*, ed. N. Kretzmann, A. Kenny, J. Pinborg, Cambridge 1982, 358-381; T. Rudavsky, ed., *Divine Omniscience and Omnipotence in Medieval Philosophy. Islamic, Jewish, and Christian Perspectives*, Dordrecht 1985 (Synthese Historical Libary, 25); W.L. Craig, *The Problem of Divine Foreknowledge and Future Contingents from Aristotle to Suarez*, Leiden 1988 (Brill's Studies in Intellectual History, 7).

[18] Unless otherwise indicated, the biographical data provided here are based on G. Ritter, *Studien zur Spätscholastik I: Marsilius von Inghen und die okkamistische Schule in Deutschland*, Heidelberg 1921 (Sitzungsberichte der Heidelberger Akademie der Wissenschaften, Philosophisch-historische Klasse, 1921/4), 7-44, which is still the best documented account of Marsilius's life.

[19] Nijmegen as place of birth is argued for, with a discussion of the literature, in H.A.G. Braakhuis and M.J.F.M. Hoenen, 'Marsilius of Ighen. A Dutch Philosopher and Theologian', *Marsilius of Inghen. Acts of the International Marsilius of Inghen Symposium*, Nijmegen, 18-20 December 1986, ed. H.A.G. Braakhuis and M.J.F.M. Hoenen, Nijmegen 1992 (Artistarium Supplementa).

From 1362 onward, Marsilius is mentioned in the acts of the *natio anglicana* of the University of Paris. On September 27 of that year, he started his career as *magister artium* under the tutelage of his countryman William Buser of Heusden († after 1413). Marsilius adopted much of the latter's views in his *Obligationes*.[20] We do not know whether Marsilius had been studying in Paris before. Also in 1362, his name appeared on the roll of the *natio anglicana* for a prebendaryship, together with that of Geert Groote († 1384), initiator and inspiration of the *Devotio moderna*. The two must have been personally acquainted, or at least have communicated with one another. This may be gathered from a letter, probably dating from 1374, written by Geert Groote to Henry (?) de Lippia, canon of St. Severin in Cologne, in which Marsilius is mentioned.[21] Marsilius became a canon of this church in 1362. Also, Groote maintained contacts with Henry of Oyta († 1396), who like Marsilius was of great importance for the young German universities.[22]

From ca. 1366 onward, Marsilius studied theology in Paris. He was not to finish this study until thirty years later in Heidelberg. In Paris Marsilius became acquainted with the ideas of men like Ockham, Gregory of Rimini, Buridan († 1358), and Albert of Saxony († 1390). He knew Nicholas Oresme († 1381) personally. The views of Gregory of Rimini, Buridan, and Albert of Saxony recur in Marsilius's works, often in the form of *verbatim* quotations.

Next to his office as magister, Marsilius held many administrative assignments. In 1367 and again in 1371, he was rector of the University of Paris. In 1363 and from 1373 to 1375, he was procurator of the Anglican *natio*. In 1369 and in 1377-1378 he was representative of the University at the papal court in Avignon. The offices of president and delegate at the papal court were particularly honored assignments, testifying that Marsilius must have been highly regarded in Paris.

As a teacher, Marsilius was much esteemed as well, as is indicated by the (unsuccessful) attempt of Pope Urban V in 1369 to persuade him to accept a chair at the University of Montpellier. We also know that in Paris Marsilius's lectures drew large audiences.

In 1378, Marsilius found himself as the University's delegate at the court of Pope Urban VI in Tivoli. In 1379, he instructed one of his colleagues, Hugh of Hervort, to look after his interests in Paris. After 1379, Marsilius's name is no longer mentioned in the acts of the University of Paris. It is not

---

[20] For Buser and his influence on Marsilius, see C.H. Kneepkens, 'The Mysterious Buser Again: William Buser of Heusden and the 'Obligationes' Tract *Ob rogatum*', *English Logic in Italy in the 14th and 15th Centuries. Acts of the 5th European Symposium on Medieval Logic and Semantics*, Rome, 10-14 November 1980, ed. A. Maierù, Napoli 1982, 147-166.

[21] Geert Groote, *Epistolae*, ed. W. Mulder, Antwerp 1933 (Tekstuitgaven van Ons Geestelijk Erf, 3), 8.

[22] This can be gathered from a sermon by Jan Brugman († 1473), in Am. van Dijk, ed., *Verspreide Sermoenen*, Antwerp 1948 (Klassieke galerij, 41), 157.

inconceivable that he turned away from Paris because of the imbroglio of the Schism in 1378. The German students at the University of Paris, including Marsilius, opposed the University's official support of the Anti-Pope. They were subsequently made the object of boycotts and minor harassment — a climate Marsilius must have found thoroughly disagreeable. This may have been his reason for not returning to Paris, unless in fact he was not allowed to return.

Between 1379 and the year the University of Heidelberg was founded (1386), Marsilius's whereabouts are virtually unknown. Anneliese Maier surmised that he stayed in Italy, basing her opinion on the fact that Giovanni Marliani († 1483), professor at the University of Pavia, spoke of 'Marsilius noster'.[23] As William J. Courtenay has rightly pointed out, this expression probably means only that Marsilius's views were much esteemed in Pavia; it is certainly insufficient ground for claiming that Marsilius had been teaching in Italy.[24] The only thing known with certainty of the period 1379-1386 is that Marsilius was in Nijmegen in 1382, where he was treated to a banquet by the town council.[25]

From 1386 onward, Marsilius was magister at the University of Heidelberg. There, as before in Paris, he held a number of administrative offices. He was one of the founders of the University of Heidelberg, of which he was rector no less than nine times, from 1386-1392 and in 1396. In 1389-1390, as the University's nuncio together with Conrad of Soltau († 1407), he was responsible for transferring the university *rotulus* to Rome (Boniface IX).[26]

At the beginning of the 1390s, Marsilius took up his study of theology again at the then small Heidelberg faculty of theology. Among his fellow students were Heilmann of Wunnenberg and Johannes Holzadel. They were the *socii* with whom Marsilius debated during the opening lecture (*principium*) of his commentary on the *Sentences*. Wunnenberg assisted him at his lectures in the faculty of arts. The suggestion made by Franz Pelster in 1944, that Wunnenberg was Marsilius's teacher in theology, has recently been duly challenged.[27] The magisters who taught theology at the time Marsilius took his doctoral degree were Conrad of Soltau (from 1387) and Matthew of

---

[23] A. Maier, *Ausgehendes Mittelalter II. Gesammelte Aufsätze zur Geistesgeschichte des 14. Jahrhunderts*, Rome 1967 (Storia e letteratura, 105), 332-334.
[24] W.J. Courtenay, 'Marsilius von Inghen († 1396) als Heidelberger Theologe', *Heidelberger Jahrbücher* 32 (1988), 30.
[25] Cf. the entry in the records of the City of Nijmegen, *Rekeningen der stad Nijmegen 1382-1543. Vol. I: 1382-1427*, ed. H.D.J. van Schevichaven and J.C.J. Kleijntjes, Nijmegen 1910, 28 (1382, propinationes): 'magistro Marcelio de Ingen de 4 quartalibus vini 2 [librae] 13 sol. 4 d.'
[26] On Marsilius as founder and rector of the University of Heidelberg, see most recently J. Miethke, 'Marsilius von Inghen als Rektor der Universität Heidelberg', *Ruperto Carola* 76 (1987), 110-119.
[27] Courtenay, 'Marsilius von Inghen', 29.

Krakau (from 1394), both from the University of Prague. In 1395/1396, Marsilius concluded his study of theology and so became the first theologian to obtain his doctorate in Heidelberg. Shortly after, he died, on August 20, 1396.

The influence of Marsilius has been considerable, particularly through his logical works and his commentaries on Aristotle. This may be gathered not only from the large number of manuscripts that have been preserved, but also from several other considerations.[28] Marsilius's commentary on Aristotle's *Prior analytics* was used in Prague in the 1380s. His logical works, including the *Obligationes* and the *Consequentiae*, were used as textbooks in Vienna in the 1390s.[29] His commentaries on Aristotle's *Metaphysics* and *Physics* were read in Krakau during the first sixty years of the fifteenth century. At the universities of Heidelberg, Erfurt, Basel, and Freiburg, his works were studied throughout the fifteenth century, in particular as part of the university curriculum.[30] In 1499, *doctores* and *magistri* of the *via moderna* at the University of Heidelberg published a volume that included epigrams on Marsilius by well-known humanists such as Jacob Wimpfeling, as well as a defence of nominalism in the style of Marsilius (the *via marsiliana*).[31] Praise in the form of epigrams can also be found in the 1501 Strasbourg edition of Marsilius's commentary on the *Sentences*. The *Obligationes*, printed in 1489 under the name of Peter of Ailly, were used by Thomas Bricot († 1516), John Major († 1550), and Domingo de Soto († 1560). The commentary on the *Prior analytics* was quoted by Agostino Nifo († 1538).[32] Jodocus Trutvetter († 1519) and Bartholomew of Usingen († 1532), who consolidated nominalism in Erfurt, repeatedly mentioned Marsilius in their works. Both Leonardo da Vinci († 1519) and Galileo Galilei († 1642) referred to Marsilius's commentary on *De generatione et corruptione*.

---

[28] The most extensive catalogue of extant manuscripts of Marsilius's writings is M. Markowski, 'Katalog dziel Marsyliusza z Inghen z ewidencja rekopisow', *Studia Mediewistyczne* 25/2 (1988), 39-132.

[29] G. Ritter, *Studien zur Spätscholastik*, 33 (Prague); E.J. Ashworth, 'Traditional Logic', *The Cambridge History of Renaissance Philosophy*, ed. Ch.B. Schmitt et al., Cambridge 1988, 150 (Vienna). For Vienna, see also *Acta facultatis artium universitatis Vindobonensis 1385-1416*, ed. P. Uiblein, Graz 1968 (Publikationen des Instituts für Oesterreichische Geschichtsforschung, 6/2), 79.

[30] S. Wlodek, 'Quelques informations sur les commentaires médiévaux de la Métaphysique d'Aristote conservés dans les manuscrits de la Bibliothèque Jagellone à Cracovie', *Die Metaphysik im Mittelalter*, ed. P. Wilpert, Berlin 1963 (MM, 2), 769 (Krakau); M. Markowski, 'Die neue Physik an der Krakauer Universität im XV. Jahrhundert', *Antiqui und Moderni. Traditionsbewußtsein und Fortschrittsbewußtsein im späten Mittelalter*, ed. A. Zimmermann, Berlin 1974 (MM, 9), 502 and 506 (Krakau); G. Ritter, *Studien zur Spätscholastik*, 37f (Heidelberg); A.L. Gabriel, ''Via antiqua' and 'via moderna' and the Migration of Paris Students and Masters to the German Universities in the Fifteenth Century', *Antiqui und Moderni*, 468 (Erfurt) and 476 (Basel); E.J. Ashworth, review of *Marsilius of Inghen*, by E.P. Bos, *Vivarium* 24 (1986), 159-160 (Freiburg, Krakau).

[31] Cf. A.L. Gabriel, ''Via antiqua'', 463f.

[32] E.J. Ashworth, review (see our note 30), 160.

The theological views of Marsilius appear to have had some circulation as well. His commentary on the *Sentences* was known in Krakau in the first half of the fifteenth century, and was used by Thomas de Strampino († 1460) in his *principia* (1441-1442).[33] The University of Salamanca had a theological chair (*cátedra de nominales*) for commentary on the works of Marsilius of Inghen and Gabriel Biel († 1495).[34] His commentary on the *Sentences* was quoted by Spanish theologians such as Francisco de Vitoria († 1546), Domingo de Soto, Luis de Molina († 1600), and Francisco Suárez († 1619), usually in connection with questions about divine foreknowledge and grace.[35]

The number of manuscripts of Marsilius's commentary on the *Sentences* appears to be larger than was previously assumed. Nine extant manuscripts have been recorded so far. It is interesting to note that among the former owners of these manuscripts were two libraries for preachers (Ansbach and Isny), and two libraries of faculties of arts (Erfurt and Leipzig).[36] The education in Erfurt and Leipzig included the reading of nominalist writers. It seems reasonable to assume that the *artistae* became interested in Marsilius's theological work after studying his writings on logic and physics. The presence of Marsilius's commentary on the *Sentences* in preachers' libraries bears witness to the fact that the influence of his work streched beyond university circles.

Marsilius and late medieval thinking
1. Nominalism

Fifteenth- and sixteenth-century sources

In the fifteenth and sixteenth centuries, as noted above, Marsilius of Inghen was classified among the nominalists. A large number of contemporary sources attest to the fact. Shortly after his death, in a treatise written by Johannes de Nova Domo († 1418) entitled *De universali reali* (ca. 1406-1418), Marsilius was ranked with Buridan in the line of Ockham, and was included among the *epicuri litterales*, a group that was some years later referred to as *epicurei nominales* by Johannes's former pupil Heymericus a Campo († 1460).[37] In the official documents issued in Cologne, Louvain and

---

[33] M.J.F.M. Hoenen, 'Einige Notizen über die Handschriften und Drucke des Sentenzenkommentars von Marsilius von Inghen', *RThAM* 56 (1989), 117-163, esp. 122-127.

[34] F. Ehrle, *Der Sentenzenkommentar Peters von Candia des Pisaner Papstes Alexander V. Ein Beitrag zur Scheidung der Schulen in der Scholastik des 14. Jahrhunderts und zur Geschichte des Wegestreites*, Münster 1925 (FzS Beihefte, 9), 246.

[35] M.J.F.M. Hoenen, 'Der Sentenzenkommentar des Marsilius von Inghen. Aus dem Handschriftenbestand des Tübinger Wilhelmsstifts', *Theologische Quartalschrift* 171 (1991), 114-129, esp. 118 n. 30.

[36] Hoenen, 'Einige Notizen', 133-141 and 145f.

[37] Z. Kaluza, *Les querelles doctrinales à Paris. Nominalistes et réalistes aux confins du XIVe et du XVe siècles*, Bergamo 1988 (Quodlibet, 2), 20.

Paris (in 1425, 1427, and 1474, respectively) pertaining to the so-called 'Wegestreit' at the universities, Marsilius was counted as a nominalist in the tradition of the *via moderna*. This picture carried over into the sixteenth century. The *Annales ducum Boiariae* by chronicler Johannes Aventinus († 1534) mentioned Ockham, Buridan, Gregory of Rimini, and Marsilius of Inghen as the *antesignani* of the nominalists.[38]

The sources focused in particular on the logical views of Marsilius and the others, most notably their denial of the universal's reality outside the human mind. In the fifteenth century this was the main issue between nominalists and realists. The theology of Marsilius was also seen as nominalist. As mentioned above, the University of Salamanca maintained a nominalist chair called the *cátedra de nominales*, set up for commentary on the theological works of Marsilius and Gabriel Biel. It is not difficult to understand why Biel's commentary on the *Sentences* was considered 'nominalistic'. Biel himself, who also wrote a series of logical works, called his commentary an *abbreviatura* of Ockham's *Scriptum*, which indeed it clearly resembled in structure as well as in content. Although nominalism in the fifteenth and sixteenth century was not automatically identified with the thought of Ockham, the resemblance still suggested a connection between nominalism and Biel's commentary on the *Sentences*.

More difficult to understand is why Marsilius's commentary on the *Sentences* was considered to be a nominalist work in Salamanca. Nowhere in the commentary did Marsilius refer to himself as a 'nominalist', nor did he qualify himself as a follower of Ockham. Quite the contrary, he criticized Ockham on several points. But perhaps the reason for his nominalist image should be understood from a broader perspective. As a logician and philosopher of nature, Marsilius had an established reputation. As we have seen, his logical treatises and his commentaries on Aristotle formed part of the curriculum of the *via moderna* at several universities in the fifteenth and sixteenth centuries. This philosophical reputation, we may reasonably suppose, aroused an interest in his theological works as well, and especially in the nominalist views to be found there.

The interest in Marsilius's commentary on the *Sentences* was of course quite justified. In several places the work reverted to discussions from the logical works and from the commentaries on Aristotle, applying them to the solution of various theological problems. Two nominalist positions in the commentary are of particular importance here. First, that universals have existence only in the human mind, and not outside. Second, that the order of language is not the same as the order of reality. Both tenets qualified as

---

[38] See the text cited in A.D. Trapp, 'Augustinian Theology of the 14th Century. Notes on Editions, Marginalia, Opinions and Book-Lore', *Augustiniana* 6 (1956), 146-274, esp. 183f n. 43.

typically nominalist in the fifteenth and sixteenth centuries. In Marsilius's commentary on the *Sentences*, the first point was made in the context of his theory of ideas, the second in the discussion of divine attributes.

These considerations show that the characteristic logico-semantic outlook of nominalism was easily brought to bear on certain positions in theology. That this is what in point of fact happened is clear from the reaction of the Paris nominalists to the prohibition of nominalism of 1474. In this reaction it is stated that according to the nominalists (*nominales*), deity and wisdom are one, whereas according to the realists (*reales*), divine wisdom is distinct from the deity.[39] Marsilius's commentary on the *Sentences* contained opinions that were standardly attributed to the nominalists. We may be sure that this was the reason why it was called 'nominalist' in the sixteenth century.

Nominalism and the developments in the fourteenth century

The view that Marsilius was a nominalist occurs in much of the modern literature. It is based essentially on the fifteenth- and sixteenth-century sources discussed above. The 'nominalism' found there is then projected back into the fourteenth century.[40] This procedure suffers from two flaws, one historical, the other critical.

In the first place, a concept that has developed within a certain historical context cannot simply be transferred from one period of time to another regardless of context. The sources mentioned in the previous section all date from *after* the death of Marsilius. They stem from a climate that was entirely different from that of the second half of the fourteenth century. The so-called 'Wegestreit' was a product of the fifteenth century, even though its roots lie in the century before. The first public conflict between a 'via antiquorum' and a 'via modernorum' of which we have documentation, occurred at the University of Cologne in 1425.[41] In the fourteenth century, expressions like 'via moderna', 'nominalism', and 'schola nominalistarum' were never used as labels for contemporary views or clusters of then existing positions.[42] (Of course, this is not to deny that views called 'nominalist' in the fifteenth

---

[39] This document is edited in F. Ehrle, *Der Sentenzenkommentar*, 322-326.

[40] The modern historiographical understanding of nominalism is discussed in W.J. Courtenay, 'In Search of Nominalism. Two Centuries of Historical Debate', *Gli studi di filosofia medievale fra otto e novecento. Atti del convegno internazionale*, Roma, 21-23 settembre 1989, ed. R. Imbach and A. Maierù, Rome 1991 (Storia e letteratura, 179), 233-251.

[41] A.L. Gabriel, "Via antiqua", 439 (with refences to the sources). E. Meuthen, *Die alte Universität*, Cologne-Vienna 1988 (Kölner Universitätsgeschichte, 1), 172, refers to a document of 1414. However, this document does not mention a 'via antiquorum' and a 'via modernorum'. See the edition of this document in A.G. Weiler, *Heinrich von Gorkum († 1431). Seine Stellung in der Philosophie und der Theologie des Spätmittelalters*, Hilversum 1962, 57f.

[42] W.J. Courtenay, 'The Role of English Thought in the Transformation of University Education in the Late Middle Ages', *Rebirth, Reform, and Resilience. Universities in Transition 1300-1700*, ed. J.M. Kittelson and P.J. Transue, Columbus 1984, 146 n. 5 and n. 6.

century were often held by fourteenth-century thinkers.) Calling Marsilius or his views 'nominalist', then, is historically speaking an anachronism in the context of fourteenth-century developments.

In the second place, recent research has brought to light that the views of fourteenth-century thinkers such as Ockham, Gregory of Rimini, and Marsilius of Inghen, all of whom were called 'nominalist' in the fifteenth century, were actually in important respects too different to allow us to speak of a single school or movement.[43] We must conclude that the fifteenth-century use of the concept 'nominalism' bears only on a limited number of points in the field of logic, and should not be taken to refer to a comprehensive and elaborate philosophical system. This means that the concept carried little informational content. It tells us little, if anything at all, about the views that were taken with regard to other, non-logical points. Hence, for an inquiry into the philosophical developments of the fourteenth century, expressions such as 'nominalism' are not very useful. If they are used in the fifteenth-century manner, they are simply too vague, lumping together thinkers who happened to share some views in logic, but whose outlooks may otherwise have had little or nothing in common. On the other hand, should we try to make the expressions more specific, redefining them by adding new components and criteria, we are confronted with two other problems. First, it is far from clear how we could give a historically justified redefinition of a typically fifteenth-century concept, especially if its original logical meaning is of little use to us in this context. Secondly, we are faced with the confusing situation in which a thinker called 'nominalist' by fifteenth-century standards, may cease to be a nominalist in this new terminology, or vice versa.

Marsilius and the moderni

Although the term 'modernus', unlike 'nominalist', was actually employed in the fourteenth century, it suffers from much the same historical and critical defects when used as a label for pigeonholing the position of philosophers and theologians. As has been established by Neal W. Gilbert and William J. Courtenay, the term 'modernus' usually meant nothing more than 'contemporary'.[44] More particularly, it did not refer to a particular group of philosophers or theologians, nor did it stand for the followers of Ockham, as has long been thought. The use of the term in the sense of 'contemporary' has a long tradition, going back at least to the second century.[45] This means that

---

[43] Courtenay, 'Late Medieval Nominalism Revisited: 1972-1982', *JHI* 44 (1983), 164.

[44] N.W. Gilbert, 'Ockham, Wyclif, and the 'via moderna'', *Antiqui und Moderni. Traditionsbewußtsein und Fortschrittsbewußtsein im späten Mittelalter*, ed. A. Zimmermann, Berlin 1974 (MM, 9), 85-125, esp. 106-107; W.J. Courtenay, ''Antiqui' and 'moderni' in Late Medieval Thought', *JHI* 48 (1987), 3-10, esp. 3.

[45] Gilbert, 'Comment', *JHI* 48 (1987), 41-50, esp. 44.

generally speaking the term carried little information about the concrete views of the philosophers referred to.

In a recent paper by Courtenay (1987), however, attention has been drawn to an important shift in the meaning of the term as it was used in the fourteenth century. From ca. 1310 onward, writers of that time were not only referred to as 'modernus' in the period they were actually teaching, but also thereafter. The term assumed a broader meaning and began to denote several generations of fourteenth-century philosophers and theologians. Moreover, its connotation seems to have slightly shifted to what was associated in the fifteenth century with the views of the *via moderna*. So it came to be that Scotus was called 'antiquus' at the end of the fourteenth century, when Ockham was still called 'modernus'.[46]

The turning point of ca. 1310 is of importance for our inquiry. Various opinions and positions concerning divine knowledge that were attributed to *moderni* after 1310 were connected with the new developments that occurred after the time of Scotus, viz., the emphasis on the incomprehensibility of the combination of certainty and contingency, the logico-semantic approach, and the role of man in determining divine foreknowledge. As we shall see later, there is indeed a striking connection between these new developments and the views attributed to the *moderni* in the fourteenth century. This is important for our understanding of the way the historical development of certain opinions and positions in the fourteenth century was actually perceived at the time. We in our turn may compare this perception with fourteenth-century developments discovered by historical research.

The above considerations have the following consequences for the study of Marsilius of Inghen. If we can work out which views on divine knowledge were attributed to the *moderni* in the fourteenth century, which of them were endorsed by Marsilius, and from which he took distance, we may be able to get a clear picture of the different traditions in which he was standing, and of the understanding of those traditions by his contemporaries. As we proceed, we shall see that on some points Marsilius clearly reverted to traditions that went back to the thirteenth century. On other points, most notably with regard to God's knowledge of future contingents, he endorsed opinions that were explicitly attributed to the *moderni* by various theologians in the second half of the fourteenth century. This last aspect is of particular importance. It gives us reason to assume that Marsilius was seen by his contemporaries as a champion of the 'modern', typically fourteenth-century way of thought, in the tradition of Ockham, Wodeham, and Gregory of Rimini.

---

[46] Courtenay, "Antiqui", 4-6.

2. COMMENTATOR ARISTOTELIS

Like many of his contemporaries, Marsilius was thoroughly familiar with the works of Aristotle. This can be gathered from the many places in his commentary on the *Sentences* where he is quoting and often critically discussing the views of Aristotle. Much of his extensive knowledge he had no doubt acquired as a *magister* at the faculties of arts in Paris (1362-1378) and Heidelberg (1386-1396). His lectures in that capacity included commentaries on Aristotle's *Organon, Physics, De anima,* and *Metaphysics*.

It has been suggested that Marsilius virtually ceased work on his commentaries on Aristotle after 1367, due to his many administrative occupations in Paris, and later his study of theology in Heidelberg.[47] This view is probably false. University documents testify that he was still giving lectures at the faculty of arts in Paris in 1374-1375, and at the faculty of arts in Heidelberg in 1389. Moreover, his commentary on the *Metaphysics* was composed in Heidelberg. Incidentally, it is interesting to note that the autograph of his commentary on *De generatione et corruptione* was bequeathed by him to the University Library of Heidelberg. A copy of the *Reportata Metaphysicae a magistro Marsilio in Heidelberga* was handed down to the same library by Gerhardus Emelissa in 1396.

The influence of Buridan

Much of what Marsilius had asserted in his commentaries on Aristotle is found again in his commentary on the *Sentences*, which was written later. This also holds good for the topic of divine knowledge. Moreover, in many places there is a striking, sometimes word-for-word resemblance between parts of Marsilius's commentaries on Aristotle and those of Buridan, which may indicate that Marsilius used Buridan's commentaries as a point of departure in his lectures. This seems to have been true especially of the commentary on the *Metaphysics*. The titles of the *quaestiones* discussed there are virtually identical to those of Buridan. Often the expositions run parallel to each other. Marsilius gave more commentary, however, and discussed aspects of questions or themes that are not found in Buridan. Through the commentaries on Aristotle, much of Buridan's thought worked its way into Marsilius's commentary on the *Sentences*. This is of interest not only for our general understanding of the historical mechanism of textual tradition, but also more specifically because of the fact that Buridan, unlike Marsilius, was not a theologian but a philosopher.

One idea Marsilius took over from Buridan, and which is of special importance for our inquiry, is that God according to Aristotle and Averroes

---

[47] E.P. Bos, *Marsilius of Inghen. Treatises on the Properties of Terms. A First Critical Edition*, Dordrecht 1983 (Synthese Historical Library, 22), 8f.

is not only the final cause of the heavens and of the separate substances, but also their efficient cause. On this point Buridan and Marsilius were following the line of Scotus and Ockham as against that of John of Jandun, Johannes Baconis, and Gregory of Rimini. Noteworthy in this connection is the fact that in the *Puncta super libros Metaphysicae* (brief abstracts of Aristotle for teaching purposes), attributed to Johannes de Slupcza and written in Krakau in 1433, some of the views that Marsilius adopted from Buridan, such as the one just mentioned, were attributed to Marsilius instead of Buridan, notwithstanding the fact that the author was familiar with both Marsilius's and Buridan's commentaries.[48] This offers a fine illustration of Marsilius's particular influence in the fifteenth century.

Aristotle and natural reason

Marsilius treated the teachings of Aristotle as equal to those of natural reason itself. Unlike thinkers such as Gregory of Rimini, he rarely pitted the views of Aristotle against the natural reason of man. He firmly believed that just about everything a human being is capable of knowing about God by means of the limited natural capacities endowed to him had already been discovered by Aristotle.

In his commentary on the *Sentences*, Marsilius criticized the view of Hugolin of Orvieto that Aristotle's statements about God mean something different from the same statements as expressed by a Christian theologian. Hugolin was of the opinion that every purely philosophical proposition about God contains a falsity, based as it is on an incorrect and unreal, i.e., non-Christian, image of God. If there happens to be more than mere verbal identity between the claims of the (non-Christian) philosophers and those of the theologians, this is not because human reason as such is capable of discovering the truth, but rather because those philosophers have been illuminated by the *lumen theologicum*. (Hugolin was here adopting a line of thought that was defended by Henry of Ghent at the end of the thirteenth century.) Against this view, Marsilius contended that natural reason as such is capable of forming some adequate and true concepts of God (*conceptus proprii et veri*), and also of forming true propositions about God. This, he claimed, also held good for philosophers such as Aristotle.[49]

Yet, Marsilius also believed that there are things that cannot be known to man by natural reason alone. Aristotle and natural reason may be able to prove that God exists, that he has knowledge, and that he has will, but not that God has free will, that he has infinite power, or that he can create from nothing. For

---

[48] See the texts edited in R. Tatarzynski, 'Le commentaire à la 'Metaphysique' d'Aristote attribué à Jean de Slupcza. La choix des questions relatives à la causalité', *MPhP* 24 (1979), 133-168. These *Puncta* are preserved in Kraków, Bibl. Jag. 2099.

[49] *Quaestiones super quattuor libros Sententiarum*, I q. 5 a. 1, Strasbourg 1501, repr. Frankfurt a/M 1966, fol. 34rb.

man to know these things he needs the supernatural light of faith (*lumen supernaturale*). If he uses only the natural light, man finds the exact opposite of the above, i.e., that God acts of necessity, that his power is limited, and that he cannot create from nothing. The reason for this, according to Marsilius, is that natural reason starts from observation, and is based on principles that are derived from observation. In the observable world nothing happens from nothing, and nothing disappears into nothingness; therefore, it is necessary that there is always something. This means that, by the light of natural reason alone, we must conclude that God necessarily keeps the world in existence, that he has not made the world from nothing, and that therefore he has only limited power.[50]

Several of Marsilius's commentaries on Aristotle discussed the problem of divine (fore)knowledge, viz., the *Quaestiones veteris artis*, the *Abbreviationes super octo libros Physicorum Aristotelis*, and the *Quaestiones super librum Metaphysicorum*. Of course, the problem was also treated in the commentary on the *Sentences*, to which we shall shortly turn.

The *Quaestiones veteris artis* is a commentary in the form of *quaestiones* on Porphyrius's *Isagoge* and Aristotle's *Categories* (*Praedicamenta*) and *De interpretatione* (*Perihermeneias*). The work has been preserved in seven manuscripts. In all probability, it originated in Paris, perhaps as early as 1363.[51] The commentary on the *Perihermeneias* is especially important for our subject here.

The *Abbreviationes super octo libros Physicorum Aristotelis* are a commentary on the eight books of Aristotle's *Physics*. The work consists of a large number of short *quaestiones*. It was probably composed during Marsilius's time in Paris, as may be gathered from the frequent use of examples involving this city. The *Abbreviationes* have been preserved in a number of manuscripts, and were printed several times: in Pavia in 1480 (?), and in Venice in 1490 and 1521.[52] Marsilius's commentary on the *Sentences* makes several references to arguments and expositions found in the *Abbreviationes*.

Finally, the *Quaestiones super librum Metaphysicorum* is a series of longer *quaestiones* which originated in Heidelberg. From Marsilius's introduction to the work we learn that one of its objects was to prepare (*adaptare*) the *scolares* for the study of theology. The commentaries on books III, XI, XIII and XIV are missing, as is also the case in Buridan's commentary. This

---

[50] Ibid., I q. 42 a. 2, fol. 177ra-va.

[51] M. Markoswki, 'Die handschriftliche Überlieferung der Werke des Marsilius von Inghen', *Marsilius of Inghen. Acts of the International Marsilius of Inghen Symposium*, Nijmegen, 18-20 December 1986, ed. H.A.G. Braakhuis and M.J.F.M. Hoenen, Nijmegen 1992 (Artistarium Supplementa).

[52] Ch.H. Lohr, 'Medieval Latin Aristotle Commentaries. Authors: Johannes de Kanthi-Myngodus', *Traditio* 27 (1971), 329.

is further proof of the fact that the work was primarily intended for teaching, since knowledge of these books was not required of students at the University of Heidelberg.[53]

3. THE COMMENTARY ON THE SENTENCES AND ITS SOURCES

We now turn to Marsilius's theological work, the *Quaestiones super quattuor libros Sententiarum*, which will be our chief source in this study. The work covers all four books of Peter Lombard, and consists of a series of *quaestiones*, rather than *distinctiones*. Divine knowledge is discussed in book I, questions 38 and 40, as was customary in continental commentaries on Lombard. Marsilius's views on divine ideas were put forward in his *principium* (opening lecture) to book I, which was included there as the first *quaestio*. The *principia* to books II and III were similarly incorporated as separate *quaestiones* into the *Sentences* commentary. From the list of books Marsilius left to the University of Heidelberg at his death in 1396, we know that these *principia* also existed as separate works.[54]

The order in which the subject matter is dealt with in the commentary followed that of Lombard's *Sentences*. As was the custom in many fourteenth-century commentaries from the second decade onward, Marsilius's *quaestiones* consist largely of *suppositiones* and *conclusiones* with extensive proofs. The *conclusiones* are sometimes deduced from each other, which is probably why the incipit of the printed edition of 1501 speaks of an 'ordo optimus quasi mathematicalis certissimus'.

The actual presentation of the commentary took place in Heidelberg in 1392-1394. As we shall see later, however, it is not unlikely that Marsilius had already been working on it before, perhaps even in Paris. It was not unusual for a future *sententiarius* in those days to start collecting material for his commentary at an early stage of his study of theology.

Only one version of Marsilius's commentary on the *Sentences* is known to us. Other versions have either not been preserved, or never existed. I have shown elsewhere that Marsilius left his work unfinished when he died.[55] In all textual witnesses known to us, some responses to *rationes principales* are missing in books I and II, e.g., in the discussion of predestination. In the printed edition of 1501, the death of Marsilius is given as an explanation of

---

[53] Cf. B. Michael, *Johannes Buridan: Studien zu seinem Leben, seinen Werken und zur Rezeption seiner Theorien im Europa des späten Mittelalters*, Vol. 2, Berlin 1985 (Inaugural-Dissertation Berlin), 808 (with references to the documents).

[54] On the *principia* of Marsilius, see my 'Neuplatonismus am Ende des 14. Jahrhunderts. Die Prinzipien zum Sentenzenkommentar des Marsilius von Inghen', *Acta Mediaevalia*, ed. S. Wielgus et al., Lublin 1992, (in print). For a discussion of late medieval *principia*, see also M.H. Shank, *"Unless You Believe, You Shall Not Understand": Logic, University, and Society in Late Medieval Vienna*, Princeton, New Jersey 1988, esp. 207-210.

[55] Hoenen, 'Einige Notizen', 148-153.

the omissions, which is probably correct. It is interesting to note that each of the four known manuscripts of book I has blank pages at the place of the omissions. We may assume that these go back to blank pages in Marsilius's autograph, which remained in Heidelberg until 1489. If this surmise is correct, it means that Marsilius had probably been engaged in editing his commentary until his death in 1396. And this in turn means that the one version handed down to us is an *ordinatio*, which also seems to be confirmed by the terms 'ordinata' and 'edita' in respectively the *incipit* of the Kraków manuscript (Bibl. Jag. 1581), and of the printed edition of 1501.

Marsilius had a library that was unusually large for its time. It consisted of no less than 237 volumes, including works of thirteenth- and fourteenth-century writers on philosophy and theology, as well as works on grammar, logic, mathematics, astronomy, law, medicine, and hermetical writings, together with works of Plato, Cicero, Ovid, Seneca, Augustine, Bernard of Clairvaux, Richard of St. Victor, and Alan of Lille. The influence of many of these works on the commentary on the *Sentences* is unmistakable. This is also true of the Neoplatonic and hermetical writings. As we shall see later, the *Liber XXIV philosophorum* was quoted by Marsilius in his discussion of divine knowledge, and his exposition of the ideas drew heavily on Neoplatonic thought.[56]

In addition to thirteenth- and early fourteenth-century thinkers such as Thomas Aquinas, Bonaventure, Henry of Ghent, Duns Scotus, Giles of Rome, Peter Aureoli, Durand of St. Pourçain, and William of Ockham, Marsilius also quoted theologians of later date such as Bradwardine, Thomas of Strasbourg, Adam Wodeham, Gregory of Rimini, Hugolin of Orvieto, and John of Ripa. Although Marsilius often referred to his sources by name, the same sources were sometimes quoted anonymously, so that it is often only by a careful comparison of texts that we see that he borrowed (long) passages from the work of others.

Thomas of Strasbourg, Adam Wodeham, and Gregory of Rimini especially influenced Marsilius's views on divine knowledge, although Thomas of Strasbourg was of a distinctly different persuasion here than Adam Wodeham and Gregory of Rimini. His views on divine attributes, for instance, go back to all three of them, and his logico-semantic approach, in a somewhat adapted form, goes back to Adam Wodeham and Gregory of Rimini.

It is not difficult to understand why Marsilius was familiar with the works of these three theologians. Adam Wodeham's commentaries on the *Sentences* attracted the attention of several theologians at the end of the fourteenth

---

[56] The 237 volumes of Marsilius's library are listed in *Die Rektorbücher der Universität Heidelberg*, Vol. 1/2, ed. J. Miethke, Heidelberg 1990 (Die Amtsbücher der Universität Heidelberg, A), 475-507 passim.

century, as is clear from the *abbreviatio* of Henry of Oyta (Paris, ca. 1375), and from quotations in various works of that period.[57] Much the same goes for the commentary on the *Sentences* by Gregory of Rimini. As for Thomas of Strasbourg, his *Sentences* commentary was one of the most influential works of its kind of the late Middle Ages, and was used as a textbook at some universities. Conrad of Soltau, theologian in Prague and later (1387) in Heidelberg, followed it very closely in his own commentary on the *Sentences*.[58]

Remarkably, in Marsilius's *Sentences* commentary no theologians writing after 1370 are quoted by name, with the exception of Heilmann of Wunnenberg and Johannes Holzadel, who are mentioned as *socii* at the beginning of the first book.[59] Even Conrad of Soltau, with whose work Marsilius was surely familiar, is not mentioned anywhere. The reasons for this are unknown. It has been suggested that Marsilius had already finished (part of) his commentary when he was still a student of theology in Paris (1366 and after).[60] A problem with this explanation is that it presumes that Marsilius made no substantial changes to his commentary before its presentation in 1392-1394, nor even after that. This does not sit comfortably with the fact that the work was left unfinished by Marsilius at his death, which seems to imply that he kept working at it until 1396.

Perhaps the explanation should be sought in a different direction. There may be some significance in the fact that the case of Marsilius is no isolated phenomenon in this connection. The same pattern is found in the work of other theologians, especially at the beginning of the fifteenth century. In the commentary on the *Sentences* of Johannes Capreolus (written 1409-1432), for instance, practically no theologians of the second half of the fourteenth century are mentioned, with the exception of John of Ripa. Capreolus discussed almost exclusively theologians of the first half of the fourteenth century, such as Scotus, Aureoli, Durand of St. Pourçain, Adam Wodeham, and Gregory of Rimini. The same holds for the commentary on the *Sentences* of Johannes Bremer (1429), who mostly quoted Bonaventure and Scotus, and sometimes also later theologians such as Peter of Candia.[61] Our understand-

---

[57] Cf. W.J. Courtenay, *Adam Wodeham. An Introduction to His Life and Writings*, Leiden 1978 (Studies in Medieval and Reformation Thought, 21), 140-152 (with references to the sources). Wodeham wrote three different commentaries on the *Sentences*.

[58] On the influence of Thomas of Strasbourg, see A. Zumkeller, 'Die Augustinerschule des Mittelalters. Vertreter und philosophisch-theologische Lehre', *Analecta Augustiniana* 27 (1964), 167-262, esp. 212-214.

[59] *Sent.*, I q. 1 (Strasbourg 1501), fol. 1vb. Heilmann of Wunnenberg is also mentioned in q. 2 a. 5, fol. 20ra.

[60] Courtenay, 'Marsilius von Inghen', 38.

[61] Cf. Johannes Capreolus, *Defensiones theologiae divi Thomae Aquinatis*, 1-7, ed. C. Paban and Th. Pèques, Tours 1900-1908; L. Meier, 'Der Sentenzenkommentar des Johannes Bremer', *FzS* 15 (1928), 161-169, esp. 167 (contains list of authors cited by Johannes Bremer).

ing of the fact that Marsilius quoted only theologians writing before ca. 1370 therefore should not be based on his earlier Parisian education, but clearly requires a broader scientific-cultural perspective.

Some methodological remarks

As we observed above, at the turn of the thirteenth century the views of Thomas, Scotus and Ockham had developed into three distinct and competing lines of thought that determined the outlook on the problem of divine knowledge for a considerable period of time. The fourteenth-century writer on this subject found his discussion partners in this theological *troika* or from some of their many followers. Marsilius of Inghen was no exception. His *principium* to the first book of Lombard's *Sentences*, addressing the problem of divine ideas, refers to Henry of Ghent as well as to Thomas, Scotus, and Ockham. As late as 1486, in the first book of Gabriel Biel's *Collectorium*, and even in 1520, in the *Libri quinque de fato, de libero arbitrio et de praedestinatione* by Pomponazzi († 1525), the question of divine knowledge was largely a discussion of the views of Thomas, Scotus, and Ockham. Obviously, a study of the position of Marsilius must deal with the views of this theological triad.

The views of Thomas, Scotus and Ockham concerning divine knowledge have been the subject of much thorough inquiry in present-day secondary literature. Here we should mention the well-known studies by Gilson (on Thomas and Scotus), by Wippel (on Thomas), Schwamm (on Scotus), Boehner and McCord Adams (both on Ockham), to name only some of the most important.[62] Yet, the present study will be concerned in particular with primary sources. The field of problems opened up by divine knowledge is of dazzling complexity, to the modern mind as much as to that of medieval writers. As an illustration of this last point it is significant that Thomas in his *Summa contra gentiles* rephrased his answer to the question of how God can know a multitude of things no less than three times. In his *Ordinatio*, moreover, Duns Scotus left the *quaestiones* on divine knowledge unanswered, probably because he was not content with his treatment of this difficult problem.[63]

The aim of this study is to set out the range of opinions concerning divine knowledge Marsilius was confronted with. This means, in the first place, that we should attempt to provide a coherent picture of the views of the most influential thinkers. But, secondly, we must also try to bring out whatever

---

[62] Full references for these studies can be found in the bibliography.
[63] On Thomas, cf. L.B. Geiger, 'Les rédactions successives de Contra Gentiles, I, 53 d'après l'autographe', *Saint Thomas d'Aquin aujourd'hui*, Paris 1963 (Recherches de philosophie, 6), 211-240. On Scotus, cf. A.B. Wolter, *The Philosophical Theology of John Duns Scotus*, ed. M. McCord Adams, Ithaca-London 1990, 285f.

ambiguities and contradictions we can find, insofar as they are of historical and systematical significance. It is often from the vague and the inconsistent that unexpected but interesting connections between apparently incompatible views have developed. We can find numerous examples of this seemingly self-contradictory phenomenon. How was it possible, for instance, that within the genre of *Correctoria corruptorii* (ca. 1278-1286) one group vindicated as the view of Thomas that God knows future contingents through the ideas, while another group denied that this was the opinion of the *doctor angelicus*? How was Robert Cowton able to unify the positions of Thomas and Scotus? Or how was Marsilius able to equate Ockham's and Scotus's theories of ideas?

Questions such as these can be answered only by detailed research of the sources, and by closely attending to the various lines of development in the fourteenth century that originated from Thomas, Scotus, and Ockham. In this way we may hope to attain a view of the problem and its solutions that can reasonably be assumed to resemble the view of a fourteenth-century philosopher and theologian like Marsilius of Inghen.

Much attention has been given lately to the logico-semantic aspects of the philosophical methods used in the fourteenth century. Although the discussion about the origin, status and significance of those methods has only just started (examining such issues as whether the use of logico-semantic analysis was specific to one movement or rather a more general phenomenon), it has already been established beyond doubt that the semantic approach made important contributions to problems in various domains.[64] This also holds for the problem of divine knowledge. The history of that problem in the fourteenth century shows the rise of a mode of thought in which the relation between divine knowledge and human freedom is no longer treated metaphysically by speculative means, but rather formally by logico-semantic means. This latter mode of thought was employed by Marsilius. We shall examine in this study where this new analysis came from, and whether the thinkers who used it share relevant metaphysical or speculative views in addition to this formal approach.

This study will only tangentially touch on the epistemic-logical aspects of the problem. Epistemic logic is concerned with the logic of terms expressing various epistemic attitudes such as knowing, believing, and doubting. As will become apparent, the theologians and philosophers studied here only rarely addressed the problem of divine knowledge in terms of this kind of logic. There seems to have been good reason for that. God's knowledge, according to most medieval writers, is absolutely infallible; consequently, he does not 'believe' or 'doubt' as we do. The medieval analysis of the truth-conditions

---

[64] For bibliographical references, see W.J. Courtenay, *School and Scholars in Fourteenth-Century England*, Princeton 1987, 239 n. 38.

of proposition *Know*(p), 'God knows that the Antichrist will sin', boils down to an analysis of the conditions under which proposition p is true, 'The Antichrist will sin'. Similarly, the hypothetical proposition h*Know*(p), 'If God knows that the Antichrist will sin, then the Antichrist will sin', was basically tantamount to the trivial implication h(p), 'If the Antichrist will sin, then the Antichrist will sin'. Virtually all medieval theologians deduced the necessity of h*Know*(p) from that of h(p). This shows unequivocally that they were convinced that the modal operator 'knowing' does not affect the truth-conditions of propositions concerning divine knowledge.

CHAPTER TWO

ARGUMENTS FOR DIVINE KNOWLEDGE

Most commentaries on the *Sentences*, which are the chief sources on our subject, start their discussion of divine knowledge with the question of whether God can be said to have knowledge at all. We will accordingly have to deal with this problem first.

In the thirteenth and fourteenth century there were three major proofs of the claim that God has knowledge, based on the three *viae* of pseudo-Dionysius: the argument from immateriality, the argument from perfection, and the argument from causality. Although they were also used in the much quoted texts of Avicenna and Anselm of Canterbury, and in the *Liber de causis*, the arguments came to be part of the late medieval stock of standard knowledge chiefly through the work of Thomas Aquinas. His was the formulation of the arguments that was adopted by various theologians, sometimes even *verbatim*, and that was scrutinized in the writings of Scotus and Ockham.

THE ARGUMENT FROM IMMATERIALITY

The argument from immateriality, which went back to Avicenna, was based on a close connection between immateriality and the possession of knowledge.[1] A high degree of immateriality was supposed to imply a high degree of knowledge, as (conversely) materiality was supposed to interfere with the power to receive the intelligible forms. God is immaterial; therefore he has knowledge. From the beginning of the fourteenth century, this argument tended to be used less frequently, and was not used by Marsilius. Its gradual disappearance was probably influenced by the criticism of Scotus found in the *Reportata Parisiensia*, as well as that of Ockham and others.[2] Scotus, e.g., argued that materiality is not an impediment to knowledge, nor immateriality the ultimate ground (*ratio*) of intelligibility. As witnessed in remarks of

---

[1] Cf. Avicenna, *Liber de philosophia prima sive scientia divina*, VIII c. 6, ed. S. van Riet, Louvain-Leiden 1977-1980 (Avicenna Latinus), 414. Thomas used this argument for instance in *STheol.*, I q. 14 a. 1 c. (ed. Leon., 4), 166a-b. In the commentary on the *Sentences* of John of Paris, the argument from immateriality was called the 'ratio Avicennae', *Commentaire sur les Sentences, Reportation*, I q. 113, ed. J.-P. Muller, Rome 1961 (Studia Anselmiana, 47), 344.

[2] Cf. Scotus, *Reportata Parisiensia*, I d. 35 q. 1 a. 1 n. 9, ed. Wadding, Vol. 11/1, Lyon 1639, repr. Hildesheim 1969, fol. 193a; Ockham, *Scriptum in librum primum Sententiarum. Ordinatio*, I d. 35 q. 1, ed. G.I. Etzkorn and F.E. Kelly, St. Bonaventure, New York 1979 (OTh, 4), 425-427. Although the first book of Scotus's *Reportata Parisiensia* in the edition of Wadding is an abbreviation made by William of Alnwick, it presents the authentic position of Scotus. See most recently A.B. Wolter, *The Philosophical Theology*, 286 n. 5.

Hervaeus Natalis (who sided with Thomas on this issue) and Peter Aureoli, criticism of Thomas's link between immateriality and intellectuality was a widespread phenomenon at the beginning of the fourteenth century.[3]

THE ARGUMENT FROM PERFECTION

The argument from perfection, on the other hand, occurred in a large number of works throughout the years 1250-1400. In Thomas it ran as follows. Knowledge is the most eminent perfection. Since God is the first principle, he does not lack any perfection. Therefore, God has knowledge.[4]

The best known source for this line of reasoning was certainly Anselm, whose influence in the twelfth, thirteenth and fourteenth century was considerable. In his *Monologion*, he made the well–known claim that whatever is as such more apt to belong to something than to nothing, is a perfection as such (*simpliciter*). Perfections of this kind necessarily belong to God, because God is that than which nothing more perfect can be thought.

The above characterization of 'perfection *simpliciter*' recurred in Thomas's *De veritate* together with a reference to Anselm, at the point where the question of whether God has knowledge is broached. Anselm's definition was well-known, as may be gathered from the fact that Scotus called it a 'descriptio famosa' in his *De primo principio*. Also, in the *Sentences* commentary of Giles of Rome (ca. 1276–1277, † 1316), Anselm is credited as the author of the rule that whatever is more apt to be than not to be, belongs to God.[5] Anselm, however, was by no means the first to describe God as the being than which nothing better can be thought. A similar idea had been voiced earlier by Cicero, Seneca, Augustine, and Boethius. For this reason some medieval authors attributed it not (or not only) to Anselm, but rather to Augustine.

A second source for the argument from perfection, next to Anselm, was the *Metaphysics* of Aristotle and the commentary on it by Averroes. Thomas referred to the latter work in his *Sentences* commentary, with regard to the question of whether God has knowledge, as well as in the *Summa theologiae*, in connection with the question of whether God has the perfections of all beings. According to Book V of Aristotle's *Metaphysics*, which contains a chapter on the meaning of 'being perfect', things are called perfect if they do not lack anything good and are not surpassed by anything else, and if they

---

[3] Cf. Hervaeus Natalis, *Sent.*, I d. 33 q. 1 a. 1, Paris 1647, repr. Westmead Farnborough 1966, fol. 137aA-C; Peter Aureoli, *Sent.*, I d. 35 a. 2, Rome 1596, fol. 758a-759a.

[4] *ScG*, I c. 44 n. 377, ed. C. Pera, Vol. 2, Turin-Rome 1961, 57b.

[5] Thomas Aquinas, *De veritate*, q. 2 a. 1, Rome 1975 (ed. Leon., 22/1), 38b (sed contra); Duns Scotus, *De primo principio*, c. 4 n. 53, ed. W. Kluxen, Darmstadt 1974 (Texte zur Forschung, 20), 64; Giles of Rome, *Sent.*, I d. 35 a. 1 q. 3, Venice 1521, repr. Frankfurt a/Main 1968, fol. 181rbE.

cannot be surpassed by anything in their *species*. In his comment on this passage, Averroes remarked that the first of these descriptions applies to God. This comment was adopted by Thomas. The first description of 'being perfect', Thomas wrote, truly describes the state God is in; the second description does not apply, since there is no species of 'God'. God is surpassed by nothing else in goodness, nor does God need any good from outside. Each perfection to be found in the world also exists in God. Of course this also includes the perfection of knowledge.[6]

Like the argument from immateriality, the argument from perfection was criticized by Duns Scotus. He objected to the way the argument proceeded, rather than to the premise that the possession of knowledge is a perfection. His criticism can be put as follows. The criterion for being a complete perfection is God himself. If something belongs to God, then it is a complete perfection; otherwise it is not a complete perfection. But this means that we should first establish *whether or not* God has knowledge, before arguing that knowledge is a complete perfection.[7]

From the fact that intelligibility is bound up with being, which is the most general notion *überhaupt*, and that knowledge as a quiddity cannot be reduced to something else, Scotus inferred the impossibility of an *a priori* proof of God's intelligibility and intellectuality. He did think it possible to prove that knowledge belongs to created beings and to God, but denied that this attribute can be derived from something higher, since all quiddities are irreducible.[8]

This last point was also made by Ockham. He claimed that intellectuality is an irreducible property for which no further ground (*ratio*) can be given. Being intellectual is a property that cannot be derived from anything else. It does not come to a thing through something else, but rather is an aspect of the thing itself: by its very nature something either has a faculty of knowledge, or it has not.[9]

THE ARGUMENT FROM CAUSALITY

Of the three arguments, the argument from causality is the one that figured most in works of the thirteenth and fourteenth century. Many writers considered it to be the most powerful argument in support of the claim that God has knowledge. Thomas's version of the argument can be summarized as follows.

---

[6] Aristotle, *Metaphysics*, V c. 16, 1021b30ff; Averroes, *In Metaphysicam*, V t. 21, Venice 1562, repr. Frankfurt a/Main 1962 (ed. Iuntina, 8), fol. 131raB; Thomas Aquinas, *Sent.*, I d. 35 q. 1 a. 1, ed. P. Mandonnet, Vol. 1, Paris 1929, 808 (sed contra); id., *STheol.*, I q. 4 a. 2 c. (ed. Leon., 4), 51b; id., *In Metaphysicam*, V lect. 18 n. 1040, ed. M.–R. Cathala, Turin 1926, 325a.
[7] *Reportata Parisiensia*, I d. 35 q. 1 a. 1 n. 14 (ed. Wadding, 11/1), fol. 193b.
[8] Ibid.
[9] *Scriptum*, I d. 35 q. 1 (OTh, 4), 427.

Natural things, being without knowledge, are unable to direct themselves towards a goal; they must be directed towards their end by something else. God is the author of everything. He is also the author of all natural things, and has directed each of them towards its goal by giving it a nature of its own. This means that God knows their goal. Therefore, God has knowledge.[10]

Some medieval writers associated the argument from causality with the *dictum* that the work of nature is the work of intelligence (*opus naturae est opus intelligentiae*). Various philosophers were (and still are) credited with the authorship of this idea, including Anaxagoras, Protagoras, Plato, Aristotle, Themistius, and Averroes. From the second half of the thirteenth century on, it was considered more or less as indisputable. The meaning of the *dictum*, however, is rather ambiguous. It may be taken either as saying that the structure of nature itself is inherently rational, or as saying that nature is guided by an outside intelligence. The first interpretation was endorsed by Albert the Great and Thomas Aquinas. The second we find in various writers of the fourteenth century, such as Gregory of Rimini.[11]

Gregory's argument from causality differed from that of Thomas in that it did not rely on the assumption that creatures without knowledge must have a general nature, made by God, which determines their actions and guides them toward their goal. It was based instead on the assumption that no creature, not even the rational ones, could produce anything at all without God's direct assistance. The common universal nature of a cause, according to Gregory, is unable to determine the production of a particular (singular) effect. The fact that a cause produces a certain singular effect A rather than a similar but numerically distinct effect B, cannot be accounted for in terms of the cause's universal nature. It must therefore be assumed that a higher cause is co-operating, determining whether A or B should be produced, that is, determining the singularity of the effect. According to Gregory this applies equally to natural causes and to free will.[12]

The reason that Gregory restructured the argument from causality in this way may have been influenced by the fourteenth century's increasing emphasis on the particular, or perhaps by Ockham's criticism of the 'old' argument, to the effect that the teleology of common nature does not allow any inference to the existence of a higher cause directing that nature to its goal.[13] As for the background of Gregory's argument, we should bear in mind

---

[10] *Sent.*, I d. 35 q. 1 a. 1 c. (ed. Mandonnet, 1), 809f; *ScG*, I c. 44 n. 378 (ed. Pera, 2), 57f.

[11] On this dictum, see J.A. Weisheipl, 'The Axiom 'Opus naturae est opus intelligentiae' and its Origin', *Albertus Magnus Doctor Universalis 1280/1980*, ed. G. Meyer and A. Zimmermann, Mainz 1980 (Walberger Studien, Philosophische Reihe, 6), 441-463.

[12] *Lectura super primum et secundum Sententiarum*, I d. 35-36 q. 1, ed. A.D. Trapp and V. Marcolino, Vol. 3, Berlin 1984, 216-218.

[13] Cf. Ockham, *Quodlibeta septem*, IV q. 2, ed. J.C. Wey, St. Bonaventure, New York 1980 (OTh, 9), 303. Also: II q. 2, 115.

that similar arguments from causality based on singularity had been used by other theologians before Gregory, among others by Adam Wodeham, Francis of Mayronnes, and William of Rubione (OFM, commentary on the *Sentences* before 1334). They used the argument to prove that God's actions are free and that God co-operates with all created causes in producing their effects.[14] In the course of time, similar arguments were applied to the problem of divine knowledge by Hugolin of Orvieto and by Marsilius of Inghen.

MARSILIUS OF INGHEN

Turning now to Marsilius of Inghen, the first thing to notice is that he used only the arguments from causality and from perfection. He did not employ the argument from immateriality, unlike the influential *Sentences* commentary of Thomas of Strasbourg, who read at Paris from 1335 to 1337, and that of Johannes Capreolus, which was completed more than a generation after Marsilius composed his commentary. The fact that the argument did occur in these works, notwithstanding the widespread criticism of it in the early fourteenth century, indicates that its absence in Marsilius may well be more than an insiginificant omission. While it is tempting to see here the influence of Scotus and Ockham, there is no direct evidence for that in Marsilius's work.

The argument from perfection

Marsilius's argument from perfection was as follows. Each perfection of the created world exists preeminently (*supereminenter*) in God. Knowledge is a perfection, so God has knowledge in a perfect way (*perfectissime*).[15]

That all perfections of the created world are true of God, Marsilius proved in the first *principium* of his *Sentences* commentary. He based his argument on two unexpected *auctoritates* that are only rarely quoted in this connection,

---

[14] Adam Wodeham, *Lectura Oxoniensis*, III q. 2 (Paris, Bibl. Maz., 915), fol. 175va: "(N)ullum agens naturale potest aliquid producere sine contingenti concausatione principii liberi infiniti, quia sine eius libera concausatione non plus produceret unum de numero infinitorum producibilium ab hoc activo creato naturali vel libero in hoc passo (! = passivo?) quibuscumque demonstratis, quam aliud (...)"; Francis of Mayronnes, *Sent.*, I d. 9 q. 4, Venice 1520, repr. Frankfurt a/Main 1966, fol. 55raB; William of Rubione, *Sent.*, I d. 38 q. u. a. 1, Paris 1518, fol. 221rb, cited from H. Schwamm, *Das göttliche Vorherwissen bei Duns Scotus und seinen ersten Anhängern*, Innsbruck 1934 (Philosophie und Grenzwissenschaften, 5/1-4), 264: "(N)ulla causa secunda determinatur a seipsa nec ab alia causa secunda, sed a prima, cum omnis causa secunda sit ex se ad omnes effectus eiusdem rationis consimiliter indeterminata (...)."

[15] *Sent.*, I q. 38 a. 1, ed. M. Hoenen, published in M.J.F.M. Hoenen, *Marsilius van Inghen over het goddelijke weten*, Deel 2: Tekstuitgave van Marsilius van Inghen, *Quaestiones super quattuor libros Sententiarum*, Lib. I qq. 38 en 40, Nijmegen 1989, 12: "(Q)uicquid est perfectionis in rebus dependentibus supereminenter est in Deo. Sed cognoscere est in rebus dependentibus. Ergo perfectissime est in Deo."

viz., Richard of St. Victor (*De trinitate*, I c. 20), 'All good must be attributed to God,' and the *Liber XXIV philosophorum*, prop. 5, 'God is that than which nothing better can be thought' (*quo nihil melius excogitari potest*). Other commentaries from the thirteenth and fourteenth century usually quote only the well–known classical texts by Augustine and Anselm.

One of the reasons why Marsilius used some rather unusual *auctoritates* in this context may have been the fact that he was giving a *principium*. Being public addresses, *principia* were scheduled so as to enable all students and *magistri* to attend. The *sententiarius* might use the opportunity to put all his intellectual power and erudition on display before the assembled university community. Marsilius was no exception. He seized upon the *principia* to show that he was a man of wide reading, by basing his argument on two uncommon sources. As a matter of fact, we also know from the catalogue of his books bequeathed *post mortem* to the Heidelberg University library that he possessed a large number of works by Richard of St. Victor, as well as one attributed to Hermes Trismegistus. This latter reference should probably be understood as the *Liber XXIV philosophorum*, which in several manuscripts is attributed to Hermes Trismegistus.[16]

God's knowledge as perfection

Each of God's perfections, Marsilius argued, accrues to God in an infinite, immeasurable and incomprehensible way (*infinite, immense, incomprehensibiliter*). Of course, this also holds true for God's knowledge. Calling divine knowledge immeasurable and incomprehensible, Marsilius was following the line of Adam Wodeham and Gregory of Rimini.[17]

According to Marsilius, God's perfections are perfections *simpliciter*, which means that qua perfection they cannot be surpassed. In God, everything belonging to a perfection is actually contained in it, including its being. Marsilius held that perfection coincides with being. Being perfect *simpliciter*, God's perfections are unsurpassable qua perfection. Creatures lack these complete perfections that only God can have. The perfections of created beings do not of themselves contain their own being, so they cannot be complete.[18]

---

[16] Cf. M.-Th. d'Alverny in *Catalogus translationum et commentariorum: Mediaeval and Renaissance Latin Translations and Commentaries. Annotated Lists and Guides* I, ed. P.O. Kristeller, Washington, D.C. 1960 (Union académique internationale), Appendix 1, 151-154, esp. 151. The *Liber XXIV philosophorum* was probably written in the second half of the twelfth century.

[17] *Sent.*, I q. 1 a. 1 (ed. Strasbourg 1501), fol 3rb. Cf. Adam Wodeham, *Lectura Oxoniensis*, III q. 2 (Paris, Bibl. Maz., 915), fol. 175ra-rb; Gregory of Rimini, *Lectura*, I d. 38 q. 2 a. 2 (ed. Trapp-Marcolino, 3), 283.

[18] Cf. *Sent.*, I q. 1 a. 2 (ed. Strasbourg 1501), fol. 4va; *Quaestiones super librum Metaphysicorum*, VIII q. 2 (Wien, Oesterr. Nationalbibl., CVP, 5297), fol. 123va.

In his commentary on Aristotle's *Metaphysics*, the argument from perfection was the *only* proof of God's knowledge Marsilius gave. This tells us something of the evident weight he attached to this argument. In this connection he quoted from the commentary on Aristotle's *Metaphysics* by John Buridan.[19] In the same work he also remarked that it can be proven by the light of natural reason that God has knowledge. Marsilius here referred to Aristotle, natural reason incarnate, who had argued that without knowledge God would be asleep, which is contrary to the perfection of the divine life.[20]

The argument from causality

Marsilius's argument from causality was identical to that of Gregory of Rimini. The causality of a natural cause, for instance that of fire, is of a general sort, directed indiscriminately toward all effects it could possibly produce. The fact that the fire produces a certain singular effect A as against a similar but numerically distinct effect B, cannot be explained by the causality of the fire as such (for this is indifferent as to the singularity of the effect produced), but only by introducing a higher cause that directs the fire's causality toward the singular effect. This higher cause must therefore have knowledge of all the effects that can be produced by the fire. This higher cause can only be God. Therefore, God has knowledge. In support of this argument, Marsilius cited the *dictum* referred to above, viz., *opus naturae est opus intelligentiae* (the work of nature is the work of intelligence), which was attributed by him to Averroes.[21]

God's causality

Marsilius accepted without criticism the implicit premise in the argument from causality, viz., that God is the efficient cause of the created world. Ockham, as is well-known, severely criticized the provability of this premise,

---

[19] Marsilius of Inghen, *Quaestiones super librum Metaphysicorum*, XII q. 2 (Wien, Oesterr. Nationalbibl., CVP, 5297), fol. 174va (= 175va): "*Prima* (propositio): *Deus intelligit. Patet quia intelligere est praedicatum perfectionale* simpliciter nullam importans imperfectionem." Cf. John Buridan, *Kommentar zur Aristotelischen Metaphysik*, XII q. 13, Paris 1518, repr. Frankfurt a/Main 1964, fol. 75va-vb: "Prima (conclusio) est quod Deus intelligit, quia intelligere est praedicatum perfectionale sine connotatione alicuius diminutionis." The passages Marsilius borrowed *verbatim* from other authors are indicated by *italics*. This convention will be observed throughout the book.

[20] Marsilius, *Quaestiones*, XII q. 2 (Wien, Oesterr. Nationalbibl., CVP, 5297), fol. 174va (= 175va). Cf. Aristotle, *Metaphysics*, XII c. 9, 1074b18.

[21] *Sent.*, I q. 38 a. 1 (ed. Hoenen), 12-14: "(O)mne dirigens appetitum naturalem cognoscit. Sed Deus dirigit appetitum naturalem, igitur. Patet maior quia certum est quod ignis non est plus determinatus ad producendum sua caliditate caliditatem 'a', quam quamlibet illi consimilem quam postea producit in eodem vel in alio subiecto. Nisi igitur dirigeretur ab aliquo agente cognoscente 'a' caliditatem et volente illam produci, non plus produceret 'a' quam aliquam aliam ad cuius productionem ignis indifferens est. (...) Unde dicit Commentator quod opus naturae est opus intelligentiae."

arguing that natural reason is unable to prove that God has produced the celestial bodies as an efficient cause.

The absence of criticism in Marsilius is not difficult to explain. Unlike the *venerabilis inceptor*, Marsilius thought it possible to demonstrate by natural reason that the intelligences, the celestial bodies and the sublunar creatures are dependent upon God in their being as well as in their activity (*agere*). This dependency is partly immediate, partly it is mediated by the being and activity of other creatures. The being and activity of the intelligences are received immediately from God. The celestial bodies receive their being immediately from God, but their activity is directed by God through the intelligences. Moreover, the being and the activity of the sublunar creatures, which are subject to change, are derived from the celestial bodies, although these creatures are properly and principally (*principalius*) directed by God.[22] Finally, as noted in the previous chapter, Marsilius believed that it was the view of Aristotle and Averroes that God is the final cause as well as the efficient cause of the celestial bodies and the intelligences. He therefore had no reason to doubt the basic premise of the argument from causality.[23]

God's modes of knowledge

As Marsilius put it, God's knowledge is certain and infallible (*certe et infallibilis*). In support of this he pointed out that all perfections exist in God in the most eminent way, and that God is the first cause directing the universe. Nothing can be hidden from him, for whatever happens in any way whatsoever is directed by God; therefore, God must have knowledge of all that happens.[24] Moreover, God's knowledge is said to be a perfect unity, equal to God himself, as well as eternal. From these three characteristics or modes Marsilius concluded that nothing is prior to God's knowledge, from which or by which this knowledge would come to be. In this respect divine knowledge is fundamentally different from human knowledge, which receives its knowledge from outside.

Also, from the attributes of unity, identity and eternity Marsilius inferred that God's knowledge is neither discursive nor abstractive (*abstractive*). By 'abstractive' knowledge Marsilius meant knowledge that is derived from other, prior knowledge. As God's knowledge is a perfect unity, it cannot be composed of different acts of knowledge, nor can it be derived from other

---

[22] *Sent.*, I q. 39 a. 2 (ed. Strasbourg 1501), fol. 162vb-163ra.
[23] Marsilius, *Quaestiones super librum Metaphysicorum*, XII q. 6 (Wien, Oesterr. Nationalbibl., CVP, 5297), fol. 155vb-156ra (= 156vb-157ra): "Conclusio responsalis est ista: De mente Aristotelis et sui Commentatoris fuit *quod Deus moveat* primum mobile sive totum *caelum active*. Ista conclusio probatur per *auctoritates* allegatas post oppositum. Secundo probatur sic ratione: *Intelligentia movens* primum mobile *active*, tunc *etiam movet ut finis*." Cf. John Buridan, *Metaphysik*, XII q. 6 (ed. Paris 1518), fol. 68rb.
[24] *Sent.*, I q. 38 a. 1 (ed. Hoenen), 14.

knowledge. Marsilius agreed with Ockham and Gregory of Rimini that God's knowledge is intuitive, always being immediately directed at its object without any intervening medium.[25]

He explicitly denied that the proper object (*objectum proprium*) of God's knowledge is the proposition.[26] His motive was probably once more to distinguish divine knowledge from human knowledge, as he took the proposition to be the proper object of human knowledge. In this latter respect, Marsilius belonged to the tradition of William of Ockham and Robert Holcot, criticizing the view of Gregory of Rimini that the proper object of human knowledge is the *complexe significabile*.[27]

The relation between God's knowledge and God's essence

Marsilius believed that God has perfect knowledge of his own essence, which is known to him immediately and without the intervention of a medium. This knowledge is *primo et principaliter* knowledge of itself; like God's essence, it is infinite. From these modes, Marsilius concluded that divine knowledge is the most splendid form of knowledge (*cognitio delectabilissima*), and that God loves himself infinitely, taking infinite delight in himself. Divine knowledge (*cognitio*), the divine act of understanding (*intellectio*), divine (self-)love (*dilectio*), and divine delight (*delectatio*) all coincide, and are formally identical with divine essence.[28]

Marsilius paid much attention to these last two modes, viz., that God's knowledge is most splendid and that God takes infinite delight in himself. There is an obvious affinity here with the terminology used by Aristotle in his *Metaphysics* to describe the divine life (1072a19–1073a13). Such expressions do not occur in the expositions on divine knowledge by Thomas Aquinas, Scotus, Ockham, and Gregory of Rimini.

The reason why Marsilius made much of these modes can probably be traced back to the fact that he wanted to establish not merely which properties could be attributed to divine knowledge on the basis of faith alone, but also to establish whether they could be validated by natural reason (i.e., Aristotle). Significant in this respect are the last words of the article in which the attributes are derived. There Marsilius wrote, "I believe that the Philosopher

---

[25] Ibid., 16. Cf. William of Ockham, *Scriptum*, I d. 38 q. u. (OTh, 4), 585; Gregory of Rimini, *Lectura*, I d. 38 q. 2 a. 2 (ed. Trapp-Marcolino, 3), 283.

[26] Ibid., I q. 38 a. 1 (ed. Hoenen), 16f.

[27] For extensive discussion of the views of Holcot, Rimini, and Marsilius, see G. Nuchelmans, *Theories of the Proposition. Ancient and Medieval Conceptions of the Bearers of Truth and Falsity*, Amsterdam-London 1973 (North-Holland Linguistic Series, 8), 204f (Holcot), 227-237 (Rimini) and 251-254 (Marsilius). Marsilius's criticism, to the effect that the *complexe significabile* was introduced by writers ignorant of logic, was quoted approvingly by Bartholomew of Usingen in the *Exercitium physicorum* (Erfurt 1507).

[28] Cf. *Sent.*, I q. 38 a. 2 (ed. Hoenen), 20-27, and 27: "Corollarium: Essentia divina est formaliter cognitio, intellectio, dilectio et delectatio."

on the basis of natural light alone would have granted these conclusions, which are each of them evident in the light of faith, and it is therefore that he said in book XII of his *Metaphysics* that God (himself) is the act of understanding and the life."[29]

Virtually the same list of the modes of divine knowledge was given by Marsilius in his commentary on the *Metaphysics*. He particularly mentioned the fact that God's knowledge is most perfect, and that everything is known by God immediately through his essence. He also pointed out that God takes delight in himself and that this delight coincides with God himself.

Most of the modes we have discussed can be found *verbatim* in John Buridan's commentary on the *Metaphysics*. Like Marsilius, Buridan thought that these modes were valid not only for believers, but also for philosophers. From this it is clear that Buridan's commentary was one of the main sources from which Marsilius drew his view on the modes of divine knowledge.[30]

---

[29] Ibid., 27.

[30] Cf. Marsilius, *Quaestiones super librum Metaphysicorum*, XII q. 12 (Wien, Oesterr. Nationalbibl., CVP, 5297), fol. 174va-175ra (= 175va-176ra): "*Secunda conclusio: Intellectio Dei est perfectissima* (...). *Tertio conclusio: Deus intelligit se* (...). *Quarta conclusio: Intellectio Dei est Deus* (...). Quinta conclusio: Deus intelligit se quantum est intelligibilis (...). Corollarium: Deus intelligit comprehensive se (...). Sexta conclusio: Deus non intelligit se intellectione superaddita sibi (...). Septima *conclusio: Deus* non *intelligit per repraesentativum* sui *distinctum ab* eo (...). Octava *conclusio: Quicquid Deus intelligit*, hoc *intelligit per simplicissimam suam essentiam sine discursu alterius intellectionis vel repraesentativi* (...). Nona conclusio: In Deo est idem repraesentativum, repraesentatum, repraesentatio, intellectio, intellectus, intellectum (intellectus, *ms.*) et intelligibile (...). Duodecima *conclusio: Deus* non (*bis, ms.*) *intelligit complexe* (...)." Also: XII q. 8, fol. 161ra-rb (= 162ra-rb): "Decima quarta *conclusio: Deus* summe *delectatur* (...). Decima quinta *conclusio: Delectatio* Dei *est ipsemet Deus.*" Cf. John Buridan, *Metaphysik*, XII q. 13 (ed. Paris 1518), fol. 75vb; XII q. 8, fol. 71ra.

CHAPTER THREE

DIVINE ATTRIBUTES

INTRODUCTION: THOMAS AQUINAS

According to Thomas Aquinas, knowledge is not a distinct part of God, but is altogether identical with God himself: God just *is* his knowledge. His essence is one uninterrupted act of knowledge, for God is immutable.[1] Thomas inferred this identification of essence and knowledge in God from the fact that God is pure act and that he is the first principle. What is perfect in act and lies at the basis of all things cannot be composite or divided. For what is composed and divided is dependent upon something else, viz., that from which it is so composed, and the cause that holds the parts together.

God's knowledge, his volition, his creatorship, and the other divine perfections, were called 'attributes' by Thomas. The use of this term as a technical expression for God's properties and perfections seems to go back to the 40s and 50s of the thirteenth century, where it made its first appearance in the commentaries on the *Sentences* by Albert the Great and Thomas Aquinas. The *Sentences* of Peter Lombard, written in the period 1155-1157, did not speak of an *attribute* but rather of the *name* 'knowledge'. The same goes for the *Glossa in libros Sententiarum* (1223-1227) by Alexander of Hales, as well as for the *Summa halensis* and the commentary on the *Sentences* by Bonaventure. In the first part of Thomas's *Summa theologiae*, too, divine perfections were still called 'names' of God. From the last decades of the thirteenth century onward, however, the term 'attribute' tended to become common currency.

Harry A. Wolfson has suggested that the origins of the technical use of 'attribute' for divine perfections lie in the reception (after 1230) of the Latin translation of Maimonides's († 1204) *Guide for the Perplexed*. In this connection, Wolfson also drew attention to an interesting remark made by Ockham, who attributed the use of the term 'nomen' to the *antiqui*, and that of 'attributum' to the *moderni*.[2]

The work of Maimonides, which was quoted by Thomas in his commentary on the *Sentences* in the context of divine attributes, contained a discus-

---

[1] *ScG*, I c. 45 n. 383 (ed. Pera, 2), 58b: "Intelligere ergo Dei est divina essentia, et divinum esse, et ipse Deus."

[2] H.A. Wolfson, *The Philosophy of the Kalam*, Cambridge, Mass. 1976 (Structure and Growth of Philosophic Systems from Plato to Spinoza, 4), 350-352. Cf. Ockham, *Quodlibeta*, III q. 2 (OTh, 9), 209. On the reception of Maimonides, see W. Kluxen, 'Maimonides and Latin Scholasticism', *Maimonides and Philosophy*, ed. S. Pines and Y. Yovel, Dordrecht 1986 (Archives internationales d'histoire des idées, 114), 224-232.

sion of Islamic controversies concerning the status of divine attributes, as well as an elaborate exposition of his own view that the attributes have no reality of their own. Maimonides's opinion was judged erroneous by Giles of Rome in his widely read *Errores philosophorum*, written about 1270. In the Latin West, discussions on the status of the divine attributes were pursued most frequently from the second half of the thirteenth century onward, examining such issues as the problem of how a multiplicity of attributes can be combined with God's simplicity. Thus Thomas inserted a *quaestio disputata* on this problem into his commentary on the *Sentences*.[3] It is therefore very plausible, as has been suggested by Wolfson, that it was precisely the translation of Maimonides and the technical use of the term 'attribute' that kindled discussions on the status of divine perfections, which were to last throughout the fourteenth century.

Thomas's theory of the attributes has been excellently described in several other studies; we shall thus content ourselves here with some brief remarks.[4] Distinction between the attributes does not express distinction in God, but only between the concepts or modes of knowledge (*rationes*) employed by man in his description of God. Because of his limited capacity of knowledge, man can know God, who is infinite, only by analogy, viz., through creation. Every concept inferred by man from creation is as such insufficient for knowing God (this is why we always use several attributional names at a time), but each of these concepts expresses an aspect of God's perfection because the perfections in creation derive from God. Distinction between the attributes was called 'rational' by Thomas, to express that such distinction exists between modes of knowledge (*rationes*).[5]

Significant in this connection is the question of whether Thomas believed that the rational distinction introduced by man at the conceptual level corresponds to a rational distinction in God. The problem was put most succinctly by the Dominican theologian John of Paris: would there still be a distinction in God even if there were no human beings to distinguish the attributes conceptually?[6]

In the *Summa theologiae*, Thomas denied that the attributes are rationally distinct in God. In the commentary on the *Sentences*, however, he emphatically maintained that the conceptual determinations applied by man to the

---

[3] *Sent.*, I d. 2 q. 1 a. 3. This *quaestio* was written in the years 1265-1267, cf. B.M. Lemaigre, 'Perfection de Dieu et multiplicité des attributs divins', *Revue des sciences philosophiques et théologiques* 50 (1966), 198-227, esp. 223.

[4] Thomas's theory of divine attributes is discussed in J.F. Wippel, *Metaphysical Themes in Thomas Aquinas*, Washington, D.C. 1984 (SPhHPh, 10), 215-241, esp. 228-239; R.M. McInerny, *Being and Predication. Thomistic Interpretations*, Washington, D.C. 1986 (SPhHPh, 16), 259-278.

[5] *Sent.*, I d. 2 q. 1 a. 2 ad 1 (ed. Mandonnet, 1), 63.

[6] John of Paris, *Sent.*, I q. 10 (ed. Muller), 35.

attributional names correspond to rational distinctions in God himself. Each attribute has its immediate *fundamentum proximum* (the *significatum* of the attributional name or term) existing outside the human mind in divine essence, just like the term 'man' has its immediate *fundamentum* in man. In support of this view, Thomas claimed that whatever exists in God must exist there in its most genuine form; therefore, in God, who because of his infinity contains all perfections, the form (*ratio*) of wisdom must be distinct from the form of goodness. The rational distinction between the attributes is not simply *produced* by someone reflecting on it, that is, *ex parte ratiocinantis*, but also exists because of the perfection itself, that is, *ex proprietate ipsius rei*.[7] Both lines of argument, that of the *Summa* and that the commentary on the *Sentences*, were elaborated by later theologians of Thomistic signature.[8]

From the notion that God is pure act and that he is the first principle, Thomas also concluded that God in his knowledge depends on nothing else. God knows by himself. He does not receive intelligible species from outside, since this is impossible because God is pure act. Rather, because God is immaterial he acts as the intelligible species himself. Being immaterial, therefore fully intelligible, God has perfect knowledge of himself.[9] That is why Thomas believed that the divine act of knowledge is altogether different from that of the human intellect, which is not identical with man's essence but is attached to a body. Unlike God, man is cognitively speaking dependent upon things outside of him. He needs an active intellect (*intellectus agens*) to render immaterial the intelligible species received from outside. Also, man knows himself only indirectly through knowledge of other things. In God, by contrast, knower and known are perfectly one. According to Thomas they could only be distinguished *secundum rationem*, or as he also put it *secundum*

---

[7] Compare the following two texts: *STheol.*, I q. 3 a. 3 ad 1 (ed. Leon., 4), 40b: "Quod ergo dicitur deitas vel vita, vel aliquid huiusmodi, esse in Deo, referendum est ad diversitatem quae est in acceptatione intellectus nostri; et non ad aliquam diversitatem rei."; *Sent.*, I d. 2 q. 1 a. 2 c. (ed. Mandonnet, 1), 62: "(Q)uia unumquodque eorum est in Deo secundum sui verissimam rationem, et ratio sapientiae non est ratio bonitatis, inquantum huiusmodi, relinquitur quod sunt diversa ratione, non tantum ex parte ipsius ratiocinantis, sed ex proprietate ipsius rei (...)."

[8] The *Summa* line was followed by John of Paris, Thomas of Sutton, and Hervaeus Natalis, partly in opposition to Henry of Ghent. Many Franciscan theologians (William de la Mare, Duns Scotus, William of Nottingham, Robert Cowton) took this line to be the actual view of Thomas. The line of the commentary on the *Sentences* was followed by the Thomists Peter of Tarantasia (the future Pope Innocentius V, † 1276) and the author of the commentary on the *Sentences* from the manuscript Brugge, Stadsbibliotheek, 491. It was defended by Robert of Orford (fl. 1285-1293) in the Thomistic defense against Giles of Rome entitled *Reprobationes dictorum a fratre Egidio in primum Sententiarum* (1289-1293). For an overview of the early discussions on divine attributes, see L. Hödl, 'Die philosophische Gotteslehre des Thomas von Aquin O.P. in der Diskussion der Schulen um die Wende des 13. zum 14. Jahrhunderts', *Rivista di filosofia neo-scolastica* 70 (1978), 113-134; H.G. Gelber, *Logic and the Trinity: A Clash of Values in Scholastic Thought, 1300-1335*, Ann Arbor, Michigan 1981 (Ph.D. Thesis 1974, University of Wisconsin), 12-59.

[9] *ScG*, I c. 46 n. 389 and c. 47 n. 397 (ed. Pera, 2), 59a-b.

considerationem, viz., in the thought of man reflecting on the immateriality of God's essence. Focusing on the immateriality of God's essence, we call his essence 'knower', whereas focusing on the fact that it is known qua immaterial, we call his essence 'known'.[10]

The identification of essence and knowledge in God, as we find it in Thomas, doubtless goes back to Aristotle and Avicenna. In his *Metaphysics*, Aristotle had argued that the first principle is an immaterial spirit (νοῦς). Being immaterial and perfect this spirit has no parts and depends upon nothing else for its knowledge. It is thinking about its own thought (νόησις νοήσεως), and coincides with what is thought (νόησις τῷ νοουμένῳ μία). That Thomas used Aristotle as a source for the equation of essence and knowledge in God is clear from several references and quotations, notably in the *Summa theologiae* and *De substantiis separatis*.[11]

God's immateriality and unity were also important themes in the *Metaphysics* of Avicenna (tract. VIII c. 6). It is certain that Thomas used Avicenna's exposition of divine knowledge in his earlier works. In the commentary on the *Sentences*, he borrowed part of Avicenna's demonstration on this point without mentioning his source, including the unmistakably Avicennian argument that the fact that a knower needs an object of knowledge does not imply that they are different, no more than the fact that a mover needs an object of motion implies that the two are different; in either case the difference stands in need of independent proof. Furthermore, as was already mentioned, in his commentary on the *Sentences* Thomas used the expression 'secundum considerationem', which derived from the Latin translation of Avicenna, instead of 'secundum rationem', which he used in other works. Finally, he explicitly mentioned Avicenna in *De veritate*, where he quoted his view on God's knowledge. The fact that Thomas referred to Avicenna in connection with divine knowledge in his early works and not in his later works squares with his general tendency to decrease the number of quotations from Avicenna in the later work.[12]

---

[10] *Sent.*, I d. 35 q. 1 a. 1 ad 3 (ed. Mandonnet, 1), 812: "(I)ntellectum ab intellectu nullo modo differt re in eo, sed consideratione tantum: quia prout consideratur essentia eius ut immunis a materia, sic est intelligens (…), sed prout consideratur essentia sua secundum quod intellectus accipit eam sine materia, sic est intellectum (…)."; *De veritate*, q. 2 a. 2 ad 1 (ed. Leon., 22/1), 45a-b.

[11] *STheol.*, I q. 14 a. 4 c. (ed. Leon., 4), 171a; *De substantiis separatis*, c. 14, Rome 1969 (ed. Leon., 40), D65a. Cf. Aristotle, *Metaphysics*, XII c. 9, 1074b15-1075a10.

[12] Thomas Aquinas, *Sent.*, I d. 35 q. 1 a. 1 ad 3 (ed. Mandonnet, 1), 812; cf. Avicenna, *Liber de philosophia prima*, VIII c. 6 (ed. van Riet), 415; Thomas Aquinas, *De veritate*, q. 2 a. 2 (ed. Leon., 22/1), 45a. On the quotations from Avicenna in the works of Thomas, see G.C. Anawati, 'Saint Thomas d'Aquin et la Métaphysique d'Avicenne', *St. Thomas Aquinas 1274-1974. Commemorative Studies*, Vol. 1, Toronto, Canada 1974, 449-465, esp. 454.

Knowledge as an attribute: the positions in the period 1280-1310
1. Unity vs. plurality

At the turn of the thirteenth and fourteenth century, a good deal of the discussion on divine attributes concerned their epistemological and metaphysical status. This can be seen in the works of Henry of Ghent, Godfrey of Fontaines, Thomas of Sutton, and Duns Scotus. If God is perfectly one, then how can different attributes be predicated of him? Two things were taken for granted in this discussion: first, that God is one, and second, that he has properties that are not identical with each other (God's knowledge is not equal to his will, for he knows the sins of man and yet he does not will them). The question was how to reconcile these two assumptions. This raised an epistemological problem — how can a unity be distinguished into different aspects? — as well as an ontological problem—what is the ground for these differences?

The solution offered by Scotus, to which we shall return shortly, involved the notion of a 'formal distinction'. Scotus was not the first to use a notion of this kind. Similar concepts had been invoked earlier by several Franciscan thinkers, including Bonaventure, Peter of John Olivi, and Peter of Trabibus. That the formal distinction was nonetheless generally treated as exclusively Scotistic in the fourteenth century, was caused by the enormous influence of Scotus at the time, and by the thoroughness with which he and his followers studied the formal distinction, extending its application to the doctrine of Trinity and the status of the divine attributes.

The formal distinction was seen as a halfway house between the real distinction and the rational distinction. It was more than a mere conceptual construct, but less than the distinction between two real things.

That the attributes were not really distinct was a *communis opinio*: the attributes coincide with God's essence, which is undivided. God is not made up of separate parts. Yet the obvious alternative, that the attributes are distinct only in the thought of man (the line of Thomas in the *Summa theologiae*, as we have seen), was equally unsatisfactory in the eyes of some, for reasons that involved the Trinity. The persons in the Trinity are really distinct from one another, notwithstanding the fact that each of them coincides with divine essence. This was the only real distinction in God allowed, and even required, by faith.[13] Some theologians, including Scotus, saw the difference between the Son and the Holy Spirit as grounded in the difference between divine

---

[13] Interest in this ancient Trinitarian dogma was rekindled in the thirteenth century. It was emphatically vindicated in the case of the condemnation of Joachim of Fiore († 1202) at the fourth Lateran Council in 1215, cf. *Constitutiones Concilii quarti Lateranensis una cum Commentariis glossatorum*, ed. A. García y García, Vatican City 1981 (Monumenta iuris canonici, A/2), 41-47. Throughout the second half of the thirteenth century the dogma was discussed in almost every commentary on Lombard's *Sentences*, with reference to the Council.

intellect (Son) and divine will (Holy Spirit). If God's intellect and God's will are distinct only for an act of the human intellect, then how can they be the source of the real distinction between the persons in God's essence? These considerations led some theologians to the conclusion that the attributes of God should be more than mere products of the human mind, that is, that they should be distinct *ex natura rei* in a way that precedes human thought. This is the distinction that was called 'formal' by Scotus and many of his followers.

Henry of Ghent

Apart from Scotus, important contributions to the discussion of divine attributes were also made by Henry of Ghent and Godfrey of Fontaines. In his fifth *Quodlibet*, written in 1280 or 1281, Henry of Ghent criticized the *Summa* line of Thomas Aquinas, although he agreed with Thomas that the distinction between the attributes is rational.[14] The difference between their positions consisted in the fact that Thomas saw the rational distinction as a product of human thought, whereas Henry of Ghent saw it as a product of divine thought. Henry tried to escape from a difficulty he saw in Thomas's position: would there still be a distinction between the attributes even if there were no creatures, or would divine will and intellect be identical then?

Henry argued that the relation between the divine persons is grounded in the difference between the attributes. Now, this relation is not arbitrary, for the Son is produced by an act of the intellect, whereas the Spirit is produced by an act of the will, and not the other way round. This would be impossible without some kind of difference in God himself.[15]

The derivation of distinct attributes from divine unity reveals the Neoplatonic background of Henry of Ghent's position. It resembles the emanation of a plurality (the lower intelligences) from a unity (the first intelligence) found in Avicenna's *Metaphysics* and in the *Liber de causis*: the unity's reflection on itself unfolds the plurality implicitly contained in it. In Henry of Ghent the reasoning was as follows. As an immaterial substance God has perfect self-knowledge. In this self-knowledge several stages can be distinguished. First, God knows his essence as essence. Secondly, reflecting on his essence, he knows it as known, as knower, and as mode of knowledge (*ratio intelligendi*). This is why God has the attribute 'knowledge'. Now, because God takes delight in his essence, which he knows to be the highest good, he also knows it as willed, as willing, and as mode of willing (*ratio volendi*). This is why God has the attribute 'will'.[16]

---

[14] For the date of Henry's fifth *Quodlibet*, see the introduction to Henry of Ghent, *Quodlibet* I, ed. R. Macken, Leuven-Leiden 1979 (Opera omnia, 5), XVII.

[15] Henry of Ghent, *Quodlibeta*, V q. 1, Paris 1518, repr. Louvain 1961, fol. 152rP.

[16] Ibid., fol. 153rV: "(S)umuntur omnes respectus attributorum verissime ad intra, inquantum videlicet intellectus divinus concipiens divinam essentiam, concipit seipsum et omnia concipienda circa eam (...). (P)rimo et simplici intelligentia concipit ipsam essentiam sub

The difference between Henry and Thomas (in the *Summa*) can succinctly be put as follows. What in Thomas's view is accomplished by man's reflection on the real plurality of perfections in creation, in Henry's view is accomplished by God through his self-knowledge, that is, through the discovery and determination of distinct attributes.

Godfrey of Fontaines

The view of Henry of Ghent was quoted at length and criticized in detail in the *Quodlibeta* of Godfrey of Fontaines, particularly in the seventh *Quodlibet* of the early 1290s.[17] Against the Neoplatonicizing argument discussed above he launched a fundamental objection: it is impossible to derive a difference, rational or otherwise, from that which is one. A difference can only derive from a relation of the one to an external manifold, for only then does the intellect have a point of reference for conceiving of a plurality of aspects within the one. Godfrey's objection, which was of a most fundamental nature, was not motivated by a lack of understanding of the Neoplatonic aspects of Henry of Ghent's thought. Godfrey of Fontaines was the author of a critical annotation to Avicenna's *Metaphysics* (the original basis of the view advocated by Henry), which had the form of a confrontation between Avicenna and other thinkers, Averroes among them.[18]

According to Godfrey, the attributes in God are one. If God knows only himself, then he knows only the unity of his perfections and not the differences between them. Therefore he must first know the creatures and their differences before he can conceive of the distinction between the attributes as rational differences in his essence. For only in the created world are the perfections distinct from one another. This knowledge does not add to the perfection of God, nor does God become dependent upon the creatures: the distinction is merely rational, while the content of his perfection remains the same.[19] This position was also endorsed by Godfrey in his *Quodlibeta* 14 and 15, dating from the late 1290s and 1303-1304, respectively.

---

ratione essentiae, et deinde negotiando circa essentiam conceptam concipit eam ut intellecta est, et ut intelligens est, et ut ratio intelligendi. Et quia in cognoscendo et intelligendo seipsam complacet ei in seipsa, deinde concipit eam ut volitum, volens et ratio volendi."

[17] For the date of Godfrey's *Quodlibeta* and for a discussion of his view on the divine attributes, see J.F. Wippel, *The Metaphysical Thought of Godfrey of Fontaines. A Study in Late Thirteenth-Century Philosophy*, Washington, D.C. 1981, XXVIIf (date), and 115-123.

[18] For Godfrey's criticism of the position of Henry of Ghent, see Godfrey of Fontaines, *Les Quodlibet cinq, six et sept*, ed. M. de Wulf and J. Hoffmans, Louvain 1914 (Les philosophes Belges, 3), VII q. 1, 270: "Quod enim in uno omnino simplici et indistincto secundum rem ponantur aliqua plura et distincta pure secundum rationem absque comparatione ad aliqua, quae aliquo modo differunt ab eo in quo huiusmodi distincta sola ratione ponuntur, est impossibile (…)." For Godfrey's annotation to Avicenna's *Metaphysics*, see Avicenna, *Liber de philosophia prima*, V-X (ed. van Riet), 86*-114*.

[19] Godfrey of Fontaines, ibid., 271.

From a remark in the commentary on the *Sentences* of Pierre Roger (the future Pope Clemens VI, † 1352), we learn that the views of Godfrey of Fontaines were not uncommon in Paris in the years 1320-1321, and that they played a role in the discussion then going on between Pierre Roger and Francis of Mayronnes concerning the status of *rationes* in God. In this context, Godfrey's views were classified as Thomistic. (Peter of Aquila also equated the views of Thomas Aquinas and Godfrey of Fontaines.) In the course of this debate, Francis of Mayronnes sought to reconcile Thomists and Scotists by associating one of the meanings of the term 'ratio' given by Thomas (*ratio definitiva non ab anima fabricata*), with the Scotistic view of the formal distinction *ex natura rei*. The fact that the parties to this debate wore the colours of Thomists and Scotists shows us that the formal distinction was at that time a point of public controversy between the two factions.[20]

2. Duns Scotus

It has recently been established that Scotus's notion of formal distinction was not as static as has been assumed, but underwent some changes in the course of his career. This development took place not so much in the basic idea of a distinction *a parte rei* itself, but rather in the particular significance given to the aspect of 'distinction'.[21] Simply stated, in the *Lectura* it was the *distinction* that Scotus stressed, while in his Parisian period the emphasis shifted from formal distinction or difference to formal *non-identity*. Subsequently, in the *Ordinatio* Scotus seems to have fallen in again with the line of the *Lectura*, rather than with his Parisian view. Both the line of *Lectura/ Ordinatio* and that of the Parisian period were taken up by Franciscan thinkers at the beginning of the fourteenth century.[22]

---

[20] Cf. Francis of Mayronnes and Pierre Roger, *Disputatio (1320-1321)*, ed. J. Barbet, Paris 1961 (Textes philosophiques du Moyen Age, 10), n. 237, 168 (= Pierre Roger, *Sent.*, II, secunda replicatio contra fratrem Franciscum): "(D)octrina enim magistri Go<dofridi> reputatur Parisius satis communis (...)."; Peter of Aquila, *Quaestiones in 4 libros Sententiarum*, I d. 8 q. 4, Speyer 1480, repr. Frankfurt am Main 1967, coll. 1-2 (not foliated): "(E)st una opinio Thomae et Gotfridi quod inter attributa est tantum distinctio per actum intellectus sive rationis." On the use of the term *ratio* by Francis of Mayronnes, see F. Ruello, 'La notion 'thomiste' de 'ratio in divinis' dans la Disputatio de François de Meyronnes et de Pierre Roger (1320-1321)', *RThAM* 32 (1965), 54-75.

[21] F. Wetter, *Die Trinitätslehre des Johannes Duns Scotus*, Münster 1967 (BGPhThMA, 41/5), 74; H.G. Gelber, *Logic*, 101.

[22] The *Lectura/Ordinatio* line is found in Alexander of Alessandria († 1314, 1307-1308 magister in Paris), and in the Scotists Francis of Mayronnes and Peter of Aquila. It is clear from Alexander of Alessandria's work that he was acquainted with the objection that every distinction is either rational or real (but not formal), and that a formal distinction implies a real distinction; these objections were raised against Scotus by Thomas of Sutton and by the author of the *Liber propugnatorius*.
The more reticent line of the Parisian period was followed by William of Alnwick (secretary to Scotus in Paris) and by the Scotist Landulph Caracciolo († 1351). William of Alnwick contended in his *Quodlibet* (q. 2) that the attributes in God are not formally or *simpliciter ex*

Scotus used various terms for referring to formally distinct things such as the attributes. In the *Lectura* and in the *Ordinatio* his expressions included *realitates, formalitates, rationes, rationes formales, intentiones,* and *rationes reales.* The distinction itself was called a 'formal distinction' and a 'formal non-identity', as we have seen, but also a *differentia secundum rationem quiditativam, differentia secundum rationem,* or a *differentia virtualis.* In Paris, Scotus most notably used the expression *secundum quid distinctio ex natura rei,* the emphasis on *secundum quid* reflecting the fact that the distinction was not real.[23]

Scotus's view, particularly as expressed in the *Lectura*, could easily be construed as a denial of God's unity, which was indeed the usual criticism of the formal distinction. As has been suggested by Friedrich Wetter and Hester G. Gelber, Scotus's reticence in Paris with regard to the aspect of distinction may have been caused by the debate on the formal distinction in 1302-1303, which involved the Paris Chancellor, among others.[24]

The formal distinction between the attributes

According to Scotus, for two things, for instance two attributes, to be formally distinct or formally non-identical, it is required that they are really the *same* thing or *in* the same thing, and that the definition of the one does not include the definition of the other, provided the things under consideration admit of a definition in the Aristotelian sense. This last clause was added by Scotus because he did not believe that pure perfections could be defined (because of their simplicity), though they are still distinct from one another. Every perfection has its own irreducible quiddity. The difference between these quiddities is not caused by the intellect, but exists *ex natura rei*. If an intellect, reflecting on the irreducibility of the quiddities, forms the proposition that 'wisdom is not formally identical with goodness', then the truth of this proposition is not caused by the intellect that forms it (for in that case all truth would be subjective), but by wisdom and goodness itself.[25]

---

natura rei distinct, but only *secundum quid ex natura rei.* Landulph Caracciolo, like Alnwick, distinguished between formal non-identity and formal difference, the first of which does not imply a real difference and can hence be predicated of the attributes without endangering divine unity. For Landulph, see Gelber, *Logic,* 105.

[23] The relevant places in Scotus's works are mentioned in M. McCord Adams, 'Ockham on Identity and Distinction', *FcS* 36 (1976), 5-74, esp. 31f and 33 n. 84; F. Wetter, *Die Trinitätslehre,* 62; Gelber, *Logic,* 82-85.

[24] Wetter, *Die Trinitätslehre,* 64, and Gelber, *Logic,* 71 and 85. Scotus's denial of the existence of a formal distinction in God, and the fact that he devoted a *quaestio* to this matter in Paris because some took him to be introducing an inadmissible difference in God, were mentioned in the *Reportatio* of Walter Chatton's (OFM, † 1343) commentary on the *Sentences* (London?, ca. 1321-1323), I d. 34 q. 1, see the text quoted in Gelber, *Logic,* 535 n. 59. For the date of Chatton's *Reportatio,* see Walter Chatton, *Reportatio et Lectura super Sententias: Collatio ad Librum Primum et Prologus,* ed. J.C. Wey, Toronto 1989 (Studies and Texts, 90), 1.

[25] Duns Scotus, *Ordinatio,* I d. 8 p. 1 q. 4 n. 193, Vatican City 1956 (ed. Vat., 4), 262.

That all perfections exist in God, and that they are formally distinct in him even before any operation of the divine intellect, Scotus argued as follows. In the first place, if not *all* perfections existed in God, then God would not be perfect, which is impossible because of the Anselmian rule that God is the most perfect being. Secondly, the perfections in God must exist in a perfect way, for else they would not exist perfectly (i.e., infinitely) anywhere at all, since perfections in the created world are without exception finite. The perfections that have perfect existence in God must have *real being* and not just *being-as-known* in God's intellect, as Henry of Ghent had thought: for real being is more perfect than being-as-known. Finally, if the perfections, such as knowledge and will, were to exist formally only in the creatures and not in God, then they would exist formally only in the participants, and not in the cause of the formal participation. But this is impossible: for how could the creatures participate in something of the first principle that the first principle itself does not have?[26]

Infinity leaves the formal distinction intact

According to Scotus, the proper conceptual content of each of the quiddities is not in the least affected by God's infinity. Thus it is not the case, as Thomas had claimed in the *Summa theologiae*, that the perfections, which are formally distinct in the creatures, form a single indiscriminate perfection in God. 'Knowledge' and 'will' are so-called *transcendentalia*, which transcend the distinction between finite and infinite. Their unique conceptual content is the same whether they are attributed to God or to the creatures; only their mode is changed. On this account Scotus believed that man has univocal knowledge of divine perfections. Man's conception of 'knowledge', acquired by abstraction from the finiteness of the notion of 'knowledge' as drawn from the created world, is the very concept that applies to the infinite deity.[27]

The distinction precedes knowledge, and is not constituted by it

Against Henry of Ghent, Scotus argued that the intuitive knowledge God has of his essence implies that the distinction between the attributes must precede knowledge and cannot be constituted by it. Intuitive knowledge is knowledge of something as existing. Therefore, if God has intuitive knowledge of distinctions in his essence, as was admitted by Henry of Ghent, then these distinctions must exist in reality, as opposed to being mere products of an act of knowledge. If the attributes were only the product of an act of knowledge,

---

[26] Ibid., n. 185, 252f.

[27] On Scotus's notion of *transcendentalia*, see A.B. Wolter's still very useful work, *The Transcendentals and Their Function in the Metaphysics of Duns Scotus*, St. Bonaventure, New York 1946 (Franciscan Institute Publications Philosophy Series, 3); T.A. Barth, 'Being, Univocity, and Analogy According to Duns Scotus', *John Duns Scotus, 1265-1965*, ed. J.K. Ryan and B.M. Bonansea, Washington, D.C. 1965 (SPhHPh, 3), 210-262.

then God would know something as existing which in reality has only being-as-known; obviously, the falsity of this knowledge is inconsistent with God's perfection.[28]

This criticism clearly shows in which respect Scotus differed from Godfrey of Fontaines as well as from Henry of Ghent. His view was the exact opposite of that of Godfrey of Fontaines: in order to know the differences between his attributes, God must turn his knowledge inward, not outward. The difference with Henry of Ghent, who also held that God knows the attributes through inward knowledge, was largely about the nature of this knowledge, which according to Scotus was direct and not reflexive.

The formal distinction and God's unity

From the concept of divine infinity, Scotus inferred that the formal distinction between the attributes did not contradict God's unity. All perfections in God are infinite; hence they are identical with one another, for nothing infinite can contain a potentiality. This is why 'knowledge' and 'will' can be predicated of each other, even though they are not formally identical.[29] The case is different with created perfections, which can only come together because of some third thing. According to Scotus, what we have here is a fundamental difference between the unity of perfections in the infinite deity and in the finite creature. *Animal* and *rationalis* are identical only insofar as they are both predicated of man; taken by themselves as abstract quiddities there is no identity at all. *Animalitas* contains no trace of *rationalitas*; 'Man is a rational living being' is true, but '*Animalitas* is *rationalitas*' is not.[30]

3. Thomistic criticism

The views of Henry of Ghent and Duns Scotus were severely criticized in a Thomistic vein by Thomas of Sutton. His criticism of Henry of Ghent as delivered in the second *Quodlibet*, written in the 1280s or 1290s, essentially agreed with that offered by Godfrey of Fontaines, claiming that God knows his essence only as a unity. Like Godfrey, Thomas of Sutton relied here on the idea that from a unity only a unity can follow. God can know the differences between the attributes only through his knowledge of the human intellect, which distinguishes between various attributes in God on the basis of differences in the world of creation.[31] This knowledge is eternal and immu-

---

[28] *Ordinatio*, I d. 8 p. 1 q. 4 n. 187 (ed. Vat., 4), 257.
[29] Ibid., n. 215, 273: "(B)onitas et sapientia et cetera huiusmodi, sunt eadem quasi identitate mutua, quia utrumque est formaliter infinitum, propter quam infinitatem utrumque est idem alteri (...)."
[30] Ibid., n. 219, 274f.
[31] Thomas of Sutton, *Quodlibeta*, II q. 2, ed. M. Schmaus and M. González-Haba, München 1969 (VKHUTMG, 2), 167 and 168: "(N)on cognoscit distincta attributa, nisi inquantum

table (in spite of the fact that human knowledge is not), for God knows everything in his eternity.

The criticism of Scotus, put forward in the third *Quodlibet* (written after 1311), focused on the attributes being distinct *ex natura rei*. Sutton acknowledged only two basic types of distinction, rational and real. All distinctions that are not produced by the intellect alone are real. Seen from this angle, the position of Scotus implies the existence of a composition in God.[32]

In his treatise *Contra Robert Cowton*, Sutton sought to support his position by reference to the view of Thomas Aquinas in the *Summa theologiae*: the concepts of divine attributes formed by man have their foundation in the perfection of divine essence, yet their differences do not in any way imply a difference in God.[33]

The formal distinction was also severely criticized by the author of the *Liber propugnatorius*, written ca. 1310.[34] The main point of criticism here was that a formal distinction between the attributes is inconsistent with God's unity. This is certainly one of the most crucial objections with which the position of Scotus was confronted, and as we shall presently see, it was also raised by Ockham. The author of the *Liber propugnatorius* was following here the line set out by Thomas Aquinas in the *Summa theologiae*, and by Godfrey of Fontaines.[35]

WILLIAM OF OCKHAM

Ockham's criticism of the theories of divine attributes as proposed by Henry of Ghent and Scotus started from two basic points: first, that all being (*entia*) is either real or rational, and second, that real beings can only differ in reality, and that rational beings can differ only rationally.[36]

---

cognoscit suam essentiam sub diversis rationibus intelligibilem ab intellectu creato (...)." The date of Sutton's *Quodlibeta* is according to pp. XVI-XXII. See also J.F. Wippel, 'Thomas of Sutton on Divine Knowledge of Future Contingents', *Knowledge and the Sciences in Medieval Philosophy. Proceedings of the Eight International Congress of Medieval Philosophy*, Vol. 2, ed. S. Knuuttila, R. Työrinoja, and S. Ebbesen, Helsinki 1990, 364-372, esp. 364 n. 1.

[32] Ibid., III q. 1, 340. For a discussion of Thomas of Sutton's view on the formal distinction, see Thomas of Sutton, *Contra Quodlibet Iohannis Duns Scoti*, ed. J. Schneider, München 1978 (VKHUTMG, 7), 21-56.

[33] See the texts quoted in Thomas of Sutton, *Contra Quodlibet* (ed. Schneider), 32-36.

[34] In the printed edition, *Liber propugnatorius super primum Sententiarum contra Johannem Scotum*, Venice 1523, repr. Frankfurt a/Main 1966, I d. 8 q. 5, the discussion took no less than nine columns: fol. 70vb-72vb. On the (unknown) author of this treatise, see Thomas of Sutton, *Quaestiones ordinariae*, ed. J. Schneider, München 1977 (VKHUTMG, 3), 63*-66*.

[35] Cf. *Liber propugnatorius*, ibid., fol. 72ra: "(E)x hoc quod ad extra in creatura distinguuntur realiter intellectus et voluntas, habet ortum distinctio istorum secundum rationem in Deo."

[36] For a discussion of Ockham's criticism of the formal distinction, see M. McCord Adams, *William Ockham*, Vol. II, Notre Dame, Ind. 1987 (Publications in Medieval Studies, 26/2), 934-941; R. Schönberger, 'Realität und Differenz. Ockhams Kritik an der distinctio formalis', *Die Gegenwart Ockhams*, ed. W. Vossenkuhl and R. Schönberger, Weinheim 1990 (Acta humaniora), 97-122.

Criticism of Scotus's formal distinction

Ockham believed that formal non-identity of the divine attributes implied real non-identity, a point also made by Thomistic writers, such as Thomas of Sutton and the author of the *Liber propugnatorius*.[37] Ockham argued as follows. If there is non-identity with regard to two beings, then it is possible to find (*verificari*) contraries. These contraries are either real, or rational, or composed of something real and something rational. Now, if we assume with Scotus that the attributes are distinct because of their nature (*ex natura rei*), then the contraries in this case can neither be rational nor composed of something rational and something real. For that which is rational cannot exist in the nature of a real being, since it is produced by the intellect. The non-identity envisaged by Scotus must therefore be a distinction between real things.[38]

The nature of Ockham's argument is better appreciated if we take a look at some of its background. Ockham was of the opinion that there are only four ways for two things to be different from one another. A difference may occur between (1) real beings, or (2) rational beings, or (3) a real being and a rational being, or (4) a composition of a real being and a rational being on the one hand, and, on the other hand, either a similar composition, a real being, or a rational being. In the first case, he claimed, we have a real distinction, while in the second case we have a rational distinction. The third case and the fourth case he treated as some kind of intermediate, being neither rational nor real, because the entities in question are neither fully real nor fully rational. The name to be accorded to this 'mixed' kind of distinction, Ockham claimed, was of no consequence, since it depends entirely on the language user's will.[39]

In sum, we can say that Ockham acknowledged only two kinds of being (apart from the mixed kinds composed of those two), viz., rational being and real being. A difference between real beings is always real, while a difference between rational beings is always rational. The Ockhamist rationale behind this view is clear enough. There is no third entity that causes the difference between two things; things are different by themselves and not through something else. Therefore, the ontological status of a distinction is simply that of the things distinguished. Ockham also applied this line of reasoning

---

[37] In this connection, it is worth noting the interesting parallel between the views of the Dominican school and those that are currently seen as the hallmark of late medieval nominalism, cf. W.J. Courtenay, *Capacity and Volition. A History of the Distinction of Absolute and Ordained Power*, Bergamo 1990 (Quodlibet, 8), 73f. M. Jordan, 'What's New in Ockham's Formal Distinction?', *FcS* 45 (1985), 97-110 esp. 102, writes: "That William of Ockham was one of the first, and continues to be one of the most important, critics of the formal distinction should come as no suprise to anyone with even superficial knowledge of 13th and 14th Century Western Thought." The first part of this claim is surprising, in the light of the sources mentioned above.
[38] William of Ockham, *Scriptum*, I d. 2 q. 1 (OTh, 2), 14.
[39] Ibid., q. 3, 78f.

to matters of identity: real identity is always between real things, rational identity is always between rational things.[40]

The view that the mode of being of a relation follows that of the things related is also found in the work of William of Alnwick and James of Ascoli. In William of Alnwick, the argument was structured to the effect that the attributes in God are not formally and *simpliciter ex natura rei* distinct, but only *secundum quid*. The argument was as follows. Things that are really different have different realities, while things that are rationally different have different *rationes*; likewise, things that are formally different have different formal natures. In God there can be no different formal natures, as this would imply an absolute distinction, which is contrary to God's unity. Therefore, the attributes cannot be formally distinct. Yet the distinction between the attributes precedes any activity of the divine intellect (a typically Scotistic point). Hence the attributes must be *ex natura rei* distinct, not *simpliciter* or formally, but only *secundum quid*.[41]

James of Ascoli used the view of the relation following the relata to argue that if, for example, a stone is represented by God's essence, we can neither say that it is really identical with divine essence, nor that it is really distinct from it. Unlike divine essence, James claimed, such a stone does not have real being. Therefore it cannot be compared to the essence. We can only say that the stone and the essence are neither really identical nor really distinct.[42]

Against this background, Ockham's criticism of Scotus is easy to situate. According to Scotus the attributes really coincide with God's essence, which makes them as real as divine essence. Now, if they are also (formally) *different*, as Scotus assumed, then this must be a difference between *real* beings. Therefore, Ockham concluded, attributes that are *distinct* in God, must be *really* distinct, because a distinction between real beings is always a real distinction.[43]

The difference between the positions of Scotus and Ockham ultimately went back to a difference in their general ontological outlook. Ockham admitted only two kinds of being, rational and real. Scotus, however, admitted a third kind, that of formalities. Standing halfway between real

---

[40] Ibid., 75: "(S)icut distinctio rationis et identitas rationis se habent ad entia rationis, ita differentia realis et identitas realis se habent ad entia realia (...)."

[41] William of Alnwick, *Quaestiones disputatae de esse intelligibili et de quolibet*, Quodl. q. 2, ed. A. Ledoux, Florence 1937 (BFSMA, 10), 232 and 244f.

[42] *Quaestiones ordinarie*, q. 5, as edited in T. Yokoyama, 'Zwei Quaestionen des Jacobus de Aesculo über das esse obiectivum', *Wahrheit und Verkündigung*, Vol. I, ed. L. Scheffczyk, W. Dettlof, and R. Heinzmann, München 1967, 31-74, esp. 49.

[43] The view that there are only two kinds of being, real and rational, and correspondingly only two kinds of distinction, was a principal point in the criticism of Scotus. It was used by several writers other than Ockham, including Godfrey of Fontaines, Thomas of Sutton, Hervaeus Natalis, and Durand of St. Pourçain. For references to the germane passages, see R. Schönberger, 'Realität und Differenz', 118 nn. 68-71.

being and rational being, these were supposed to have a determinate formal nature independent of either the being they belong to or the intellect that knows them. One and the same real being can contain more than one formal being. Accordingly, Scotus held that in addition to real and rational distinctions, things can also be distinct formally.

Although Ockham rejected the formal distinction with regard to the divine attributes, he retained it with regard to the Trinity. Each of the divine persons coincides with the essence, yet they are really distinct, being three hypostases with irreducible properties. In this one special case of a real being (the essence) that is at the same time three real beings (the persons), Ockham saw it proper to speak of a formal distinction. Thus the Father and the essence are formally distinct, yet really identical. Some real properties accrue to the Father that do not accrue to the reality of the essence. Therefore, we discover here a difference between real beings. Yet, as these real beings are also one, their difference is not real, but formal. Ockham's use of the formal distinction, then, was limited to real beings that are one, and did not apply to formalities.[44] In the case of the attributes we do not have one being (the essence) that is at the same time more beings (the attributes), for the attributes are indiscriminately one. Hence Ockham refused to speak of a formal distinction in this case. The same goes for the creatures, none of which is at once one real being and many real beings.

Criticism of Henry of Ghent

Ockham's criticism of Henry of Ghent drew on the same basic points. Because distinctions follow the status of the things they distinguish, it is impossible for a real being to be rationally distinct from itself, or for two rational beings to be really distinct. Now, if we assume with Henry of Ghent that the attributes are rationally distinct, then they cannot coincide with God's essence. Alternatively, if they are said to be really identical with God's essence, as also assumed by Henry of Ghent, then they cannot be rationally distinct.[45]

The background of Ockham's basic objections becomes particularly clear in his criticism of Henry of Ghent. The difference between a rational being and a real being is greater than that between two real beings. For being is first divided into real and rational being (the well-known division of existence inside and outside the soul). Subsequently, further divisions may be brought to bear, such as those between two real beings. Now, differences with regard to the prior and more general division cut deeper than differences with regard to the posterior and more shallow division. This is why something that has

---

[44] *Scriptum*, I d. 2 q. 1 (OTh, 2), 19. For Ockham's teachings on the Trinity and his use of the formal distinction, see M. McCord Adams, *William Ockham*, II, 996-1007.

[45] *Scriptum*, ibid., q. 2, 63.

only being-as-known does not have real being. Therefore, if the attributes only have being-as-known and thus are rational, as Henry of Ghent claimed, they cannot *really be* the divine essence itself.[46]

Unlike the *Scriptum*, Ockham's *Quodlibeta* no longer mentioned the notion of a rational distinction as one between *rational* entities having objective being, speaking instead of a distinction between *real* entities, viz., between written, spoken, or thought definitions and descriptions. Also, the *Quodlibeta* no longer grouped rational beings into a separate kind next to real beings, but included them as a subgroup among the real beings. Marilyn McCord Adams has rightly argued for a connection between these two significant changes and the fact that Ockham, in the *Quodlibeta*, no longer saw concepts in the mind (*entia rationis*) as objective beings, identifying them rather with the acts of knowledge themselves, which as such have real being.[47]

The position of Ockham

The division between real and rational being was not only central to Ockham's criticism but also to the development of his own view on the attributes. According to Ockham, divine attributes can be taken in either of two ways: firstly, as an attributional perfection that is really identical with God; secondly, as something in the human mind that is predicated of God. Taken in the first sense, the attributes belong to the realm of reality; taken in the second sense they belong to the realm of man's speech and thought *about* reality. Depending on the level that is intended, the question of the attributes's plurality and ontological status requires a different approach. We shall consider each of the levels in turn.[48]

The attribute as (real) perfection

At the level of reality there is no plurality of attributes: there is only a single perfection that is a perfect unity and coincides with God.[49] Ockham's reason for this was quite straightforward. God is a simple, non-composite, real being.

---

[46] Ibid., 55.
[47] Cf. M. McCord Adams, 'Ockham on Identity and Distinction', 24f (contains references to the relevant passages in Ockham).
The sharp division between rational and real being made by Ockham in the *Scriptum* is also found in Henry of Harclay's *quaestio* on the ideas (Città del Vaticano, Bibl. Apost., Borgh., 171). There it is argued that the ideas used by God in creating things cannot be rational entities, because there is no similarity (*nulla similitudo*) between a rational entity and the real substance of the thing produced. No two things can be more different than a rational entity and a substance: since they belong to different *genera*, they cannot be similar in any respect except the most general, viz., qua being. See the edition of this *quaestio* in A.A. Maurer, 'Henry of Harclay's Questions on the Divine Ideas', *Med. Stud.* 23 (1961), 163-193, esp. 170.
[48] Cf. Ockham, *Scriptum*, I d. 2 q. 2 (OTh, 2), 61f. For Ockham's view on divine attributes, see A.A. Maurer, *Medieval Philosophy*, Toronto ²1982 (The Gilson Series, 4), 271-275, and M. McCord Adams, *William Ockham*, II, 941-952.

An attributional perfection that coincides with God must be as real as God himself. If there were more than one attribute, each as real as God himself, God would consist of more than one reality, which is contrary to his simplicity.

Because the attributional perfection completely coincides with God, Ockham was of the opinion that it is properly speaking (*de virtute sermonis*) incorrect to say that the attribute is *in* God, as this would apparently imply that the attribute is different from the essence (for nothing is *in* itself). This point was also made in other contexts: knowledge, for example, is not *in* God, but knowledge *is* God.[50]

The attribute as (conceptual) predicate in the human mind

If the attributes are taken as something at the level of our speech and thought *about* reality, by contrast, they are not really identical with God. They are mere concepts or tokens in the human mind that are predicated of God. In this case, Ockham claimed, it is more proper to speak of an attributional *name* or attributional *concept* than of an attributional *perfection*, which is always a thing (*res*), whereas concepts are neither things nor perfections as such (*perfectiones simpliciter*). Taken as a predicate, more than one attribute can be attributed to God; the plurality of attributes does not exist in God, but only in the human mind.[51]

Depending on the status accorded to concepts, the attributes are either rationally or really distinct. In the *Scriptum*, Ockham gave the following two

---

[49] *Scriptum*, I d. 2 q. 2, 61: "Primo modo dico quod non sunt plures perfectiones attributales, sed tantum est ibi una perfectio indistincta re et ratione (...)."

[50] *Scriptum*, I d. 35 q. 1 (OTh, 4), 432f. For a discussion of the notion 'de virtute sermonis', see W.J. Courtenay, 'Force of Words and Figures of Speech. The Crisis over 'virtus sermonis' in the Fourteenth Century', *FcS* 44 (1984), 107-128.
Remarks on the use of *esse in* with regard to God are also found in the *Lectura* of Walter Chatton (Oxford 1328-1330). When theologians use the expression *esse in* in propositions such as 'Wisdom is in God' or 'Divinity is in God', they mean something different from ordinary usage. In these phrases, wisdom or divinity should not be taken to belong to God in the way parts belong to a whole, or accidents belong to a substance; rather, they betoken the fact that wisdom and divinity coincide with God, in the way Socrates's humanity coincides with Socrates himself. According to Chatton, different terms predicated of God refer to one and the same object, yet they are not synonymous, because they signify God according to different formal definitions, thus creating the (false) impression that there are differences in God. See the relevant passages cited in H.G. Gelber, *Logic*, 606, n. 89 (= *Lectura*, I d. 2 q. 6 a. 4), and n. 88 (= a. 2). The date of the *Lectura* is according to Walter Chatton, *Reportatio* (ed. Wey), 1.
These remarks by Ockham and Walter Chatton illustrate their critical attitude toward theological language. None of the theologians of the thirteenth and early fourteenth century *intended* to say that the attributes are somehow contained in God as separate parts, yet this is precisely what most of them were *actually* saying with the expression 'in God' (cf., for example, Thomas Aquinas, *Sent.*, I d. 2 q. 1 aa. 2-3). Ockham and Chatton drew attention to the inadequacy of this expression, because it did not say what was intended.

[51] *Scriptum*, I d. 2 q. 2 (OTh, 2), 61f and 66: "(D)ico quod attributa divina quae sunt plura non sunt realiter essentia divina, sed attributa, quae sunt conceptus."

possibilities. First, if concepts have only rational being (being-as-known), then the attributes are rationally distinct, for rational beings can differ only rationally. Second, if concepts are taken as real qualities of the human mind, then the attributes have real being and are really distinct. In this case they are really distinct from divine essence, since both the concepts as acts of knowledge and divine essence are real. Whichever way concepts are understood, as being-as-known or as real being, the attributes can be predicated of God, because the attributional concepts stand for (*supponunt pro*) God's essence, although they are distinct from it.[52]

As we have already seen, in the *Quodlibeta septem* Ockham settled for the second of these options as his canonical view on concepts. It implies that the attributes, taken as attributional names, are both really and rationally distinct: *really*, because each attribute has existence in the mind as a distinct act of knowledge; and *rationally*, because each attribute has its own definition. Notice that in the *Quodlibeta* entities and relations are no longer 'rational' because of the ontological status of being-as-known (as they would be according to the first of the two options given in the *Scriptum*), but rather because of the definition (*ratio*) expressed by the act of knowledge that apprehends the entities and relations.[53]

We noted earlier that, in the *Quodlibeta*, Ockham attributed the use of 'nomen' for divine perfections to the *sancti antiqui*, and associated the use of 'attributum' with the *moderni*. According to Ockham, the *antiqui* acknowledged only a distinction between the names, not between what the names signify (i.e., God) — which was also exactly Ockham's own view. Ockham's position with regard to the attributes was criticized in Avignon by John Lutterell and the papal committee, whose exposition made reference to the saints.[54] Since Ockham finished the *Quodlibeta* in Avignon, his reference to the *sancti antiqui* should probably be seen in light of his defense against the accusation of heresy and modernism. It is thus worthwhile to examine the criticism by John Lutterell and the papal committee.[55]

The criticism by John Lutterell

In the so-called *Liber contra doctrinam G. Occam*, two articles (aa. 9-10) were devoted to Ockham's position on divine attributes. The author, John Lutterell, framed his criticism of Ockham from a point of view similar to that

---

[52] Ibid., 66.
[53] *Quodlibeta*, III q. 2 (OTh, 9), 209f.
[54] Cf. J. Koch, *Kleine Schriften*, Vol. 2, Rome 1973 (Storia e letteratura, 128), a. 1 (= R), and a. 15 (= V), 342: "Dicimus quod negare attributa divina differre ratione (scl., *in* God, MH) est falsum in philosophia et in theologia et est (*om.*, V) clare contra dicta sanctorum."
[55] For the dating of the *Quodlibeta*, see ibid., (OTh, 9), 36*-38* and 41* (introduction). See also recently William of Ockham, *Quodlibetal Questions*, Vol. 1, transl. by A.J. Freddoso and F.E. Kelly, New Haven-London 1991, xxiv.

of Thomas Aquinas in the commentary on the *Sentences*, although he did not mention Aquinas by name. The fact that Lutterell wrote his work shortly after Thomas's canonization (July 18, 1323) may be significant here. The occasion surely boosted the position of Thomas as an authority to be used in discerning heresies in other thinkers, which was exactly what Lutterell had in mind for Ockham. Moreover, Lutterell wrote his libel as a court document for John XXII, who is known to have adopted Thomas as an authority.[56]

Lutterell's criticism was directed against Ockham's fundamental distinction between *reality* (God) and our thinking *about* reality. His criticism developed two main points. First, Lutterell rejected the view that real beings cannot be rationally distinct. He argued that God's wisdom and his goodness are one *in re*, yet rationally distinct, since these attributes have different meanings. This difference does not exist only in the human mind as a difference between concepts, but exists also in God himself as that to which the conceptual difference corresponds.[57]

Secondly, Lutterell took exception to Ockham's contention that the attributes predicated of God in a proposition are not the same as divine essence. According to Lutterell, the propositional structure of subject and predicate corresponds to a similar structure in reality. If a predicate is veridically affirmed of a subject in the intellect (*per intellectum*), then the one thing (*res*) must belong to the other in reality as well. The attribute predicated of God in a proposition must therefore really exist in God: it is not a mere concept, but rather the thing (*res*) grasped by the concept.[58]

The criticism by the papal committee

Both points of criticism recurred in the two lists of errors drafted by the special committee of theologians enrolled by John XXII for inspecting Ockham's works with an eye to heresies. Members of the committee included John Lutterell and Durand of St. Pourçain. Although the order of the articles in the two lists is totally different, they show many literal similarities. One list (the so-called *Responsiones*, abbreviated here as 'R') was submitted to John XXII in a public meeting; the other was submitted later, under seal ('V').[59]

One of the views the committee took exception to was that the attributes in God are not rationally distinct. This was judged to be *falsum in philosophia*

---

[56] Cf. J. Miethke, *Ockhams Weg zur Sozialphilosophie*, Berlin 1969, 61 esp. n. 215.

[57] *Libellus contra doctrinam G. Occam*, a. 9 n. 62, as edited in F. Hoffmann, *Die Schriften des Oxforder Kanzlers Iohannes Lutterell*, Leipzig 1959 (Erfurter theologische Studien, 6), 32f.

[58] Ibid., a. 10 n. 68, 35.

[59] The process against Ockham is discussed by J. Koch, *Kleine Schriften*, II, 286-95; J. Miethke, *Ockhams Weg*, 58-74; F.E. Kelly, 'Ockham: Avignon, before and after', *From Ockham to Wyclif*, ed. A. Hudson and M. Wilks, Oxford 1987 (Studies in Church History, Subsidia 5), 1-18; G. Knysh, 'Biographical Rectifications Concerning Ockham's Avignon Period', *FcS* 46 (1986), 61-91.

et theologia. What is more, it led to errors with regard to the Trinity. If the divine attributes cannot be rationally distinct, since they are *idem re*, then surely it is also impossible for the divine persons (which coincide with God's essence) to be *really* distinct, since a real distinction cuts much deeper than a rational one.[60]

The second list ('V') reveals that one of the arguments endorsed as normative by the committee was similar to that of Thomas in the commentary on the *Sentences*: the plurality of attributes does not exist in the essence as either a plurality of the essence itself (*subiective*), or as something existing formally, but rather as the ground for the distinction between the attributes (*fundamentaliter*).[61] This last term was used in the sense of Thomas's *fundamentum proximum*, referring to the *significatum* of the attributional terms in God.

Secondly, the committee saw a contradiction in the fact that Ockham claimed on the one hand that the intellect is God's essence (which was not disputed), while at the same time maintaining that the proposition 'God's intellect is God's essence' is about two distinct concepts rather than about a real unity. If this were correct, so the committee argued, then no proposition would ever be true. Obviously, the sounds (*voces*) in the positions of subject and predicate are always different, and so are the concepts. Thus the requirement for truth, viz., coincidence of subject and predicate, would never be fulfilled.[62]

This objection makes clear that the members of the committee, quite on a par with Lutterell in his libel, believed that the relation of the terms in a proposition reflects a subject-predicate structure in reality. Unity at the level of reality implies unity at the level of the proposition, and vice versa. Ockham, by contrast, sharply distinguished between the two levels. What is one in reality (divine essence and intellect), can be referred to by different terms (subject and predicate).

Robert Holcot

In England, the criticism of Lutterell and the papal committee probably had little or no influence. (In fact, Ockham was never officially condemned for his theological views.) This may be gathered from the fact that Ockham's views on divine attributes were adopted by several English writers. We shall briefly review the position of one of them, Robert Holcot.[63]

---

[60] J. Koch, *Kleine Schriften*, II, (edition of both lists) a. 1 (= R), and a. 15 (= V), 342.
[61] Ibid., a. 15 (= V), 343.
[62] Ibid., a. 2 (= R), and a. 26 (= V), 343f.
[63] On Ockham's influence in England, see W.J. Courtenay, 'The Reception of Ockham's Thought in Fourteenth-Century England', *From Ockham to Wyclif* (see our note 59), 89-107; G.J. Etzkorn, 'Codex Merton 284: Evidence of Ockham's Early Influence in Oxford', *From Ockham to Wyclif*, 31-42.

In one of Holcot's *quaestiones quodlibetales*, which originated in 1333-1334, the influence of Ockham's views on attributes is unmistakable. According to Holcot, to speak of attributes is to speak of language. The term 'attribute', he claimed, is a second-level term, a term in meta-language: it designates the names and concepts we use when speaking about God and the creatures. Essential attributional perfections, such as wisdom and justice, Holcot described as words (i.e., attributes) signifying perfections, that can be predicated of terms signifying divine essence. For words can only be attributed to other words. Nothing can be attributed to God, since that would impugn his immutability.[64]

Holcot made a sharp distinction between real attributes and predicates. He also distinguished between two ways in which something may 'be in something', viz., the sense in which a part is really contained in a whole, or a form is really in a subject, and the sense in which a predicate is logically contained in a subject.[65]

Starting from these premises, Holcot drew up twelve *conclusiones*, which we shall briefly review.[66] Again, the twelve theses and their proofs clearly bear witness to the influence of Ockham.

> 1. No attribute is really *in* God. *Proof*: if it coincides with God, it is not *in* God, since nothing is *in* itself. Alternatively, if it does not coincide with God, then it is a creature, which is not *in* God either.
> 2. No attribute is a perfection as such (*perfectio simpliciter*). *Proof*: spoken sounds (*voces*) and concepts never are perfections as such. The proposition 'Wisdom is an attribute' is only true in case the term 'wisdom' does not stand for real wisdom (i.e., does not have personal supposition), but for the word or concept 'wisdom' (having *suppositio materialis* or *simplex*). If 'wisdom' refers to real wisdom, then the above proposition is false, because 'wisdom' then refers to a real perfection, while 'attribute' stands for a concept or word.
> 3. No attribute is identical with divine essence. *Proof*: all attributes are *voces* or concepts. Moreover, if some attribute were identical with the essence, then the essence would be an attribute of itself, which is impossible.
> 4. In God, the attributes cannot be distinguished. *Proof*: the attributes are not in God; therefore, they are not distinct in God. It is quite pointless to speak of a formal (or other) distinction between the attributes in God.
> 5. The attributes are really distinct from one another. *Proof*: *voces* and concepts are real (etc.).

---

[64] Robert Holcot, *Utrum perfectiones attributales essentiales in divinis distincte praecedant omnem operationem intellectus*, as edited by H.G. Gelber, *Exploring the Bounderies of Reason. Three Questions on the Nature of God by Robert Holcot OP*, Toronto 1983 (Studies and Texts, 62), 55-61. For the date of Holcot's *Quodlibeta*, see the introduction to the forthcoming edition by P.A. Streveler, K.H. Tachau, H.G. Gelber, and W.J. Courtenay, *Seeing the Future Clearly. Quodlibetal Questions on Future Contingents by Robert Holcot*. Cf. also K.H. Tachau, *Vision and Certitude in the Age of Ockham*, Leiden 1988 (STGM, 22), 244.
[65] Holcot, in H.G. Gelber, *Exploring*, 56.
[66] Ibid., 56-61.

6. Attributes that have different meanings qua *ratio* (definition or description) are rationally different. This holds good for 'intellect', 'will', and 'wisdom', for instance.
7. Some attributes are not rationally distinct, but only really so. *Proof*: this happens when the same attribute is pronounced in different languages. In cases like these, the words have the same *ratio* (and do not differ rationally), but are still different real words.
8. Attributes are not distinct without some prior operation of the intellect (*ante omnem operationem intellectus*). *Proof*: no meaningful word or concept can exist without intellectual activity.
9. Attributes can be really distinct without (actual) activity of the human intellect. *Proof*: this happens when someone forms a word in the imagination without using his intellect. Also, when two attributes are mentioned in a book.
10. Whatever is distinct, is really distinct. *Proof*: according to the grammarians, 'everything' means 'all things' (*omnes res*).
11. That every distinction is real does not mean that it is a third entity next to the things so distinguished. *Proof*: one thing is different from another through its essence.
11a. There is no middle ground between a rational distinction and a real one.
12. The proposition 'Divine essence and divine goodness are one thing' is false. *Proof*: two singular terms combined with a verb in plural always have supposition for two things.

Marsilius of Inghen

In his study on Marsilius's doctrine of Trinity, Wilhelm Möhler found a notable difference ("einen bemerkenswerten Unterschied") between the views on divine attributes of Marsilius and Ockham. According to Möhler, whose interpretation is still the most recent, Marsilius was of the opinion that the divine attributes are formally distinct.[67]

This interpretation does not strike us as correct, however. As we shall presently see, there is basically no difference between the views of Marsilius and Ockham with regard to divine attributes. Marsilius explicitly denied that the attributes in God are formally distinct. Like Ockham and many other non-Scotists, he insisted that the formal distinction is dependent upon the real distinction: things that are formally distinct must be really distinct as well.

Moreover, Marsilius taught that *within* God's essence there is no difference whatsoever *ex parte rei* between the attributes, therefore also no rational difference, and that the attributional differences conceived by man are actually differences between human concepts. Like Ockham and Holcot, Marsilius sharply distinguished between conceptual being on the one hand (human concepts), and real being on the other (God's essence).

---

[67] W. Möhler, *Die Trinitätslehre des Marsilius von Inghen. Ein Beitrag zur Geschichte der Theologie des Spätmittelalters*, Limburg/Lahn 1949, 134.

Attributional ratio vs. attributional perfection

Marsilius differentiated between two levels of discourse on the attributes, that of the attributional *ratio* and that of the attributional *perfectio*. The first level deals with the concept in the human mind that expresses what the attribute, e.g., wisdom, signifies. The second level refers to the thing itself that is signified by the attributional name, that is, the thing for which the name stands (*supponit*). The first level is concerned with something in the human mind, the second refers to divine nature.[68] This distinction corresponds to that made by Ockham between, on the one hand, the attributional perfection that is identical with God, and on the other hand, the attributional name that is a mere concept or sign that can be predicated of God.

The immediate source for Marsilius's distinction, however, was not Ockham but rather Gregory of Rimini, who was quoted by Marsilius, though without mentioning him by name. A distinction similar to Gregory's was used by Hugolin of Orvieto.[69]

In sum, Marsilius wanted to establish the following claim: the attributional perfections in God are neither really, nor formally, nor rationally distinct. Only the attributional concepts in the human mind are distinct. He made his point in several *conclusiones*, which we shall now examine.

The attributional perfections in God

First, Marsilius submitted the *conclusio* that God's intellect, his wisdom, and all of his other perfections are neither distinct from each other, nor from divine nature. He proved this claim by reference to a rule he attributed to Anselm, viz., that everything in God that does not specifically belong to one of the persons of the Trinity is one (Anselm, *De processione spiritus sancti*, c. 1). From the wording and proof of this *conclusio* it is clear that Marsilius used the *Lectura Oxoniensis* of Adam Wodeham.[70]

The second *conclusio* also made use of Wodeham's work. Divine will, divine wisdom, and all the other attributes of God, are not distinct formal

---

[68] *Sent.*, I q. 12 a. 3 (ed. Strasbourg 1501), fol. 60rb: "*Ratio attributalis* vocatur *ratio* vel *conceptus animae, explicans quid per attributum significatur. Perfectio attributalis vocatur entitas quam significat principaliter, et ex qua supponit abstractum attributum Deo* et *de eo dictum.*" For the source used by Marsilius, see the passage from Gregory of Rimini's *Sentences* commentary referred to in the following note.

[69] Gregory of Rimini, *Lectura*, I d. 8 q. 2 (ed. Trapp-Marcolino, 2), 75; Hugolin of Orvieto, *Commentarius in quattuor libros Sententiarum*, I d. 8 q. u. a. 1, ed. W. Eckermann, Vol. 2, Würzburg 1984, 192.

[70] Marsilius, *Sent.*, I q. 12 a. 3 (ed. Strasbourg 1501), fol. 60va: "*(P)rima conclusio* huius articuli: *Dei intellectus*, scientia, *sapientia*, et *volitio quae Deus est* et sic de ceteris perfectionibus designatis per attributa *non sunt res distinctae inter se vel a Dei natura.* Patet per *regulam venerabilis Anselmi*: 'quia *in divinis omnia sunt* idem, *ubi non obviat relationis oppositio'.* Et haec non est inter aliqua istorum, igitur." Cf. Adam Wodeham, *Lectura Oxoniensis*, I d. 6 q. 1 (Paris, Bibl. Maz., 915), fol. 72ra.

natures of the same thing, viz., divine essence. They are not different forms, or perfections, or formal *rationes*, or real *modi*, or intelligibilities or quiddities, or whatever other name they are given, of one and the same thing.[71]

We find a similar list of terms in Gregory of Rimini and later in Jean Gerson, who criticized Scotus and John of Ripa in particular, calling them *formalizantes*. The fact that so many different terms were used may indicate a lack of agreement or clarity among the Scotistic theologians on the question of how their formal distinction of the divine attributes should be understood. In this connection, Gregory of Rimini distinguished no less than six different senses of formal non–identity in Scotus alone.[72]

The opinion of Scotus was called an *opinio famosa* by Gregory of Rimini. Peter of Candia, in his commentary on the *Sentences* (Paris, ca. 1378), also spoke of the view of Scotus as a 'famous' opinion, setting it against another 'famous' opinion, that of Ockham and his followers (*sequaces*). Among these followers, he mentioned Adam Wodeham and Gregory of Rimini in particular. We may glean from this remark that the line of thought followed by Marsilius with regard to the divine attributes was probably a well–known opinion at the time Marsilius was studying theology in Paris.[73]

The Marsilian proof of the claim that the attributes in God are formally distinct neither from each other nor from divine essence, was based on the identification of reality and formality. The proof went as follows. If the formalities in God are really identical, as was assumed by Scotus and the Scotists, and if the *formality* of God's essence (F_1) is identical with the *reality* of God's essence (R_1), and if furthermore the formality of God's wisdom (F_2) is identical with the reality of God's wisdom (R_2), then it follows that F_1 and F_2 are identical: their realities R_1 and R_2 are by assumption identical with each other and with God's essence. If it is assumed, however, that formalities F_1 and F_2 are *not* identical with their respective realities, and if it is said that, for example, formality F_2 is formally distinct from its reality, then we are caught

---

[71] Marsilius, *Sent.*, I q. 12 a. 3, fol. 60va: "*Secunda conclusio: Sapientia divina, volitio divina*, et deitas, et ita de aliis attributis *non sunt* in Deo *distinctae formalitates inter se* unius et *eiusdem rei* absolutae. Puta, non habent se sic, quasi in *eadem re sint distinctae formalitates, vel* distinctae *perfectiones* seu diversae *rationes formales, vel modi reales eiusdem rei inter se* et *a parte rei distincti* (distinctae, *ed.*) seu etiam *distinctae cognoscibilitates, vel quiditates. Vel* quocumque alio modo eas *placuerit* appellari." Cf. Adam Wodeham, *Lectura Oxoniensis*, I d. 6 q. 1 (Paris, Bibl. Maz., 915), fol. 72ra-rb.

[72] Gregory of Rimini, *Lectura*, I d. 8 q. 1 a. 1 (ed. Trapp-Marcolino, 2), 29f; also: a. 2, 32; Jean Gerson, *Contra vanam curiositatem*, quoted by Z. Kaluza, *Les querelles*, 40f, and 68 n. 14. On the use of the term *formalizantes* for Scotus and the Scotists, see A. Combes, *Jean Gerson. Commentateur Dionysien. Pour l'histoire des courants doctrinaux à l'université de Paris à la fin du XIVe siècle*, Paris ²1973 (Etudes de philosophie médiévale, 30), 568-607, and Z. Kaluza, *Les querelles*, esp. 41 and 65.

[73] Gregory, *Lectura*, I d. 8 q. 1 a. 1 (ed. Trapp-Marcolino, 2), 26. For Peter of Candia, see the text cited by F. Ehrle, *Der Sentenzenkommentar*, 62. The dating is according to W.J. Courtenay, *Adam Wodeham*, 148.

in the following infinite regression. In order to show that there is a formal distinction between formality F_2 and its reality, a third formality F_3 must be posited. With respect to this new formality F_3, the question of its identity with the reality of F_2 recurs. If it is identical, then we may as well say that formality F_2 is identical with reality R_2, and that formalities F_1 and F_2 were identical to start with. If, however, formality F_3 is *not* identical with the reality of F_2, a fourth formality F_4 must be introduced, et cetera.[74]

The same proof appeared almost *verbatim* in Adam Wodeham's *Lectura Oxoniensis*. It is quoted in brief by Thomas of Strasbourg as one of the arguments adduced by *aliqui doctores* against the opinion of Scotus and his followers.[75]

Adam Wodeham, Gregory of Rimini, and Marsilius of Inghen all concurred that positing distinct formalities in God would imply the existence of distinct realities in God, which in turn would seriously compromise God's simplicity.[76] In addition, they did not share the feeling of the Scotists that without a formal distinction between the divine attributes it would not be possible to explain the differences between the divine persons in the Trinity. They all endorsed Ockham's argument that it is not impossible for one and the same principle (divine essence) to produce altogether different effects (Son and Holy Spirit). The different ways of production of the Son and the Holy Spirit can be explained without recourse to a formal distinction between God's intellect and God's will.[77]

In a third *conclusio*, Marsilius submitted that divine wisdom and all other attributional perfections are in reality as identical with divine essence as divine essence is identical with itself. *A parte rei* there is no distinction or non–identity whatsoever between the attributes of God.

---

[74] Marsilius, *Sent.*, I q. 12 a. 3 (ed. Strasbourg 1501), fol. 60va.

[75] Adam Wodeham, *Lectura Oxoniensis*, I d. 6 q. 1 (Paris, Bibl. Maz., 915), fol. 72rb; Thomas of Strasbourg, *Commentaria in IIII libros Sententiarum*, I d. 6 q. 1 a. 2, Venice 1564, repr. Ridgewood, New Jersey 1965, fol. 44rb.

[76] Adam Wodeham, *Lectura Oxoniensis*, I d. 6 q. 1, fol. 72rb: "(H)oc dato, sequeretur processus in infinitum in distinctis formalitatibus in qualibet earum contentis, vel dabitur quod sint inter se distinctae res (...)."; Gregory, *Lectura*, I d. 8 q. 1 a. 1 (ed. Trapp-Marcolino, 2), 30: "(O)stendam quod ipse (scl., Scotus, MH) posuit et ponere habuit consequenter ad dicta sua quod in deo est quaedam multitudo entitatum (...)."; Marsilius, *Sent.*, I q. 12 a. 3 (ed. Strasbourg 1501), fol. 60va-vb: "(S)i sint distinctae formalitates, erunt et similiter distinctae realitates." It should be noted, however, that this implication of the Scotist position was not universally agreed upon. Henry of Oyta, for instance (*Quaestiones Sententiarum*, I q. 7, Paris, ca. 1378–1380), while like Marsilius denying the existence of a formal distinction between the attributes in God, did not believe that God's simplicity was compromised by the Scotist opinion. See the relevant passages quoted by A. Lang, *Heinrich Totting von Oyta. Ein Beitrag zur Entstehungsgeschichte der ersten deutschen Universitäten und zur Problemgeschichte der Spätscholastik*, Münster 1937 (BGPhThMA, 33/4-5), 177.

[77] Adam Wodeham, *Lectura Oxoniensis*, I d. 6 q. 1, fol. 73ra; Gregory, *Lectura*, I d. 8 q. 1 a. 2, 44; Marsilius, *Sent.*, I q. 12 a. 3, fol. 63ra. Cf. Ockham, *Scriptum*, I d. 2 q. 1 (OTh, 2), 34-36.

The proof of this claim is of significance with respect to the relation between faith and natural reason: Marsilius argued that a conclusion on which all *sancti doctores* agree, and which is also validated by natural reason, and the contrary of which is not supported by urgent reasons, should always be granted as true.[78]

That natural reason does not distinguish between God's various attributes was supported with references to two philosophers *par excellence*, Aristotle and Averroes. Aristotle, Marsilius held, was of the opinion that God is identical with his delight, and that there is no non–identity whatsoever in God.[79]

As in the previous *conclusiones*, Marsilius quoted here from the *Lectura Oxoniensis* of Adam Wodeham, although the proof given above and the reference to Aristotle and Averroes did not occur at that place in Wodeham.[80]

The attributional rationes in the human mind

We have just seen that, taken as attributional perfections, the divine attributes are perfectly one with God's essence. Taken as attributional *rationes*, however, they are distinct in the human mind. God's perfection being infinite, man is unable to know this perfection by means of a single concept. Marsilius concurred with Thomas Aquinas and other theologians in the opinion that human beings in this life form their conception of God by means of notions taken from the finite world of creation. These notions are of necessity inadequate, since they can only express one aspect of God's infinite perfection at a time. There is unity with regard to the thing for which man's concepts stand (*supponunt*), but there is difference with regard to the way they signify this self-same thing. Divine essence is called 'intellect' by man when considered as an essence that has knowledge; it is called 'will' when considered as an essence that has volition. The differences between the attributes are therefore reflections of the different modes of knowledge and the corresponding names by which God's perfection is known to man and signified by him.[81]

---

[78] Marsilius, *Sent.*, I q. 12 a. 3 (ed. Strasbourg 1501), fol. 60vb: "*Tertia conclusio: Sapientia divina omnibus modis a parte rei est essentia divina, vel eadem essentiae* divinae, *quibus* scilicet *essentia est eadem* sibi ipsi, *et ita dicatur de qualibet alia perfectione* attributali. *Nec aliqua est inter eas distinctio, vel non identitas ex natura rei*. Probatur sic: Illud quod *sancti* doctores communiter dicunt, ratio naturalis quoque concludit, et cuius contrarium nulla ratio cogit, est semper tenendum." For Marsilius's source, see the passage from Adam Wodeham referred to in n. 80 below.

[79] Ibid.

[80] Adam Wodeham, *Lectura Oxoniensis*, I d. 6 q. 1 (Paris, Bibl. de l'Univ., 193), fol. 86ra. Wodeham refers to Averroes in the proof of the first *conclusio*, see fol. 85vb, and Paris, Bibl. Maz., 915, fol. 72ra.

[81] Marsilius, *Sent.*, I q. 12 a. 3 (ed. Strasbourg 1501), fol. 61ra: "(E)x parte rei sign<ific>atae pro qua termini supponunt et rationes ipsae, omnimode est identitas, et idem pro quo attributa supponunt, quia est essentia divina; sed res attributorum quoad nostram cognitionem sunt

It should be clear that this view was shared by several other theologians, in particular by Thomas of Sutton and Godfrey of Fontaines. In this respect Marsilius belonged to an old tradition. Yet his immediate sources were probably of later date: opinions similar to those of Marsilius were held by the Augustinian theologians Thomas of Strasbourg and Gregory of Rimini, with whose works Marsilius was well aquainted.[82]

---

diversae, quia nobis eandem rem diversimode significant."

[82] According to Thomas of Strasbourg, *Sent.*, I d. 6 q. 1 a. 4 (ed. Venice 1564), fol. 45vb-46ra, the attributes are not formally distinct or *ex natura dei* distinct, but only rationally. Their differences are bound up with the way perfections exist in the created world, and with the way man talks about God. In created beings perfections exist separately. Man has no other way of talking about God but in terms of what he sees in creatures. If man speaks of God, he speaks of him in terms of the differences among creatures. Even God himself has knowledge of the attributes as different only when he is addressing the various perfections in the creatures. Without these differences, divine attributes simply cannot be conceived of. This opinion is referred by Thomas to Giles of Rome (*doctor noster*), cf. Giles of Rome, *In primum librum Sententiarum*, I d. 2 q. 3 a. 3, Venice 1521, repr. Frankfurt a/Main 1968, fol. 18va-vb.

Thomas of Strasbourg criticized the view that, abstracting from all relations to the world of creation, the divine attributes could be distinguished by God by mere contemplation of his own essence. In a marginal remark to the 1564 edition, possibly based on marginal remarks in the manuscripts used for the edition, such a view is attributed to Henry of Ghent and to the Augustinian Alexander of San Elpidio († 1326, commentary on the *Sentences* 1299–1300 in Paris). From the quotations used by Thomas of Strasbourg we may deduce that Alexander of San Elpidio, of whose *Sentences* commentary we have no direct knowledge, held that God's essence virtually contains all the different attributes. These attributes become actual when God's essence is known by his intellect. Cf. Thomas of Strasbourg, *Sent.*, I d. 6 q. 1 a. 3, fol. 45ra-vb. On Alexander of San Elpidio, see A. Zumkeller, 'Die Augustinerschule', 199. Opinions of Alexander were also quoted by Alfonsus Vargas, see J. Kürzinger, *Alfonsus Vargas Toletanus und seine theologische Einleitungslehre. Ein Beitrag zur Geschichte der Scholastik im 14. Jahrhundert*, Münster 1930 (BGPhThMA, 22/5-6), 77. On the nature of marginal notes, see A.D. Trapp, 'Augustinian Theology of the 14th Century. Notes on Editions, Marginalia, Opinions and Book-Lore', *Augustiniana* 6 (1956), 146-274.

Also, according to Gregory of Rimini, *Lectura*, I d. 8 q. 2 a. 2 (ed. Trapp-Marcolino, 2), 88f, the attributes are rationally distinct when considered as attributional *rationes*. Considered as attributional perfections in God, however, they are one. Their differences as attributional *ratio* reflect the way each *ratio* signifies divine essence. What the attributional *rationes* stand for (*supponunt*) is one and the same thing, viz., divine essence, but what they connote is different, viz., created beings. For instance, 'God's justice' stands for God, but connotes the merits of created beings and their corresponding reward or punishment.

CHAPTER FOUR

GOD'S KNOWLEDGE OF CREATION

INTRODUCTION

After the more general questions concerning divine knowledge and God's attributes discussed in the two foregoing chapters, we now turn to the specific problem of whether and, if so, in what manner God has knowledge of *creatures*. As we saw earlier, the way the problem was approached by Thomas Aquinas set the example for subsequent generations of theologians and philosophers. We shall accordingly start our discussion with the position of Thomas. We shall then turn to Aristotle, Avicenna, and Averroes, and to the various interpretations their works received in the thirteenth and fourteenth centuries. Subsequently, we shall discuss the positions of Scotus, Ockham, Peter Aureoli, Gregory of Rimini, and Marsilius of Inghen, all of whom critically evaluated and, each in his own way, elaborated upon the arguments set out by Thomas Aquinas.

That God has knowledge of creatures, Thomas inferred from his earlier considerations that God has knowledge at all (see chapter 2). God's knowledge of the creatures differs from his self-knowledge only in its object, not in its intelligible species: in both cases, the species is God's essence itself. According to Thomas, the fact that God knows the creatures is a direct consequence of the fact that he knows himself. Divine essence he called the primary object of God's knowledge (*intellectum primum*), the creatures he called the secondary object (*intellectum secundum*).[1]

More particularly, Thomas submitted three arguments to prove that God has knowledge of the creatures. First, God's essence is an immaterial form that is the first cause, and as such it encompasses all forms and perfections existing in the created world. This all-comprehensive, altogether immaterial form is completely intelligible; it acts as the intelligible species of God's knowledge, and it coincides with God's knowledge. Therefore, God has knowledge not only of himself, but of the creatures as well.

Secondly, God has knowledge because he guides the natural beings toward their goal. This he does by alotting to each being its proper nature. But this again means that God must know the nature of each thing in order to lead it to its goal.

---

[1] *Sent.*, I d. 35 q. 1 a. 2 c. (ed. Mandonnet, 1), 814f. With slight modifications, this terminology was employed by various other writers too, as we shall see below.

Finally, to have knowledge of other things is a perfection in the world of creation. As he is the most perfect being, God has all the perfections of the creatures. Therefore, he also has knowledge of other things.[2]

Thomas made use of the first two arguments in particular. They were both based on God's causality, and on the presumption that perfect self-knowledge of the cause (God) implies knowledge of the effect (creatures). Nothing is known completely unless its power is known, and that power is not known unless the things affected by it are known as well. God knows himself (first argument), and God's power affects the creatures (first and second argument); therefore, God knows the creatures.

The two arguments from causality, in connection with the idea that knowledge of the cause implies knowledge of the effect, were also employed by other theologians and philosophers such as Peter de Falco (OFM?, *fl.* 1279-1281, whose sources included Bonaventure, Thomas Aquinas, and Henry of Ghent), the Franciscan Richard of Middleton († 1302-1308, influenced by Thomas on several points), and the Dominicans John of Paris and Hervaeus Natalis.[3] This dissemination evinces the influence of the arguments from causality and their underlying assumption. Yet, this fundamental assumption was not universally accepted. It was criticized on epistemological grounds by Duns Scotus, and later by William of Ockham.

A thorough discussion and clear appreciation of the problems involved in God's knowledge of the creatures, as found in Thomas and others, is totally absent in the work of Peter Lombard and of writers of the early thirteenth century such as William of Auxerre and William of Auvergne, even though they did touch on the subject. The first thorough discussion did not appear until ca. 1220-1236 in the *Quaestiones antequam esset frater* of Alexander of Hales. In this connection, Ruedi Imbach has rightly pointed out that the way God's knowledge of the creatures was discussed by Thomas and others should historically be understood against the background of the reception and increasing influence of Aristotle's *libri naturales* from the second quarter of the thirteenth century onward.[4]

---

[2] First argument: *De veritate*, q. 2 a. 3. c. (ed. Leon., 22/1), 51a-b; *STheol.*, I q. 14 a. 5 c. (ed. Leon., 4), 172b. Second argument: *Sent.*, I d. 35 q. 1 a. 2 c. (ed. Mandonnet, 1), 814; *De veritate*, q. 2 a. 3 c., 50b-51a. Third argument: *De veritate*, q. 2 a. 5 c., 62a; *STheol.*, I q. 14 a. 11 c., 183a.

[3] Peter de Falco, *Questions disputées ordinaires*, q. 4 a. 1, Vol. 1, ed. A.-J. Gondras, Louvain-Paris 1968 (Analecta Mediaevalia Namurcensia, 22), 162; Richard of Middleton, *Super quatuor libros Sententiarum*, I d. 35 a. 1 q. 6, Brescia 1591, repr. Frankfurt a/Main 1963, fol. 305b; John of Paris, *Sent.*, I q. 115 (ed. Muller), 350; Hervaeus Natalis, *Sent.*, I d. 33 q. 1 a. 2 (ed. Paris 1647), fol. 138aA.

[4] R. Imbach, *Deus est intelligere. Das Verhältnis von Sein und Denken in seiner Bedeutung für das Gottesverständnis bei Thomas von Aquin und in den Pariser Quaestionen Meister Eckharts*, Freiburg 1976 (Studia Friburgensia, NF 53), 41-49, with refences to the sources mentioned above.

The discussion of Aristotle's naturalist works, particularly with regard to his views on divine knowledge, reached a climax around the years 1270-1277. This may be gathered from *De quindecim problematibus* (probll. X-XI) written by Albert the Great before 1270, the *Errores philosophorum* by Giles of Rome, and the Parisian condemnations of 1270 (prop. 11) and 1277 (prop. 3). In the *Errores philosophorum*, the view that God knows the creatures only partially, or not at all, which was censored in 1270 and 1277, is explicitly associated with Avicenna (partial knowledge), and with Aristotle and Averroes (no knowledge).[5] The issues raised in these and similar works of the period significantly shaped the framework within which the question of God's knowledge of the creatures was to be discussed for the remainder of the thirteenth century and throughout the fourteenth century. It is therefore important to consider first the views of Aristotle, Avicenna, and Averroes.

Aristotle

In the thirteenth and fourteenth centuries, interpretations of Aristotle's view on divine knowledge were based almost exclusively on the *Metaphysics* (XII c. 9, 1074b15-1075a10). Aristotle argues there, in very dense terms, that the first principle (νοῦς) can think only about itself, and that thinking about the lower beings is contrary to its divinity. This passage proved particularly hard to interpret, in part because of the unfortunate brevity of the exposition: was the expression 'thinking about itself' meant to imply that the first principle has no knowledge of other things? Opinions were divided on this issue, as we learn from several works of Thomas, in particular from his commentary on the *Metaphysics* and his *De substantiis separatis*, and from the *Errores* of Giles of Rome. Some read in these words the view that God does not know the creatures. Others, however, among them Albert the Great, Thomas Aquinas, Peter de Falco, and Richard of Middleton, were of the opinion that Aristotle's 'thinking about itself' did not mean that the first principle has no knowledge of the creatures, but rather that it does not know them through something other than itself.

One influence in the explanation of Aristotle's position no doubt was the commentary of Averroes. This Arabian thinker had stated Aristotle's problem in a clear formula: that which is known is the perfection of the knower: *intellectum est perfectio intelligentis*.[6] The first principle cannot know (through) something else, since then it would be perfected by something else and hence cease to be the first principle. This rendering of the problem was

---

[5] Giles of Rome, *Errores philosophorum*, critical text with notes and introd. by J. Koch. English transl. by J.O. Riedl, Milwaukee, Wisc. 1944, 12 (Aristotle), 24 (Averroes), 36 (Avicenna).

[6] Averroes, *In Metaphysicam*, XII t. 51 (ed. Iuntina, 8), fol. 335vaG.

adopted by many writers of thirteenth century, such as the authors of the *Summa halensis*, Bonaventure, Thomas Aquinas, and Roger Bacon.[7]

In the fourteenth century, the question of Aristotle's position was frequently tied in with that of Averroes. Peter Aureoli († 1322), Johannes Baconis († 1348), Matheus de Eugebio (*magister artium* in Bologna, 1333-1347), and Gregory of Rimini did not even distinguish between the views of Aristotle and Averroes, speaking generally of the view of 'the philosophers'. Yet, this equation of Aristotle and Averroes did not mean that fourteenth-century thinkers concurred in one unique interpretation of them. According to Peter Aureoli and Johannes Baconis, the God of Aristotle and Averroes did have knowledge of the creatures; according to Matheus de Eugebio and Gregory of Rimini, however, he did not. Thus, the interpretation of 'thinking about itself' was still an open question in the fourteenth century.

ARABIAN PHILOSOPHY

The problem of whether God has knowledge of the creatures through his knowledge of himself, was magnified not only by Aristotle but also by the Arabian philosophers Avicenna and Averroes. Although this originally Neoplatonic theme of knowledge through self-knowledge was also present in *De divinibus nominis* (c. 7) and in the *Liber de causis*, it was especially in reaction to the views of Avicenna and Averroes that many theologians and philosophers of the thirteenth century addressed this subject.

Avicenna

Almost an entire chapter of Avicenna's *Metaphysics*, as it was known in the Western world, was devoted to a discussion of how God has knowledge of creation through his knowledge of himself (Tract. VIII c. 6).[8] Like Aristotle, Avicenna believed that God's knowledge cannot be derived from other things. God is a necessary being of pure perfection; as such, he cannot be influenced by anything outside himself. Anything God knows, he must know through his knowledge of himself, thereby including the things outside. That God has knowledge of things outside himself, Avicenna inferred from divine necessity: by knowing himself as a necessary cause, God has knowledge of things. And because Avicenna held that God is the cause of *all* being, he believed that God can know *all* things.[9]

---

[7] The relevant passages are referred to by R. Imbach, *Deus est intelligere*, 47-49.

[8] On the influence of Avicenna in the Latin West, see A.–M. Goichon, *La philosophie d'Avicenne et son influence en Europe médiévale*, Paris ²1951 (Forlong lectures 1940); id., *The Encyclopaedia of Islam*, New Edition, s.v. 'Ibn Sina'; E. Gilson, 'Avicenne en Occident au Moyen Age', *AHDLMA* 44 (1969), 89-121; Avicenna, *Liber de philosophia prima*, I-IV (ed. van Riet), 123* and 135*-136* (S. van Riet).

[9] Avicenna, *Liber de philosophia prima*, VIII c. 6 (ed. van Riet), 417.

A special problem was that of the knowledge of singular things, particularly insofar as these things are tied up with matter, with time, and with mutability. God does not have senses; the use of sensory species in the process of knowledge is ruled out by his simplicity. But matter can only be perceived by means of the senses. Therefore God cannot know matter. Being immutable, moreover, God cannot have changing knowledge of the things as they change. He cannot at one moment know that a thing exists, and at another moment that it does not exist, at least not by means of distinct acts of knowledge. For distinct acts of knowledge would require distinct intelligible species that cannot exist simultaneously, which is contrary to God's immutability. From these considerations Avicenna concluded that God knows the singular things only generally, that is, by their essence and universal properties. But this does not mean, Avicenna added, that something about the singular things goes unnoticed; on the contrary, God knows everything, each singular thing.[10]

This problem was solved as follows. Avicenna first distinguished between two kinds of singular things: those in which species and individual coincide (which he thought was the case with universal principles and species that consist of a single individual, such as the sun), and those in which the species consists of more than one individual. Now, this distinction was brought to bear on the explanation of God's knowledge of singular things. Things of the first kind God knows through knowledge (by his essence) of the principles that have emanated from him, and the things produced by them. God has knowledge of the consequences of the combined action of these principles, knowing how often something is produced and how much time elapses in between. Those principles are universal yet also individual, since they are one of a kind. Therefore, God has universal knowledge of these principles, even though they are individual. The same applies to the effects of the combined action of the universal principles, insofar as they also have universal properties and are one of a kind, as in the case of the sun.[11]

The second kind of singular things is material and subject to change. According to Avicenna this poses a double problem: first, can God have universal knowledge of every individual of a species in all its particular details, and second, can he know of every individual whether it exists or not? The solution of the first problem was based on the well-known example of the solar eclipse: even man can have complete knowledge of a singular thing by means of universal knowledge of its causes. We are able to know when and how a solar eclipse will take place, and how long it will take before the next occurrence. All properties of a solar eclipse can be ascertained from our knowledge of the movements of the celestial bodies. Although this knowl-

---

[10] Ibid., 418.
[11] Ibid., 419f.

edge universally applies to all eclipses of the sun, we are also sure that it applies to this one event in particular.¹² In similar manner, God can have knowledge of the solar eclipse and of any other singular event or thing. Being the cause of all causes, his knowledge of himself at once affords perfect knowledge of all the properties that make a thing the particular, singular thing it is. Since this thing is known by its universal properties, it is known to God in a universal way.

Avicenna's response to the second aspect of the problem also involved an example. God's knowledge is like that of a person who always exists and who knows all the properties of a given individual or particular event, such as a solar eclipse. Not only does he know when and how a particular eclipse of the sun will take place, but also *that* it takes place at that particular moment in time. This knowledge is unchanging. Should his knowledge have been in time (knowing now that a thing is, and later that it is not), then it would be subject to change. But God is not in time, nor does his judgment of the existence of a thing or the occurence of an event take place in time. His set of judgments is always the same, therefore his knowledge does not change.¹³

Avicenna's solution was often criticized in the Middle Ages, by Arabian as well as Western thinkers. Al-Gazali († 1111), one of the best-known champions of Islamic orthodoxy and foe to philosophical theology, launched a heavy attack on the view of Avicenna in his *Tahafut* (translated as *Destructio philosophorum* in 1328). He objected both to its theological and its philosophical implications. Avicenna's view, he argued, leads to the destruction of the laws of Faith. For if God knows the singular things in a universal (hence, Al-Gazali inferred, imperfect) manner, then how can he have knowledge of the personal acts of human individuals, as is taught in the Koran? How can he know that someone is true to Islam, or that Mohammed has prophesied? As for its philosophy, Al-Gazali objected to Avicenna's claim that God has no distinct knowledge of distinct moments in time. If distinct knowledge of distinct moments implies changes in knowledge, as Avicenna assumed, then we should also deny that God knows the various distinct universal principles (*genera* and *species*). For the difference between moments in time is surely less deep than that between universal principles. Conversely, if God does know distinct universal principles, then why should he not know distinct moments in time?¹⁴

---

¹² Ibid., 420.
¹³ Ibid., 421-422: "Tu enim, si scires de eclipsi quomodo invenitur, et tu esses semper, profecto esset tibi scientia non de eclipsi absoluta, sed de omni eclipsi quae fit, et tamen esse illam eclipsim et non esse non variaret in te aliquid. (...) Primus vero, qui non subest tempori nec eius iudicio, multo remotior est ab hoc quod ipse iudicet in hoc tempore, vel in illo, secundum quod eclipsis est in illo, et secundum quod iudicium de ea est novum vel cognitio nova."
¹⁴ See Al-Gazali, *Tahafut al-falasifah* <*Incoherence of the Philosophers*>, transl. S.A. Kamali, Lahore ²1963 (Pakistan Philosophical Congress Publications, 3), Prob. XIII, 153-162.

If we now turn to the Latin West, it is interesting to note that the discussion of Avicenna's views on divine knowledge was almost exclusively restricted to the thirteenth century, when, in addition to its critics, it also had some advocates, as seen in the position of Robert Grosseteste.[15] In the fourteenth century, when the position of Averroes was still the focus of attention, Avicenna was mentioned very rarely. Averroes, who had laid down his position in an authoritative commentary on Aristotle's *Metaphysics*, probably benefited from the more lasting attention, institutionalized at the universities, paid to the works of Aristotle.

Many writers in the second half of the thirteenth century concurred in the stereotypical version of Avicenna's view: that God has knowledge of the creatures, but that he knows them only universally, not singularly. This is the formula we find in Thomas Aquinas, Giles of Rome, Peter de Falco, and John of Paris.[16] This agreement on Avicenna's position starkly constrasted with the controversy surrounding the interpretation of Aristotle and Averroes. The agreement was not necessarily a consequence of the lucidity of Avicenna's text. Such unanimity may also have been due to a common secondary source: both Peter de Falco and John of Paris demonstrably based themselves on the commentary on the *Sentences* of Thomas Aquinas. Another contributing factor may have been the rendering of Avicenna's position in Averroes's widely read commentary on the *Metaphysics*: God knows all things in a universal way, not in a singular way. A similar formula was used by Giles of Rome in the *Errores*.[17]

Despite their use of similar formulae, Thomas Aquinas and Giles of Rome disagreed on the philosophical foundation of Avicenna's position. From his criticism of Avicenna, it is clear that Thomas took the following two interrelated (though in his view erroneous) tenets to be fundamental: first, that God is not the cause of matter, and second, that God does not produce all things immediately, but by means of the general principles as intermediate causes. Thomas criticized the view that perfect knowledge of singular things

---

On Al-Gazali and the *Tahafut*, see M. Fakhry, *A History of Islamic Philosophy*, New York-London 1970 (Studies in Oriental Culture, 5), 244-261, esp. 255f; O. Leaman, *An Introduction to Medieval Islamic Philosophy*, Cambridge 1985, passim, esp. 108-120.

[15] See Robert Grosseteste, as quoted in C. Bérubé, *La connaissance de l'individuel au Moyen Age*, Montréal-Paris 1964 (Université de Montréal, Institut d'Etudes Médiévales), 15 nn. 1 and 2.

[16] Thomas, *Sent.*, I d. 38 q. 1 a. 3 c. (ed. Mandonnet, 1), 903, and *De veritate*, q. 2 a. 5 c. (ed. Leon., 22/1), 62a; Giles of Rome, *Sent.*, I d. 36 q. 1 (ed. Venice 1521), fol. 185rbH-vaI; Peter de Falco, *Questions disputées ordinaires*, q. 4 a. 3 (ed. Gondras, 1), 166f and 170; John of Paris, *Sent.*, I q. 118 (ed. Muller), 362f.

[17] Averroes, *In Metaphysicam*, XII t. 51 (ed. Iuntina, 8), fol. 337raA: "(D)ixerunt quidam, quod ipse scit omnia, quae sunt hic, scientia universali, non scientia particulari."; Giles of Rome, *Errores philosophorum* (ed. Koch), 32 n. 13. The terms 'particularis' and 'singularis' were used interchangeably not only by Averroes but also by Avicenna, Thomas Aquinas, Giles of Rome, and Peter de Falco.

can be universal. Singularity is caused by matter, not by a combination of universal properties. If God knows something by its universal properties, then he does not know it as being singular. Moreover, Thomas believed that God is immediately active in every being: he is the cause of matter as well as of the universal principles. Therefore, God can know each thing immediately in his self-knowledge, and in particular insofar as it has been individualized by matter.[18]

Giles of Rome disagreed with this interpretation. As he saw it, the roots of Avicenna's position were neither the status of matter nor the manner of creation, but rather the connection of singularity and actuality. Should God know singular things in a singular fashion, then (according to Avicenna) his knowledge would be changing as things come to be or pass away. Giles thought that the proper response to Avicenna was not to point out that God is the cause of matter, but that he is pure act, and therefore able to cause all beings, including the changeable ones, without changing himself.[19]

The interpretation and criticism offered by Thomas were adopted by Peter de Falco, Roger Marston (OFM, † ca. 1303), and John of Paris.[20] Peter de Falco, it should be noted, also mentioned the point made by Giles of Rome. If we compare the criticisms of Thomas and Giles with the original claims made by Avicenna, we find that they can only partly be justified: in point of fact, it is incorrect to attribute to Avicenna the view that God is not the cause of matter (Thomas) or of being (Giles). Avicenna did not deny God's causality on these points; he only denied that God is the *immediate* cause of matter. On the other hand, however, the criticism highlighted precisely what the critics themselves were after, viz., that God has immediate knowledge of the singular beings, as opposed to some sort of *quasi* discursive knowledge by means of universal causes and their combinations.

In this connection, it is remarkable that no writer of the thirteenth century, as far as we know, ever raised the question of whether Avicenna's idea of a *quasi* discursive mode of knowledge is in agreement with divine simplicity (also assumed by Avicenna). Thomas and others emphatically defended God's simplicity and denied that God has discursive knowledge, but apparently it never occurred to them to use either of these points against Avicenna.[21]

---

[18] Thomas, *Sent.*, I d. 36 q. 1 a. 1 (ed. Mandonnet, 1), 832. See also *De veritate*, q. 2 a. 5 c. (ed. Leon., 22/1), 62b; *STheol.*, I q. 14 a. 11 c. (ed. Leon., 4), 183b.

[19] Giles of Rome, *Sent.*, I d. 36 q. 1 (ed. Venice 1521), foll. 185va<M>-186raA.

[20] In addition to the sources referred to above, n. 16, see Roger Marston, *Quodlibeta quattuor*, I q. 4, ed. G.F. Etzkorn and I.G. Brady, Florence 1968 (BFSMA, 26), 15, quoting *verbatim* Thomas Aquinas, *Sent.*, I d. 36 q. 1 a. 1 c.

[21] Most modern literature on Avicenna is focused on the question of whether universal knowledge of singular things is at all possible within Avicenna's general frame of thought. Opinions are divided. M. Marmura and B.S. Kogan defend the view that Avicenna's position here is at variance with some of his other tenets, to the effect that individual, sublunar objects can never be identified individually by means of universal properties. Universal properties can

Averroes

In the thirteenth and fourteenth centuries, what was known about Averroes's views on divine knowledge came from his commentary on Aristotle's *Metaphysics* (XII t. 51), where the problematic 'thinking about itself' passage, referred to above, is discussed. Averroes's commentaries were translated into Latin in the years 1220-1235. Other works from his hand, such as the *Epistula ad amicum*, translated 1278, and the *Destructio destructionum* (*Tahafut al-Tahafut*), translated 1328, in which he expressly stated, unlike the commentary on the *Metaphysics*, that God has complete knowledge of the singular things, were virtually unknown. The scantness of information here was no doubt the cause of the controversy over his position. Indeed, it is bound to have contributed to the negative assessment of what was taken to be his view: one of the theses censored in 1270 and 1277, viz., that God does not have knowledge of the creatures, in all likelihood goes back to Averroes.

Averroes's commentary on the *Metaphysics* discussed the views on divine knowledge of Themistius and Avicenna. Compared to the latter, Averroes did not weave many neoplatonic elements into his philosophy. He criticized the emanationism of Al-Farabi and Avicenna. His position in the commentary on the *Metaphysics*, to the effect that God does not have singular knowledge of singular things, concurred with that of Alexander of Aphrodisias, mentioned in chapter 1, whom he quoted in this connection in the *Epitome*.[22]

---

only single out species. Identification of individuals is thus only possible if they are one of a kind, which is not the case with the sublunar things distinguished by matter. Hence, God cannot have universal knowledge of singular sublunar things (in Avicenna's terms: singular objects of the second kind). See M. Marmura, 'Some Aspects of Avicenna's Theory of God's Knowledge of Particulars', *Journal of the American Oriental Society* 82 (1961), 299-312, esp. 312; id., 'Divine Omniscience and Future Contingents in Alfarabi and Avicenna', ed. T. Rudavsky, *Divine Omniscience*, 81-94, esp. 91; B.S. Kogan, 'Some Reflections on the Problem of Future Contingency in Alfarabi, Avicenna, and Averroes', ed. T. Rudavsky, *Divine Omniscience*, 95-101, esp. 97. Cf. Avicenna, *Liber de philosophia prima*, V c. 5 (ed. van Riet), 276-278.

The conclusion is denied by L. Gardet and O. Leaman, who argue that there is no contradiction in Avicenna here. When Avicenna claims that God knows singular things by universal means, he also means to say that God knows everything there is to know. According to Gardet, Avicenna's philosophical system implies that there is no other knowledge of singular things than universal knowledge based on universal properties. As opposed to this, there is also singular, 'experimental' knowledge by which a thing is known in its material singularity, but which is not really knowledge at all. This general theory of Avicenna is in perfect unison with his claim that God's knowledge of singular things is universal, since he is able to know even their smallest details without entering into their singularity. The problem according to Gardet is not in the system, but in Avicenna's appreciation of *singularia*. Being the products of a complex concourse and harmony of causes, they have no unique or irreducible properties. This view of Gardet, though not the most recent one but certainly very well documented, strikes us as still the most plausible interpretation of Avicenna available. See L. Gardet, *La pensée religieuse d'Avicenne (Ibn sina)*, Paris 1951 (Etudes de philosophie médiévale, 41), 82f and 85 n. 1; O. Leaman, *An Introduction*, 117f.

[22] Cf. *Die Epitome der Metaphysik des Averroes*, übersetzt und mit einer Einleitung und Erläuterungen versehen von S. van den Bergh, Leiden 1924 (Veröffentlichungen der 'De

A highly regarded commentator of Aristotle, indeed, affectionately known as 'the Commentator', Averroes's influence on thirteenth- and fourteenth-century philosophy can hardly be overrated. Like Avicenna and others, Averroes believed that God can know the things outside him only through knowledge of himself.[23] God's essence is being qua being. Since he knows his own being, he also knows that of all other things. According to Averroes, God's knowledge of the things is neither singular nor universal. Singular knowledge of singular things is impossible, for God as well as for other knowing subjects, because there are infinitely many singular beings, and the infinite cannot be known. Universal knowledge of singular things (the position of Avicenna) is contrary to divine perfection: universal knowledge implies a potentiality, because there is still something left to be known.[24]

What became of the argument from self-knowledge in the hands of Averroes, and the way in which it differed from Avicenna's argument, is best seen in his criticism of Themistius († ca. 390), the ancient Greek commentator of Aristotle. Themistius had claimed that Aristotle was saying that God knows all things individually by knowing himself as a cause. To this interpretation Averroes objected that it contradicted certain other views of Aristotle, in particular those on divine simplicity. If God has knowledge of other things by his being a cause, then knower and known do not coincide in God.[25]

The background of Averroes's objection may be understood from the *Tahafut-al-Tahafut*, where the same question was raised. 'Being-a-cause', Averroes argued, is a relational concept. To have knowledge of a relation, is to have knowledge of both terms of that relation. If God knows himself as a cause, then he also knows that which he is causing. But this means that God's knowledge is dependent upon something outside him, and that he does know something other than himself.[26]

Averroes also thought that Themistius's view that God knows things individually is contrary to divine simplicity. All that is known to God

---

Goeje-Stiftung, 7), 145; *Ibn Rushd's Metaphysics. A Translation with Introduction of Ibn Rushd's Commentary on Aristotle's Metaphysics, Book Lam*, by Ch. Genequand, Leiden 1984 (Islamic Philosophy and Theology, 1), 52 (introduction).

[23] Averroes, *In Metaphysicam*, XII t. 51 (ed. Iuntina, 8), fol. 337raA: "(P)rimum scit omnia, secundum quod scit se tantum scientia in esse (...)."

[24] Ibid., fol. 337raB.

[25] Themistius, *In Aristotelis Metaphysicorum librum lambda paraphrasis hebraice et latine*, latine expressa c. 9, ed. S. Landauer, Berlin 1903 (Commentaria in Aristotelem Graeca, 5), 32; Averroes, *In Metaphysicam*, XII t. 51 (ed. Iuntina, 8), fol. 336vbL-M. For a discussion of Themistius's view on divine knowledge and the reply of Averroes, see S. Pines, 'Some Distinctive Metaphysical Conceptions in Themistius' Commentary on Book Lamba and Their Place in the History of Philosophy', *Aristoteles. Werk und Wirkung*, Vol. 2, ed. J. Wiesner, Berlin-New York 1987, 177-204, esp. 194-196.

[26] *Averroes' Tahafut al-Tahafut (The Incoherence of the Incoherence)*, Vol. 1, transl. with introd. and notes by S. van den Bergh, London 1954 (Unesco Collection of Great Works, Arabic Series), 122.

coincides with his essence; therefore, it must be perfectly one. It follows that God cannot know a multiplicity of different objects, for that would mean that his essence would be divided too.[27]

Averroes's solution was that God does not know things because of his being-a-cause, but because his essence as being-qua-being contains everything that exists in the world (where it becomes differentiated). He knows all things, not by knowing himself as a cause, but simply by knowing his essence: what exists in God also exists in the world. Averroes tried to drive this point home by means of the following example. Someone who knows only the nature of heat, by the same token knows heat in concrete existing hot things, even though his knowledge is not directed at any of them individually.[28]

The debate carried on in the thirteenth and fourteenth century with regard to Averroes was in particular about the meaning of 'being-qua-being', that which God was supposed to know in his essence. Finding its correct interpretation proved to be extremely difficult, as is testified by the despairing remark of Matheus de Eugubio, who confided that he had consulted every commentary in Bologna in an attempt to procure a reliable reading of Averroes.[29] Opinions on what was the proper view of Averroes were indeed highly divided. We shall briefly review some of the options that were taken.

According to Giles of Rome, William of Ockham, Gregory of Rimini and Matheus de Eugebio, Averroes believed that God knows nothing other than himself.[30] This interpretation relied in particular on remarks to the effect that knower and known are one in God, and that God does not depend on something else by which his knowledge is determined. The comments of the interpreters indicate that they did not read Averroes as saying that God knows all things through the knowledge of his essence. Their response was precisely that God *does* know the creatures in his self-knowledge, and that this affects neither his simplicity nor independence. They fully accepted Averroes's emphasis on divine simplicity and perfection, but objected to (what they took to be) the negative conclusions he drew from it. Interesting in this connection are the multiple positions of Giles of Rome. In his commentary on the *Sentences* he not only gave the above interpretation, which he claimed

---

[27] Averroes, *In Metaphysicam*, XII t. 51 (ed. Iuntina, 8), fol. 336vbL-M.

[28] Ibid., fol. 337raA: "(Q)ui scit calorem ignis tantum, non dicitur nescire naturam caloris existentis in reliquis calidis, sed iste est ille, qui scit naturam caloris, secundum quod est calor. Et similiter primus scit naturam entitatis (unitatis, *ed.*) in eo quod est ens simpliciter, quod est ipsum."

[29] *Averroïsme Bolonais au XIVe siècle. Editions des textes*, ed. Z. Kuksewicz, Wroclaw 1965 (Institut de philosophie et de sociologie de l'academie polonaise des sciences), 260: "(L)ittera sic debet iacere, nam in hoc passu examinavi et vidi quasi omnia commenta concepta et alia, que potui invenire Bononie."

[30] Giles of Rome, *Sent.*, I d. 35 a. 1 q. 3 (ed. Venice 1521), fol. 181rbF; Ockham, *Scriptum*, I d. 35 a. 2 (OTh, 4), 434-436; Gregory of Rimini, *Lectura*, I dd. 35-36 q. 1 (ed. Trapp-Marcolino, 3), 211-213; Matheus de Eugubio, as edited by Z. Kuksewicz, *Averroïsme Bolonais*, 254-262.

follows the literal meaning of Averroes's text, but two other interpretations as well. First, that God does not know singular things because there are infinitely many of them (this is also found in the *Errores*), and second, that God knows the creatures only uniformly and without distinction. With regard to this second interpretation, Giles noted that it may have been the position of Averroes himself or that of someone quoted by Averroes (referring here to the example of heat and hot things).[31]

According to Thomas Aquinas, Averroes held that God knows the being of things by means of his essence; he does not have knowledge of things as distinct and individual. This view he expressly attributed to Averroes. He also mentioned the argument that God does not know singular things because of their infinite number, but this time without attributing it to Averroes.[32]

Thomas understood Averroes's 'being' of things as the most general being. This is plain from his reply to the Commentator: God is not only the cause of general being (*esse commune*), but of everything existing in a thing. This is why he knows his creatures completely, and not only insofar as they are all beings (*communicant in ratione entis*).[33]

A significantly richer interpretation of Averroes's 'being' was given by Peter Aureoli and Johannes Baconis. In their opinion, Averroes was saying that God, by the knowledge of his being, knows all the particular forms and all the essences of the singular things, with the exception of their individuality. He knows everything *about* the lion and the ox, but he does not know *this* lion or *this* ox, because of their infinite number.[34]

Peter Auroli explicitly rejected the interpretation given by Thomas Aquinas, because, he argued, Averroes claimed that God contains *all* being in an eminent way. It is interesting to note that Aureoli here deployed an argument that Thomas had used *against* Averroes, viz., that of the fullness of God's being. Johannes Baconis also availed himself of arguments given by Thomas. He drew his support for the view that Aristotle and Averroes believed that God has knowledge of the creatures from the *Summa contra gentiles*. This implies that he saw Thomas's arguments with regard to divine knowledge of the creatures as entirely in line with the position of Aristotle and Averroes. He even referred to Thomas's arguments as the 'rationes Philosophi et Commentatoris'.[35]

---

[31] Respectively, Giles of Rome, *Sent.*, I d. 35 a. 1 q. 3 (ed. Venice 1521), fol. 181rbF; *Sent.*, I d. 36 q. 1, fol. 185rbH; *Errores philosophorum* (ed. Koch), 22 n. 8; *Sent.*, I d. 35 a. 1 q. 4, fol. 182raBC.

[32] Thomas, *Sent.*, I d. 35 q. 1 a. 3 c. (ed. Mandonnet, 1), 816, and *ScG*, I c. 63 n. 525 (ed. Pera, 2), 74a.

[33] *Sent.*, I d. 35 q. 1 a. 3 c., 817; *STheol.*, I q. 14 a. 6 c. (ed. Leon., 4), 176a.

[34] Peter Aureoli, *Sent.*, I d. 35 p. 3 a. 1 (ed. Rome 1596), fol. 790aB-C; Johannes Baconis, *Quaestiones in quatuor libros Sententiarum*, I d. 39 q. u. a. 1 par. 3, Cremona 1618, repr. Westmead, Farnborough 1969, fol. 382aA (= 378aA); and a. 2, fol. 382aE.

[35] Peter Aureoli, *Sent.*, I d. 35 p. 2 a. 2, fol. 777aC. Cf. Thomas Aquinas, *ScG*, I c. 50 nn.

Even for present-day researchers, the interpretation of Averroes's commentary on the *Metaphysics* on this point has proved persistently difficult. On the basis on the Arabic text, some have suggested a reading similar to that of Thomas Aquinas: God knows only the general being of things, not their individual differences. Other scholars, by contrast, who take their lead from different works, including the two mentioned at the beginning of this section, claim that Averroes believed that God also has individualized knowledge of the things.[36] Leaving these modern-day interpretations aside, we shall more than once in this chapter have occasion to come back to the medieval readings of Averroes.

Duns Scotus

In this section we shall consider the criticism offered by Duns Scotus of the argument from causality and of the views of Bonaventure and Henry of Ghent in particular. We will also examine the reception of Scotus's views by subsequent thinkers. Like Thomas Aquinas and other thirteenth-century thinkers before him, Duns Scotus used arguments from perfection and from causality in support of the claim that God has knowledge of all creatures. Scotus's argument from perfection was essentially as follows. God knows the created things effectively and distinctly, for this mode of knowledge is one of the perfections that belong to the intellect. God has intellectual knowledge of *all* things, for the intellect *qua* intellect is necessarily directed at being in the fullness of its extension. God's intellect is perfect. Therefore it knows all things towards which it is directed.[37] Note that this argument does not contradict Scotus's earlier objection to the argument from perfection as an a priori demonstration of God's knowledge. The question there was *whether* God has knowledge (which is assumed here), whereas we are now dealing with the question *what* is known by God and in what *manner* it is known by him.

Scotus used two arguments from causality. First, God is compared to a perfect artist, who has the most detailed knowledge of each individual thing before he actually creates it. Secondly, Scotus argued that each thing is dependent upon God as the cause of its being. Therefore God necessarily has

---

418 and 422 (ed. Pera, 2), 62a-b; *STheol.*, I q. 14 a. 6 c. (ed. Leon., 4) 176a-b. Johannes Baconis, *Sent.*, I d. 35 q. u. a. 2 (ed. Cremona 1618), fol. 360aB-bA. Cf. Thomas, *ScG*, I c. 50.

[36] For the first reading of Averroes, see *Ibn Rushd's Metaphysics*, 52 (Ch. Genequand, Introduction). The second reading is defended by M. Fakhry, *A History of Islamic Philosophy*, 317f; A. Badawi, *Histoire de la philosophie en Islam*, Vol. 2, Paris 1972 (Etudes de philosophie médiévale, 60), 807-809; L. Gardet, 'Thomas et ses prédécesseurs Arabes', *St. Thomas Aquinas 1274-1974. Commemorative Studies*, Vol. 1, Toronto, Canada 1974, 426 n. 23, and 427.

[37] Duns Scotus, *Ordinatio*, I d. 2 p. 1 qq. 1-2 n. 106 (ed. Vat., 2), 187f; *De primo principio*, c. 4 concl. 8 n. 66 (ed. Kluxen), 84.

knowledge of each thing. This second argument, which hinges on God's causality as the mediating principle of knowledge, is a clear example of the influence of Avicenna.[38]

Criticism of the argument from causality

In the *Reportata Parisiensia*, the argument from causality was subjected to closer scrutiny and made more precise. Scotus here distinguished between two possible ways to understand the argument, one of which he rejected. If the argument is taken to imply that God knows himself and creation in one and the same act of knowledge, then it is false. Knowledge of God cannot be formally identical with knowledge of the creatures. This claim was explained epistemologically. Complete knowledge of the principles does not always carry with it knowledge of the conclusion; similarly, knowledge of the cause does not always imply knowledge of the effect. Knowledge of what is prior is independent of knowledge of what is posterior.[39]

This epistemological objection had a deeper ontological motivation (possibly directed against Avicenna) in considerations concerning divine freedom. God is completely independent of creation, with regard to his knowledge as well as in other respects. This last point was also stressed in the *Lectura* and in the *Ordinatio*: what is known depends upon God, and never vice versa. We find an even stronger emphasis on divine independence in Peter Aureoli, who unlike Scotus went so far as to deny that God can know anything other than divine essence itself, even if it were known through divine essence.[40]

Summarizing the above, we can say that Scotus's argument from causality must be understood as follows. Knowledge of the effects does not coincide with knowledge of the cause, nor is it a part of it; rather, it follows upon it. Only thus construed can God's self-knowledge be independent of his knowledge of creation, and yet the latter be effected through the first.

Although the above position with regard to the argument from causality did not occur in the *Lectura* or the *Ordinatio*, it was known to Johannes Baconis, who quoted it in his commentary on the *Sentences*.[41] Baconis also sketched several objections that had been raised by others (*anonymi*) against the argument from causality. God is only the efficient and final cause of creation, not the formal or material cause (the two internal principles of sublunar things). Therefore God cannot know the quiddity of things through his causality, for quiddity involves the formal cause. He can only know *that*

---

[38] *De primo principio*, c. 4 concl. 8 n. 66, 84.
[39] *Reportata Parisiensia*, I d. 36 q. 2 n. 9 (ed. Wadding, 11/1), fol. 201a.
[40] Scotus, *Lectura*, I d. 35 q. u. n. 22 (ed. Vat., 17), 452; *Ordinatio*, I d. 35 q. u. n. 32 (ed. Vat., 6), 258, and I d. 36 q. u. n. 43, 288; Peter Aureoli, *Sent.*, I d. 35 p. 2 a. 1 (ed. Rome 1596), fol. 771bE.
[41] Johannes Baconis, *Sent.*, I d. 35 q. 1 a. 4 par. 1 (ed. Cremona 1618), fol. 362aF-bA.

the thing exists (because he is its efficient cause) and *what* it exists *for* (because he is its final cause). As far as his causality is concerned, the objection concluded, God cannot have complete knowledge of creation. Other critics objected that God's essence is a complete unity. Hence, knowledge of the essence's causality can only yield non-distinct knowledge. It follows that God does not know the creatures through his essence, but through his ideas.[42]

We thus see that the use of the argument from causality was far from uncontroversial at the beginning of the fourteenth century. Now, one might well expect from the above that Scotus's criticism of it was endorsed in particular by Scotists themselves. Yet, interestingly, this expectation is not borne out by the facts. Criticism of the argument was completely absent in the commentaries on the *Sentences* of Scotist authors such as Francis of Mayronnes (the version printed in 1520 and reprinted in 1966 originated in Paris, 1320/1) and Peter of Aquila. They did not even refer to Scotus's criticism from the *Reportata Parisiensia*.[43]

According to Francis of Mayronnes, the argument from causality as it was employed by Thomas Aquinas was valid (*demonstrative*). God knows himself as a cause, therefore he also knows his causal relation to the creatures. Knowledge of this relation implies knowledge of the creatures. This is precisely the form of the argument that was criticized by Duns Scotus. Francis thought that it was one of the most powerful arguments against those who deny that God has knowledge of the creatures. In particular, he thought it was more convincing than Scotus's argument, viz., that God knows being in its entirety, and therefore also all creatures.[44]

Like Francis of Mayronnes, Peter of Aquila simply presented Thomas's version of the argument without further comment.[45] He added a discussion of Averroes's view, however, which is not found in Scotus. According to Peter, Averroes's position was that God does not know the creatures. One of the six arguments of Averroes discussed by him was that God cannot be perfected by anything but himself — the classical point that in the thirteenth century was taken to be Averroes's key argument. Notice that Peter attributed four other arguments against God's knowledge of the creatures to so-called *artistae* (Masters of the Faculty of Arts). The background of this 'philosophical' line of criticism was the classical Platonic-Aristotelian view that intellectual knowledge is of the universal and the immutable, not of the singular. The four

---

[42] Ibid., par. 6, foll. 364bC-365aE.

[43] On the different versions of the *Sentences* commentary of Francis of Mayronnes, see H. Rossmann, 'Die Sentenzenkommentare des Franz von Meyronnes OFM', *FzS* 53 (1971), 129-227, esp. 135 and 219.

[44] Francis of Mayronnes, *Sent.*, I d. 36 q. 4 (ed. Venice 1520), foll. 109vbQ and 110raA-B.

[45] Peter of Aquila, *Sent.*, I d. 35 a. 3 (ed. Speyer 1480) col. 1, not foliated: "Cognoscens perfecte virtutem suam cognoscit omnia ad quae virtus illa se extendit".

arguments in question are the following:[46]

> 1. Singular things are known by means of the senses, whereas God does not have senses.
> 2. Singular things can only be known by reflection upon what is known by the senses.
> 3. Singular things are not always in act, whereas God's knowledge is.
> 4. The intellect only knows the abstract, whereas singular things are concrete *hic et nunc*.

From this list of arguments we learn that certain older issues, which had been discussed during the second half of the thirteenth century, were still relevant in the controversy over God's knowledge among theologians of the 1330s, in particular with regard to the views of Averroes.

God's knowledge is non-reflective

Scotus believed that God knows individual things directly, without an intermediate reflection on the imitability of his essence, that is to say, without the intervention of ideas or differences on the part of the act of knowledge. It is sufficient, he thought, that God has knowledge of his own essence. In this connection he criticized the views of Bonaventure and Henry of Ghent.

In the *Reportata Parisiensia*, the view that God knows things individually only if his knowledge is based on rational relations (i.e., ideas) that specify the knowledge, was attributed to all the *doctores moderni*.[47] This, however, is not quite correct. Thomas of Sutton, Hervaeus Natalis, as well as John of Paris denied the need for such rational relations. The fact that Scotus mistakenly referred to it as the received view was probably due to the enormous influence of Godfrey of Fontaines and Henry of Ghent, who indeed endorsed the requirement of rational relations.[48]

The tension between God's knowledge of individual things on the one hand, and the unity of his essence on the other as put forward by Godfrey of Fontaines and Henry of Ghent, was felt as a really pressing problem at the beginning of the fourteenth century, as we learn from the commentary on the *Sentences* of Jacob of Metz (second redaction 1304/6), and from an early *quaestio disputata* by Henry of Harclay, possibly written before 1313, in which the problem was discussed at length.[49]

---

[46] Ibid., a. 2, coll. 1-2. Cf. J. Hamesse, *Auctoritates Aristotelis. Un florilège médiéval. Etude historique et édition critique*, Louvain-Paris 1974 (Philosophes Médiévaux, 17), 142 (27), 318 (87), and 319 (93): "Sensus est singularium, scientia vero universalium."

[47] Scotus, *Reportata Parisiensia*, I d. 36 q. 2 n. 14 (ed. Wadding, 11/1), fol. 202a.

[48] For a discussion of the views of Godfrey of Fontaines, see J.F. Wippel, *The Metaphysical Thought*, 124. As to Henry of Ghent, see below. On the influence of Henry of Ghent, see J.I. Catto, 'Theology and Theologians 1220-1320', *The Early Oxford Schools*, ed. J.I. Catto, Oxford 1984 (The History of the University of Oxford, 1), 471-517, esp. 504f.

[49] Cf. Jacob of Metz, *Sent.*, I d. 35, as cited by B. Decker, *Die Gotteslehre des Jacob von*

Criticism of other views

The position of Henry of Ghent was that God knows all things individually because his intellect reflects on the imitability of his essence, thus producing specific, rational relations, that is: ideas. Scotus objected to this view because it tacitly presupposed that God knows all things individually. For where would different rational relations come from if God knew only his simple essence? Clearly there must be knowledge of the individual creatures before God can know his essence as imitable.[50]

Another view criticized by Scotus was that of Bonaventure. His position was that God has knowledge of individual things because the essence contains different *rationes* (forms of knowledge, ideas) produced by the expressiveness of God's essence as the first cause, and not (contra Henry of Ghent) by the reflective act of the divine intellect. The *rationes* are where knower and known come together. Thus God can have perfect knowledge of the creatures.

Scotus objected to two points in this position. In the first place, the forms of knowledge cannot determine knowledge. As they are the consequence of an act of knowledge, they cannot precede knowledge. Secondly, if there were *rationes* (or *relationes* — the terms are used interchangeably by Scotus in this context) that precede knowledge, they could not be rational but would have to be real. What precedes knowledge cannot be a product of knowledge; therefore it cannot be rational.[51] Curiously enough, Scotus did not consider the possibility that Bonaventure's *rationes* might be formally distinct (as was proposed by Peter Thomae and others). Instead, he used a fork that he himself rejected elsewhere, and that was frequently used by critics of the formal distinction, viz., that every relation is either rational or real. In his criticism of the views of others, Scotus appears to have proceeded independently of his own views, as did Ockham, as we shall see.

The third and last position rejected by Scotus is the view that God knows the differences between things through differences in the acts of knowledge.

Metz. Untersuchungen zur Dominikanertheologie zu Beginn des 14. Jahrhunderts, Münster 1967 (BGPhThMA, 42/1), 167: "Sed adhuc manet dubium. Cum essentia dei sit simplex, quomodo deus per essentiam suam potest plura distincte cognoscere, nisi intelligatur in eo aliqua distinctio secundum rationem." For Henry of Harclay, see A.A. Maurer, 'Henry of Harclay's Questions', 168 (= Città del Vaticano, Bibl. Apost., Borghese, 171, fol. 12va). The dating of the last text is according to Maurer, 'Henry of Harclay's Questions', 165. However, compare the critical remarks by M. Henninger, 'Henry of Harclay's Questions on Divine Prescience and Predestination', *FcS* 40 (1980), 168 n. 5.

[50] Scotus, *Lectura*, I d. 35 q. u. n. 20 (ed. Vat., 17), 451; *Ordinatio*, I d. 35 q. u. n. 25 (ed. Vat., 6), 254f. Cf. Henry of Ghent, *Quodlibeta*, VIII q. 1 (ed. Paris 1518), fol. 299vB, and VIII q. 8, fol. 313rF; *Quodlibet* IX, q. 2, ed. R. Macken, Opera Omnia, Vol. XIII, Leuven 1983, 44f. This line of criticism is similar to that of Thomas of Sutton against Henry of Ghent.

[51] Scotus, *Ordinatio*, I d. 35 q. u. n. 21, 253. Cf. Bonaventura, *Commentaria in IV libros Sententiarum*, I d. 35 a. u. q. 1, Florence 1934 (Opera Theologica Selecta, 1), 479b-480a.

If the acts can differ by themselves, so can the objects in God's essence. Alternatively, if they do not differ by themselves, they must be distinct on account of something else. But what could this be if everything in God's essence is one?[52]

The relation between God and the thing known

With regard to God's knowledge of individual things, Scotus thought, the detour via rational relations or *rationes* was completely unnecessary. Individual things can be known directly: divine essence as such, qua essence, is the form of knowledge by which God knows himself as well as all other things. When God's intellect is actualized by the essence, this act is sufficient for producing in the intellect knowledge of all things. For God's essence contains all possible perfections.

That the above account of direct knowledge of particulars is indeed possible, Scotus inferred from the immediacy with which God knows himself. Self-knowledge does not involve a relation to something else. It does not need a rational relation, as there is no comparative act of knowledge involved. God only knows his essence, nothing else. Nor does it need a real relation, as everything in God is one. This means that an act of knowledge as such does not need a preceding relation in the intellect or object.[53]

The relation between God's knowledge and that which is known (the things), was qualified by Scotus as a *relatio tertio modo*, that is, a non-reciprocal relation in which one relatum is determined by the other, but not vice versa. This type of relation derives from Aristotle's *Metaphysics* (1021a26-30), where it is applied for instance to the relation between the measure (the independent) and the measured (the dependent). Thomas Aquinas, Henry of Ghent, and Duns Scotus applied it in particular to the relation between creator and creature: the creature is completely dependent upon God, while God remains completely independent.[54]

According to Duns Scotus, the divine intellect is the measure, and the thing known is the measured. In the divine act of knowledge the thing receives its intelligibility (*esse intelligibile*). *That* something is known does not depend upon the thing, but rather upon divine knowledge which 'collects' it, so to speak, from within God's essence, thereby producing it as a separate *esse intelligibile*. The process of knowledge in God is therefore the exact opposite

---

[52] Scotus, *Ordinatio*, I d. 36 q. u. n. 43 (ed. Vat., 6), 287f.

[53] *Lectura*, I d. 35 q. u. n. 19 (ed. Vat., 17), 451: "Igitur videtur quod non est necessarium propter actum intelligendi, in quantum est actus intelligendi, esse aliqua relatio in intellectu vel in obiecto (...)."

[54] Cf. K. Bannach, *Die Lehre von der doppelten Macht Gottes bei Wilhelm von Ockham. Problemgeschichtliche Voraussetzungen und Bedeutung*, Wiesbaden 1975 (Veröffentlichungen des Instituts für Europäische Geschichte Mainz, 75), 144 and 161, with references to the germane passages in the works of the authors mentioned.

of that in man. When God knows a thing, his knowledge remains unchanged and independent; only that which is known is changed. On the other hand, when man knows a thing, his knowledge is changed because it is determined by the thing he knows; the thing however remains unchanged. In man, the relation between knower and known is still a *relatio tertio modo*, but now the thing known is the measure, whereas knowledge is what is measured.[55]

From the fact that God's knowledge is to its object as a measure is to its measured, Scotus concluded that we need only a relation from the known to God, and not from God to what is known. Therefore God can know a thing without being antecedently related to it. Scotus thus rejected the view of Henry of Ghent and others who claimed that a preceding relation is involved. Scotus admitted that God can be related to the things, in the sense of Henry of Ghent, *after* he has knowledge of the individual things. In this respect, God's intellect is capable of no less than the human intellect. It can relate the divine essence to anything man can relate God's essence to. Man can relate it to each intelligible thing, and so can God. In the case of God, the divine intellect produces rational relations that exist in God. These relations can be known by God (for he can know everything), but should not be seen as a condition for his knowledge. They do not precede his knowledge, but are consequent upon it. Scotus here endorsed the view, which we find in other philosophers as well, that a relation cannot be known unless the relata are also known.[56]

As we have seen above, there is a certain tension between God's knowing individual things, and the simplicity of the divine intellect. To illustrate how these two can be accomodated, in the *Ordinatio* Scotus invoked a distinction between God's essence as univocal and equivocal principle. A univocal principle does not produce different effects, whereas an equivocal principle does. Taken as a univocal principle, God's essence moves the knowledge of the essence qua essence (the *obiectum primum*); taken as an equivocal principle, it moves the knowledge of the individual things (the secondary objects). In both cases the acts of knowledge have the same principle, viz., God's essence, but different things are known. Knowledge of the secondary objects immediately follows upon knowledge of the essence, giving expression to what is univocally known in the primary object.[57] The plurality of secondary objects does not occur in the essence but in the intellect, when it has been actualized by the simple essence. The intellect does not come to know different things by virtue of differences in the primary object; rather,

---

[55] Scotus, *Lectura*, I d. 35 q. u. n. 22 (ed. Vat., 17), 452. Also: I d. 39 qq. 1-5 n. 93, 510, and I d. 35 q. u. n. 18, 450.

[56] Ibid., d. 35 q. u. n. 14, 449; *Ordinatio*, I d. 35 q. u. n. 33 (ed. Vat., 6), 259. For a discussion of the medieval theories of relations, see M. Henninger, *Relations. Medieval Theories 1250-1325*, Oxford 1989.

[57] *Ordinatio*, I d. 36 q. u. n. 41, 287.

the differences are produced by the intellect as separate *intelligibilia*.

In the *Reportata Parisiensia*, Scotus distinguished between the object of knowledge as the mover and as the target of the act of knowledge, that is to say, as that *by which* something is known, and as that *which* is known. No creature is able to move God's intellect; only God's essence is capable of doing so. God's intellect being infinite, it can only be moved by an infinity. Therefore, no creature can ever be the cause of God's act of knowledge. As for the target of the act of knowledge, Scotus further distinguished between a primary and a secondary object. The primary object is the target that delimits the act of knowledge by virtue of the object's intrinsic nature; therefore, Scotus claimed, it is a correlate of the act of knowledge itself, without which no knowledge is possible. The secondary object is the target that does not delimit the act by itself, but by virtue of that in which it is contained.[58]

According to Scotus, divine essence is the primary, immediate target of knowledge. Only the essence is necessary for knowledge, not the finite creatures. God's infinite act of knowledge could not possibly have a finite being as its primary target, for that would limit its infinity. Finite beings can therefore act only as secondary, mediate targets. They are not necessary for the act of knowledge, nor do they delimit it by themselves; rather, they are known when the primary target is known. These considerations from the *Reportata* did not go by unnoticed. They were quoted in the commentaries on the *Sentences* of Peter Aureoli, Johannes Baconis, and Peter of Aquila.[59]

As we have seen, the emphasis on divine independence with regard to the finite objects of knowledge is also found in Scotus's *Lectura* and in the *Ordinatio*. Although he did not discuss the position of Averroes in either of these works, nor in the *Reportata*, his expositions clearly amounted to a reflection on Averroes's view and on the criticism of Themistius as found in Peter Aureoli and Johannes Baconis: divine unity and perfection are inconsistent with the idea of God's knowledge being immediately directed at the finite things, even if they were to be directly known in the essence. Therefore they can only be known as a consequence of God's knowledge of the essence.

In the *Lectura* and the *Ordinatio*, Scotus epitomized his view on God's knowledge of the creatures by distinguishing four conceptually successive stages. The following passage, which bears quoting, is taken from the *Lectura*:[60]

---

[58] *Reportata Parisiensia*, I d. 36 q. 2 nn. 5-6 (ed. Wadding, 11/1), fol. 200b.
[59] Ibid., n. 7, fol. 200b; Peter Aureoli, *Sent.*, I d. 35 p. 2 a. 4 (ed. Rome 1596), fol. 784a-b; Johannes Baconis, *Sent.*, I d. 35 q. 1 a. 4 par. 1 (ed. Cremona 1618), foll. 361b-362a; Peter of Aquila, *Sent.*, I d. 35 a. 3 (ed. Speyer 1480), col. 2.
[60] Scotus, *Lectura*, I d. 35 q. u. n. 22 (ed. Vat., 17), 452f.

"First, the divine intellect knows the essence.
In the second instance it knows the creature as an intelligible being (*in esse intelligibili*), not by an act of comparison, but he knows the stone in a direct act, followed by a relation of the third kind [between the stone and] the divine intellect or divine knowledge. For the stone, which then exists as an intelligible being, is brought into relation with divine knowledge like the measured is brought into relation with the measure. Thus, knowledge of the stone means only that the stone, produced as an intelligible being, is related to divine knowledge insofar as divine knowledge is independent, and not insofar as it is related to something. Similarly, the fact that God creates the stone means only that the stone, produced as an existing being, is brought into relation with God, who is conceived as independent insofar as he delimitates this relation.
In the third sign (*signum*), however, or in the third instance qua nature, the divine intellect relates its essence to the stone that exists as an intelligible being. This relationship causes a certain ideal relation (*relatio quaedam idealis*).
In the fourth instance, however, it reflects upon this relationship and upon the act of relating. Thus the idea is known, such that the idea, insofar as it is a being (*ens*), follows upon the knowledge of the creature in the third sign, and in another instance (viz., the fourth) follow the cognition (*cognitio*) and the understanding (*intellectio*) of the idea and of the relationship."

The equivalent text in the *Ordinatio* has somewhat different accents, but conveys substantially the same thought. Differences occur on the following three points:[61]

1. The *Ordinatio* is more pronounced on the fact that the intelligible being (*esse intelligibile*) is produced by God. Right at the outset of the second stage we read: "In the second instance God produces (*producit*) the stone as an intelligible being, and knows the stone."

2. In the *Ordinatio*, the first and second instances are more clearly distinguished from the third and fourth ones. The last two stages are of a different order than the first two: they *might* take place. "In a third instance, the divine intellect might (*forte*) relate its knowledge to each intelligible thing we can relate it to. Thus it could (*potest*) effect a rational relation within itself, by relating itself to the stone that is known. And in the fourth instance it could (*potest*), so to speak, bend itself over this relationship caused in the third instance, and then this relationship would be known. Thus it is not a relationship that is necessary for the knowledge of the stone." The fact that the third instance is not a necessary condition for knowledge of things was also stressed in the *Reportata Parisiensia*.[62]

3. In the first versions of the *Ordinatio*, Scotus made no reference to ideas. In a later annotation, however, he added, "Along this way (*via*), it appears of which thing there is an idea."[63]

---

[61] Cf. *Ordinatio*, I d. 35 q. u. n. 32 (ed. Vat., 6), 258.
[62] *Reportata Parisiensia*, I d. 36 q. 2 n. 34 (ed. Wadding, 11/1), fol. 206b.
[63] *Ordinatio*, I d. 35 q. u. n. 32 (adnotatio Scoti), 258, and the critical apparatus to the lines 20-23.

Although Scotus usually stated that the known, in the second stage, is related to divine knowledge, there are places in the *Reportata Parisiensia* and in the *Ordinatio* where he denied this. In the *Reportata*, he distinguished between two views (*viae*) in this regard. A similar distinction does not occur in the *Lectura*. According to the first view, the known in the second instance is related to and dependent upon God's knowledge. This matches the account of the four stages in the *Lectura* and the *Ordinatio*. According to the second view, however, there is no dependency, because the stone is still nothing. This second view was favoured in the *Reportata*. It also occurred in the *Ordinatio*, but there it was not preferred by Scotus. It was merely mentioned as an alternative to what the *Reportata* called the first view.[64] In Ockham, we will again find the notion that the object known by God is nothing.

Some controversial issues

In the first half of the fourteenth century, several aspects of Scotus's position were the subject of intense debate. We will discuss the following four areas in some detail:

1. The distinction of successive conceptual stages in God.
2. The point that God can know things without ideas.
3. The object of God's knowledge.
4. The production of the thing known.

1. Stages in God

The distinction of conceptual stages (*signa naturae, signa originis, instantia naturae, instantia originis*), discussed above with regard to God's knowledge of singular things, was also applied by Scotus in other contexts, viz., that of knowledge of the contingent, the theory of the Trinity, and the theory of predestination. Its use was typical of Scotus and of Scotists generally. In the debate between Pierre Roger and Francis of Mayronnes (1320/1) mentioned earlier, the latter remarked that two issues controlled the better part of theology at the time: the *rationes formales* and the *signa originis*. In this debate, Francis of Mayronnes defended the Scotist doctrine of distinct stages in God's essence, especially with regard to the Trinity.[65]

From the manuscript Oxford, Merton College, 284, we learn that the stage theory was being discussed at Oxford as early as 1314. The Thomistic *Liber propugnatorius* also raised objections against Scotus on this same point. We

---

[64] *Reportatio Parisiensia*, I d. 36 q. 2 n. 26 (ed. Wadding, 11/1), fol. 204b (first view); n. 34, fol. 206a-b (first view); n. 29, fol. 205a-b (second view): "Nec etiam mihi videtur quod ibi sit relatio aliqua (...) propter aliquam dependentiam (...) in lapide respectu intellectionis, quia ab aeterno intellectus non est aliquid, sed nihil (...)." See also *Ordinatio*, I d. 35 q. u. n. 51 (ed. Vat., 6), 267.

[65] Francis of Mayronnes and Pierre Roger, *Disputatio (1320-1321)*, n. 94, 101.

know that Ockham as well criticized the stage theory.[66] On the other hand, there have also been Thomistic writers who endorsed the idea of a conceptual order in divine knowledge similar to the one proposed by Scotus. So the theory was not the exclusive property of Scotists. In his commentary on the *Sentences*, e.g., the Thomist Hervaeus Natalis proposed the following five instances in divine knowledge as they are distinguished by man:[67]

> 1. First God knows his essence as the primary object (*obiectum primum*). The intellect is moved by this object as if it were a possible intellect. The choice of the terms 'moving' and 'possible intellect' merits some attention. Scotus, too, spoke of the essence as 'moving' knowledge, as we have seen. The reference to the divine intellect as 'possible intellect' later recurs in the commentary on the *Sentences* of the Scotist Francis of Mayronnes.[68]
> 2. Next comes the act of knowledge, caused by the primary object.
> 3. Then the act of knowledge is directed at God's essence as its primary object. At this stage the intellect knows that all things can be known through God's essence, because all things illuminate (*relucere*) in God's essence when it is known.
> 4. In the next instance the creatures are known.
> 5. Finally the intellect explicitly knows divine essence as the idea of each individual creature. This was not possible at earlier stages, for God must first know the creatures individually, which was not yet the case at the third stage.

The exposition of Hervaeus was quoted by Johannes Baconis, and therefore appears to have been noticed at the time.[69] It resembled that of Scotus in two respects. First, the plurality of known things does not exist in God's essence, but only in his intellect. God's essence, which remains absolutely one, acts as the cause of the differences because it contains all perfections. Secondly, Hervaeus and Scotus concurred on the view that the ideas are a consequence of God's knowledge of things, and not a condition for it. The creatures can be known individually without positing a plurality of ideas. The above considerations sufficiently show that, although certain views about divine knowledge have been typical of specific lines of thought, they were by no means restricted to them.

2. *God can know things without ideas*

The position Scotus took against Henry of Ghent, viz., that God can know the things without the aid of ideas, was adopted by the author of the *Liber propugnatorius* and by William of Ockham — both of them philosophers who

---

[66] See G.J. Etzkorn, 'Codex Merton 284', 32f; *Liber propugnatorius*, I prol. q. 5 (ed. Venice 1523), fol. 4b; M. McCord Adams, *William Ockham*, II, 1044-1048.
[67] Herveaus Natalis, *Sent.*, I d. 34 q. 1 a. 3 (ed. Paris 1647), fol. 143aC-D.
[68] Francis of Mayronnes, *Sent.*, I d. 36 q. 1 a. 3 (ed. Venice 1520), fol. 108vbP-109raB.
[69] Johannes Baconis, *Sent.*, I d. 36 q. 4 a. 3 par. 1 (ed. Cremona 1618), fol. 368bC-E.

criticized Scotus on many other counts.[70] It was also taken up by Henry of Harclay, a philosopher whose early career was strongly influenced by the views of Scotus, especially in the first book of his commentary on the *Sentences* (Paris, ca. 1300). In an early *quaestio* mentioned above (Città del Vaticano, Bibl. Apost., Borgh., 171), he endorsed the position that God's knowledge of the creatures can be explained without recourse to rational relations. He argued his view as follows. All relations, including the rational ones, need a foundation on which they are based. Rational relations must therefore follow upon knowledge, and not vice versa. Also, if ideas were to precede the knowledge, they would determine it and cause it. A plurality of ideas would thus imply a plurality of acts of knowledge, which is false.[71]

In a later *quaestio ordinaria* (Worcester, F. 3) Henry appears to have relinquished the view of Scotus in favour of that of Henry of Ghent and Godfrey of Fontaines. The old issue of simplicity returns here. Knowledge is a species of assimilation. That which contains no distinction whatsoever (divine essence) cannot be assimilated to contraries (the variety of things). So if God has knowledge of contraries, this must be by means of distinct *rationes*.[72]

3. The object of God's knowledge

Scotus's *Reportata* view on the object of God's knowledge was criticized in the commentary on the *Sentences* of Peter Aureoli. In a recent study by Katherine H. Tachau, it is shown that the thought of Peter Aureoli played a greater role in the first half of the fourteenth century than had previously been assumed.[73] With regard to divine knowledge (a subject not covered by Tachau), this is true in particular of his view of the object of knowledge. Can God's knowledge be directed at individual things? Aureoli's position was that it cannot. His arguments recurred in many commentaries on the *Sentences*, including those of Gregory of Rimini and Marsilius of Inghen. They were based in particular upon the presumed impossibility of actually knowing an infinite set of things, thus also rekindling the older question of God's knowledge of the infinite.

Peter Aureoli's criticism of Scotus focused on two points: that God's essence moves the intellect, and that the secondary objects are a target of God's knowledge. First, if God's essence is more than merely the target of his knowledge, if it is what moves the knowledge, then there must be potentiality in God. This contradicts his perfection, therefore the antecedent must be false.

---

[70] *Liber propugnatorius*, I d. 35 q. u. (ed. Venice 1523), fol. 114vb; Ockham, *Scriptum*, I d. 35 q. 4 (OTh, 4), 467.
[71] See the text edited in A.A. Maurer, 'Henry of Harclay's Questions', 169f. For literature on Harclay, see M. Henninger, *Relations*, 98 n. 1.
[72] See the text in Maurer, 'Henry of Harclay's Questions', 187.
[73] K.H. Tachau, *Vision and Certitude*, 85f and 315f.

God's knowledge is completely in act and completely subsistent; it cannot be moved, but can only have a target.[74] Although Aureoli did not go into it, this must also mean that the distinction of stages is pointless.

Concerning the second objection, Aureoli criticized the view that God's knowledge of the essence is distinct from his knowledge of the creatures. According to Aureoli, the acts by which essence and creatures are known are formally identical insofar as their target is equally God's essence. Yet God knows all things. The creatures are known *aequipollenter* in God's essence. Because God contains all perfections, when he knows his essence, he has knowledge of all things as similar to his essence. Moreover, Aureoli argued that Scotus had not sufficiently accounted for God's independence with regard to the objects of knowledge. If God does not know the creatures at the instant he knows his essence, but only after, then he somehow needs the creatures. For suppose that there are no secondary objects. Now, can God know the creatures by knowing his essence? If so, then there is no need to assume secondary objects as targets for God's knowledge. If not, however (as Scotus claimed), then God indeed needs the secondary objects. But then his perfection is necessarily dependent upon the knowledge of the creatures.[75]

A defense of Scotus against Aureoli's objections was undertaken by Johannes Baconis. He argued that Aureoli confused the position of Scotus with that of Themistius: as if God, when he knows himself, immediately passes into (*subito transit*) knowing the creatures as secondary objects, which delimit the knowledge and act as its target (viz., as the immediate target of Scotus). If this were correct, Baconis admitted, then God would indeed be dependent upon the secondary object.[76]

Baconis submitted, however, that there is yet another way in which creatures can be the secondary object and target of knowledge: they can also be known as a consequence (*consecutive et resultative*) of the knowledge of some other thing that is a proper target. Thus the creatures can be the secondary object, one which God will not be dependent upon; the secondary object thus acts as an indirect target.[77]

Although Baconis was correct in pointing out that Scotus's secondary objects were not themselves the direct target of God's knowledge, he did not do full justice to Aureoli's objection. Aureoli was striving to hold on to divine simplicity: even when he has knowledge of the creatures, God must be a perfect unity. There is in God no plurality of things known, there is but a single act of knowledge, identical with God, by which only the perfect essence is known. The assumption of secondary objects of any kind whatsoever would

---

[74] Peter Aureoli, *Sent.*, I d. 35 p. 2 a. 4 (ed. Rome 1596), fol. 785aF-bC.
[75] Ibid., foll. 785bD-F; 786bA-B.
[76] Johannes Baconis, *Sent.*, I d. 35 q. 1 par. 3 (ed. Cremona 1618), fol. 363aC, and I d. 39 q. 1 par. 8, fol. 381aC-D.
[77] Ibid., d. 39 q. 1 par. 8, fol. 381aD.

be a violation of this unity, Aureoli argued.⁷⁸ He believed that this was also the view of Aristotle and of Averroes, which he thought were in complete agreement with faith in this respect.

We learn from the reaction of Johannes Baconis that Aureoli's criticism of Scotus with regard to divine knowledge was well-known at the time. Curiously, there is no defense of Scotus against Aureoli in the work of Peter of Aquila, even though the latter, a Scotist, did quote Scotus's view of the object of God's knowledge and also discussed the view of Averroes. Perhaps the explanation for this is simply that he was not familiar with the first book of Aureoli's commentary on the *Sentences*.⁷⁹

4. *The production of the thing as intelligible being*

In the *Ordinatio*, Scotus stated that the thing is 'produced' by God as an intelligible being. In the *Reportata*, he spoke rather of its being 'constituted'. Things are not intelligible by themselves, but receive intelligibility in the divine intellect when it is moved by God's essence. This account sits well with the remarks Scotus made elsewhere concerning God's independence with regard to the known, and concerning God's intellect acting as a measure in the relation of knowledge. If created things were intelligible by themselves, then qua direct objects they would be the immediate target of knowledge, thus making God dependent upon them.

This point was criticized by William of Alnwick, who confessed that he had initially been a follower of Scotus here.⁸⁰ Alnwick's objection was closely connected with his view on the things that are known, which he believed to be both really and formally identical with God. Divine essence is infinitely perfect by itself, and not by an act of the intellect. Therefore, by itself it represents infinitely many intelligible things. As God does not produce the primary object of his knowledge (i.e., the essence), Alnwick argued, so he does not produce the secondary object either.⁸¹

Noteworthy is Alnwick's remark on the question why Scotus did not attribute a proper intelligibility to the things. As Alnwick saw it, Scotus joined in with the then popular view that creatures do not have being by themselves. Therefore, he submitted, Scotus was forced to the position that even their intelligibility was produced by something else, viz., God.⁸² If this diagnosis is correct, it would mean that Scotus tried to stress the *creatureliness* of

---

⁷⁸ Peter Aureoli, *Sent.*, I d. 35 p. 2 a. 2 (ed. Rome 1596), fol. 775aF-bB.
⁷⁹ Yet, he did know the second book of Aureoli's commentary, see K.H. Tachau, *Vision and Certitude*, 319 n. 14.
⁸⁰ William of Alnwick, *Quaestiones disputatae*, VI (ed. Ledoux), 161: "(S)olebam cum eis dicere quod creatura secundum suum esse intelligibile aeternum producitur a Deo, sed nunc veritatem diligentius inquirendo contrarium mihi omnino apparet."
⁸¹ Ibid., V, 125; VI, 165f.
⁸² Ibid., VI, 161.

creatures in all its aspects, including their quiddity and intelligibility, and thus their difference from God.

A similar criticism is found in the work of Peter Thomae (OFM, † ca. 1337), whose views were aimed explicitly against Scotus. Divine essence is the exemplar containing all perfections. The quiddities of things are not produced because God's essence causes them in the intellect, as Scotus believed; rather, the essence gives the things their intelligibility.[83]

Another critic of Scotus's view was Francis of Mayronnes, who frankly confessed that he did not see the point of it (*non capio*).[84] He distinguished between two approaches to discussing the quiddities, viz., the theological approach and the metaphysical approach. Theologically speaking — that is, according to Augustine — the quiddities are the highest things, the immutable *rationes* in God on account of which he is called wise. If they were produced by God, however (as Scotus claimed), then they would have a diminished being (*esse secundum quid et diminutum*) and could no longer be said to be the highest things. Metaphysically speaking — that is, according to Plato — the quiddities signify the definitions of things. A definition, however, is far removed from any question of being produced or not; it merely indicates a quiddity, and that is all. Whichever way we take the quiddities, Francis concluded, it does not make sense to speak of them as being produced.[85]

WILLIAM OF OCKHAM

A highly critical attitude with regard to the then current views of God's knowledge of creatures was assumed by William of Ockham. His position is particularly important with respect to the provability of God's knowledge of creatures. Ockham did not believe it possible to *prove* that God knows the creatures, at least not in the strict sense of the word (*sufficienter*); nor, indeed, did he believe the opposite to be possible, that is, to prove that God has *no* knowledge of the creatures. Yet he also thought that philosophy can still somehow settle the matter: probable arguments can be given to the effect that God has knowledge of the creatures (*probabiliter*). Ockham criticized the validity of the arguments put forward by Thomas Aquinas and Duns Scotus on this point, as well as the position of Averroes.

---

[83] See the text cited by O. Wanke, *Die Kritik Wilhelms von Alnwick an der Ideenlehre des Johannes Duns Scotus,* Bonn 1965 (Inaugural-Diss. Bonn), 293 n. 13, and 294 n. 23.

[84] Francis of Mayronnes, *Sent.*, I d. 47 q. 2 (ed. Venice 1520), fol. 133vbQ. For Mayronnes's criticism of Scotus, see also P. Vignaux, 'L'être comme perfection selon François de Meyronnes', *Etudes d'histoire littéraire et doctrinale,* Montréal-Paris 1962 (Université de Montréal, Publications de l'Institut d'Etudes Médiévales, 17), 277f.

[85] Francis of Mayronnes, *Sent.*, I d. 47 q. 2, 133vbQ-134raA. Also: I d. 42 q. 3 a. 3, foll. 119vbQ-120raB.

Ockham on Averroes

Many philosophers, Ockham remarked in the *Quodlibeta*, subscribe to the view (*multi philosophi posuerunt*) that God has no knowledge at all of the things beyond himself. It appears from the *Scriptum* that he was thinking in particular of Averroes and his interpretation of Aristotle. Averroes, as read by Ockham, not only held that we cannot *prove* that God knows things beyond himself, but also that he *really* knows nothing beyond himself. This additional claim Ockham called manifestly (*manifeste*) false.[86]

Ockham's reading of Averroes was clearly at odds with that of Peter Aureoli and Johannes Baconis (according to whom Averroes's position was that God knows all things), as well as with that of Thomas. Ockham followed the interpretation that Giles of Rome called the 'literal' reading of Averroes.

It is a curious fact that Ockham spoke here of "*many* philosophers". It nowhere appears that he was thinking of anyone other than Averroes. The use of 'posuerunt' may be an indication that he did not have contemporary thinkers in mind, but 'classical' ones. It is not very likely that he was thinking of Aristotle in this connection: in the *Scriptum* he said essentially that this view (that God has no knowledge of the creatures) was read into the words of Aristotle by Averroes.[87] Apparently, then, Ockham believed that Aristotle's own view differed from that of Averroes.

Ockham discussed eight arguments that Averroes purportedly used to prove that God has no knowledge of the created world. These arguments all derive from the twelfth book of Averroes's *Metaphysics*, and are based on his discussion of the object of God's knowledge: the object can be nothing but divine essence itself, since God would otherwise be dependent upon something else which perfects him. We shall review two characteristic arguments here.

The first argument is as follows. God is infinitely perfect, whereas all other things are less perfect. It is imperfect to know an imperfect thing. Therefore God does not have knowledge of other things than himself. This argument Ockham took to be the most powerful of the eight: if any argument could demonstrate that God does not know things, then it would be this one. Unfortunately, however, it is not valid. Ockham's criticism was that it is pointless to compare the act and the object of knowledge qua perfection. An act of knowledge is not equally perfect to, neither is it more nor less perfect than, the object of knowledge. Hence, the knower's perfection does not preclude that an imperfect object can be known.[88]

Ockham did not explain on what considerations his criticism was based. We may guess, however, that they involved the distinction between the status

---

[86] Ockham, *Quodlibeta*, I q. 1 (OTh, 9), 6f; *Scriptum*, I d. 35 q. 2 (OTh, 4), 434 and 436.
[87] *Scriptum*, I d. 35 q. 2, 434f.
[88] Ibid., 435 and 440f.

of real beings and that of concepts, as in the *Scriptum*'s discussion of the attributes. When an object is known and exists in the mind, it is no longer a thing (*res*), but a concept. Only things can be more or less perfect, not concepts. It is therefore pointless to compare things and concepts in this respect.

The second argument attributed to Averroes starts from the observation that every act of knowledge depends upon the object. As God depends upon nothing else, he cannot have knowledge of other things. To this Ockham objected that the first premise cannot be proved, and offered two examples to drive his point home. First, it cannot be proved that the act of knowledge by which the intelligence moves heaven depends upon heaven as it is moved. Also, Ockham claimed, even in man the act of knowledge does not always depend upon the object of knowledge.[89]

Again, these arguments were given without further explanation. The first example may have been intended as an *argumentum ad hominem*. Averroes believed that heaven has two movers: a soul directly connected to it, and an intelligence that is apart from it. The intelligence's act of knowledge does not by itself cause heaven to move, but acts through the soul that is directed toward the intelligence's knowledge, conveying it to heaven in the form of eternal motion. This means that the intelligence's act of knowledge is independent of heaven, and yet is responsible for moving it.[90] Thus Ockham could show that, even within Averroes's own frame of thought, not every act of knowledge depends upon its object.

As for his second example, Ockham may have been thinking of so-called abstractive knowledge which abstracts from the existence or non-existence of the thing known, or of the situation in which God causes in us intuitive knowledge of an object, without the object existing.[91]

Although Ockham was regrettably short in his comments, the general direction of his argumentation was straightforward enough: some acts of knowledge do not depend upon their object, therefore Averroes's premise is false, and his argument does not hold.

Ockham on Thomas Aquinas

Of the three arguments that Thomas used to prove that God has knowledge of the creatures, the first to be discussed by Ockham was the one that God knows creation through his powers. Ockham had two objections to this argument: first, that it did not sufficiently (*non sufficienter*) establish the

---

[89] Ibid., 435 and 441.
[90] For a discussion of Averroes's view, see A. Badawi, *Histoire de la philosophie en Islam*, II, 818f, with references to the relevant passages in Averroes's work.
[91] Ockham's view on abstractive knowledge and on intuitive knowledge of non-existents is dealt with in K.H. Tachau, *Vision and Certitude*, 117f, and 119 and 126, respectively. See also W. Vossenkühl, 'Ockham on the cognition of non-existents', *FcS* 45 (1985), 33-45.

claim that perfect knowledge of a power implies perfect knowledge of whatever the power is capable of, and secondly, that it did not sufficiently prove that God is the cause of all things.[92]

By 'sufficient proof' Ockham meant a proof that is based either on self-evident principles or on experience.[93] If a proof is insufficient, this means that it can be inferred neither from self-evident principles nor from experience. Ockham undertook to show that this was the case with Thomas's argument.

As for the first objection, he drew attention to two matters of experiential fact. First, non-complex knowledge of one thing does not yield non-complex knowledge of something else. This is clear from experience: no matter how immediate and perfect our knowledge of a thing is, it never gives us knowledge of another thing, unless that other thing was already known before. Hence, knowledge of one thing's power, viz., the power of God's essence, does not establish knowledge of its effects, viz., of the creatures.[94]

Moreover, our senses can have perfect knowledge of an object as well as of its power, for object and power are not distinct (it is the object's power that causes knowledge in the senses). Yet, no individual sense knows what else the object's power is capable of; it is ignorant of the other things (viz., the other senses) that can be touched by the object's power. Hence Ockham concluded that experience does not establish that Thomas's argument is universally and necessarily valid.[95] As we have seen above, this criticism resembles that of Duns Scotus in the *Reportata Parisiensia*: knowledge of the anterior does not necessarily include knowledge of the posterior.

Ockham's second objection, that God's universal causality is insufficiently proved, was of more substantial import. The argument from causality, Ockham believed, was the most powerful argument for God's knowledge: if it could at all be shown that God knows the creatures, then it would be by this argument.[96]

The question of whether God's causality can be proved was discussed in particular in the *Quodlibeta*. There Ockham came to the conclusion that the matter cannot be proved by natural reason. He used the phrase 'proof by natural reason' as synonymous with 'sufficient proof'. Ockham pointed out that it cannot be sufficiently proved that the celestial bodies and the separate substances (intelligences) were produced by an efficient cause. Celestial

---

[92] Ockham, *Scriptum*, I d. 35 q. 2 (OTh, 4), 436f.

[93] The germane texts are referred to in my 'Can God be proved to act freely? Ockham's criticism of an argument in Thomas', *Ockham and Ockhamists*, Acts of the Symposium organized by the Dutch Society for Medieval Philosophy, Leiden, 10-12 September 1986, ed. E.P. Bos and H.A. Krop, Nijmegen 1987 (Artistarium Supplementa, 4), 19.

[94] Ockham, *Scriptum*, I d. 35 q. 2 (OTh, 4), 436: "(I)llud quod est causa potest perfecte cognosci, nullo effectu cognito."; *Scriptum*, I prol. q. 9 (OTh, 1), 240f.

[95] *Scriptum*, I d. 35 q. 2 (OTh, 4), 437.

[96] Ibid., 441: "(S)i posset probari quod Deus intelligit omnia alia a se, hoc maxime esset per hoc quod Deus est causa omnium aliorum."; *Quodlibeta*, II q. 2 (OTh, 9), 115.

bodies and separate substances are immutable, and only of mutable, sublunar things can it be proved that they were produced. Moreover, the generation and corruption of sublunar things, Ockham argued, can be explained without recourse to God, viz., with reference to the causality of the celestial bodies and sublunar causes alone. For our experience tells us that the celestial bodies are the causes of things on earth. In short, this means that experience is unable to establish that God is the efficient cause of *anything*, let alone of *all* things.[97]

The alternative route to a sufficient proof would be by means of self-evident principles, but this option is not available with regard to God's causality. According to Ockham, God's existence is not self-evident; *a fortiori*, neither is God's causality.[98] In sum, neither self-evident principles nor experience can establish God's universal causality; therefore, it cannot be sufficiently proven.

The question of whether the celestial bodies and the intelligences can be produced by an efficient cause was often raised at the beginning of the fourteenth century, usually with regard to the opinions of Aristotle and Averroes. In his commentary on the *Metaphysics*, Averroes submitted as Aristotle's view that efficient causes can only produce composite substances (compounded of matter and form). The efficient cause works on the matter until it assumes a given form. This activity necessarily implies that the effect is subject to change. Celestial bodies and separate substances are not subject to change; hence they cannot have been produced by an efficient cause.[99]

Averroes's interpretation induced several philosophers and theologians to believe that Aristotle and Averroes claimed that God is not the efficient cause of the celestial bodies and the separate substances. Such was the view of John of Jandun (†1328, philosopher at Paris), of Johannes Baconis, and later also of Gregory of Rimini. According to John of Jandun, Averroes used 'causing' in the sense of 'bringing forth the form out of matter' (*abstrahere* and *educere*). Others, however, endorsed the opposite view: that Aristotle and Averroes believed that God is the efficient cause of celestial bodies and separate substances. Such was the opinion of Scotus and Hervaeus Natalis.[100]

Ockham followed the interpretation of Scotus and Hervaeus, as we learn from the *Reportatio* of his commentary on the second book of the *Sentences*, and from the *Quodlibeta*: Aristotle and Averroes held that God moves the

---

[97] *Quodlibeta*, II q. 1, 108 and 111.
[98] For pertinent references, again see my 'Can God be proved to act freely?', 19.
[99] Cf. Averroes, *In Metaphysicam*, XII t. 18 and t. 44 (ed. Iuntina, 8), fol. 304vaH and 328rbD.
[100] John of Jandun, *Quaestiones in duodecim libros Metaphysicae*, II q. 5, Venice 1553, repr. Frankfurt a/M 1966, fol. 27raA and 27rbG; Johannes Baconis, *Sent.*, II d. 1 q. 1 a. 2 par. 1 (ed. Cremona 1618), fol. 424bC; Gregory of Rimini, *Lectura*, II d. 1 q. 1 (ed. Trapp-Marcolino, 4), 8f. For the opposite view, see Scotus, *Lectura*, I d. 8 p. 2 q. u. (ed. Vat., 17), 77ff; Hervaeus Natalis, *Quodlibeta*, II q. 1, Venice 1513, repr. Ridgewood, New Jersey 1966, fol. 31rbff.

heaven as its efficient cause (*effective*).¹⁰¹ To explain how Aristotle could come to this position, Ockham attributed to him a second view of efficient causality, in addition to the one attributed by Averroes: sometimes Aristotle means by 'efficient cause' that which takes the form out of the matter (*extrahit*, the interpretation of Averroes), but sometimes he means that which is followed by the existence of something else. In this second sense, Aristotle could indeed claim that intelligences and celestial bodies are 'caused', for they exist because God exists. But, Ockham added, this kind of efficient causality cannot be proved by natural reason.¹⁰²

Notwithstanding Ockham's suggestion to the contrary, this alternative notion of efficient causality was not Aristotle's. In point of fact it derived from the *Metaphysics* of Avicenna.¹⁰³

Ockham on Duns Scotus

Of Scotus's arguments for God's knowledge of the creatures, Ockham criticized the one based on the assumption that God directs all things towards their goals. Ockham objected that it does not sufficiently establish the claim that God is the first efficient cause.¹⁰⁴ Surprisingly, he did not discuss God's finality in connection with his criticism of Scotus. For that we must turn to another context.

One *quaestio* of the *Quodlibeta* was devoted to God's finality in particular (Quodl. IV, q. 2). We learn there that Ockham did not think that God's finality could be proved. He argued as follows. Things that produce their effects without knowledge always act in similar fashion. By their nature they are determined to produce certain effects. Their activity does not change unless they themselves change, or that upon which they act changes (e.g., if the wood becomes damp, the fire will go out). Hence it is unwarranted to infer that unknowing things are directed by something else that lies beyond their own nature, including a cause that knows their end. Only things that can be directed towards their end in more than one way (such as spears) and are thus not constrained by their nature to produce a given effect, require some other

---

¹⁰¹ Ockham, *Quaestiones in secundum librum Sententiarum (reportatio)*, q. 5 (OTh, 5), 84 and 87; *Quodlibeta*, VII q. 16, (OTh, 9), 763: "(I)ntentio Philosophi et Commentatoris est quod Deus moveat caelum effective." In light of this passage, the view of A.A. Maurer in 'Ockham on the Possibility of a Better World', *Being and Knowing. Studies in Thomas Aquinas and Later Medieval Philosophers*, Toronto 1990, 383-402, esp. 387 (originally published in *Med. Stud.* 38 (1976), 291-312), to the effect that Ockham's position in the *Quodlibeta* was that the Aristotelian God is not the efficient cause of heaven, stands in need of correction. For further discussion, see my 'Can God be proved to act freely?', 20-21 n. 27.

¹⁰² Ockham, *Quaestiones*, q. 5, 85f.

¹⁰³ Cf. Avicenna, *Liber de philosophia prima*, VI c. 1 (ed. van Riet), 292. For a recent discussion of Ockham's view on causality, see E.P. Bos, 'William of Ockham's interpretation of the first proposition of the 'Liber de causis'', *On Proclus and His Influence in Medieval Philosophy*, ed. E.P Bos and P.A. Meijer, Leiden 1992 (Philosophia antiqua, 53), 171-189.

cause that knows their end and leads them to it.[105] This line of thought, which Ockham admittedly did not use against the above argument from Scotus, clearly shows that Ockham rejected not only the assumption that God's *causality* can be proved (as we have seen), but also the assumption that God's *finality* can be proved.

Ockham's alternative

As an alternative to the unsuccessful attempts of Thomas Aquinas and Duns Scotus, Ockham proposed a probable argument based on God's causality. His position, in short, was that it is probable that God is the immediate cause of some effect, and that he knows what he is the cause of. Therefore it is probable that God has knowledge of the effect.[106] The arguments Ockham gave in support of the two premises tended to differ in his various works. We shall review some of these arguments here.

Ockham's first premise was that God is probably the immediate cause of some effect. In the *Scriptum*, he argued this claim from what can be described as an 'extrinsical' description of causality: one thing is the cause of another thing, if destruction of the former is followed by destruction of the latter. This phrase was also used in the commentary on the second book of the *Sentences*, where it figured in the demonstration of the view that not only secondary causes can be the immediate cause of the creatures, but God too. If God exists there may be creatures, but not if he does not exist. In the *Quodlibeta*, however, the premise is proved in a different manner. There Ockham emphasized the significance of God's being a cause: it is more probable that God produced something than nothing, because otherwise it would be pointless to assume that he exists.[107]

Ockham's second premise was that God probably knows that of which he is the cause. In the *Scriptum* this claim was explained as follows. It is improbable that the first cause is ignorant of its effect, for that would mean that it produces something without knowing what. In the *Quodlibeta*, however, Ockham based his premise on God's perfection: because God is the most perfect being that moves all things intellectually and rationally, it is reasonable (*rationabiliter*) to assume that he knows what he produces.[108]

The underlying assumption on which Ockham's second premise was based, viz., that God's productivity needs an intellect, was not universally accepted as self-evident at the beginning of the fourteenth century. One of its critics was Henry of Harclay, who in a *quaestio ordinata* on ideas (Worcester, F. 3) objected that even if God had neither intellect nor will, yet was in act,

---

[104] Ockham, *Scriptum*, I d. 35 q. 2 (OTh, 4), 440; *Quodlibeta*, II q. 2 (OTh, 9), 116.
[105] *Quodlibeta*, IV q. 2 (OTh, 9), 303. See also II q. 2, 115.
[106] *Scriptum*, I d. 35 q. 2 (OTh, 4), 441f; *Quodlibeta*, II q. 2, 115.
[107] *Scriptum*, I d. 35 q. 2, 441f; *Quaestiones*, II qq. 3-4 (OTh, 5), 60f; *Quodlibeta*, II q. 1, 109.
[108] *Scriptum*, I d. 35 q. 2, 442; *Quodlibeta*, II q. 2, 115.

he would still be capable of producing all things. The reason for this is that a being's activity depends on its actuality. Intellect and will are needed only for *freely* (*libere*) producing an effect, not for the production as such. Harclay inferred that the ideas are not needed for the production of things, but only for the intellectual *manner* of production. Existing in God's intellect, the ideas are not *causa per se*, but only *causa sine qua non*: without ideas, God cannot be productive in an intellectual manner.[109]

How does God know the creatures?

Regarding the question of *how* God knows the creatures, Ockham's position was akin to that of Scotus: there is no need of rational relations or ideas because God has direct knowledge of the creatures. Ockham criticized the view of Henry of Ghent on this point. Unlike Scotus, however, he did not distinguish between different stages in God, nor did he treat God's essence as the cause of God's knowledge of the creatures. The one cannot be the cause of the other: God's essence is itself the knowledge of all things.[110] Both points on which Ockham departed from the position of Scotus had been made by other theologians before him, as we have seen above.

That God does not need rational relations in order to know the creatures (as was maintained by Henry of Ghent), Ockham inferred from the manner in which God has knowledge of himself. If two things are really identical, what is not needed for one thing is not needed for the other thing. The act by which God knows himself is the same as that by which he knows the creatures. Rational relations are not needed for God's knowledge of himself, so they are not needed for his knowledge of the creatures either.[111] This argument is obviously very similar to the one Scotus used in the *Lectura*.

Furthermore, Ockham pointed out that there are two contradictions in the position of Henry of Ghent. It was Henry's view, we may recall, that God's knowledge of divine essence causes his knowledge of all other things. In the first instance, the creatures are known without distinction as being identical with the essence. It is only in the second instance, when he knows his essence as imitable, that God knows all creatures distinctly. Against this view, Ockham objected that if there is something that causes and something that is caused, there is a plurality, because nothing can cause itself. This plurality can only be on the part of the object, considering that God's essence, his intelligence, and his act of knowledge are one. It follows that the object *by* which God has knowledge (the essence) is different from the object *of* which he has knowledge (the creatures), which is in contradiction with Henry's tenet that in the first instance the creatures are known as identical with God's

---

[109] See the text edited in A.A. Maurer, 'Henry of Harclay's Questions', 190f.
[110] Ockham, *Quodlibeta*, IV q. 3 (OTh, 9), 310: "(S)ua essentia est cognitio omnium (...)."
[111] *Scriptum*, I d. 35 q. 4 (OTh, 4), 465.

essence.¹¹²

The second contradiction involved that the very notion that God has knowledge of the things by knowing his own essence is incoherent, because nothing in God can be caused. The primary tenet of Henry of Ghent and many other theologians, viz., that something that is one cannot represent a plurality of things, Ockham simply dismissed as untrue. It is quite possible, he argued, for one and the same thing to simultaneously and without internal distinction be the cause of different effects; it is thus that the sun produces light and warmth. Similarly, one and the same thing may without internal distinction represent a plurality of things.¹¹³

This same consideration was used by Ockham to explain the distinction in the Trinity between Son and Father as being the result of a natural act of the intellect, and of a free act of the will, respectively. One and the same principle (God's essence) can have a natural action toward one effect (the Son), yet at the same time be free with regard to the other effect (the Spirit). Within God's essence no distinction is required, but only in the effects.¹¹⁴

Scotus's distinction between knowledge of the essence and knowledge of the creatures was another target of Ockham's criticism. If by one and the same act several things can be known (essence and creatures), then the one is not known before the other. Hence, Ockham concluded, God does not know himself before he knows the creatures.¹¹⁵ This objection did *not* carry with it a rejection of the distinction between primary and secondary object, as it did for Peter Aureoli. The objects of knowledge may be different, and one object may be antecedent to the other, but that does not affect the manner in which they are known. From the fact that there is an order in the objects it does not follow that there is a similar order in the modes of knowledge, especially not if the objects are known in the same act.¹¹⁶

Another objection Ockham raised against Scotus concerned his doctrine of stages. Keeping with the above line of thought, Ockham argued that there is no reason to postulate stages in God, neither because of the relation to the things that are known, nor because of the divine act of knowledge. Furthermore, he criticized Scotus's view that God's intellect is moved by the essence. According to Ockham, the expression is simply misplaced in this context, and serves no purpose in furthering the study of the divine. Ockham also objected to the view that the things qua intelligible are produced by God. His argument here was like that of William of Alnwick: as divine essence does not receive

---

¹¹² Ibid., 466f. Cf. Henry of Ghent, *Quodlibeta*, VIII q. 1 (ed. Paris 1518), fol. 299vA.
¹¹³ *Scriptum*, I d. 35 q. 4, 466f.
¹¹⁴ *Scriptum*, I d. 2 q. 1 (OTh, 2), 34-36, and I d. 7 q. 3 (OTh, 3), 141-147. In Adam Wodeham's *Lectura Oxoniensis*, I d. 6 q. 1 (Paris, Bibl. Maz., 915), fol. 73ra, this view was attributed specifically to William of Ockham.
¹¹⁵ Ockham, *Scriptum*, I d. 35 q. 3 (OTh, 4), 455f, and q. 4, 469.
¹¹⁶ Ibid., q. 3, 460.

intelligibility by virtue only of the intellect's activity, so neither do things receive their intelligibility merely from this activity.[117]

PETER AUREOLI: THE ARGUMENTS FROM INFINITY

In his *Sentences* commentary of 1317, Peter Aureoli submitted four arguments for the claim that God's knowledge is not directed toward the creatures, but toward divine essence alone. The arguments, which were to become very influential, are all of the same typical form: if it is admitted that God knows the creatures as secondary objects, one encounters certain aporias involving the notion of infinity. To illustrate the nature of Aureoli's reasoning, we give here the first two of his arguments.

First, if God has direct knowledge of the creatures, then he also knows the continuum which is infinitely divisible. If God knows the continuum in *all* of its parts, then it cannot be divided any further, which contradicts its infinite divisibility. On the other hand, if God does not have full knowledge of the continuum, then his knowledge is limited, incomplete, and imperfect, which contradicts God's perfection. Hence God cannot have direct knowledge of the continuum as a secondary object; therefore he cannot have direct knowledge of the creatures as secondary objects.[118]

Secondly, if we attribute to God direct knowledge of a certain magnitude, then we must also attribute to him the capacity for knowing a still greater magnitude: for any given magnitude, man can always conceive of a greater one; therefore, so can God. In God this possibility is always realized, as his intellect is perfect and always in act. But this means that God knows an actually infinite magnitude, which is impossible because such a thing cannot possibly exist. (The underlying idea here is that God is always able to create what he knows.) On the other hand, if we were to assume that God knows only potentially infinite magnitudes, then his knowledge would be incomplete, hence imperfect. In sum, God cannot have direct knowledge of magnitudes; therefore he cannot have direct knowledge of the creatures.[119]

The remaining two arguments are variations on the second. In the third, it is argued that God cannot have direct knowledge of numbers (because there does not exist an infinite number), while in the fourth it is argued that he cannot have direct knowledge of species (because there cannot be an infinitely perfect species).[120]

---

[117] Ibid., q. 4, 468f; also q. 3, 458, and d. 43 q. 2, 646.
[118] Peter Aureoli, *Sent.*, I d. 35 p. 2 a. 1 (ed. Rome 1596), fol. 772bB-E: "(...) (E)rgo impossibile est quod aliquid aliud a Deo ponatur in eius intuitu, vel prospectu in actu; qua ratione namque aliquid poneretur, omnes partes continui ponerentur." For the dating of Aureoli's commentaries on the *Sentences* and for further secondary literature, see K. Tachau, *Vision and Certitude*, 85-89, esp. nn. 2 and 11.
[119] *Sent.*, I d. 35 p. 2 a. 1, fol. 773aA-D.
[120] Ibid., fol. 773aE-bF.

As far as we have been able to ascertain, Peter Aureoli was the first to articulate these arguments from infinity in the context of a discussion of God's knowledge. Questions involving God's knowledge of the infinite had been discussed before by Thomas and other theologians, but never in connection with these particular problems. Even the very extensive exposition by Durand of St. Pourçain in the third draft of his commentary on the *Sentences*, written in 1317-1327, *after* Aureoli's commentary had been finished (1317), did not apply the arguments in this context.[121] Later in the fourteenth century, Aureoli's arguments were quoted and discussed by various commentators on the *Sentences*. Some examples are Gregory of Rimini, Alfonsus Vargas, Hugolin of Orvieto, Gottschalk of Nepomuk (commentary on the *Sentences*, Paris 1365-1366, close to Gregory of Rimini on many points), and Marsilius of Inghen.[122] In short, we can say that Peter Aureoli made an important and original contribution to the discussion of God's knowledge, at least as it was conducted toward the end of the fourteenth century.

Gregory of Rimini presented Aureoli's arguments as proof of the claim that God does not know the creatures.[123] Notice, however, that this was not how Aureoli had intended them. He merely wanted to show that the act by which God knows the creatures cannot be directed at the creatures themselves, but only at divine essence. According to Peter Aureoli, God does not know the creatures *terminative* (the act of knowledge does not terminate in the creatures), but rather *aequipollenter* (he knows them when he knows his essence). Aureoli rejected the received distinction between primary and secondary objects of knowledge.

The fact that Gregory took Aureoli's arguments to be proof of the claim that God has no knowledge of the creatures may at least partly be understood from the context in which Aureoli developed his view, viz., as an interpretation of the position of Averroes. This may have put Gregory on the wrong track, leading him to read Aureoli from the viewpoint of his (Gregory's) own interpretation of Averroes, which was quite different from Aureoli's, as we have seen above.

---

[121] Cf. Durand of St. Pourçain, *In Sententias commentariorum libri IIII*, I d. 39 q. 2, Venice 1571, repr. Ridgewood, New Jersey 1964, foll. 106va-107rb. The dating of Durand's commentary is according to B. Decker, *Die Gotteslehre*, 77-87.

[122] Gregory of Rimini, *Lectura*, I dd. 35-36 q. 1 (ed. Trapp-Marcolino, 3), 213f and 223-226; Alfonsus Vargas, *In primum Sententiarum*, I dd. 35-37 q. 1 a. 2, Venice 1490, repr. The Meriden Gravure Co. 1952, coll. 605f; Hugolin, *Sent.*, I d. 35 q. u. a. 3 (ed. Eckermann, 2), 302f, Gottschalk of Nepomuk, *Sent.*, I dd. 35-40 (Kraków, Bibl. Jag., 1499), fol. 44ra: "Arguit unus doctor Petrus Aureoli sic: Si Deus omnia distincte cognosceret, tunc sequeretur quod possibile esset divisionem continui totaliter evacuari."; Marsilius, *Sent.*, I q. 38 a. 3 (ed. Hoenen), 34-38. For the dating of Gottschalk's commentary, see W.J. Courtenay, *Adam Wodeham*, 141.

[123] See *Lectura*, I dd. 35-36 q. 1, 213 and 214.

Yet, Gregory seems to have had some grasp of the point Aureoli wanted to make. In his response to the first argument, he claimed that if the argument were valid, it would imply that Aureoli's view is false. For it is irrelevant to the argument, Gregory said, whether God knows the continuum directly or through divine essence.[124] This remark only makes sense if we assume that Gregory was aware of the fact that Aureoli wanted to equate God's knowledge of the creatures with his knowledge of himself.

We can summarize Gregory's criticism of Aureoli's arguments as follows. With regard to the first argument, Gregory distinguished between two sorts of division of the continuum: it may be divided either into indivisible points (*puncta*), or into parts that may each be divided still further, either actually or potentially (*partes actu vel potentia divisae*). In the first case no further division is possible. This, he noted, is indeed at odds with the infinite divisibility of the continuum claimed by Aureoli. In the second case, however, infinite division is still possible. Now, this second way, Gregory submitted, is the way in which God has knowledge of the continuum. The parts of the continuum that man is able to divide still further are actually divided into infinitely many parts in the mind of God. Any part that man conceives of, no matter how small it is, itself consists of infinitely many subparts in the mind of God.[125]

In response to the second argument, Gregory claimed that, *pace* Aureoli, God is really capable of knowing an infinite magnitude. Moreover, unlike Aureoli, he believed that God is capable of creating an infinite magnitude or an infinite body, because the notions of 'infinity' and 'magnitude' do not contradict one another. Elsewhere in his commentary on the *Sentences* (Lib. I, dd. 42-44) Gregory extensively controverted Aureoli on this issue.[126] His criticism of the third and fourth argument was similar to that of the first. God knows infinitely many numbers, but that does not mean that there is an infinite number. Whatever number man may conceive will always be followed by a larger one; therefore every number is finite. Much the same holds with regard to species: God has knowledge of actually infinitely many species; but each species is finite, as it is always surpassed by a more perfect one.[127]

Gregory's mistake concerning Aureoli's position was not repeated by Alfonsus Vargas and Hugolin of Orvieto. In their commentaries on the *Sentences* they correctly placed Aureoli's arguments in context, viz., the question of what is the terminating point of the act of knowledge by which

---

[124] Ibid., 224.
[125] Ibid. Gregory's view on infinity and on the divisibility of the continuum is dealt with in A.G. Molland, 'Continuity and Measure in Medieval Natural Philosophy', *Mensura, Mass, Zahl, Zahlensymbolik im Mittelalter*, Vol. 1, ed. A. Zimmermann, Berlin-New York 1983 (MM, 16/1), 132-144, esp. 137.
[126] Ibid., and dd. 42-44 q. 4 a. 1, 441-445. See also dd. 42-44 q. 4 a. 2, 448-473.
[127] Ibid., dd. 35-36 q. 1, 225f.

God knows the creatures. As for Alfonsus, his correct interpretation may have been facilitated by the fact that he had virtually the same view of Averroes's position as Aureoli. Yet, Alfonsus too appears to have taken the arguments as (also) showing that God does not have knowledge of the creatures.[128] We probably see here the influence of Gregory: if Aureoli's reasoning is correct, so Alfonsus seems to be arguing, then God is unable to know the creatures, even if he would know them through his essence.

Vargas's refutation of Aureoli rested on the same views as Gregory's, although he did not mention his name. God knows all parts of the continuum and all numbers, but this does not mean that the continuum is exhaustively divided or that there is a largest number. Each part itself can be divided still further, and to each number another one can be added. Here Alfonsus gave the same quotations from Augustine as had been used by Gregory. Finally, like Gregory, he also endorsed the view that God is able to create an infinite magnitude.[129]

After his criticism of the first two arguments, Alfonsus quoted some passages from the *Quaestiones ordinariae* by the Augustinian Jacobus de Appamiis, Master at Paris before 1332, who is known for his criticism of Aureoli in particular. This Jacobus may have been one of the sources from which Gregory drew his criticism of Aureoli. Either way, the passages quoted by Alfonsus Vargas show a striking resemblance to Gregory's views of the divisibility of the continuum.[130] A direct influence of Jacobus de Appamiis on Gregory of Rimini is hard to establish, however. He was not mentioned by Gregory in his commentary on the *Sentences*. Yet it is reasonable to assume that Gregory was familiar with Jacobus's criticism, considering the fact that they were fellow Augustinians who both studied in Paris.[131]

As for Hugolin of Orvieto, his view was that God has actual knowledge of all parts of the continuum, and yet each part itself is infinitely divisible. Again, he was also of the opinion that God is able to create an actually infinite magnitude.[132]

---

[128] Alfonsus, *Sent.*, I dd. 35-37 q. 1 a. 2 (ed. Venice 1490), col. 607: "(N)on solum probant quod Deus non cognoscat creaturas extra se terminative, sed quod nullo modo cognoscat eas, nec extra se nec in se, quod manifestum est catholicis esse falsum."
[129] Ibid., col. 607 and col. 608.
[130] Ibid., 608. For Jacobus de Appamiis's criticism of Aureoli, see F. Pelster, 'Zur ersten Polemik gegen Aureoli: Raymundus Bequini OP, seine Quästionen und sein Correctorium Petri Aureoli, das Quodlibet des Jacobus de Appamiis OESA', *FcS* 15 (1955), 30-47. For biographical data on Jacobus, see A.D. Trapp, *LThK*, 2th ed., s.v. 'Jacobus de Appamiis (Pamiers)'. The information provided by A. Zumkeller, 'Die Augustinerschule', 210, according to which the *Quaestiones ordinariae* of Jacobus have survived in manuscript, is not substantiated by the literature he mentions.
[131] Gregory of Rimini's first stay in Paris was from 1324 until 1329; his second stay from 1342 until 1346. On Gregory's biography, see V. Marcolino, 'Der Augustinertheologe an der Universität Paris', *Gregor von Rimini. Werk und Wirkung bis zur Reformation*, ed. H.A. Oberman, Berlin-New York 1981 (Spätmittelalter und Reformation, 20), 127-194.
[132] For further details on Hugolin's reply to Aureoli, see my 'Hugolin von Orvietos Lehre

Gregory of Rimini

Gregory of Rimini discussed the problem of God's knowledge in terms of his theory of the *enuntiabilia* and the *complexe significabilia*, according to which the object of knowledge is not the thing (*res*) or the proposition, but the state of affairs that is signified by the proposition. This theory played a role of particular importance in his discussion of the objects of God's knowledge and the way these objects are known by God.[133]

With regard to the objects of God's knowledge, Gregory distinguished between those that can be signified *simply* (that is, by means of a single term), and those that can only be signified *complexly* (that is, by means of a proposition). God has knowledge of both kinds of objects. The first kind encompasses all things that can exist by themselves, such as angels and human beings. They can be referred to by means of a single term (*incomplexe*), and are called *cognoscibilia simplicia*. Objects of the second kind cannot exist by themselves. They are 'connections' such as 'that the wood is heated by the fire'. Objects of this kind can be referred to only by means of several words (*complexe*), and are called *cognoscibilia complexe significabilia* or *enuntiabilia*.[134]

Gregory's distinction runs more or less parallel to that of Holcot and others, differentiating known things and known (pairs of contradictory) propositions.[135] His reason for postulating the second kind of objects, appears to have been the received Aristotelian notion that the object of a declarative sentence cannot be a separate entity, but only a certain state of affairs or composition of things.[136] Unlike Ockham and Holcot, Gregory did not speak of *propositions* as being the object of God's knowledge, but rather the *enuntiabilia*; in his view, the object of a judgment is not the proposition itself, but that which is signified or expressed by the proposition.[137]

---

von der scientia Dei im Rahmen der Lehrentwicklungen 1250-1350', *Augustiniana* 39 (1989), 483-501.

[133] Gregory's theory of the *complexe significabile* has received extensive scholarly attention, as is documented by the literature cited in D. Perler, *Satztheorien. Texte zur Sprachphilosophie und Wissenschaftstheorie im 14. Jahrhundert*, Darmstadt 1990 (Texte zur Forschung, 57), 344f. See also K.H. Tachau, 'Wodeham, Crathorn, and Holcot: the Development of the Complexe Significabile', *Logos and Pragma. Essays on the Philosophy of Language in Honour of Professor Gabriel Nuchelmans*, ed. L.M. de Rijk and H.A.G. Braakhuis, Nijmegen 1987 (Artistarium supplementa, 3), 161-187.

[134] Gregory, *Lectura*, I dd. 35-36 q. 1 additio 148 (ed. Trapp-Marcolino, 3), 227f; also d. 38 q. 2 aa. 1 and 3, 274 and 285 respectively.

[135] See below, p. 192.

[136] Gregory, *Lectura*, I prol. q. 3 a. 1 (ed. Trapp-Marcolino, 1), 109. Cf. *Auctoritates Aristotelis* (ed. Hamesse), 305 (2): "Circa compositionem et divisionem consistit veritas et falsitas."

[137] For a discussion of Gregory's view, see G. Nuchelmans, *Theories of the Proposition*, 227-237, with references to the germane passages.

As for the origins of the distinction, Gregory referred to the *antiqui doctores* who, he claimed, distinguished between the knowledge of things and the knowledge of *enuntiabilia*. Here he mentioned William of Auxerre and Giles of Rome, whose works he knew well, as may be gathered from literal quotations elsewhere in his commentary on the *Sentences*. Yet it is very probable that Gregory did not really derive his distinction from the sources he mentioned. The distinction, together with the very same reference to the *doctores antiqui* and to William of Auxerre, also occurred in Adam Wodeham's *Sentences* commentary, a work that was frequently quoted by Gregory. It is thus reasonable to assume that he simply adopted his presentation of the distinction from Adam Wodeham.[138]

As for the reference to Giles of Rome as his other source, we should bear in mind that Gregory, as an Augustinian, was thoroughly acquainted with Giles's widely read work, which from the thirteenth (1290) until into the sixteenth century was part of the required literature for all Augustinians.[139] The reference does not bespeak any material agreement between the two thinkers. In Giles's work, the *enuntiabilia* are discussed only in passing, and play no role of any consequence. Gregory might as well have referred, for example, to Thomas Aquinas, who also mentioned the distinction between *res* and *enuntiabile*.[140]

Both Thomas Aquinas and Giles of Rome discussed the *enuntiabilia* in their commentaries on the *Sentences* in relation to questions concerning God's knowledge, picking up elements from a twelfth-century discussion on the subject as it had crystallized in Lombard's *Sentences* and other works.[141] The fact that they even treated the *enuntiabilia* was not so much caused by a thirteenth-century interest in the matter, as by the required reading of Peter Lombard and the influence of the widely read *Summa aurea* by William of Auxerre. Equivalent to the *Sentences* in design, and written between 1215 and 1229, this work discussed many twelfth-century views, including those on the *enuntiabilia*.[142] The commentaries on the *Sentences* of Thomas Aquinas and

---

[138] Gregory, *Lectura*, I dd. 35-36 q. 1 additio 148 (ed. Trapp-Marcolino, 3), 228; Adam Wodeham, *Lectura Oxoniensis*, III q. 2 (Paris, Bibl. Maz., 915), fol. 173vb: "Quoad primum respondendum est secundum doctores antiquos quod illud vocabulum 'scientia Dei' uno modo sumitur pro notitia rerum, alio modo pro scientia vel notitia enuntiabilium. Et hanc distinctionem ponit Altissiodorensis libro suo primo cap. 43." G. Gál has shown (in his 'Adam of Wodeham's Question on the 'complexe significabile' as the immediate object of scientific knowledge', *FcS* 37 (1977), 66-102) that Gregory borrowed the notion of the *complexe significabile* from Adam Wodeham. The above mentioned passages on divine knowledge (which are not discussed by Gál), point in the same direction.

[139] See A. Zumkeller, 'Die Augustinerschule', 169f.

[140] Cf. Giles of Rome, *Sent.*, I d. 39 q. 2 (ed. Venice 1521), foll. 205vbQ-206rbH; Thomas Aquinas, *Sent.*, I d. 38 q. 1 a. 3 c. (ed. Mandonnet, 1), 903.

[141] For the twelfth-century views as reported by Peter Lombard, see G. Nuchelmans, *Theories of the Proposition*, 185-187.

[142] Cf. William of Auxerre, *Summa aurea*, I tract. 9 c. 2, ed. J. Ribaillier, Paris-Grottaferrata

Giles of Rome followed Lombard much more closely than later commentaries did. It is important to notice that discussions of the *enuntiabilia* do not recur in the later commentaries, which shows how strong the influence of Lombard was on the choice of themes in the earlier commentaries on his work. Adam Wodeham and Gregory of Rimini were the first to reintroduce the *enuntiabilia* as an important theme in the discussion of divine knowledge, in consequence of the more general epistemological debate on the object of scientific knowledge that had been carried on since the beginning of the fourteenth century. It is noteworthy, in this connection, that the *abbreviatio* of Adam Wodeham's *Lectura Oxoniensis*, which was drawn up by Henry of Oyta at Paris around 1375, did not refer to William of Auxerre but to Peter Lombard. This may be an indication that Lombard's exposition played some role in the revival of the *enuntiabilia*.[143]

The *enuntiabilia* were divided into three groups by Gregory. The first group consisted of the *enuntiabilia* whose corresponding propositions are true. Gregory called them *enuntiabilia vera*. Some of them are necessarily true, others contingently so, depending upon the nature of the corresponding propositions. The second group consisted of the *enuntiabilia* corresponding with propositions that are false, but that might have been true. They were called *enuntiabilia falsa possibilia*. The third group consisted of *enuntiabilia falsa impossibilia*, whose corresponding propositions are necessarily false.[144]

We see that the assignment of truth values and modalities to the *enuntiabilia* proceeds only indirectly, viz., via the corresponding propositions. Gregory spoke of an 'extrinsic denomination' (*denominatio extrinseca*) in this connection. When there are no propositions, as was the case before creation, the assignment of truth values proceeds by means of the uncreated truth of God, a point that was also made by Adam Wodeham.[145] According to Gregory, it follows that *enuntiabilia* have truth values only in a derivative sense. Interestingly, there is a contrast here with the views found in the logical treatises of the twelfth century. As Gabriel Nuchelmans has shown, the common view endorsed in these logical treatises was that the *enuntiabilia* are the proper bearers of truth, and that the propositions have truth value only derivatively, as signs — the exact opposite of Gregory's position. As far as we know, there is only one other place, viz., in the *Ars Meliduna* (1170/1180), where the truth value of the *enuntiabile* was derived from that of the

---

1980 (Spicilegium Bonaventurianum, 16), 180f. On William of Auxerre, see J. Ribaillier, *DS*, s.v. 'Guillaume d'Auxerre'.

[143] See *Adam Goddam super quattuor libros Sententiarum*, III q. 2, Paris 1512 (= *abbreviatio* of Wodeham by Henry of Oyta), fol. 118ra. For the dating of the *abbreviatio*, see W.J. Courtenay, *Adam Wodeham*, 146f.

[144] Gregory, *Lectura*, I dd. 35-36 q. 1 additio (ed. Trapp-Marcolino, 3), 228f.

[145] Ibid., I prol. q. 1 a. 1 (ed. Trapp-Marcolino, 1), 11; Adam Wodeham, *Lectura Oxoniensis*, III q. 2 (Paris, Bibl. Maz., 915), foll. 175vb-176ra.

corresponding proposition, as in Gregory's position.¹⁴⁶ It is not known, however, whether Gregory was really acquainted with the views of these older logical treatises.

Ways of knowledge

Like Thomas and others before him, Gregory distinguished between God's *scientia simplicis notitiae* and his *scientia visionis*. The first is the knowledge of all existing and all possible things, the latter that of the things that exist, existed, or will exist. For this second way of knowledge Gregory used the term *visio*. If the term is applied to God, it signifies (*significat*) the knowledge and connotes (*connotat*) the things that exist in present, past, or future. Furthermore, Gregory distinguished between, on the one hand, the simply apprehensive act (*actus simpliciter apprehensivus*), by which a single thing is known without something else also being known, and, on the other hand, the composite objective knowledge (*notitia iudiciaria*) by which something is affirmatively or negatively judged to be the case or not. According to Gregory, neither of these distinctions implies a difference in God.¹⁴⁷

Although Gregory was not explicit on this, we may gather from his exposition that the *scientia simplicis notitiae* and the *scientia visionis* apply to intelligible objects of the first kind only (the non-complex *res*), that the simple act of apprehension applies to intelligibles of both kinds (simple *res* and *enuntiabilia*), and that the complex knowledge that makes judgments of existence applies only to intelligibles of the second kind. Strictly speaking, however (and here Gregory *was* explicit), the simple act of apprehension applies only to intelligible objects of the first kind; knowledge of objects of the second kind, on the other hand, is always judgmental and certain in nature.¹⁴⁸

On this last point Gregory was following Adam Wodeham, according to whom God's knowledge of objects of the second kind (*enuntiabilia*), properly speaking, proceeds by means of a true judgment, and not only by means of a simple apprehensive act. With regard to the *scientia visionis*, however, there seems to be a difference between Gregory and Wodeham. According to Wodeham, the knowledge of vision is always identical with God's knowledge of judgment, which is not always the case in Gregory's view.¹⁴⁹

---

¹⁴⁶ For the opinions expressed in these twelfth-century logical treatises, see G. Nuchelmans, *Theories of the Proposition*, 172f.

¹⁴⁷ Gregory, *Lectura*, I dd. 35-36 q. 1 additio 148 (ed. Trapp-Marcolino, 3), 229f. These distinctions were adopted almost *verbatim*, with reference to the *antiqui doctores* and to Peter Lombard, by Gottschalk of Nepomuk, *Sent.*, I dd. 35-40 (Kraków, Bibl. Jag., 1499), fol. 43vb.

¹⁴⁸ Gregory, *Lectura*, I d. 39 q. 1, 313.

¹⁴⁹ Ibid.; Adam Wodeham, *Lectura Oxoniensis*, III q. 2 (Paris, Bibl. Maz., 915), foll. 173vb-174ra. Gregory's view on this point is apparent from the fact that he distinguished between *scientia simplicis intelligentiae* and *scientia visionis* concerning objects of the first kind.

God knows all intelligible objects of the first kind (*res*) by his *scientia simplicis notitiae*. Gregory's proof of this was very simple: God has knowledge of things, therefore he must have knowledge of *all* things, for there is no reason to suppose that he knows one thing but not another. Not all things are known by means of *scientia visionis*, however. For some things will never exist; hence these cannot be known by *scientia visionis*.[150]

God knows all objects of the second kind (the *enuntiabilia*) by a simple act of apprehension. Gregory's argument for this claim was based on the assumption (which he established elsewhere) that every proposition is either true or false. God necessarily knows that every *enuntiabile* can be expressed by a proposition that is either true or false. Therefore, every *enuntiabile* is necessarily known to God by a simple act of apprehension. For if every proposition is either true or false, then God must know this, and so he must also know what it is that is true or false.[151]

The intelligibles of the second kind are not always known by means of judgmental knowledge, because not every *enuntiabile* is true. If proposition P, 'Peter will be seated at time t', is true, then proposition –P, 'Peter will not be seated at time t', must be false. No two contradictory propositions P and –P can be true at the same time. Hence, neither can the corresponding *enuntiabilia* be true at the same time. From this argument we learn that Gregory restricted the objects of judgmental knowledge to true *enuntiabilia* only.[152]

In the same context, Gregory discussed the modalities of God's knowledge. Objects of the first kind are known of necessity insofar as God's *scientia simplicis notitiae* is concerned. God knows everything that is knowable, and whatever God does not know is not knowable. Gregory proved these claims by pointing out that God has knowledge of *all* non-complex things.[153] The necessity referred to appears to be absolute necessity, not necessity *ex suppositione*: the fact that God knows all non-complex things, Gregory argued, flows from divine nature itself, and not from a particular determination of his will or from the existence of particular creatures.[154]

By contrast, the things are *not* known of necessity insofar as God's *scientia visionis* is concerned. Some of the things God knows by *scientia visionis* he might also *not* have known by *scientia visionis*: a thing disposed by God to exist, might as well have *not* been so disposed.[155]

---

[150] Gregory, *Lectura*, I dd. 35-36 q. 1 additio 148, 148b, and 148c (ed. Trapp-Marcolino, 3), 229f.
[151] Ibid., d. 39 q. 1 a. 2, 317.
[152] Ibid., dd. 35-36 q. 1 additio 148c, 231, and d. 39 q. 1 a. 2, 318. Compare Ockham's use of *scire* as discussed on p. 190 below.
[153] Ibid., dd. 35-36 q. 1 additio 148c, 231 and 233.
[154] Cf. ibid., d. 38 q. 2, 305.
[155] Ibid., dd. 35-36 q. 1 additio 148c, 232 and 234.

Intelligible things of the second kind (*enuntiabilia*) are known of necessity by a simple act of apprehension, as God has knowledge of every *enuntiabile*. By contrast, not all of them are known of necessity insofar as (affirmative) judgmental knowledge is concerned. Something that is now true may at some earlier time have been false, and something that is now false may at some earlier time have been true. If this mode of knowledge were necessary, then the judgment would not be able to follow the *enuntiabile*'s change of truth value.[156]

All the things God knows, so Gregory continued, he knows intuitively and not abstractively. In other words, he knows all things immediately, in the literal sense: without any medium. As is well-known, Gregory's conception of intuitive and abstractive knowledge differed from that of Ockham, who also held that God's knowledge is intuitive, notwithstanding his different use of the term.[157] In Gregory's opinion, the fact that God knows all things by intuition ultimately derives from divine unity, which makes it impossible for divine knowledge to employ any kind of medium. Gregory rejected the idea that divine essence represents the creatures: God's intellect, his act of knowledge and his essence are completely indistinct and perfectly identical. God knows the creatures not *via* his essence, but immediately. In this criticism of the view that God uses some kind of representation of the creatures, Gregory was clearly following Ockham again.[158]

Marsilius of Inghen

In his discussion of the problems concerning God's knowledge of the creatures, Marsilius elaborated upon material found in particular in Thomas of Strasbourg, John Buridan, and Gregory of Rimini. The general background and frame of reference for this discussion, however, was determined by the views of Thomas Aquinas, Scotus, and Ockham discussed earlier in this chapter.

According to Marsilius, all things are known to God in his essence, possible things (*producibilia*) as well as actual things (*producta*). As he thought that this could be proved by natural reason, Marsilius concurred with Gregory of Rimini and Hugolin of Orvieto, and clearly disagreed with Ockham.[159]

---

[156] Ibid., d. 39 q. 1 a. 2, 317, and d. 38 q. 2 a. 3, 286.
[157] Ibid., dd. 35-36 q. 1, 234f. Gregory's notion of intuitive cognition and his criticism of Ockham's view is discussed in J. Würsdörfer, *Erkennen und Wissen nach Gregor von Rimini. Ein Beitrag zur Geschichte der Erkenntnistheorie des Nominalismus*, Münster 1917 (BGPhThMA, 20/1), 47f; K.H. Tachau, *Vision and Certitude*, 363.
[158] Cf. Ockham, *Scriptum*, I d. 35 q. 4 (OTh, 4), 477.
[159] Marsilius, *Sent.*, I q. 38 a. 3 (ed. Hoenen), 28: "(E)tiam in puro lumine naturali concedendum est Deum in sua essentia cognoscere omnia alia (...)." Cf. Gregory, *Lectura*, I dd. 35-36 q. 1 (ed. Trapp-Marcolino, 3), 222; Hugolin of Orvieto, *Sent.*, I d. 35 q. u. a. 1 (ed.

Marsilius's interpretation of Aristotle and Averroes

The opinion of Aristotle and Averroes, Marsilius thought, was that God has knowledge of the things outside himself. According to some interpreters, Marsilius wrote in his commentary on the *Sentences,* possibly with Gregory of Rimini in mind, the opinion of Aristotle and Averroes was quite the opposite; but they do not do justice to Aristotle and Averroes (*iniuriam faciunt*). Marsilius referred to the well–known passage from Aristotle's *Ethica Nicomachea* (X c. 9, 1179a22-24) and to Averroes's commentary on this text, where it is said that man, if he develops his intellectual faculty of knowledge, is loved by the gods and rewarded with happiness. From this Marsilius inferred that, according to the philosophers, the gods have knowledge. This same view supported by the same reference is found in the work of Thomas of Strasbourg, who may have been one of Marsilius's sources here.[160]

Apart from the textual support of his interpretation, Marsilius based his view on the fact that God, according to Aristotle and Averroes, is the first efficient cause, and that he has knowledge of himself. God knows himself to be the efficient cause; therefore he must have knowledge of all the things of which he is the efficient cause.[161]

With regard to Averroes, however, Marsilius's commentary on the *Metaphysics* seems to have endorsed a different interpretation. Here it is said that Averroes, judging by the literal meaning of his words (*ut verba sua sonant*), was of the opinion that God does *not* know anything apart from himself. Marsilius informs us that many philosophers followed Averroes in this respect, as did some *catholici*, who said that God according to the light of natural reason does not know created being. Marsilius may have been referring here to the *artistae* mentioned by Peter of Aquila.[162]

Eckermann, 2), 299. Unlike Gregory, however, Marsilius thought that natural reason coincides with the teachings of Aristotle and Averroes.

[160] Marsilius, *Sent.*, I q. 38 a. 3, 31; Thomas of Strasbourg, *Sent.*, I d. 35 q. 1 (ed. Venice 1564), fol. 103ra. Cf. Averroes, *In Ethicam*, X, Venice 1562, repr. Frankfurt a/M 1962, ed. Iuntina, Vol. 3, fol. 156raC.

[161] Marsilius, *Sent.*, I q. 38 a. 3, 30: "Philosophus et Commentator volunt quod Deus sit primus motor sicut prima causa efficiens, ut praemissum est. Vel ergo volunt quod novit se movere, et si sic, novit motum et mobile, ergo aliquid extra se, et ultra, ergo omnia extra se, cum non sit maior ratio de uno quam de alio, eo quod in essentia infinitae perfectionis omnis finita perfectio eminenter aequaliter est inclusa. Vel volunt quod Deus quamvis movit tamen nec motum nec mobile novit. Contra, quia dicunt eum movere per intellectum et voluntatem respectu mobilis et motus. Hoc esse non possit nisi motum et intelligeret et vellet similiter et mobile sic mutari."

[162] Marsilius, *Quaestiones super librum Metaphysicorum*, XII q. 12 (Wien, Oesterr. Nationalbibl., CVP, 5297), fol. 175ra (= 176ra): "Dixerunt enim quidam quod Deus nihil intelligit a se, de quorum opinione videtur fuisse Commentator, ut verba sua sonant super isto textu 'dignius est quaedam non videre quam videre' (= *In Metaphysicam*, XII t. 51), et ipsum plurimi philosophi fuerunt secuti et etiam catholici dicentes quod in lumine naturali Deus nihil intelligeret extra se (...)."

The arguments of Averroes and the philosophers mentioned by Marsilius consisted of the familiar points put forward in Averroes's commentary on the *Metaphysics*. These included the argument that every act of knowledge depends upon that which is known, whereas God depends upon nothing else (therefore God cannot have knowledge of created being, but only of himself), and the argument that God's knowledge is neither universal nor singular (therefore God cannot know individual creatures).

Other philosophers however, Marsilius suggested, believed that natural reason teaches us that God *does* know the things outside him. Marsilius considered this to be the more probable view (*opinio probabilior*).[163] The fact that Marsilius spoke of 'probability' does not mean that he thought the issue could not be proved, a view we encountered earlier in Ockham. On the contrary, his discussion of the matter later continued with a *conclusio* in which it is demonstrated by natural reason that God has knowledge of the things outside himself.[164]

The above points also occurred in John Buridan's commentary on the *Metaphysics*. Like Marsilius, Buridan distinguished between two groups of philosophers. He too believed that God, according to Averroes, does not have knowledge of anything outside himself. Again, Buridan mentioned the same point with regard to probability; yet, he was of the opinion that only probable arguments can prove that God has knowledge of things other than himself.[165]

From this we may conclude that Marsilius had presumably been drawing from Buridan's commentary on the *Metaphysics* at these points when preparing the draft of his own commentary. This would also account for the difference between his interpretations of Averroes in his commentaries on the *Metaphysics* and on the *Sentences*.[166]

Arguments for God's knowledge of the creatures

Marsilius's arguments for the claim that God has knowledge of created being were thoroughly traditional, as were his arguments for God having knowledge at all. Again, his arguments elaborated on points we have met before in our discussion of Thomas and Scotus. Marsilius gave two arguments, one from causality and one from perfection.

The argument from causality was based on two premises: first, that God has perfect knowledge of himself, and second, that God is the cause of

---

[163] Ibid.
[164] Ibid.
[165] Buridan, *Metaphysik*, XII q. 13 (ed. Paris 1518), fol. 75vb and fol. 76ra.
[166] In spite of the fact that Marsilius's commentary on the *Metaphysics* was very likely directly dependent upon Buridan's, we should not rule out the possibility that it was also, though perhaps less directly, inspired by the *Sentences* commentary of Giles of Rome, a work with which Marsilius was thoroughly familiar (see W. Möhler, *Die Trinitätslehre*, 126). This suggestion is supported by the fact that Marsilius's rendering of the position of Averroes closely resembled that of Giles discussed above, p. 73f.

everything. It ran as follows. God has perfect knowledge of himself. Therefore he knows that he can produce every thing. If God knows that he can produce all things, he must also know all things, for it would be contradictory for God to know that he can produce a thing without knowing the thing.[167] As we have seen, a similar argument from causality was used by Thomas Aquinas, and was subsequently adopted by many other thinkers.

In his commentary on the *Metaphysics*, Marsilius used the same argument from causality in a number of versions that remind of Buridan.[168] A similar argument from causality was used by Thomas of Strasbourg.[169] In the same work, Marsilius also gave a different though no less traditional argument from causality, however, referring to Averroes: God has knowledge of the things outside himself because he directs all things that do not have knowledge themselves. This argument also came from Buridan.

Unlike Scotus and Ockham, neither Buridan, Thomas of Strasbourg, nor Marsilius criticized the premises of the argument. In the case of Marsilius this is not difficult to understand. Elsewhere in his work he made it clear that he does not share the basic assumptions behind Ockham's criticism of the argument from causality. In the first place, as we have seen above, Marsilius believed that it can be proved that God is an efficient cause. Secondly, he rejected Ockham's view that from simple knowledge of one thing no simple knowledge of another thing can be obtained. This is especially clear from the *Abbreviationes super octo libros Physicorum Aristotelis*, where he claimed that simple knowledge of the one can be gained from simple knowledge of the other. In proof of this claim he argued that all of man's intellectual knowledge, both composite and non–composite (of propositions and concepts, respectively), is ultimately based on non–composite sensory knowledge. In this context, Marsilius criticized the anonymous view that knowledge derived from simple knowledge is always produced by means of a discursive process involving propositions.[170]

---

[167] Marsilius, *Sent.*, I q. 38 a. 3 (ed. Hoenen), 29f.
[168] Marsilius, *Quaestiones super librum Metaphysicorum*, XII q. 12 (Wien, Oesterr. Nationalbibl., CVP, 5297), foll. 175rb-va (= 176rb-va): "Secundo sic arguitur: Quicquid movet active per intellectum et voluntatem intelligit aliquid extra se. Deus est huiusmodi, igitur. (...) Tertio sic: Quicquid perfectissime cognoscit causam sufficientem alicuius et eo modo quo est sufficiens ad illud producere, illud cognoscat etiam illum effectum. (...) Quarto arquitur: Vel Deus intelligendo perfecte suam essentiam intelligit eam posse in aliquid effectum vel non. Si primum, sequitur quod Deus intelligit effectum necessario (...)." Cf. Buridan, *Metaphysik*, XII q. 13 (ed. Paris 1518), foll. 75vb-76ra.
[169] Thomas of Strasbourg, *Sent.*, I d. 35 q. 1 (ed. Venice 1564), fol. 102vb.
[170] Marsilius, *Abbreviationes super octo libros Physicorum Aristotelis*, Prohemium (ed. Venice 1521), fol. 2va: "Aliqua notitia incomplexa potest fieri ex alia notitia. (...) Nec valet ratio alterius opinionis. Dicit enim quod quando debet fieri una notitia ex alia, oportet quod hoc fiat mediante discursu. Hoc est falsum, si per discursum intelligunt complexam propositionem." The same point was made in the *Quaestiones libri Physicorum* (Cuyk en St. Agatha, Kruisherenklooster, C 12 II), foll. 5vb-6ra, which may have been written by Marsilius: "Ponunt *quidam* istam conclusionem responsalem quod *nunquam una notitia incomplexa* generatur ex

Marsilius's argument from perfection was based on the following two premises: first, that God's essence contains all perfections, and second, that God has perfect knowledge of his essence. The argument is as follows. Each entity (*entitas*) has a certain degree of perfection. The perfection of an entity is proportional to its (the entity's) being. The amount of being determines the degree of perfection of an entity, thus determining the extent to which it is a resemblance of God. As God knows himself, he knows every possible degree of perfection, for as the first being he contains all perfections; therefore he knows every possible entity.[171]

That God knows all things through his own simple essence should not be taken in the sense that he knows the creatures without any distinction. Marsilius believed that God knows that one being is more perfect than another. Divine knowledge as such is one, but because of the perfection of its object, viz., God's essence, it exists as an infinitely multiple (*multiplex*) representation of all different things that can be produced.[172]

The residual problem of how something that is perfectly one (divine knowledge and divine essence) is able at the same time to represent infinitely many things as *different* things (the creatures), was solved by Marsilius by analogy to the causality of divine essence. Just as God's causal power (*vigor*), which is perfectly one in itself, is infinitely multiple with regard to the things it produces (because God can create infinitely many things), so too is God's act of knowledge one in itself, yet it includes knowledge of infinitely many things.[173] Unlike such writers as Henry of Ghent and Duns Scotus, Marsilius did not postulate distinct stages in God here, nor did he distinguish between God's essence as a univocal and an equivocal principle of God's knowledge.[174]

---

alia notitia in nobis incomplexa. Probatur, *quia nunquam* generatur in nobis *una notitia* ex *alia nisi* in bona *consequentia*. Et hoc supponunt ipsi, quod (sed, *ms.*) omnis notitia generata in *virtute consequentiae* est *complexa*, quia est notitia (est notitia, *bis*) propositionis et per consequens est notitia complexa, quia omnis notitia propositionis est complexa. Sed contra hanc *opinionem* per rationem probatur talis *conclusio*: In nobis una *notitia incomplexa* potest generari ex *alia* notitia incomplexa.' Cf. Buridan, *Physik*, I q. 4 (ed. Paris 1509), 5ra. On the authenticity of the *Quaestiones libri Physicorum*, see E.P. Bos, 'A Note on an Unknown Manuscript Bearing Upon Marsilius of Inghen's Philosophy of Nature. Ms Cuyk and St. Agatha (The Netherlands), Kruisherenklooster C 12', *Vivarium* 17 (1979), 61-68. For a different account, see Th. Dewender, 'Einige Bemerkungen zur Authentizität der Physikkommentare, die Marsilius von Inghen zugeschrieben werden', *Acta Mediaevalia*, ed. S. Wielgus et al., Lublin 1992 (forthcoming).

[171] Marsilius, *Sent.*, I q. 38 a. 3 (ed. Hoenen), 28 and 30. See also I q. 1 a. 2 (ed. Strasbourg 1501), 4vb; *Quaestiones super librum Metaphysicorum*, VIII q. 2 (Wien, Oesterr. Nationalbibl., CVP, 5297), fol. 123va.

[172] *Sent.*, I q. 1 a. 1 (ed. Strasbourg 1501), fol. 3va.

[173] Ibid., fol. 3rb-3va.

[174] The solution that God knows all things individually because he can produce all things individually, was also given in Marsilius's commentary on the *Metaphysics*, XII q. 12 (Wien, Oesterr. Nationalbibl., CVP, 5297), fol. 175vb (= 176vb), as well as in his treatment of divine ideas in the commentary on the *Sentences*, I q. 1 a. 1 (ed. Strasbourg 1501), fol. 4ra-rb. The

112   CHAPTER FOUR

Two problems

The solution by analogy between God's (infinite) knowledge and the causal vigour of God's essence touches on two other important problems: first, how God has knowledge of evil which is obviously not caused by him, and second, whether the infinity of God's vigour can be proved.

1. *God's knowledge of evil*

Before addressing the question of how God's knowledge of evil (sin), Marsilius distinguished between the *malum poenae* and the *malum culpae*. The distinction was not invented by Marsilius: inspired by St. Augustine, it is found in the *Sentences* of Peter Lombard, as well as in Bonaventure, Thomas Aquinas, Gregory of Rimini, and many others.[175]

Malum poenae is the evil inflicted by God upon man as punishment and remedy against sin. This kind of evil poses no special problem for God's knowledge. It is not evil in the proper sense, but rather is something good, for it is a benefit to man. Being caused by God, it is also known by God through his causality.

Malum culpae is the sinful act of man himself. Here Marsilius distinguished between the act of sinning and the sin itself. The first is a being (*ens*), and therefore it is something good (*quoddam bonum*). Hence it is produced by God and known by him. The sin itself, on the other hand, is not a being but a pure *privatio*. It is not made by God. It is produced by the human will, when man turns away from the good. This kind of evil cannot be known by God through his causality.

Marsilius's solution to the problem of how the *malum culpae* can be known by God followed the same lines as those of Thomas Aquinas, Thomas of Strasbourg, Henry of Oyta, and others: God knows evil and sin *privative*, that is, as the absence of good. Marsilius gave the following explanation. Through the knowledge of his own essence, God has knowledge of all rational creatures. (According to Marsilius only rational creatures are capable of sin.) Moreover, he knows all perfections that can belong to rational creatures. Now, because God knows how rational creatures can be perfected by good actions, he also knows how they can be deformed by contrary actions; in this sense he also knows the deformations (*deformitates*) themselves.[176]

---

same solution is found in Thomas of Strasbourg, *Sent.*, I d. 35 q. 1 (ed. Venice 1564), fol. 103ra.
[175] Marsilius, *Sent.*, I q. 38 a. 4 (ed. Hoenen), 39, and q. 45 a. 2 (ed. Strasbourg), fol. 191rb; Augustine, *De libero arbitrio*, Lib. I, I n. 1, ed. W.H. Green, Opera Pars 2/2, Turnhout 1970 (CCSL, 29), 211; Lombard, *Sententiae in IV libris distinctae*, II d. 37 c. 2 n. 4, editio tertia, Vol. 1/2, Grottaferrata 1971 (Spicilegium Bonaventurianum, 4), 546; Bonaventura, *Sent.*, I d. 46 a. u. qq. 2-3 (Opera Theologica Selecta, 1), 652a-656a; Thomas Aquinas, *STheol.*, II-II q. 19 a. 1 c. (ed Leon., 8), 138a-b; Gregory of Rimini, *Lectura*, II dd. 34-37 q. 1 a. 2 (ed. Trapp-Marcolino, 6), 252.
[176] Marsilius, *Sent.*, I q. 38 a. 4 (ed. Hoenen), 39f. Cf. Thomas Aquinas, *Sent.*, I d. 36 q. 1

With regard to the problem of God's knowledge of evil, Marsilius further distinguished between the knowledge of simple understanding, the knowledge of seeing, and the knowledge of approbation (*scientia simplicis intelligentiae, scientia visionis, scientia approbationis*). In God, Marsilius claimed, these three kinds of knowledge coincide, but they can be distinguished in terms of differences in what is known. God's knowledge of evil is of the first and of the second kind, but never of the third kind. God does not know evil by knowledge of approbation, because he cannot and will not produce evil.[177]

This distinction between three kinds of knowledge is found in virtually all thirteenth- and fourteenth-century commentaries on the *Sentences*. It goes back to Lombard, Lib. I d. 35 cc. 1–6, and Lib. I d. 36 c. 2. Yet we may suppose that it was in particular the commentary on the *Sentences* of Thomas of Strasbourg that Marsilius consulted on this issue. The resemblance between the design of their texts is certainly striking: they both place the point of God's unity in a *nota* before proceeding to distinguish the three kinds of knowledge.[178] Moreover, it may be significant that Marsilius, in that particular article, also remarked that evil does not have an idea in God, whereas there is no mention of ideas in the remainder of the *quaestio*. Thomas of Strasbourg, for that matter, devoted a separate, short article to the subject, immediately followed by the article on the three kinds of knowledge.[179] Elsewhere in his commentary on the *Sentences*, Marsilius seems to have borrowed other anonymous short passages from Thomas's work, for example in his treatment of God's power.[180]

---

a. 2 (ed. Mandonnet, 1), 834; Thomas of Strasbourg, *Sent.*, I d. 36 q. 1 a. 4 (ed. Venice 1564), fol. 106rb; Henry of Oyta, *Lectura textualis* (München, Bayer. Staatsbibl., CLM 5590), fol. 95r: "Conclusio prima: Capiendo malum abstractive pro malitia ipsum simpliciter nihil est et per consequens non est cognoscibile per se. Sic tamen Deus cognoscit mala, quod cognoscit creaturas rationales et cognoscit quantum eis deficit de rectitudine (…)." Henry of Oyta's *Lectura textualis* originated in Prague in 1369–1371, see A. Lang, *Heinrich Totting von Oyta*, 49.

[177] Marsilius, *Sent.*, I q. 38 a. 4, 40f.

[178] Ibid., 40: "Secundo noto *quod quamvis* scientia *Dei sit una* in se, *tamen* ut distinctius eam exprimere valeamus in ordine ad *scita, tripliciter* nominatur. Nam inquantum est *omnium possibilium* et productorum ac producendorum vocatur *scientia simplicis notitiae*. Inquantum autem est *omnium* productorum et producendorum vocatur *scientia visionis*. Sed inquantum est scientia eorum *quae* approbat et *sibi sunt grata* vocatur *scientia approbationis*. Cf. Thomas of Strasbourg, *Sent.*, I d. 36 q. 1 a. 4 (ed. Venice 1564), fol. 106rb.

[179] Marsilius, *Sent.*, I q. 38 a. 4, 40: "Secunda propositio: Huiusmodi *mala* (scl., mala culpae, MH) *non habent ideam* propriam eorum proprie repraesentativam *in Deo*." Cf. Thomas of Strasbourg, *Sent.*, I d. 36 q. 1 a. 3, fol. 106rb.

[180] Marsilius, *Sent.*, I q. 42 a. 1 (ed. Strasbourg 1501), fol. 176ra: "*Duplex* sit *potentia*, scilicet *activa* quae est principium transmutandi alterum inquantum alterum. *Alia* est *passiva* quae est principium transmutandi ab altero. Potentia *passiva* omnino a *Deo* secluditur quoad naturam divinam, *quia* cum sit summe *simplex* (…) omnino *repugnat* ei recipere (…)." Cf. Thomas of Strasbourg, *Sent.*, I dd. 42-43 q. 1 a. 1, fol. 114ra.

2. Provability of God's infinite power

With regard to the problem of God's vigor, Marsilius distinguished between two kinds of divine infinite power (*vigor*): first, the effective power by which God can always create different and better beings, and second, the intrinsic power of God's perfection on account of which he is different qua perfection from all creatures. Only the second aspect of God's infinite power can be proved by natural reason, Marsilius claimed, but not the first.[181]

2.1 The unprovable infinite effective power of God

'Infinite effective power' was defined by Marsilius as 'always being able to produce more than has been produced.' Virtually the same definition is found in the works of Buridan, Thomas of Strasbourg, and Conrad of Soltau. The definition goes back to Averroes, who in his commentary on the *Physics* distinguished between a power that is infinite because its activity never stops, and a power that is infinite because it can always make a thing move faster than it actually does. The fourteenth-century thinkers mentioned above associated this second power with the infinite effective power of God, and in particular with the infinite power to produce ever better species.[182]

That God is infinite in power, Marsilius inferred from the claim that God is an infinite spiritual magnitude, as he had established elsewhere in his commentary on the *Sentences*. According to Marsilius, God's infinite spiritual magnitude entails that he is infinite not only in duration, but also in power.[183]

Marsilius believed that it cannot be proved by natural reason that God's power is infinitely efficacious. This he argued as follows. First, it is not by itself evident to man in his earthly existence that God is infinite in power. This is clear from the observation that some writers, notably Aristotle and Averroes, denied that God has this property. Moreover, there can be no a priori proof of the infinite efficacy. God's infinite power being one with his essence, it is impossible to derive either his essence or his power from something higher or prior, because God is the first cause. Furthermore, it is impossible to give an a posteriori proof of God's infinite power, that is, a

---

[181] Marsilius, *Sent.*, I q. 42 a. 2, fol. 180ra-rb.

[182] Ibid., a. 1, fol. 176rb. See also *Quaestiones super librum Metaphysicorum*, XII q. 6 (Wien, Oesterr. Nationalbibl., CVP, 5297), fol. 157rb (= 158rb); *Abbreviationes super octo libros Physicorum Aristotelis*, VIII (ed. Venice 1521), fol. 39vb. Cf. Buridan, *Physik*, VIII q. 11 (ed. Paris 1509), fol. 119rb; *Metaphysik*, XII q. 6 (ed. Paris 1518), 69rb; Thomas of Strasbourg, *Sent.*, II d. 1 q. 2 a. 4 (ed. Venice 1564), 129vb; Conrad of Soltau, *Sent.* (Stuttgart, Württ. Landesbibl., Cod. Theol. Fol. 118), fol. 51va; Averroes, *In Physicam*, VIII t. 79 (ed. Iuntina, 4), fol. 427raB-C.

[183] Marsilius, *Sent.*, I q. 42 a. 1, fol. 176rb; *Abbreviationes super octo libros Physicorum Aristotelis*, VIII (ed. Venice 1521), fol. 40ra. See also *Quaestiones libri Physicorum* (Cuyk en St. Agatha, Kruisherenklooster, C 12 II), fol. 120vb. On Marsilius's notion of an infinite spiritual magnitude, see my 'Der Sentenzenkommentar', 122-125.

proof that is based on the effects of God's power. All effects accessible to human perception are finite, and it is impossible to prove the infinity of the cause from the finiteness of the effects. This exhausts the possibilities for a proof by natural reason.[184]

This same view is also found in the works of Ockham, Buridan, and Michael Aiguani. Advocates of the opposite view included the Augustinians Giles of Rome, Thomas of Strasbourg (who called the issue a generally acknowledged problem), and Gregory of Rimini.[185]

Marsilius concurred with Buridan that God's power, according to Aristotle and Averroes, is not infinite in its efficacy. He noted that Averroes had stated that by the infinity of the first mover both Aristotle and he himself meant only that the first mover moves the celestial bodies incessantly, and that the first mover is infinite only in duration. Furthermore, Marsilius remarked, Averroes stated that the first mover is the form of the first thing moved. Now, should the first mover be infinite in power, then the right proportion (*proportio*) between the first thing moved and its form would be lost, and the first mover could no longer be the form of the first thing moved.[186]

What Marsilius had in mind here was probably the following. Averroes's commentary on the *Metaphysics* criticized the view of Avicenna, who had insisted on a separate first unmoved mover, in addition to the soul or mover of the first celestial body. Averroes found this to be an unnecessary assumption: the first unmoved mover itself is the form of the first celestial body.[187] Presumably it was this criticism of Avicenna that gave Marsilius the idea that Averroes thought that the power of the first mover (God) is associated with, and proportional to, the first thing moved, and that it is therefore not infinite

---

[184] *Sent.*, I q. 42 a. 2, fol 176vb; *Abbreviationes super octo libros Physicorum Aristotelis*, VIII, fol. 39vb. See also *Quaestiones libri Physicorum*, fol. 120vb.

[185] Ockham, *Quodlibeta*, III q. 1 (OTh, 9), 199f; Buridan, *Physik*, VIII q. 11 (ed. Paris 1509), fol. 120ra; Michael Aiguani, *Sent.*, I (Kraków, Bibl. Jag., 1459), fol. 66ra: "Tertia conclusio est quod non probatur evidenter increatum esse simpliciter causam potestatis infinitae. Probatur sic conclusio: Hoc non est evidenter probatum nec a priori nec a posteriori (...). Quod non a priori: cum ipso nihil sit prius; nec a posteriori: cum omnis effectus sit finitus." For the opposite view see Giles of Rome, *Sent.*, I d. 43 q. 1 (ed. Venice 1521), fol. 233rb-va; Thomas of Strasbourg, *Sent.*, I dd. 42-43 q. 1 a. 3 (ed. Venice 1564), fol. 114rb-va: "Utrum autem evidenter et philosophice probari possit Deum esse infinitae virtutis, seu potentiae in vigore, multo doctorum antiquorum et modernorum in dubium posuerunt. Determino tamen me ad partem affirmativam, videlicet, quod possit evidenter et philosophice probari."; Gregory of Rimini, *Lectura*, I dd. 42-44 q. 3 a. 2 (ed. Trapp-Marcolino, 3), 424. On Michael Aiguani and his *Sentences* commentary, delivered in Paris 1362-1363, see W.J. Courtenay, *Adam Wodeham*, 139.

[186] Marsilius, *Sent.*, I q. 42 a. 2 (ed. Strasbourg 1501), fol. 178va. Cf. Buridan, *Physik*, VIII q. 11 (ed. Paris 1509), 120ra; Averroes, *In De coelo*, II t. 39, Venice 1562, repr. Frankfurt a/M 1962, ed. Iuntina, Vol. 5, fol. 123rbE.

[187] Averroes, *In Metaphysicam*, XII t. 44 (ed. Iuntina, 8), foll. 327vaH-328raC, esp. 327vaH; Avicenna, *Liber de philosophia prima*, IX c. 4 (ed. van Riet), 479f.

in power. We find a similar interpretation of Averroes in Gregory of Rimini.[188]

2.2 The provable infinite intrinsic power of God

Beside the infinite power to produce things, Marsilius distinguished in God the infinite intrinsic power of his essential perfection (*perfectio essentialis*).[189] In the *Abbreviationes super octo libros Physicorum*, Marsilius claimed that this type of infinity can be ascribed to God on the basis of natural reason. This amounts to the idea that no created perfection can come close to the uncreated perfection of God. Following Buridan, Marsilius spoke here of infinity *per similitudinem*: God's infinite perfection has the same attributes as the infinite magnitude. Infinite magnitude is greater than any finite magnitude; no matter how many finite magnitudes are taken together, they will always be less than an infinite magnitude. The same goes for the infinite perfection of God: no matter how many finite perfections are taken together, they will never add up to an infinite perfection.[190]

In his commentary on the *Sentences*, Marsilius repeated the claim that God's infinite perfection can be proved by natural reason. There it was taken as a token of divine power (*vigor*), not insofar as the power is productive, but insofar as it is completely independent (viz., uncreated), and insofar as it cannot be equalled by any created being. According to Marsilius, this infinite essential perfection of the divine essence enables us to state that God's act of knowledge is at once a knowing of infinitely many things.[191]

Thus we see that the infinity of God's act of knowledge was associated by Marsilius not only with God's power to produce infinitely many things, as we saw earlier, but also with the intrinsic power of divine perfection. His reason for doing so was surely the aspect of provability: the first association cannot be proven, whereas the second one can.

It is interesting to observe that Marsilius expressed some doubt with regard to the question of whether Aristotle thought that God knows infinitely many things by his perfection.[192] This hesitation would seem to imply that,

---

[188] See Gregory of Rimini, *Lectura*, II d. 1 q. 1 a. 2 (ed. Trapp-Marcolino, 4), 24 and 34. In this context, Marsilius criticized the interpretation of Averroes given by Thomas of Strasbourg in *Sent.*, I dd. 42-43 q. 1 a. 3 (ed. Venice 1564), fol. 114va. The latter had submitted that Averroes assumed the existence of an independent mover of infinite power, in addition to the mover of the first celestial body. Marsilius tersely commented, *Sent.*, I d. 42 a. 2 (ed. Strasbourg 1501), fol. 179va: "I do not recall anything of the sort from the work of Averroes."
[189] Marsilius, *Sent.*, I q. 42 a. 2 (ed. Strasbourg 1501), fol 180ra-rb.
[190] *Abbreviationes super octo libros Physicorum Aristotelis*, VIII (ed. Venice 1521), fol. 40ra. Cf. Buridan, *Physik*, VIII q. 11 (ed. Paris 1509), fol. 119.
[191] *Sent.*, I q. 42 a. 2 (ed. Strasbourg 1501), fol. 180rb.
[192] Ibid., q. 38 a. 3 (ed. Hoenen), 32: "(D)ifficile est quod Philosophus concederet Deum esse infinitae virtutis in actualiter cognoscendo distincte et semper infinita distincta, immo infinities infinita."

on this one issue at least, Marsilius believed that natural reason was capable of more than had been claimed or would have been claimed by Aristotle. Why Aristotle had not said as much, Marsilius did not make clear. Perhaps there is a connection with the fact that Aristotle, according to the interpretation of Averroes vindicated by Marsilius, believed that God is associated with the first celestial body, and that hence his perfection is bounded.

MARSILIUS'S RESPONSE TO PETER AUREOLI

The distinction between primary and secondary object

Like many thirteenth- and fourteenth-century theologians, Marsilius distinguished between the primary and the secondary object of God's knowledge. The primary object is God's essence itself (*obiectum primarium*), the secondary object is created being (*obiectum secundarium*). Creatures are given the status of secondary object because God's knowledge of them does not derive from the creatures themselves but from his own essence, which is the primary and proper object of his knowledge.[193]

This distinction was criticized by Peter Aureoli against Duns Scotus, as we have seen, on the grounds that God's perfection would be dependent upon the creatures if they were the secondary object of his knowledge. This criticism was mentioned in Marsilius's commentary on the *Sentences* as an *alia opinio*. It was also quoted by Thomas of Strasbourg, who referred to it as the opinion of *quidam doctor*.

Interestingly, the reply to Aureoli was almost identical in Thomas and Marsilius, and Marsilius presumably drew from the former. Their response was as follows. The claim that God's perfection depends on something else (viz., a creature) may be taken in either of two ways. First, it may mean that God depends upon the creature itself, or second, it may mean that the creature as a possible creature is necessarily represented and known if God knows his own essence. Now, both Marsilius and Thomas argued that God cannot be dependent upon created being in the first sense, for he can exist without the creatures existing. Therefore it is possible for God to know the creatures even when they don't exist, and without him being dependent upon their existence. In the second sense of dependency, however, the creatures, known as possible beings, may necessarily go with God's perfection. If God has perfect knowledge of his essence, then he knows it as a cause, and therefore he must also know all possible things from which it is the cause.[194]

---

[193] Ibid., 33f.

[194] Ibid., 35f: "(P)rimam intellectionem sive scientiam aliquid coexigere ad suam perfectionem *potest intelligi dupliciter. Uno modo quod* ipsa illud *coexigat* tamquam aliquo modo ab eo dependens. (...) (S)ic *creaturae non coexiguntur* ad perfectionem cognitionis *divinae*. (...) Secundo *modo* potest intelligi quod sic aliquid *coexigatur* tamquam id quod in ipsa perfecta

The argument from infinity

As we have indicated earlier, the arguments from infinity given by Aureoli were discussed in many fourteenth-century commentaries on the *Sentences*. The first argument mentioned by Marsilius is the argument from number: God cannot have knowledge of the individual numbers, for this would imply the existence of an infinite number.[195]

Like Thomas of Strasbourg, Gregory of Rimini, and Alfonsus Vargas, Marsilius responded first with a reference to St. Augustine (*De civitate Dei*, XII c. 19).[196] He went on to give a semantic analysis of the word *omnis* ('all'), making the commonplace distinction between the distributive and collective use of *omnis*. The distinction was familiar enough from the logical textbooks of Peter of Spain and Richard Billingham that were widely used in philosophical education, and also appeared in the work of Gregory of Rimini, John Buridan, and Albert of Saxony.[197]

With *omnis* ('all') used distributively, the proposition 'God knows all numbers' means that God knows each number *1, 2, 3, ...* individually. According to Marsilius, this proposition is true: God knows each creature individually, and therefore each number as well.

With *omnis* used collectively, however, the above proposition means that God knows a number *n* which contains all numbers. According to Marsilius, this proposition is false, because there cannot be a number *n* which contains all numbers. Being a number itself, *n* should also contain itself, which is impossible, for nothing can contain itself. God cannot know the impossible. Therefore he cannot know such a number.

Furthermore, the collective use of *omnis* in this case would imply that God knows the set of all numbers, and that there cannot be a number that does not belong to the set of all numbers. But this is impossible as well, Marsilius argued. For suppose that God could produce (the set of) all numbers collec-

---

cognitione divina *necessario* sufficienter *repraesentatur* tamquam possibile ab ea dependere. Et sic creaturae ut possibiles possunt dici *coexigi* ad *perfectionem* cognitionis divinae, quia in perfecta *cognitione* divina *necessario* sufficienter *repraesentatur*. Quia quod perfecte novit causam etiam necessario cognovit effectum possibilem fieri ab ista causa (...)." Cf. Thomas of Strasbourg, *Sent.*, I d. 35 q. 1 (ed. Venice 1564), fol. 104ra.

[195] Marsilius, *Sent.*, q. 38 a. 3 (ed. Hoenen), 35.

[196] In addition to the references given in n. 122 above, see Marsilius, *Sent.*, q. 38 a. 3, 37; Thomas of Strasbourg, *Sent.*, I d. 35 q. 1 (ed. Venice 1564), fol. 104va.

[197] Cf. Peter of Spain, *Tractatus called afterwards Summule logicales*, XII n. 4, ed. L.M. de Rijk, Assen 1972 (Philosophical Texts and Studies, 22), 210; *Some 14th Century Tracts on the Probationes Terminorum. Martin of Alnwick OFM, Richard Billingham, Edward Upton, and Others*, II.1 n. 43 (= Billingham, Probationes terminorum, prior recensio) and II.2 n. 43 (= Billingham, recensio altera), ed. L.M. de Rijk, Nijmegen 1982 (Artistarium, 3), 57 and 91; G. Ritter, *Studien zur Spätscholastik*, 86 (Gregory and Albert of Saxony); J.M.M.H. Thijssen, *Johannes Buridanus over het oneindige*, Vol. I, Nijmegen 1988 (Diss.), 260 (Buridanus). The *Probationes terminorum* of Billingham was very popular among the logical works of its kind in the fourteenth century, see *Some 14th Century Tracts*, *5*.

tively. It would then be impossible for him to produce a new number. But this is contrary to God's infinite power; therefore (etc.).[198]

The semantic strategy deployed above was also used by Marsilius in solving the other arguments of Peter Aureoli, viz., the argument from continuity and the argument from infinite magnitude. With respect to the argument from continuity, Marsilius held that all parts of the continuum are known to God distributively, but not collectively. Whichever part of the continuum *a, b, c, ...* is considered, it can veridically be said to be known by God. But God does not know the parts of the continuum as a closed set. For each part of the continuum can always be subdivided into still smaller parts.[199]

That the continuum consists of infinitely many parts, each of which is itself infinitely divisible, Marsilius called the more probable opinion (*opinio probabilior*). It was the view held by Buridan, among others. The contrary opinion of the atomists, that the continuum consists of indivisible elements, was rejected by Marsilius.[200]

The two contrasting views were also mentioned by Thomas of Strasbourg. He informed us that many *doctores* rejected Aureoli's argument on the strength of the assumption that the continuum's atomic constituents are indivisible. The Peripatetics, on the other hand, endorsed the opposing view, which was also more agreeable to Thomas of Strasbourg himself.[201]

As to the question of whether God can know an actually infinite magnitude — the last of Aureoli's arguments discussed above — two anonymous opinions were quoted by Marsilius. The first is that God can know the infinite, but that he cannot make it; the second is that God can both know and make the infinite. The second view was that of Gregory of Rimini.

Both views were criticized by Marsilius. His argument was that a being of actually infinite extension (*infinitum in extensione*) cannot exist. Therefore, God cannot know an actually infinite extension, for what cannot be made by God, cannot be known by him either.

---

[198] Marsilius, *Sent.*, I q. 38 a. 3 (ed. Hoenen), 37f.
[199] Ibid., 56f. See also *Quaestiones libri Physicorum* (Cuyk en St. Agatha, Kruisherenklooster, C 12 II), fol. 19rb: "Licet Deus distinctive cognoscat omnes partes alicuius continui, tamen impossibile est Deum dividere continuum in omnes suis partes."
[200] Ibid., 57; *Abbreviationes super octo libros Physicorum Aristotelis*, III (ed. Venice 1521), fol. 13va. Also, cf. *Quaestiones libri Physicorum*, fol. 19rb. For the views of some fourteenth-century indivisibilists (Henry of Harclay, Walter Chatton, and William Crathorn) and divisibilists (Scotus, Ockham, William of Alnwick, and Walter Burleigh), see *Adam de Wodeham. Tractatus de Indivisibilibus*, ed. R. Wood, Dordrecht 1988 (Synthese Historical Library, 31), 3-13 (introduction). See also J.E. Murdoch, 'Naissance et développement de l'atomisme au bas Moyen Age Latin', *La science de la natura. Théories et pratiques*, Montréal-Paris 1974 (Institut d'Etudes Médiévales, Université de Montréal, Cahiers d'études médiévales, 2), 11-32. For Buridan, see J.M.M.H Thijssen, *Johannes Buridanus*, 251ff.
[201] Thomas of Strasbourg, *Sent.*, I d. 35 q. 1 (ed. Venice 1564), fol. 104rb.

That God is unable to produce an actually infinite magnitude, does not imply imperfection. Rather, Marsilius argued, it is a consequence of God's omnipotence. For any given extension, God can always produce a greater extension or a greater perfection. But he cannot produce a greatest one, for that would imply that he is unable to produce a yet greater perfection or extension, which is contrary to his infinite power.[202]

The view that God can always produce a greater effect was described by Peter of Candia as the received view of the *moderni* (*ruminatio communis modernorum*). As we shall also see on other occasions, Marsilius here followed a line of thought that was called 'modern' in the 1370s.[203]

---

[202] Marsilius, *Sent.*, I q. 38 (ed. Hoenen), 58f, and q. 42 (ed. Strasbourg 1501), fol. 181ra-rb; *Abbreviationes super octo libros Physicorum Aristotelis*, III (ed. Venice 1521), fol. 14rb. Marsilius's concept of infinity is discussed in G. Ritter, *Studien zur Spätscholastik*, 80-89. His view that God can always produce a greater effect, but not an infinite one, is dealt with in my 'Der Sentenzenkommentar', 122-125.

[203] Peter of Candia, *Sent.* (Erfurt, Wissenschaftl. Bibl., Cod. Amplon., Fol. 94), fol. 108, as cited by F. Ehrle, *Der Sentenzenkommentar*, 68.

CHAPTER FIVE

DIVINE IDEAS

An important aspect of the discussion on divine knowledge was the question of the nature and ontological status of divine ideas. The question was raised by many authors of the thirteenth and fourteenth centuries, inspired in particular by the works of Augustine and pseudo-Dionysius. Marsilius of Inghen was no exception in this respect. Before turning to his position, however, we must first take a look at those thinkers who were primarily responsible for setting the scene for Marsilius: Thomas Aquinas, Henry of Ghent, Duns Scotus, and William of Ockham. At the same time, we shall also have to clarify the manner in which their views were received and elaborated by those who followed them.

THOMAS AQUINAS

Thomas Aquinas based his argument for the existence of ideas on the order found in the created world. The order and design found in the world cannot be merely fortuitous; they betoken the activity of a creator-God. This means that God's mind must contain the forms in the image of which he creates the world and all things in it — for whatever exists by more than mere chance must have a form to act as its end. According to Thomas, the specific function of the ideas lies in the process of creation: in his *De veritate*, they are called *creativae et productivae rerum*. This practically oriented approach to the question of the existence of ideas, which originally goes back to Augustine, is also found in the works of Giles of Rome and Hervaeus Natalis.[1]

The ideas are formed in the mind of God when God compares his essence to the things (*res*) that are known in the essence. Divine essence contains all perfections. Therefore, when God knows the extent to which a given thing is successful at imitating the perfection of his essence, he has knowledge of its

---

[1] Thomas, *De veritate*, q. 3 a. 1 ad 5 (ed. Leon., 22/1), 101a; *STheol.*, I q. 15 aa. 1-2 c. (ed. Leon., 4), 201b-202a; Giles of Rome, *Sent.*, I d. 36 a. 2 q. 1 (ed. Venice 1521), fol. 187rbE-F; Hervaeus Natalis, *Sent.*, I d. 34 q. 1 a. 1 (ed. Paris 1647), fol. 140aD-bB. Cf. Augustine, *De diversis quaestionibus octoginta tribus*, XLVI n. 2, ed. A. Mutzenbecher, Opera Pars 12/2, Turnhout 1975 (CCSL, 44A), 71. On Thomas's theory of ideas, see L.–B. Geiger, 'Les idées', 175-209; J.P. Beckmann, 'Der Ideentheoretische Grundansatz bei Thomas von Aquin, Duns Scotus und Wilhelm von Ockham', *Tommaso d'Aquino nella storia del pensiero*, Vol. 2, Naples 1976 (Tommaso d'Aquino nel suo settimo centenario), 286-296, esp. 288-290; W. Kluxen, *HWdPh*, s.v. 'Idee'. For a discussion of medieval theories on divine ideas, see also recently M. Fattori and L. Bianchi, eds., *Idea. VI Colloquio Internazionale Roma, 5-7 gennaio 1989. Atti*, Rome 1990 (Lessico Intellettuale Europeo, 51).

bounded form and delineation. Thus, God knows the form of vegetable things by knowing his own essence insofar as it is represented by 'life that has no sensory knowledge'. Again, God knows the form of animals by knowing his own essence insofar it is represented by 'life with sensory knowledge but not intellect'; and so forth for all other forms.[2]

According to Thomas, God has knowledge of the forms of things simply when he reflects upon his knowledge of the things in his essence. By token of this knowledge of his knowledge, each individual *res* has its rational form in God's mind.[3] These rational forms are the ends to which God is directed in his creation of the world. Although the ideas coincide with God's essence, they signify not only the essence but also its relation to other things: for the ideas exist in virtue of a comparison between God's essence and the things.[4]

The plurality of ideas in God, Thomas claimed, does not contradict God's essential unity. Concerning this issue he distinguished between two senses of 'form': first, the form that is the specification and actualization of knowledge, which in God is divine essence itself, and second, the form that is the result of an act of knowledge, which is an idea. The ideas are not that *by means of which* God knows, but rather that *which* he knows, objects rather than instruments of knowledge. The unity of the subject is not compromised when it has knowledge of a plurality of things, unless the form through which it knows is itself a plurality. Because God has knowledge of the ideas through his essence, his knowledge remains a unity.[5]

The ideas were called *exemplaria* by Thomas when associated with practical knowledge, where they serve as the ends and examples in the process of creation. They were called *rationes* when considered as objects of God's speculative as well as his practical knowledge: God's power of reflection extends beyond the forms of things actually used in creation to the contemplation of all forms.[6] Whether all *exemplaria* are of necessity ideas of things actually existing in past, present or future, is a question on which Thomas was less than clear. His usage of the term tended to vary. In *De veritate* the question was answered negatively, whereas in the *Summa theologiae* the answer was affirmative. The latter, more restricted use of the term 'exemplar' was later adopted in the *Correctorium corruptorii 'Sciendum'*.[7]

---

[2] *Sent.*, I d. 36 q. 2 a. 2 c. (ed. Mandonnet, 1), 842; *De veritate*, q. 3 a. 2 c., 104b-105a; *ScG*, I c. 54 n. 451 (ed. Pera, 2), 66a; *STheol.*, q. 15 a. 2 c., 202a-b.

[3] *STheol.*, q. 15 a. 2 ad 2, 202b: "Deus autem non solum intelligit multas res per essentiam suam, sed etiam intelligit se intelligere multa per essentiam suam. Sed hoc est intelligere plures rationes rerum; vel, plures ideas esse in intellectu eius ut intellectas."

[4] *Sent.*, I d. 36 q. 2 a. 2 ad 1 (ed. Mandonnet, 1), 842; *De veritate*, q. 3 a. 2 ad 2 (ed. Leon., 22/1), 105a.

[5] See L.-B. Geiger, 'Les idées', 179 and 207, with references to the germane passages.

[6] *STheol.*, I q. 15 a. 3 c. (ed. Leon., 4), 204a.

[7] Ibid.; *De veritate*, q. 3 a. 3 ad 3 (ed. Leon., 22/1), 108b; *Le Correctorium corruptorii*

Considering his argument for the existence of ideas, we may presume that the practical aspect of ideas was more important for Thomas. Of whatever can be an independent object of his creative activity, God has *practical* ideas. This goes for particulars, of course, but it is also true of species, because nature inclines toward the preservation of the species.[8]

By contrast, God has *speculative* ideas of all possible representations or imitations of his essence, including the things that have no existence of their own. Next to things of which God has practical ideas this includes *genera*, matter (which Thomas believed can only exist together with form), and accidents.[9]

As stated above, the issue of divine ideas was the subject of extensive discussion in the thirteenth and fourteenth centuries. We shall briefly delineate three aspects of the discussion, to give an impression of the problems associated with this issue, and to situate Thomas's views in the context of intellectual exchange at that time.

1. The relation between thing and idea

A problem of special importance was the question of whether God has knowledge of things *immediately* in his essence, or only *mediately* through the ideas. The importance of this question is highlighted by the work of Henry of Ghent and the reactions it evoked. As we saw in the previous chapter, Thomas believed that God has immediate knowledge of individual things in his essence. This was denied by Henry of Ghent, who believed that God knows individuals only through the ideas (*rationes ideales*). If his knowledge is directed at divine essence only, then God knows the creatures indistinctly, for all perfections in God are one. In order to distinguish something from the essence, and thus have distinct knowledge of individuals, the intellect must first know the essence as being imitable in various ways, which is how the ideas come to be.[10]

Immediate reactions to this view came from Duns Scotus and Henry of Harclay in his work prior to 1313. They both rejected the position of Henry of Ghent. Other reactions came from so-called 'Thomistic' writers. Thus, Thomas of Sutton commented on this view in the *Quodlibeta*. Following the line of Thomas Aquinas, he argued that God knows the things directly in his

---

'Sciendum'. Les premières polémiques Thomistes, Vol. II, ed. P. Glorieux, Paris 1956 (Bibliothèque Thomiste, 31), a. 4, 47.

[8] *Sent.*, I d. 36 q. 2 a. 3 ad 3 (ed. Mandonnet, 1), 845; *Quaestiones quodlibetales*, VIII q. 2 a. 2 c., ed. Fr.R. Spiazzi, editio VIII revisa, Turin-Rome 1949, 160a; *De veritate*, q. 3 a. 8 c. (ed. Leon, 22/1), 116a. The view that God has ideas of particulars was also that of Bonaventure, *Sent.*, I d. 35 a. u. q. 2 ad 3 (Opera Theologica Selecta, 1), 483a, and q. 4 c., 486a.

[9] *De veritate*, q. 3 a. 5 c., and a. 7 c., 112a and 114b.

[10] Henry of Ghent, *Quodlibeta*, VIII q. 1 (ed. Paris 1518), 299vB, and q. 8, 313rF; *Quodlibet* IX, q. 2, ed. R. Macken, Leuven 1983 (Opera omnia, 13), 44f.

essence, and only subsequently has knowledge of the ideas. For how could God know his essence as imitable by the creatures, unless he knows the creatures themselves? This line of argument was also adopted by the Thomistic theologians Hervaeus Natalis and John of Paris.[11]

2. *Ideas of matter and accidents*

Another point of controversy concerned the question of whether God has practical ideas of matter and of the accidents, a position denied by Thomas Aquinas. Thomas's view was rejected by William de la Mare in his *Correctorium fratris Thomae*, written in 1278-1279. He argued as follows. In the sacrament of the altar the accidents, i.e., the appearances of bread and wine, continue to exist while the substance is changed into the body of Christ. From the fact that God is able to sustain the accidents without their natural substance, De la Mare concluded that God must also be able to sustain matter without form — if he can do one, then he can also do the other. Hence God has practical ideas of matter and of the accidents. Based as it was on considerations of divine omnipotence, this view of the ideas is later found in Scotus.[12]

This question of accidents existing without substance was discussed with particular zeal, both in its philosophical and its theological aspects, particularly since the time De la Mare wrote the *Correctorium*. This is attested by various philosophical and theological works, as well as by the condemnations of 1277, which censored the view that such a separation is not possible (propp. 139-141).[13]

3. *Ideas of particulars*

Another battle of minds was provoked by the question of whether God has ideas of particulars. Henry of Ghent and Godfrey of Fontaines defended the view that God has no distinct ideas of particular things, but only of species. According to Godfrey, all members of a species are equal in perfection.

---

[11] Thomas of Sutton, *Quodlibeta*, II q. 4 (ed. Schmaus), 199f; Hervaeus Natalis, *Sent.*, I d. 34 q. 1 a. 3 (ed. Paris 1647), foll. 143bD-144aA; John of Paris, *Sent.*, I q. 118 ad 2 (ed. Muller), 366, and q. 120 c., 371.

[12] The *Correctorium* of William de la Mare is edited in *Le Correctorium corruptorii 'Quare'. Les premières polémiques Thomistes,* Vol. I, ed. P. Glorieux, Le Saulchoir, Kain 1927 (Bibliothèque Thomiste, 9), a. 4, 25f.

[13] The relevant works are referred to by R. Imbach, 'Metaphysik, Theologie und Politik. Zur Diskussion zwischen Nikolaus von Straßburg und Dietrich von Freiberg über die Abtrennbarkeit der Akzidentien', *Theologie und Philosophie* 61 (1986), 359-395, esp. 365-378. The view that substance and accident are in point of fact inseparably bound up with each other, was identified as the position of Aristotle by Dietrich of Freiberg (OP, † after 1310) and by William of Ockham. See R. Imbach, 'Philosophie und Eucharistie bei Wilhelm von Ockham. Ein vorläufiger Entwurf', *Ockham and Ockhamists*, ed. E.P. Bos and H. Krop, Nijmegen 1987 (Artistarium Supplementa, 4), 43-51, esp. 45f.

Differences in perfection occur only *between* species. Consequently all individuals belonging to the same species are known in a single imitation of divine essence, that is, in a single idea. Roughly the same point was made by Henry of Ghent. He argued that particulars do not add to the essence of the species to which they belong. Therefore God has ideas of the species only.[14]

An intermediate position was taken by Hervaeus Natalis and John of Paris, who believed that God has speculative ideas of particulars, but not practical ideas. John of Paris argued that God does not have distinct practical ideas, except of things that are different in being as well as in form, that is: of the species. Practical ideas of particulars and of *genera* are ruled out: the former because they differ only in being, the latter because they differ only in form (for *genera* exist only together with a species).[15]

The position of Thomas Aquinas, as we have seen, was that God has practical ideas of each particular. Remarkably, this line was adopted in particular by non-Dominicans, such as Giles of Rome, Peter de Falco, and Richard of Middleton. They believed that God has practical ideas of each particular created by him.[16]

Duns Scotus

Another theory of great historical significance was that of Duns Scotus, particularly because of its influence on thinkers such as William of Ockham, Henry of Harclay, and James of Ascoli. According to Duns Scotus, the idea is identical with the thing known, or with the known quiddity (*quiditas*, *essentia*, or *natura*). The existence of ideas does not require a relation between the essence and that which is known: ideas are simply identical with the things God knows, including those he knows immediately. This is the position most commonly attributed to Scotus in the works of fourteenth-century theologians.[17]

Yet, the account of ideas as 'immediately known quiddities' was not the only one used by Scotus. In the previous chapter we quoted a long passage from the *Lectura* in which Scotus summarized his view of God's knowledge

---

[14] Godfrey of Fontaines, *Les quatre premièrs Quodlibets*, IV q. 1, ed. M. de Wulf and A. Pelzer, Louvain 1904 (Les Philosophes Belges, 2), 230; Henry of Ghent, *Quodlibet* VII, qq. 1-2, ed. G.A. Wilson, Leuven 1991 (Opera omnia, 11), 8. For a discussion of the views of Godfrey and Henry, see J.F. Wippel, *The Metaphysical Thought*, 124-130.

[15] Hervaeus Natalis, *Sent.*, I d. 34 q. 1 a. 4 (ed. Paris 1647), fol. 144bA-B; John of Paris, *Sent.*, I q. 122 (ed. Muller), 380.

[16] Giles of Rome, *Sent.*, I d. 36 a. 2 q. 4 (ed. Venice 1521), fol. 189rbG; Peter de Falco, *Questions disputées*, I q. 5 c. (ed. Gondras, 1), 201; Richard of Middleton, *Sent.*, I d. 36 a. 2 q. 4 c. (ed. Brescia 1591), fol. 316a.

[17] Scotus's theory of ideas is discussed by E. Gilson, *Jean Duns Scot. Introduction à ses positions fondamentales*, Paris 1952 (Etudes de philosophie médiévale, 42), 279-306; J.P. Beckmann, *HWdPh*, s.v. 'Idee'; A.A. Maurer, *Medieval Philosophy*, 230-232. The view that

of the creatures by distinguishing four successive stages. From this passage it appears that Scotus sometimes saw the idea as something that arises from the fact that God relates his essence to the things known, and has knowledge of this relationship. In the terminology of the quotation, the ideas come into being in stages three and four. This relationship between essence and thing Scotus called a *relatio quaedam idealis*; knowledge of this relationship is knowledge of the idea. This alternative account comes close to the views of Thomas Aquinas and Henry of Ghent: knowledge of the idea is knowledge of the relation between God's essence and the thing that is known in it.

Scotus did not simply juxtapose these two accounts of the nature of ideas. He tried to bring them together in the following passage from the *Lectura*, where he speaks first of the known quiddity, and then of the *relatio idealis*:

> "In the first instance the divine intellect knows its essence, and in the second it knows the quiddities of things, which (when known in this manner) are called ideas. And in a third instance the divine intellect relates its essence to the quiddities, causing rational relations, which are called certain other ideas (*quaedam aliae ideae*)."[18]

The fact that Scotus incidentally called the ideas *relationes ideales* seems to raise more questions than it answers, however. In the general framework of his thought, the alternative account served no purpose at all; only in the sense of known quiddities are the ideas related to Scotus's theory of divine knowledge and creation.

It may be significant in this connection that Scotus called upon his alternative account only when criticizing the position of Henry of Ghent. It is not inconceivable that Scotus lapsed into the idiom of *relatio idealis* only as a means of correcting and rephrasing Henry's view. Thus, if the ideas are seen as known relations, as Henry would have it, they must *follow upon* the knowledge of quiddities rather than precede them — they are known at a later stage, viz., after the third instance.

The function of the ideas

As we have seen, Thomas Aquinas presented a lucid view of the function of the ideas in his distinction between practical and speculative ideas. Duns Scotus did not mention this distinction in his *Lectura* or his *Ordinatio*. (It was

---

ideas are known quiddities was also adumbrated by Henry of Ghent, *Quodlibeta* IX, q. 2 (ed. Macken), 28f. The only difference between his position and that of Scotus was that Henry regarded the known quiddities as mere relations of imitability produced by the intellect, and not as immediately known things, which he considered to be impossible. Henry of Ghent thought a relation was required where Scotus saw an immediacy. Thus, whereas Scotus believed that God has immediate knowledge of the quiddities, Henry claimed he only has mediate knowledge.

[18] *Lectura*, I d. 35 q. u. n. 33 (ed. Vat., 17), 456; see also n. 22, 452f. Notice that the third

criticized in the *Reportata Parisiensia*, however, as we shall presently see.) His view of the function of ideas in these works is therefore less straightforward, though it can be reconstructed in an indirect way. Two passages are relevant in this respect.

First, Scotus determined that the idea is "the known quiddity in virtue of which a similar thing can come to exist (*potest oriri*) outside God". Secondly, explaining the position of Augustine, he stated that "the idea is not the form in virtue of which God has knowledge, but rather in virtue of which he forms (*format*) whatever can be formed (*formabile est*)".[19]

At first glance these passages seem to indicate that the ideas serve only a *practical* function in the sense of Thomas, viz., as correlates of things that can really exist. Yet this impression is mistaken, as is made clear by the following considerations. First, the terminology used by Scotus derives from Augustine. Both 'oriri posse' and 'formare' appear in the 46th question of Augustine's *De diversis quaestionibus* where divine ideas are discussed. The fact that Scotus used these phrases is of little consequence by itself: everything still hinges on the interpretation he gave of Augustine.

Moreover, in his reading of Augustine (the second passage quoted above), Scotus did not deny that ideas function as forms of knowledge, but only that they actualize knowledge. After the quotation his text continues: "If Augustine says somewhere that the idea is the form of knowledge in virtue of which God has knowledge, then this form must be precisely the object known, and not the object that induces God to know."[20] This is the very point Thomas Aquinas made in distinguishing that *by* which God knows from that *which* he knows.

Finally, and most important, it still remains to be established exactly what is meant, in the first quotation by the 'things' that may come to exist outside God. Are they the things that can exist by themselves, as in Thomas's definition of practical ideas? In the passages from the *Lectura* on the idea as *relatio idealis* (quoted on p. 83 and 126), Scotus merely stated that God has ideas of quiddities, without specifying the matter any further. In the *Ordinatio*, he was more explicit in claiming that God has ideas of things that can be produced independently, as well as of the things that are produced in connection with something else.[21] From this we may conclude that the 'things formed outside God' should probably be taken to encompass whatever can have a *forma* or *quiditas* of its own, and hence is conceptually independent: that is, all perfections.

---

and fourth stage, mentioned in the passage quoted in the previous chapter, are combined in this text.

[19] Ibid.
[20] Ibid. Cf. Augustine, *De diversis quaestionibus*, XLVI n. 2 (CCSL, 44A), 71.
[21] *Ordinatio*, I d. 35 q. u. n. 32 adnotatio Scoti (ed. Vat., 6), 258.

As intimated earlier, in the *Reportata Parisiensia* Scotus expressly addressed the distinction between practical and speculative ideas, criticizing in particular the restricted sense of practical ideas employed by Thomas in the *Summa theologiae*. Scotus argued as follows. The difference between existence and non-existence depends upon God's will. Now, the ideas in God are antecedent to the act of will. As such, they must be indifferent with regard to existence and non-existence. Therefore the fact that some things can be produced and others cannot, cannot serve to distinguish between two kinds of ideas, practical and speculative. A similar point was made in the *Lectura*: because the ideas precede the act of will, it cannot be through them that God has knowledge of the existence of things, unless this existence follows of necessity.[22]

The loosening of the tie between idea and actual existence, in the *Reportata Parisiensia* and in the *Lectura*, indicates that Scotus rejected practical ideas in the restricted sense of the word. In one sense, however, they were accepted in the *Reportata Parisiensia*, viz., if its being 'practical' refers to the thing's capacity for being produced by means of the idea. "An idea", Scotus stated, "is not called practical because something is at one time or another produced in virtue of it, but rather because a thing has a capacity (in virtue of the idea) for being produced; similarly, a thing is not called warm because it is actually heating something else, but rather because it is able to." This capacity is shared by all ideas. "Each idea is practical in its own way (*suo modo*) (…), for in virtue of it each object is capable of being produced."[23]

Which things are correlated with ideas?

It was already noted above that Scotus's theory of ideas accorded with that of William de la Mare. The intellectual affinity between the two thinkers is particularly clear in their criticism of Thomas Aquinas. Before Scotus, William had already commented upon Thomas's distinction between practical and speculative ideas.[24] But their views also concurred on other aspects of the theory of ideas. We shall briefly outline some of these here, concentrating in particular on the question concerning which things God has ideas of.

It was William de la Mare's view that God has distinct ideas of each essence. By 'essence' (*essentia*) he meant anything that can be understood as having being of its own. This included not only the forms of things, but their matter as well. Both form and matter have an essence of their own, therefore they must also have a proper idea in God. According to William de la Mare, matter as well as form can be produced in isolation by God. What counts in

---

[22] *Reportata Parisiensia*, I d. 36 q. 4 nn. 7f (ed. Wadding, 11/1), foll. 208b-209a; *Lectura*, I d. 39 qq. 1-5 nn. 20-22 (ed. Vat., 17), 485.
[23] *Reportata Parisiensia*, I d. 36 q. 4 n. 22 and n. 24, 211b-212a and 212b.
[24] *Le Correctorium corruptorii 'Quare'*, a. 5 (ed. Glorieux), 329 (William de la Mare).

this respect is not the natural order of things but divine omnipotence: whatever God can do by means of secondary causes, that is by means of creatures, he can also do by himself. In the natural order of things, matter gets its being only by means of the conjunction with form. But what God can do by means of form, he can also do directly, that is, give being to matter without form.[25]

Moreover, De la Mare believed that there is a separate idea of the conjunction of matter and form, as well as separate ideas of the accidents. For the essence (*essentia*) of the whole is different from that of its parts, and the essence of the accidents is different from that of the subject.[26]

Finally, De la Mare affirmed (practical) ideas of the *genera* as well. The embryo that will later become man is an individual of the genus 'living being', but not yet of the species 'man'. The form of the genus is real in that individual before the specification by the form of man. Therefore, De la Mare concluded, the form of the genus is known and produced by an idea that is different from that of the species. Closely connected with this account was De la Mare's assertion, against Thomas, that there is not just a single form in man (viz., the soul), but rather a plurality of substantial forms. This doctrine of the plurality of forms was discussed particularly during the last decade of the thirteenth century, most notably in the *Correctoria*.[27]

Duns Scotus also endorsed the view that God can produce matter without form, and that the two have (practical) ideas of their own. Both the general import and the choice of his words are remarkably similar to De la Mare's. Scotus also referred to divine omnipotence and the proper essence of matter at this point:

> "Each particular thing that God makes in the realm of creatures by means of a secondary cause, he can also make without that secondary cause. (...) The form is the secondary cause by means of which God gives being to matter. It (the form, MH) does not belong to the essence of matter insofar as it is matter. Therefore God can make matter without the form."[28]

As something that can have being of its own, matter is intelligible in its essence. Therefore it must also have an idea of its own.[29]

---

[25] Ibid., a. 3, 327, and a. 1, 390.

[26] Ibid., aa. 3-4, 327f.

[27] Ibid., a. 4, 26. For this debate, see R. Zavalloni, *Richard de Mediavilla et la controverse sur la pluralité des formes*, Louvain 1951 (Philosophes médiévaux, 2); Th. Schneider, *Die Einheit des Menschen. Die anthropologische Formel 'anima forma corporis' im sogenannten Korrektorienstreit und bei Petrus Johannis Olivi*, Münster 1973 (BGPhThMA NF, 8), discusses among others the view of William de la Mare. See also the introduction to Richard Knapwell, *Quaestio disputata de unitate formae*, ed. F.E. Kelly, Paris 1982 (Bibliothèque Thomiste, 44).

[28] *Ordinatio*, II d. 12 q. 2 n. 3 (ed. Wadding, 6/2), fol. 682.

[29] Ibid., q. 1 n. 20, fol. 676.

The question of the idea of matter was also raised in the *Reportata Parisiensia*. There Scotus also criticized the view that there can be no proper ideas of individual things because there can be no proper idea of matter, considered as the principle of individuation. Scotus objected that each individual has its own idea. In the same vein, he also rejected the alleged view of Thomas that nature is aimed at the conservation of the species and not of the individual, such that there would not be distinct (practical) ideas of the individuals in God. Scotus responded that nature produces individuals according to God's direction and divine grace, which is concerned precisely with individuals.[30]

In the *Reportata Parisiensia*, we also find De la Mare's view that God has distinct ideas of the parts (that is, of matter and form) as well as of the whole. Because the conjunction of matter and form is a separate being, it must have an idea of its own. Scotus also held that God has distinct ideas of each of the accidents, both those that can subsist without an underlying subject, and those that cannot, as for instance the floating capacity of wood. He was critical, however, of De la Mare's view that the genus can exist by itself in an individual. Although God has a distinct idea of the genus, since he separately produces each part of a whole, the nature of the genus is such that it cannot exist otherwise than in the species.[31]

Ontological status of the known in God

Scotus believed that the ideas in God, that is, the things that are known, do not share in the being of divine essence; they have neither essential being nor existential being (for that would make them eternal), but only being-as-known (*esse cognitum*), which is the diminutive grade of being (*esse deminutum*) of all objects of knowledge as they exist in the knowing subject, including man. Knowledge of a thing does not give it being (only will does), but only being-as-known.[32]

As established by Armand A. Maurer, the use of *esse deminutum* as characterizing the ontological status of the known derived from the Arabic translation of Aristotle's *Metaphysics* and from the commentary on it by Averroes. Through the Latin translation of these works, the notion spread in the West during the thirteenth century, and was used most notably by Duns Scotus.[33]

---

[30] *Reportata Parisienia*, I d. 36 q. 4 nn. 9 and 13f (ed. Wadding, 11/1), foll. 209a-210a.

[31] Ibid., nn. 11f and 19, foll. 209b and 211a.

[32] *Lectura*, I d. 36 q. u. n. 26 (ed. Vat., 17) 468f. For a discussion, see the extensive exposition of A. de Muralt, *L'enjeu de la philosophie médiévale. Etudes thomistes, scotistes, occamiennes et grégoriennes*, Leiden 1991, (STGM, 24), 90-127.

[33] A.A. Maurer, '*Ens Diminutum*. A Note on its Origin and Meaning', *Med. Stud.* 12 (1950), 216-222, esp. 221f (Scotus).

That things in God only have being-as-known, Scotus noted, does not mean that they cannot be known as real things. Knowing something diminishes only the grade of being of the thing as it is in the knowledge itself, but not its function as a representation of something real. If for instance Homer is known, then it is the real Homer that is known; yet he has only diminutive being in the intellect of the knowing subject, and there can be no inference from his being-known to his real being. To illustrate this point, Scotus resorted to the standard example of diminutive being found in the logical text books of Peter of Spain and Walter Burleigh: the case of the *homo mortuus*. The ambiguity involved in diminutive being, on the one hand referring to a reality while on the other hand not being real itself, is like the meaning of the word 'man' in the composite expression 'a dead man' (*homo mortuus*). The reference here is to a *living* man who has died (actually, Scotus remarked, 'a dead man' is a contradiction *in adiecto*), even though, as a *dead* man, he is no longer alive. For it cannot be inferred that 'the man is dead, therefore the man is'. Analogously, God has knowledge of things that really exist, yet in his knowledge they are not real.[34]

Criticism of Henry of Ghent

Henry of Ghent had claimed that the things known in God's essence, which he called *essentiae* or *naturae*, have essential being, a grade of being that makes it possible for something to (later) receive existential being, setting it apart from mere figments (*figmenta* or *chimaera*) that can never receive being. In the process of creation the creatures are endowed with existential being; they do not need to be given essential being again.[35]

Scotus objected to this view along the following lines. Essential being is a form of real being and always goes together with existential being. Both essential being and existential being are the result of God's creative activity, not of his knowledge. Assuming with Henry of Ghent that the things have essential being in God because of they are known, then they have a form of real being; this would make it impossible for them to be created from nothing. Moreover, because the things are known by God from eternity, their essential being must also be eternal, which in turn implies eternal existential being; this

---

[34] *Lectura*, I d. 36 q. u. n. 30 (ed. Vat., 17), 471. Cf. Peter of Spain, *Tractatus*, VII nn. 120-122 (ed. de Rijk), 157f. For Walter Burleigh, see the reference in *Lectura*, ibid., 470 n. 4. For the interpretation of *homo mortuus*, especially in the second half of the thirteenth century, see S. Ebbesen, 'The Dead Man is Alive', *Synthese* 40 (1979), 43-70.

[35] Henry of Ghent, *Summae quaestionum ordinarium*, a. 21 q. 4, Paris 1520, repr. Louvain-Paderborn 1953 (Franciscan Institute Publications, Text Series, 5), fol. 127rO-vO. For discussion and for further relevant passages in the works of Henry of Ghent, see W. Hoeres, 'Wesen und Dasein bei Heinrich von Gent und Duns Scotus', *FzS* 47 (1965), 153-161; J.F. Wippel, *The Metaphysical Thought*, 66-74; id., *Metaphysical Themes in Thomas Aquinas*, 173-184; S.P. Marrone, *Truth and Scientific Knowledge in the Thought of Henry of Ghent*, The Medieval Academy of America 1985 (Speculum Anniversary Monographs, 11), 105-129.

would mean that creation is from eternity.[36]

The same line of criticism against Henry of Ghent had been proffered earlier by Richard of Middleton in his commentary on the *Sentences*, which means that Scotus tied into an existing tradition on this point. Richard of Middleton argued as follows. Essential being is more than nothing (*nihil*). If the creatures have essential being in God, then they can no longer be created from nothing. Secondly, again like Scotus, he strongly connected essential being with existential being. If the creatures have eternal essential being, then they also have eternal existential being. But they do not have existential being in God, therefore they do not have essential being either. The close connection between the view of Richard of Middleton and that of Scotus was noted at least as early as the fifteenth century. Thus it was mentioned by Nicholas d'Orbellis (OFM, † 1472/1475) in his commentary on the *Sentences*, which was then the standard textbook of the Franciscan school. Nicholas approbated the criticism of Henry of Ghent.[37]

The influence of Scotus: followers and critics

The position of Scotus with regard to the ideas and the status of the known met with a varied reception among so-called 'Scotists', who endorsed some of his views while rejecting others. In the following paragraphs, we shall briefly evaluate his reception by such writers as Henry of Harclay, James of Ascoli, Francis of Mayronnes, William of Alnwick, and Peter of Aquila, in those areas pertinent to our topic.

In the Vatican *quaestio* by Henry of Harclay mentioned in the previous chapter (Città del Vaticano, Bibl. Apost., Borgh. 171), we find the view that the idea is nothing but the known object in the mind of God. The stone that is in God's knowledge is *idem in re* with the stone outside. It is also the exemplar God applies when he creates stones. The stone has *esse cognitum* in God's mind.[38]

In the *quaestio* handed down in the Worcester manuscript (Worcester, F. 3), on the other hand, Henry apparently subscribed to the more traditional account of the idea as the known *relatio idealis*. When divine essence is known as imitable, it contains the *ratio* of each object, and serves at once as the foundation of all ideal relations (*respectus ideales*). Knowledge of the *ratio* yields knowledge of the creature, knowledge of the ideal relation, and knowledge of the idea of the creature. The idea is not an object of knowledge,

---

[36] *Ordinatio*, I d. 36 q. u. nn. 13 and 17 (ed. Vat., 6), 276f.

[37] Richard of Middleton, *Sent.*, I d. 35 a. 1 q. 4 (ed. Brescia 1591), fol. 303a; Nicholas d'Orbellis, *Sent.*, I d. 36 q. u., as cited by H. Rossmann, 'Die Quodlibeta und verschiedene sonstige Schriften des Franz von Meyronnes OFM', *FzS* 54 (1972), 25 n. 66. On d'Orbellis, see V. Heynck, *LThK*, s.v. 'Nicolaus d'Orbellis (Dorbellus)'.

[38] See the edition by A.A. Maurer, 'Henry of Harclay's Questions', 171.

but rather follows as a *concomitans* upon knowledge of the *ratio* in the essence.³⁹

The view that the idea is the known thing and the exemplar in the process of creation also occurs in James of Ascoli's *Quaestiones ordinariae* and in his *Quaestiones quodlibetales* (1311-1312). The stone that is produced in time is precisely the stone that God knows from eternity, for otherwise God would produce the stone unknowingly. They are *idem numero quoad quid rei*. Unlike Scotus, however, James believed that ideas are primarily of the species and not of the individuals. Although individuality is a necessary condition for the process of creation, it does not affect the principle of creation (i.e., the idea), but only that which is created. With regard to the ontological status of the ideas, James claimed that the known stone is in God as a known object only. In particular, it cannot formally exist in God, for if that were the case then 'stone' could be predicated of God. The being of the stone is different from the being of God, for God is unbounded while the stone is not. James also accepted Scotus's position that the *esse deminutum* does not imply that real things cannot be known. Since what is known in God is more abstract than what exists as a material thing, it is far better suited as a representation than any real thing could ever be. Finally, James adopted the line of Richard of Middleton and Duns Scotus in denying that things in God have essential being. From the fact that God knows the existential being of a thing it does not follow that it exists from eternity; analogously, from the fact that God knows the essence of a thing it does not follow that this essence has some form of real being in God.⁴⁰

A defender of the essential being of the ideas in God was Francis of Mayronnes. His central argument was that there must be some foundation for the truth of necessary propositions in God's knowledge. This foundation was to be found in essential being, which he took to be formally distinct from God's essence. Unlike Scotus, he believed that essential being is not a form of real being, and that it does not imply existential being. Essential being, according to Francis, is simply the thing's quiddity. The fifteenth-century

---

³⁹ Cf. ibid., 189. In a marginal gloss to a manuscript of William of Alnwick (Città del Vaticano, Bibl. Apost., Pal. lat. 1805, fol. 28r), Harclay is mentioned as defending the view that the ideas are really distinct from God's essence. A.A. Maurer, 'Henry of Harclay's Questions', 164f, has convincingly argued that this reference was probably mistaken. A *Quaestio de ideis*, anonymously handed down in the manuscript Città del Vaticano, Bibl. Apost., Borgh. 171 (foll. 34r-36v), has been incorrectly attributed to Harclay in virtue of the above reference. The mistake was repeated in much of the secondary literature, particularly after the edition of Alnwicks *Quaestiones disputatae* by Ledoux in 1937 (cf. that edition p. 29 n. 1 and p. 30 n. 1).

⁴⁰ James of Ascoli, *Quaestiones ordinariae*, q. 5, as edited in T. Yokoyama, 'Zwei Quaestionen', 40-42 and 48; *Quaestiones quodlibetales*, q. 2, also edited in Yokoyama 'Zwei Quaestionen', 64 and 73f. On the ontological status of the known according to James, see Z. Wlodek, 'Zagadnienie *esse obiectivum* i intelektu u Jakuba z Ascoli', *Studia Mediewistyczne* 6 (1964), 3-18, with a summary in French.

Scotist William of Vaurouillon (OFM, † 1463) duly detected a connection between Francis and Henry of Ghent on this issue.[41]

According to William of Alnwick, the ideas in God cannot be distinguished from either the essence or divine knowledge itself. They do not have any being of their own, not even a diminutive being when they are known. For the known idea is identical with knowledge of the perfection in God's essence. The ideas must coincide with God's essence because they are necessary for his knowledge of the creatures, and it is impossible that God is dependent upon something that is not-God. Alnwick here expressly criticized Scotus's view of diminutive being.[42]

In the commentary on the *Sentences* of Peter of Aquila, two theories of ideas were put forth. First, the idea is the thing that is known in God. Second, it coincides with divine essence which contains all perfections, and is not an *ens rationis* or an object of knowledge (which in this view is tantamount to being an *ens rationis*), because a real being cannot be created by means of a rational being. The first view was that of Duns Scotus, while the second position was that of William of Alnwick. The fact that Alnwick was quoted alongside Scotus indicates that his position was influential among Franciscans writing in the 1330s. It is curious that Peter of Aquila neither rejected nor embraced either one of the views he was quoting, although we may detect a slight preference for the position of Scotus from the fact that Peter replied only to the arguments given by Alnwick.[43]

As regards the question of which things are correlated with ideas, Peter followed Scotus. God has ideas of the natural beings and of the artificial ones, of the *genera*, of the species, and of the individuals, of matter, of relations, of compositions (*composita*) and of their parts. In his arguments, Peter also followed Scotus. There must be a proper idea of matter, because by God's power it can exist without form. Against the view that God does not have ideas of the individuals, he quoted the argument from the *Reportata Parisiensia*. Divine grace works through nature, yet is aimed at the individual. Therefore, it cannot be right that nature is concerned only with the species and not with the individual. Finally, Peter of Aquila also followed Scotus with regard to the ontological status of the ideas, criticizing Henry of Ghent.[44]

---

[41] Francis of Mayronnes, *Sent.*, I d. 42 q. 1 (ed. Venice 1520), fol. 118rbH, and q. 3 a. 4, fol. 120raB. Considering these passages, I cannot agree with A.A. Maurer, *Being and Knowing*, 333 n. 4, who claims, without mentioning any primary sources, that Mayronnes denies that the divine ideas are not formally identical with God. On Francis's theory of essential being, see P. Vignaux, 'L'etre comme perfection', 276; H. Rossmann, 'Die Quodlibeta', 21-25, 40, and 42. For the reference to William of Vaurouillon, see Rossmann, 'Die Quodlibeta', 25. Cf. I. Brady, *LThK*, s.v. 'Wilhelm v. Vorillon'.

[42] William of Alnwick, *Quaestiones disputatae*, q. 1 and q. 2 (ed. Ledoux), 9 and 39f. Cf. O. Wanke, *Die Kritik*, 114f and 151; J.P. Beckmann, *HWdPh*, s.v. 'Idee'.

[43] Peter of Aquila, *Sent.*, I d. 36 q. 1 a. 3 (ed. Speyer 1480), coll. 2-3. Cf. Alnwick, *Quaestiones disputatae*, quodl. 7, 431.

[44] Peter of Aquila, *Sent.*, I d. 36 q. 2 and q. 3, coll. 2-3 and coll. 1-2, respectively.

It is remarkable that Henry of Harclay and James of Ascoli expressly defined their position vis-à-vis the words of Augustine. Much the same is true of Peter Aureoli and Johannes Baconis, who made much of their claim that their own position and their interpretation of Aristotle and Averroes concurred with the position of Augustine.[45] Augustine's theory of ideas was obviously influential in the first half of the fourteenth century. That this did not encumber the development of a wide variety of interpretations should be clear from the previous paragraphs.

WILLIAM OF OCKHAM

Ockham generally agreed with Scotus's view that the ideas are the things known by God. He differed however with regard to their ontological status. While Scotus believed that the ideas have a diminutive grade of being, Ockham thought they had no being at all.

In the previous section, we have seen that Scotus's view of ideas as things known was also adopted by Henry of Harclay (in the *quaestio* from the manuscript Città del Vaticano, Bibl. Apost., Borgh., 171), and by James of Ascoli. The same position was also taken by Durand of St. Pourçian. They used the characteristic form of words which we also find in Ockham, viz., that the created thing itself is the idea and the exemplar of its creation. Ockham's theory of ideas, which was criticized as erroneous by Lutterell, obviously formed part of an existing tradition.[46]

According to Ockham, the ideas are not constitutive in the process of divine knowledge. They are not necessary for knowledge of individual creatures, neither as forms of knowledge (*rationes cognoscendi*) nor as similitudes (*similitudines*). These two disclaimers, the second of which reflects the position of Henry of Ghent, were also proffered by Duns Scotus. Against the position that ideas are forms of knowledge, Ockham argued that nothing can act as the form of knowledge of a creature, except divine essence itself. God's knowledge coincides with his essence and cannot be determined or altered by something else. Furthermore, God's knowledge is one, whereas there is a plurality of ideas. Now, assuming that the ideas act as forms of

---

[45] Cf. the texts in A.A. Maurer, 'Henry of Harclay Quaestions', 173-178 (Harclay); T. Yokoyama, 'Zwei Quaestionen', 42, 55, and 63 (James of Ascoli); Peter Aureoli, *Sent.*, I d. 35 p. 2 a. 1 (ed. Rome 1596), fol. 774bB-C; Johannes Baconis, *Sent.*, I d. 39 q. u. par. 4 (ed. Cremona 1618), fol. 382aC-E (= 378aC-E).

[46] Ockham, *Scriptum*, I d. 2. q. 1 (OTh, 2), 25: "(E)adem res est idea et producta extra (...)." Also: I d. 35 q. 5 (OTh, 4), 503: '(A)liquid potest esse exemplar sui ipsius." Cf. Durand of St. Pourçian, *Sent.*, I d. 36 q. 3 n. 13 (ed. Venice 1571), fol. 98va. Lutterell's criticism will be dealt with below. For a discussion of Ockham's theory of ideas, see K. Bannach, *Die Lehre von der Doppelten Macht*, 225-239; A.A. Maurer, 'The Role of Divine Ideas in the Theology of William of Ockham', *Being and Knowing*, 363-381 (originally published in 1976); M. McCord Adams, *Willam Ockham*, II, 1033-1063; A. de Muralt, *L'enjeu*, 168-255.

knowledge, not insofar as they cause God's knowledge, but insofar as they coincide with the act by which God has knowledge of the creatures, then there would also have to be a plurality of acts of knowledge, which is in contradiction with divine simplicity.[47]

Against the position that ideas are similitudes, Ockham put forth a dilemma. The similitude must be either real or rational. If it has the status of something real and yet coincides with God's essence, then it puts divine simplicity in serious jeopardy. If on the other hand it is rational, then it is completely redundant. For God can know everything and produce everything without the help of rational entities; all he needs to do that is his essence. Like Henry of Harclay in the *quaestio* referred to above, Ockham argued in the *Scriptum* that a rational thing cannot function as the exemplar for something real. This claim was no doubt closely connected with his view, advocated in the same work, that there is a fundamental difference between real being and rational being.[48]

According to Ockham the ideas are neither subjectively nor really present in God, as they do not form part of the essence, but only objectively so, in the sense that they are the objects of knowledge in God's mind. He described the idea as something toward which the knowing subject (God) directs itself in order to produce it, or something similar to it, as a real being.[49]

As his reason for postulating the existence of ideas in God, Ockham pointed to the rationality of God's actions. Actions, he argued, require a power of production, viz., divine essence, as well as an exemplar at which they are aimed, which is the idea. To be sure, Ockham did not connect the idea with the productivity of God's actions, but only with their rationality, a link also made by Henry of Harclay. Unlike Thomas in *De veritate*, he did not take them as *creativae et productivae rerum*. God would be perfectly able to merely produce something without ideas, but then he would act unknowingly and irrationally. Knowledge of the essence alone is not sufficient to make God's actions be rational, Ockham thought. If God knew only his essence and not the idea, then he would inevitably be acting irrationally. Ockham inferred from this that the idea cannot possibly be the same as God's essence. It can only be the known creature, because only knowledge of the creature can turn the production of the creature into a rational act.[50]

Although the ideas were sharply distinguished from divine essence in the *Scriptum*, and considered only as the objects of knowledge, Ockham nevertheless maintained that the ideas exist of necessity. He cannot have meant the

---

[47] *Scriptum*, I d. 35 q. 5 (OTh, 4), 490f.
[48] Ibid., 488 and 492. For Henry of Harclay, see the edition by A.A. Maurer, 'Henry of Harclay's Questions', 170.
[49] *Scriptum*, I d. 35 q. 5, 490 and 497.
[50] Ibid., 488f and 492.

necessity of divine essence, however, because the ideas coincide neither with the essence nor with the act of knowledge. What he had in mind when he called the ideas 'necessary' was probably the fact that God, as a perfect being, always acts rationally and with knowledge of what he is producing. That this rationality cannot be strictly proven by man, does not entail that it is not a necessary attribute of God. Ockham stated elsewhere that what can only be demonstrated by means of probable arguments does not have to be (merely) probable itself, but can even be necessary, as there is a fundamental difference between the logical structure of a demonstration, and the ontological structure of what the demonstration is about.[51]

The view of Thomas Aquinas and Henry of Ghent, viz. that the ideas really coincide with God's essence and that they have separate existence in the intellect as known rational forms, Ockham called the *communis opinio*. He quoted the view of Henry of Ghent, which was apparently very influential at Oxford in the 1310s. Ockham's principal objection to this position was its fusion of real being and rational being. If ideas are forms of imitability of the essence, produced by the intellect, then they must have rational being. It is thus impossible that they coincide with the essence: the essence is real, and whatever is really identical with the essence must itself be real and not rational. Real coincidence can only occur between real beings, not between a rational being and a real being.[52]

Moreover, Ockham argued that it is ruled out by divine simplicity that the essence be called 'idea'. There are many different ideas. If they would really coincide with the essence, then there would be different realities within God, which is in contradiction with his simplicity. Ockham presumed here that the relations between real things must be real themselves.[53]

Unlike Thomas and others, Ockham never spoke of the idea as a *ratio*, but always simply of *idea* or *exemplar*. He was of the opinion that all ideas are practical, though not in the strict sense of the word. The distinction between the practical and the speculative, according to Ockham, applies only to the level of the *acts* of knowledge and not to that of the *objects*, including the ideas. Considering however that the knowledge of the things produced in virtue of the ideas is practical, the ideas can in this sense be called 'practical' too. Ockham did not subscribe to the strict interpretation of 'practical ideas' as it was developed by Thomas in the *Summa theologiae* and adopted in the *Correctorium corruptorii 'Sciendum'*. God has 'practical' ideas of things that will exist as well as of things that will never exist.[54]

---

[51] Ibid., 500. Cf. L. Baudry, *Lexique philosophique de Guillaume d'Ockham. Etude des notions fondamentales*, Paris 1958, s.v. 'probabile', 216.
[52] *Scriptum*, I d. 35 q. 5, 480f.
[53] Ibid., 487f.
[54] Ibid., 485 and 500f, and q. 6, 508 and 513.

Which things are correlated with ideas?

With regard to the question concerning which things there are ideas of, Ockham clearly followed the line of William de la Mare and Duns Scotus. God has distinct ideas of whatever can be produced as a separate creature. In the first place (*primo*) this includes the singular creatures, and not the species, for only the singular things can be produced as separate beings. Furthermore, God has distinct ideas of matter, of form, and of all other components of things. Ockham, as we know, agreed with De la Mare and Scotus that God can create matter without form, form without matter, and accidents without subject. God does not have ideas of generalities (the *genera*), except when these are taken as qualities of the human soul, that is, as concepts, which are attributed to many things by means of predication. In this sense they have a form of real being in the soul: concepts as such are singular things that can be produced by God.[55]

The ontological status of the ideas

Ideas, according to Ockham, do not have a *quid rei* but only a *quid nominis*. Not being a substantive thing with a quiddity of its own, an idea is only a relative or connotative term (*nomen connotativum*), a term that refers to a thing while indicating something else at the same time. An idea indicates that a real thing is in a certain state. It refers to a creature while indicating that the creature is known and that it serves as the exemplar in a process of creation. In God, the ideas do not have any positive being: their only status there is that of things known, while the positive being of the idea is the creature itself. Ockham compared their existence in God to the way the color of a wall exists in the eye. The color existing in the eye is nothing but its being known by the eye. The ideas in God have no real being, for they do not coincide with God's essence, nor with his act of knowledge. Nor do they have rational being, for rational beings cannot serve as exemplars. Considered as objects of knowledge, the ideas are simply nothing (*nihil*). They receive being only when the creature is created, for only then does that which the idea exemplifies really exist. This line of argument was used by Ockham to criticize the position of William of Alnwick, who held that the ideas, qua being, coincide with God and with his knowledge.[56]

As we have seen earlier, the view that the ideas in God are nothing (*nihil*) had also been defended by Scotus in his *Reportata Parisiensia* and in the

---

[55] Ibid., q. 5, 493; *Quodlibeta*, II q. 7 (OTh, 9), 142.
[56] *Scriptum*, I d. 35 q. 5, 485f and 490; also d. 36 q. u., 534 and 545-561. Cf. A.A. Maurer, *Being and Knowing*, 371 and 374f. On Ockham's theory of connotative terms, see P.V. Spade, 'Ockham's Distinctions between Absolute and Connotative Terms', *Vivarium* 13 (1975), 55-76; J. Boler, 'Connotative Terms in Ockham', *History of Philosophy Quarterly* 2 (1985), 21-37.

Ordinatio (although he usually added that the known things have a form of diminutive being). Again we find that Ockham's thought formed part of an existing tradition.

John Lutterell and the papal committee

As we have seen with regard to the attributes, the view that the ideas are identical with the creatures was also criticized by John Lutterell in his *Libellus contra doctrinam G. Occam* (a. 8). He attributed this view to William of Ockham and to others (*illi, qui hoc similiter ponunt*), by which he may have meant Henry of Harclay, who was elected Chancellor of Oxford before Lutterell in 1312, or the Paris theologians James of Ascoli and Durand of St. Pourçain.[57] This means that Ockham's position was not considered to be an isolated one.

The starting point of Lutterell's criticism was the view of Thomas Aquinas, in particular as it was elaborated in the Thomistic *Correctoria corruptorii 'Quare'* and *'Quaestione'*: the ideas are the *rationes* by virtue of which God knows and produces the things. These *rationes* are taken as coinciding with God's essence, which represents all things in the most perfect manner. In the ideas God sees all things as existing, because his knowledge is measured by the eternity that encompasses all time. As with his stance on the attributes, Lutterell assumed that a reality (God's essence) can harbor rational differences (ideas).[58]

Against Ockham, Lutterell argued that the ideas cannot possibly be created things, for the ideas are eternal and immutable, whereas creatures are not. He referred here to Augustine (*De diversis quaest.*, q. 46). Ockham himself had considered this objection in the *Scriptum*. His response focused on the *quid nominis* character of ideas that was discussed above. *De virtute sermonis* the ideas cannot be eternal and immutable, because 'idea' stands first for the creature and not for something in God. Yet the ideas can be called eternal and immutable inasmuch as they are known, for God's knowledge is eternal and immutable, which is what the saints and Augustine have claimed.[59]

The verdict of the papal committee was significantly shorter than Lutterell's. It did not address the question itself but merely stated that the view that the ideas are the things outside God was *falsa omnino et contra intentionem sanctorum et philosophorum*. It may be that the committee wanted only to criticize the disturbing form of words Ockham had chosen, with its obvious contradiction of the words of Augustine, without passing judgment on the status of ideas itself. Internal differences of opinion may have been the cause

---

[57] For Harclay as Chancellor of Oxford, see W.J. Courtenay, *Adam Wodeham*, 57.
[58] *Libellus*, a. 8 n. 60 (ed. Hoffmann), 32. Cf. *Le Correctorium corruptorii 'Quare'*, a. 3 (ed. Glorieux), 24; *Le Correctorium corruptorii 'Quaestione'. Texte anonyme du ms. Merton 267*, a. 3, ed. J.–P. Muller, Rome 1954 (Studia Anselmiana, 35), 20.
[59] *Libellus*, a. 8 n. 59, 30f; Ockham, *Scriptum*, I d. 35 q. 5 (OTh, 4), 496 and 504f.

of this, considering the fact that both Lutterell and Durand of St. Pourçain formed part of the committee.[60]

Up to and including the final (third) edition of his commentary on the *Sentences*, written between 1317 and 1327, Durand defended a view of the ideas that concurred with Ockham's on the debated issue, contrasting sharply with that of Lutterell. He claimed that although God's essence is the idea of the perfections that are common to God and the creatures (such as being, living, and knowing), the ideas of the creatures and the perfections that are proper to the creatures are nonetheless not something in God's essence; rather, they are the known things themselves. Durand also considered the Augustinian objection that the ideas are eternal. His response was the same as that of Ockham: the creature itself is not eternal, but God's knowledge of it is. Because God has knowledge of the creature, the idea of the creature is eternal insofar as it is the object of the knowledge. This view of Durand was criticized in two of the Thomistic *Irrtumslisten* directed against him in 1314 and 1316-1317, drawn up by John of Naples and others. In the second of these it is stated that Durand's position contradicts that of Thomas.[61] In view of the generally Thomistic outlook of John Lutterell and the non-Thomistic persuasion of Durand, it is very possible that the papal committee was unable to come to agreement over the ontological status of ideas, and that it therefore chose to omit a detailed consideration of the question.

Robert Holcot and Adam Wodeham

Divine ideas were not discussed at any length by Robert Holcot in his commentary on the *Sentences*. In a brief remark in a *quaestio* on the trinity (Lib. I q. 5) he merely stated that the idea is divine essence, and that there is therefore only one idea. From scattered remarks elsewhere in his commentary, we may glean that he shared Ockham's view that before creation the ideas have no being at all, not quidditative, nor potential, nor representational being. Holcot did not further elaborate on the subject.[62]

Much the same holds for Adam Wodeham, who devoted no separate *quaestiones* to ideas in any of his three commentaries on the *Sentences*. In the *Lectura Oxoniensis*, the term 'idea' was used only in a quotation concerning the question of whether the Word represents the coming of the Antichrist in a natural or in a contingent way (Lib. III q. 3).[63]

---

[60] J. Koch, *Kleine Schriften*, II, a. 31 (=R) and a. 43 (= V), 356. For a listing of the members of the papal committee, see J. Koch, ibid., 286; J. Miethke, *Ockhams Weg*, 61.

[61] The Thomistic *Irrtumslisten* against Durand are edited by J. Koch. See the relevant passages in his *Kleine Schriften*, II, 57 n. 14 (first list) and 77 n. 27 (second list). For the dating and the authors of these lists, see ibid., 21, 24-27, and 31. Cf. Durand, *Sent.*, I d. 36 q. 3 n. 17 and n. 22 (ed. Venice 1571), foll. 98va-vb and 99rb. Durand's theory of ideas is discussed by Chr. Knudsen, *HWdPh*, s.v. 'Idee'.

[62] Robert Holcot, *Sent.*, I q. 5 (ed. Lyon 1518), fol. fiibQ. Cf. Chr. Knudsen, 'Idee'.

[63] Adam Wodeham, *Lectura Oxoniensis*, III q. 3 (Paris, Bibl. Maz, 915), fol. 178vb. The

The fact that neither Holcot nor Wodeham developed any discussion of ideas should probably be seen in light of a more general historical evolution: from ca. 1330 onward the structure of Oxford commentaries on the *Sentences* began to change. The strictness with which the 'traditional' structure used to be observed came to be considerably relaxed, much more so than in Scotus or Ockham, and more attention was given to contemporary issues. This inevitably meant that the discussion of some of the more classical themes tended to be relocated, condensed, or even suppressed.[64] The commentaries of Holcot and Wodeham are examples of this new development. Divine foreknowledge, for instance, was treated by Holcot not in the first book, as had been the custom, but in the second, under the heading of the doctrine of creation (Lib. II q. 2). Similarly, Adam Wodeham did not discuss God's knowledge in the first book, but inserted it into the discussion of christology in book three (Lib. III qq. 2-3).

It is remarkable, however, that even the commentaries delivered in Paris by Gregory of Rimini (1343-1344), Alfonsus Vargas (1344-1345) and Hugolin of Orvieto (1348-1349), did not separately discuss the ideas, this in spite of the fact that they generally followed Lombard's *Sentences* much more closely than their English counterparts. In the commentaries by Peter of Aquila and Thomas of Strasbourg, on the other hand, written in Paris only slightly earlier, the ideas were still a separate topic. As has been established by William J. Courtenay, the influence of English thinkers such as Holcot and Wodeham started to show in Paris at the beginning of the 1340s, in the works of the Gregory of Rimini, Alfonsus Vargas, and Hugolin of Orvieto, among others.[65] The fact that these three Parisian writers did not include a separate discussion of the ideas is perhaps also evidence of this influence, as it may be due to the new structure of the commentaries by Holcot and Wodeham.

Marsilius of Inghen

Introduction

In the previous sections we have found that the ontological status and the epistemological as well as practical role of divine ideas were controversial issues among several writers of the thirteenth and fourteenth centuries. We have also seen that not all theologians took an equal interest in the problem of divine ideas, particularly from the 1330s onward. It would certainly be wrong to speak of 'the' medieval theory of divine ideas. Some theologians, such as Adam Wodeham and Robert Holcot, barely touched upon the

---

questions of Wodeham's commentaries on the *Sentences* are listed in W.J. Courtenay, *Adam Wodeham*, 183-214. See also recently Adam Wodeham, *Lectura secunda in librum primum Sententiarum*, ed. R. Wood and G. Gál, Vol. 1-3, St. Bonaventure, New York 1990.

[64] Cf. W.J. Courtenay, *Schools and Scholars*, 252f.
[65] Courtenay, 'The Role of English Thought', 133-137.

question of divine ideas in their *Sentences* commentaries. This is also true of some of the continental thinkers they inspired. Gregory of Rimini even expressly denied the existence of ideas.[66]

A similarly radical stance on the nonexistence of ideas was assumed in the work of Conrad of Soltau. Following Thomas of Strasbourg, whom he quoted literally, Conrad criticized the Scotist opinion that ideas are *ex parte rei* distinct in God, as well as the opinion that the ideas are made distinct by an act of the created intellect. According to Conrad of Soltau, God knows all things individually through his essence. Therefore he does not need ideas that are distinct by themselves (*ex natura rei*). Nor are the ideas made distinct by an act of the human intellect, as this would imply that they are sometimes distinct in God and sometimes not, depending on the activity of the human intellect. If there are ideas in God at all, he concluded, they must be made distinct by the divine intellect itself. Thus far Conrad was still following the commentary on the *Sentences* of Thomas of Strasbourg. His next remark is very important, however. It was not derived from Thomas of Strasbourg, and clearly shows that Conrad of Soltau belonged to the more radical line of thought.

> "I say '*If* divine ideas exist at all,' for I fail to see by what necessity (*qua necessitate*) we would be forced to hold that ideas exist in God at all. However, I do not want to contradict the saints (read: Augustine, *contra sanctos nolo loqui*)."[67]

This means that there were theologians who did not believe in divine ideas for systematic reasons, but only by reason of the authority of Augustine. Conrad of Soltau is one such theologian.

This radical stance must have existed as early as the beginning of the fourteenth century. This may be gathered from Francis of Mayronnes's remark that some theologians (whose names he did not mention) saw no evident necessity (*nulla necessitas evidens*) for assuming the existence of ideas in God. God's essence contains each creature in the most perfect way; therefore God does not need ideas to know and produce all creatures.

Although Francis of Mayronnes mentioned some systematic arguments for the existence of ideas in God, the argument from authority seems to have strongly appealed to him. In reply to the anonymous theologians mentioned above, he declared himself to be prepared to hold on to the existence of ideas in God because of Augustine (*propter dicta Augustini*).[68]

Radically opposed to the nonexistence line was the view of Henry of

---

[66] Gregory, *Lectura*, I d. 38 q. 2 (ed. Trapp-Marcolino, 3), 280f.
[67] Conrad of Soltau, *Sent.*, I (Stuttgart, Württ. Landesbibl., Cod. Theol. Fol. 118), foll. 46vb-47ra. Cf. Thomas of Strasbourg, *Sent.*, I d. 36 q. 1 a. 1 (ed. Venice 1564), fol. 105ra.
[68] Francis of Mayronnes, *Sent.*, I d. 47 q. 1 a. 1 (ed. Venice 1520), fol. 133vaI.

Ghent. His position was that ideas are necessary for God to know the creatures individually, because without ideas God would know his essence and the creatures as one.

We find the same emphasis on divine ideas in the work of Duns Scotus and that of the Scotistic theologians discussed above. Both John of Ripa, partly under the influence of Henry of Ghent, partly also in response to him, and Thomas of Strasbourg discussed the subject of divine ideas, as did Gerard of Kalkar (magister in Paris ca. 1383, later in Vienna, and in Cologne in 1388) and Peter of Candia. The latter two addressed the question of ideas in their *principia* to the Sentences. Peter of Candia extensively discussed the views of Duns Scotus (which he dubbed the *modus platonicus*), William of Ockham, and John of Ripa.[69]

In the first *principium* of Marsilius of Inghen (*Sent.*, I q. 1), the problem of divine ideas was discussed with regard to the question of whether the diversity of perfections in the created world derives from the diversity of divine ideas: *utrum ex diversitate idearum existentium in regno increato sumatur diversitas perfectionum productorum entium in regno creato.*

Virtually the same question had been raised in the commentary on the *Sentences* of John of Ripa. He based himself on *De unitate divinae essentiae et pluralitate creaturarum*, which he attributed to Anselm, but which was in fact written by Achard of St. Victor. The *explicit* of the manuscript in which *De unitate* has been handed down as a separate treatise (Padova, Bibl. Antoniana, Scaff. V, 89) tells us that the work was copied in 1352. It was also mentioned by Peter of Candia. This seems to establish that the treatise was probably well-known in the second half of the fourteenth century, especially in Paris.[70]

---

[69] John of Ripa, *Conclusiones*, I d. 35 q. u. aa. 1-4, ed. A. Combes, Paris 1957 (Etudes de philosophie médiévale, 44), 210-213; Thomas of Strasbourg, *Sent.*, I d. 36 q. 1 a. 1 (ed. Venice 1564), fol. 105ra. For Gerard of Kalkar and Peter of Candia, see the texts cited by F. Ehrle, *Der Sentenzenkommentar*, 46f. For the latter, see also the passages quoted by A. Combes, *Un inédit de Saint Anselme? Le traité 'De unitate divinae essentiae et pluralitate creaturarum' d'apres Jean de Ripa*, Paris 1944 (Etudes de philosophie médiévale, 34), 58-61. Biographical data on Gerard of Kalkar are provided by F. Ehrle, *Der Sentenzenkommentar*, 42-44.

[70] John of Ripa, *Conclusiones*, I d. 35 q. u. a. 1 (ed. Combes), 210: "(E)t hoc est expresse intentio venerabilis Anselmi in libro *de Unitate essentie et pluralitate creaturarum*, quem libellum specialiter ad hoc edidit ut ostenderet omnem creaturarum pluralitatem seu distinctionem essentialem necessario provenire ex rationibus divinis exemplativis et formativis creaturarum (...)". A recent study of the works of John of Ripa is Z. Kaluza, 'La nature des écrits de Jean de Ripa', *Traditio* 43 (1987), 257-298. On *De unitate divinae essentiae* and its author, see M.Th. d'Alverny, 'Achard de Saint-Victor. De Trinitate - De unitate et pluralitate creaturarum', *RThAM* 21 (1954), 299-306; Achard of St. Victor, *L'unité de Dieu et la pluralité des créatures (De unitate <Dei> et pluralitate creaturarum*. Texte Latin inédit du manuscrit de Padoue (Antoniana, Scaff. V, 89), établi, traduit et présenté par E. Martineau, Authentica 1987, 12-18; C. Viola, 'A propos de l' 'Inédit de Saint Anselme''', *BPhM* 33 (1991), 112-120. For the references to *De unitate* by Peter of Candia, see A. Combes, *Un inédit*, 61.

De unitate, or the commentary on the *Sentences* of John of Ripa, may have been used by Marsilius as a source of inspiration in preparing the draft of his *principium*. John of Ripa's commentary seems to be a particularly good candidate in this respect. As far as we have been able to establish, Marsilius never referred to *De unitate*, nor to a (pseudo-)Anselmian work of similar content. The treatise does not appear on Marsilius's list of books. On the other hand, it is certain that Marsilius did know the commentary on the *Sentences* of John of Ripa. In his *principium*, Marsilius referred to that commentary's view on the order of perfections in the created world. He also had in his possession a copy of John of Ripa's *Determinationes*, in which the same question was raised.[71]

John of Ripa's elaboration of the problem was adopted by many others. Exactly the same questions as posed by John of Ripa (*Sent.*, I dd. 35-36) can be found in the commentary on the *Sentences* of Francis of Perugia (magister in Paris 1368-1370), and in the *principia* of Gerard of Kalkar and Peter of Candia.[72]

We may safely conclude from these findings that the question Marsilius discussed in his first *principium* was of topical interest in Paris at the time he was a student of theology there. It is not inconceivable, then, that the material for his lecture had been assembled in the course of his studies in Paris.[73]

Given what we know of the reception of Marsilius's theology in the Middle Ages, his theory of divine ideas as explained in the *principium* can be called influential. Thomas de Strampino inserted long quotations from it in his own *principium* held at Krakau in 1441. Gabriel Biel's commentary on the *Sentences* also quoted the opinion of Marsilius at some length.[74] The strength of the reputation enjoyed by Marsilius in the fifteenth century is highlighted

---

[71] Marsilius, *Sent.*, I q. 1 a. 2 (ed. Strasbourg 1501), fol. 7ra; John of Ripa, *Determinationes*, ed. A. Combes, Paris 1957 (Textes philosophiques du Moyen Age, 4), 33. Cf. *Die Rektorbücher der Universität Heidelberg*, 1/2, 477 (95): "Item (417) determinaciones magistri Iohannis de Ripa alias de Marchia."

[72] J. Lechner, 'Franz von Perugia OFM und die Quästionen seines Sentenzenkommentars', *FzS* 25 (1938), 50f (= München, Bayer. Staatsbibl., CLM 8718, foll. 57rb-60ra); F. Ehrle, *Der Sentenzenkommentar*, 46f (Gerard of Kalkar and Peter of Candia). The influence of John of Ripa on Francis of Perugia is discussed by Lechner, 'Franz von Perugia', 29-38.

[73] This suggestion would also make good sense in connection with a surprising remark elsewhere in Marsilius's commentary on the *Sentences*. In question 38 on divine knowledge (ed. Hoenen, 33), Marsilius says he believes (*credo*) that he might (*forte*) have discussed the same problem in his *principium*. It is difficult to imagine a writer being less than certain about what he lectured on no more than half a year before at an occasion as important as a *principium*, unless of course he was discussing material that had been prepared and written down much earlier. We know that students of theology started to prepare themselves for their future lectures on the *Sentences* from the very beginning of their study, as is documented by V. Marcolino, 'Der Augustinertheologe', 148f.

[74] Compare Marsilius, *Sent.*, I q. 1 a. 1 (ed. Strasbourg), foll. 3vb and 4rb, with Thomas de Strampino, *Principium*, I (Kraków, Bibl. Jag., 1199), foll. 460f; Gabriel Biel, *Collectorium circa quattuor libros Sententiarum*, I d. 35 q. 5 a. 1, ed. W. Werbeck and U. Hofmann, Vol. I, Tübingen 1973, 647-649.

by the fact that Biel called upon Marsilius of Inghen, and not Henry of Ghent, as representative of the view that the ideas in reality coincide with divine essence. This in spite of the fact that Biel's commentary was based on the *Scriptum* of William of Ockham, which mentioned Henry of Ghent at this point.

Properties of the divine ideas

Marsilius was surprisingly comprehensive in his description and determination of the properties of divine ideas. His thoroughness was probably due to the fact that the ideas were discussed in a *principium*, a prestigious public lecture attended by almost all students and *magistri*.

Equally surprising is the rich strain of Neoplatonic themes in Marsilius's discussion. Although they play a role in many medieval works on philosophy and theology, largely due to the influence of pseudo-Dionysius, Avicenna, and the *Liber de causis*, compared to the rest of Marsilius's work their density in his *principium* is unusually high.

In his discussion of the ideas, Marsilius distinguished between three basic properties of God. These properties, Marsilius explained, were also attributed to God by Plato, Augustine, and almost all (other) magisters: *multi magistrorum nostrorum, immo fere omnes*. 'Multi magistrorum nostrorum' obviously does not refer to contemporary magisters, but to the authorities generally acknowledged at the time, such as Augustine.[75]

The first property: God is the indivisible simple principle from which (*a quo*) all things are. God is like the number 1 or numerical unity, from which all numbers derive their being.

Secondly, God is a universal principle (*principium universale*) that is universally productive in three ways. First, God contains all things in a perfect way before they exist. This mode of divine universality is called *universalitas ante rem*. Second, God coexists with all things once they have been produced. This is called *universalitas cum re*. Finally, God is the *principium universale per imitationem*. All things imitate the three divine persons. They imitate the Father in their being, the Son in their directedness toward God, and the Holy Spirit in their desire for God.

The third and final property is that God is the principle that contains all things as their efficient cause (for he makes all things), as their formal cause (for he is the form of all things, without himself being *in* those things), and as their final cause (for he moves all things by being intelligible and desirable).

---

[75] Marsilius, *Sent.*, I q. 1 a. 1, fol. 2ra-rb. For this meaning of 'magister', compare the term 'διδάσκαλος' as used in the New Testament (Rengstorf, *ThWzNT*, s.v. 'διδάσκαλος'), which came to be translated as 'magister' in Latin. For the use of the term 'magister' in the fourteenth century, see also K.H. Tachau, 'French Theology in the Mid-Fourteenth Century: Vatican Latin 986 and Wroclaw, Milich F. 64', *AHDLMA* 51 (1984), 46 n. 10.

The first of the properties is of immediate relevance to our discussion in the previous chapter. If God is one, and yet is able to produce all things individually, then he is also able to know all things and all ideas individually in a single act of knowledge. The second and third properties are connected with an issue discussed in more detail below. The ideas coincide with God's essence. They are the principles from which all things are created; they are the forms of things, not in the things themselves but in God, and thus also the end toward which all creatures strive.

The development of this theory of three divine properties was largely due to Neoplatonically leaning writers.[76] From the inventory of Marsilius's library we may infer that he took great interest in Neoplatonic thought. His books included Plato's *Timaeus* and the commentary on it by Calcidius, as well as an unknown work on Macrobius's commentary on the *Somnium Scipionis* of Cicero, as well as works of pseudo-Dionysius and Alan of Lille. Some of these works may have served as sources for Marsilius's opinion on the three properties. The triplet of God as causal, formal, and final cause, for instance, is found in pseudo-Dionysius and in Alan of Lille.[77]

On the other hand, we should not forget that the triplet was also mentioned by other theologians Marsilius knew and quoted, such as Bonaventure, Thomas Aquinas, and Duns Scotus.[78]

Special attention should be given here to the first book in Albert the Great's second commentary on the *Ethics*. of which there is as yet no critical edition. Marsilius possessed several works by Albert the Great, and his exposition on divine ideas was probably influenced, either directly or indirectly, by Albert's commentary on the *Ethics*. We shall return to this issue presently. In Albert's commentary, the view that the three causes coincide in God was attributed to Plato, as it was in Marsilius's *principium*.[79]

---

[76] Cf. R. Haubst, *Das Bild des Einen und Dreieinen Gottes in der Welt nach Nikolaus von Kues*, Trier 1952 (Trierer theologische Studien, 4), 86-92; K. Kremer, *Die neuplatonische Seinsphilosophie und ihre Wirkung auf Thomas von Aquin*, Leiden 1966 (Studien zur Problemgeschichte der antiken und mittelalterlichen Philosophie, 1), 329-332.

[77] *Die Rektorbücher der Universität Heidelberg*, 1/2, 477 (96f): "Item (*418*) maxime Alani in theologia in pergameno. Item (*419*) scriptum unum vel excerptum de Dyonisio"; 489 (191) "Item (*478*) Thymeum Platonis cum commento Calcidii"; 490 (204): "Item (*493*) scriptum super Macrobium de sompno Cypionis"; 490 (206): "Item (*497*) anticlaudianum." For the works of Alan of Lille mentioned, cf. N.M. Häring, 'Magister Alanus de Insulis Regulae caelestis iuris', *AHDLMA* 48 (1981), 97-226; Alan of Lille, *Anticlaudianus*, ed. R. Bossuat, Paris 1955 (Textes philosophiques du Moyen Age, 1). The relevant places in pseudo-Dionysius and Alan of Lille are referred to by R. Haubst, *Das Bild*, 87f.

[78] Bonaventure, *Sent.*, I d. 3 p. 1 dubb. 1 and 3 (Opera Theologica Selecta, 1), 56a-b and 57b; Thomas, *STheol.*, I q. 105 a. 5 c (ed. Leon., 5), 476a-b; Scotus, *De primo principio*, c. 3 concl. 19 n. 45 (ed. Kluxen), 54. For other authors mentioning the triplet, see S. Meier, 'Von der Koinzidenz zur *coincidentia oppositorum*. Zum philosophiehistorischen Hintergrund des Cusanischen Koinzidenzgedankens', *Die Philosophie im 14. Jahrhundert*, ed. O. Pluta, Amsterdam 1988, 321-342, esp. 332f.

[79] Albert the Great, *Ethicorum libri X*, I tract. 5 c. 12 n. 23, ed. A. Borgnet, Vol. 7, Paris

1. What ideas are not

In his *principium* Marsilius listed six properties that allegedly do not belong to divine ideas. Marsilius took his lead from Aristotle's criticism of Plato's theory of ideas. The form in which he presented these negative characteristics is more or less the same as that found in a similar list in Avicenna's *Metaphysics*.[80]

The following properties, according to Marsilius, do *not* belong to divine ideas.[81]

> 1. An idea is not an abstract universal *in essendo*.
> 2. It is not a universal that exists in things and that can be predicated of them under the form of 'humanity', e.g., in the case of man (*communitas in praedicando*).
> 3. It is not an abstract universal that must be assumed as the permanent being underlying the becoming and passing away of singular things.
> 4. It is not a quiddity that can be predicated of singular things (*quidditas singularium*).
> 5. It is not a causal principle that by its eternity produces the individual things that partake in it.
> 6. It is not a universal thing that exists next to singular things such as men, as though man qua man (*homo inquantum homo*) were not something singular, but rather something universal and detached from individual men (*universale abstractum a singularibus*).

These six points clearly show that Marsilius rejected any form of realism with regard to the ideas. Divine ideas are not abstract entities existing outside God or outside singular things in something like a separate *mundus intelligibilis* (compare Augustine's criticism of the Neoplatonic theory of ideas in *De diversis quaest.* 83 q. 46). Nor are they universal quiddities present *in* singular things. Marsilius denied that there is such a 'thing' as universal humanity. If we abstract from all individual properties of Socrates, then Socrates's

---

1891, 72a; Marsilius, *Sent.*, I q. 1 a. 1 (ed. Strasbourg 1501), fol. 2ra. Cf. *Die Rektorbücher der Universität Heidelberg*, 1/2, 498 (269), 498 (271), 499 (281), 505 (335), 506 (344). On the first book of Albert's commentary on the *Ethics*, see Cl. Vansteenkiste, 'Das erste Buch der Nikomachischen Ethik bei Albertus Magnus', *Albertus Magnus doctor universalis 1280/1980*, ed. G. Meyer and A. Zimmermann, Mainz 1980 (Walberger Studien, Philosophische Reihe, 6), 373-384.

In his *Physics*, however, and in several of his other works, Albert attributed this view to Aristotle, referring to the 'classical' locus *Phys.*, II c. 7, 198a24-25. Marsilius's commentary on Aristotle's *Physics* (*Abbreviationes super octo libros physicorum*) at this place mentioned only the coincidence of the *causa efficiens* and the *causa finalis* in the first cause, not the coincidence of the triplet of causes (which was the opinion of Plato, according to Marsilius).

[80] Avicenna, *Liber de philosophia prima*, VII c. 2 (ed. van Riet), 363-366. For Aristotle's criticism of Plato, see W.D. Ross, *Aristotle*, London ⁴1945, 157f; H. Cherniss, *Aristotle's Criticism of Plato and the Academy*, New York 1962, 174-478; W.K.C. Guthrie, *Aristotle. An Encounter*, Cambridge 1981 (A History of Greek Philosophy, 6), 243-246.

[81] *Sent.*, I q. 1 a. 1 (ed. Strasbourg 1501), foll. 1vb-2ra.

humanity will still be singular, being the humanity of Socrates alone.[82]

In his commentary on the *Metaphysics*, Marsilius gave the same negative characterizations of divine ideas, referring to them as attributed by Aristotle to Plato's ideas. He also distinguished there between two opinions (both incorrect, he thought) of writers he called the *antiqui*, concerning the *universale in essendo*. Some of the negative properties recur here. The first opinion, which Marsilius called the *modus platonicus*, is that the *universale in essendo* is a quiddity detached from singular things (compare properties 3, 5 and 6 above). The second opinion, which he attributed to Albert the Great and Thomas Aquinas, is that the *universale in essendo* is not detached from singular things, but exists in the things themselves (compare properties 2 and 4, above).[83]

2. What ideas are

Next to the above negative account, Marsilius also presented a positive account of the nature of divine ideas. He listed twelve positive properties. These were all quoted in the *principium* by Thomas de Strampino.[84]

It is not clear on which sources Marsilius was basing himself here. He himself claimed that it was Dionysius, according to whom the properties derive from the theory of Platonic ideas. Yet Marsilius's account resembles that of pseudo-Dionysius in his *De divinis nominibus* only in a very abstract sense. Moreover, Dionysius did not attribute his account to Plato.[85]

Apparently Marsilius was not drawing on Dionysius but rather on some other source. Indeed, there is remarkable resemblance between Marsilius's account and the explanation of the theory of ideas, attributed to the *platonici*, found in the Latin translation of Eustratius's commentary on the *Nicomachean Ethics*, which gives several of the properties mentioned by Marsilius.[86] We

---

[82] Ibid., fol. 2ra. Marsilius's theory of universal terms is discussed by G. Ritter, *Studien zur Spätscholastik*, 117f.

[83] *Quaestiones super librum Metaphysicorum*, VII q. 15 (Wien, Oesterr. Nationalbibl., CVP, 5297), fol. 106rb-va, and fol. 107rb: "Tertio est notandum quod de universali in essendo apud antiquos duo fuerunt modi. Unus quod essent quiditates separatae a singularibus, et fuit modus Platonis, et est reprobatus in articulo praecedente (cf. foll. 106vb-107ra). Alius modus fuit quod universalia non essent separata, sed essent in rebus singularibus inseparabilia ab eis. Et iste fuit maximorum philosophorum etiam clericorum et Alberti Magni et beati Thomae de Aquino."

[84] Thomas de Strampino, *Principium*, I (Kraków, Bibl. Jag., 1199), foll. 459f.

[85] Marsilius, *Sent.*, I q. 1 a. 1 (ed. Strasbourg 1501), fol. 2rb and fol. 2va (this text is quoted in n. 91 below). Cf. *Dionysiaca. Recueil donnant l'ensemble des traductions latines des ouvrages attribués au Denys de l'Aréopage*, Vol. I, Desclée de Brouwer et Cie 1937, 360f version R (translation of Robert Grosseteste).

[86] Cf. *The Greek Commentaries on the Nicomachean Ethics of Aristotle in the Latin Translation of Robert Grosseteste Bishop of Lincoln († 1253), Vol. I, Eustratius on Book I and the anonymous scholia on books II, III, and IV*, ed. H.P.F. Mercken, Leiden 1973 (Corpus latinum commentariorum in Aristotelem graecorum, 6/1), I c. 7, 68-71. Eustratius's theory of ideas is discussed by K. Giocarinis, 'Eustratius of Nicaea's Defense of the Doctrine of Ideas',

know that Marsilius possessed a copy of Eustratius's commentary, and that he quoted from the first book (where Eustratius explained the Platonic theory of ideas) in his commentary on the *Sentences*.[87] However striking the resemblance may be, and notwithstanding the use of characteristic phrases from the Latin translation, it is difficult to say with any certainty whether or not Marsilius really based himself on Eustratius, particularly as there are also many differences in redaction between the two texts. We should therefore consider the possibility that Marsilius did not base himself on Eustratius directly, but rather on some third text which in turn goes back to Eustratius. A candidate might be the second commentary on the *Ethics* by Albert the Great, which has already been mentioned. Several longer passages from Eustratius's discussion of the Platonic doctrine of ideas were adopted by Albert, and recur in abridged form in Marsilius's text. Moreover, there are no paraphrases from Eustratius that occur in Marsilius but not in Albert. Also, the central notion of *mensura*, not found in Eustratius at this point, occurs in both Albert and Marsilius. Furthermore, it should be noted that Albert, before discussing the properties of the ideas, stated that *Plato* believed in the existence of a divine principle that is one and universal, and that is the *agens* as well as *forma* and *finis* of all things. These are the exact points Marsilius attributed to Plato before entering *his* discussion of the ideas.[88]

All this does not mean, however, that we have now isolated all the sources on which Marsilius based himself. The fact remains that Marsilius himself (repeatedly) claimed that his list of twelve properties was attributed to Plato by Dionysius. It is not unthinkable that Marsilius referred to pseudo-Dionysius because he was using a commentary on his work. From a reference in his *principium*, we may gather that he indeed had an (anonymous) commentary on pseudo-Dionysius at hand. Judging from the quotation given, it may have been the well-known commentary by Robert Grosseteste, who not only wrote a commentary and a translation of *De divinis nominibus*, but also a translation of Eustratius's commentary on the *Ethics*.[89] Further research will be needed to establish whether Marsilius was basing himself here on Grosseteste's

---

FcS 12 (1964), 159-204; A.C. Lloyd, 'The Aristotelianism of Eustratios of Nicaea', *Aristoteles. Werk und Wirkung*, Vol. 2, ed. J. Wiesner, Berlin-New York 1987, 341-351.

[87] Marsilius, *Sent.*, I q. 2 a. 1 (ed. Strasbourg 1501), fol. 11ra. Cf. *Die Rektorbücher der Universität Heidelberg*, 1/2, 489 (190): "Item (477) Eustratius super ix libros ethicorum".

[88] Cf. Albert, *Ethicorum libri X*, I tract. 5 c. 12 n. 23 (ed. Borgnet, 7), 72ab; Marsilius, *Sent.*, I q. 2 a. 1, fol. 2ra.

[89] Marsilius, *Sent.*, I q. 1. a. 1 (ed. Strasbourg 1501), fol. 4rb: "(I)n commento super primo capitulo De divinis nominibus dicitur: '*In mente divina praeexistunt ab aeterno aeternae rationes omnium creandorum in quibus realiter omnia vivunt et ex quarum fulgoribus omnes cognitiones illustrantur*'." The text in italics recurs *verbatim* in the first chapter of Grosseteste's commentary on *De divinis nominibus* as edited in F. Ruello, 'La *divinorum nominum reseratio* selon Robert Grossetête et Albert le Grand', *AHDLMA* 34 (1959), 134-171, esp. 156 n. 59. For the works of Grosseteste, see J. McEvoy, *The Philosophy of Robert Grosseteste*, Oxford 1982, Appendix A, 455-504, esp. 470.

commentary (the edition of which is still incomplete), or on one of the other commentaries on *De divinis nominibus*.[90]

Leaving aside the question of sources, we now turn to the properties Marsilius attributed to divine ideas. He listed the following twelve. Properties that are also found in Albert as well as in Eustratius are marked with a star (*).

> 1*. The ideas are *per se stantes*: they do not exist in anything (they are one with God)
> 2*. They are distinct from the things. They exist in the divine mind before things exist (*ante rem*). When things come into existence, they do not mingle with them. When things cease to be (*post rem*), they persist.
> 3. They differ from one another because they represent different things. On account of their difference there are differences in the created world.
> 4*. They are the terminating point (*terminus*) toward which all dependent creatures are directed (*referentur*). For a creature to be perfect is for it to be as it is represented by the idea.
> 5*. The ideas are universal with regard to their causality, for all things are produced by them (that is, by God's essence).
> 6*. They are perfect (*totae*), coinciding completely with God.
> 7*. They are intellectual. They illuminate the intellects of other beings without being illuminated themselves (*illuminantes non illuminatae*).
> 8*. They stand above all things and are wholly immutable (*superstantes et supererectae*), for they exist in God.
> 9*. They depend on nothing else (they are *principales*)
> 10*. They are the formal and final cause of the creatures. They determine every creature's form and the way it strives toward God.
> 11*. They are the generating principles (*conditrices*).
> 12*. They are the examples (*notiones exemplares*) in accordance to which the things are produced.[91]

---

[90] A listing of medieval commentaries on pseudo-Dionysius is provided by B. Faes de Mottoni, *Il 'Corpus Dionysiacum' nel Medioevo, Rassegna di studi: 1900-1972*, Società editrice il mulino 1977 (Pubblicazioni del centro di studio per la storia della storiografia filosofica 3), 14f. The commentary of Albert the Great, *Super Dionysium De divinis nominibus*, ed. P. Simon, Opera omnia 37/1, Münster 1972, was not used by Marsilius on this point.

[91] *Sent.*, I q. 1 a. 1 (ed. Strasbourg 1501), fol. 2rb-va (words that appear both in Eustratius and Albert are in *italics*; words that appear only in Albert are in CAPITALS): "His praemissis Plato de ideis secundum mentem beati Dionysii has conditiones videtur attribuisse: Primam, quod sunt *hypostatice*, id *est* persistentes *sive per se* stantes, quia nulli inhaerent. Secundam, quod sunt *separatae*, quia sunt *in mente Dei* ante rem praecedentes, post rem remanentes et quando res est non commiscentur ei. Tertiam, quod sunt differentiae, quia diversa repraesentant et earum diversa repraesentatione ad extra mundus in partibus suis diversificatus est. Quartam, quod sunt terminativae dependentiae omnium rerum, quia omnia dependentia *referuntur ad eas* tamquam ad suos terminos. Tunc enim est aliquid perfectum in suo esse cum fuerit tale quale ipsum sua idea repraesentat esse debere. Quintam, quod *essent universales*, non intelligatur in essendo vel praedicando, sed causando, quia singula a sua idea producuntur. Immo ut dicetur, essentia ideae Deus est qui in causando universalissimus est. Sextam, esse *tota* non partialia, quia ex quo sunt in Deo, sunt tota. Nihil enim Dei imperfectum est sed totum est. Et merito tota vocantur, quia ab eis est tota perfectio participata, sive sit individualis sive specifica sive generalis. Ipsae vero non ab alio, sed quoad se Deus sunt, a quo omnia alia sunt. Septimam, *intellectuales esse*, id est intellectus, aliorum ILLUminantes *et non intelligibiles*, id est non illuminatae vel illuminabiles. Octavam, quod sunt *superstantes et supererectae*, id

Of particular interest is the third property in this list. This item was not given by either Eustratius or Albert the Great, but is found in John of Ripa and other Paris theologians of the second half of the fourteenth century. It was discussed at some length by Marsilius elsewhere in his *principium*.[92]

Reaction to the views of some other theologians

Apart from the twelve properties, Marsilius's *principium* also discussed the theories of the ideas of Thomas Aquinas, Henry of Ghent, Duns Scotus, William of Ockham, as well as the view of an *anonymus*. Because of the nature of the lecture, which was celebratory and public, we may assume that the views of the theologians that were mentioned by name were commonly known and respected at the time (1392), at least at Heidelberg. This was certainly true of Scotus and Ockham, whose view Marsilius called the *opinio quorundam valentium*.[93] It was therefore to Ockham's view that Marsilius devoted most of his attention; he did not discuss any arguments peculiar to Scotus, because he took Scotus's opinion to be the same as Ockham's.

The fame enjoyed by the theory of ideas of Scotus and Ockham stretched far beyond Heidelberg and the 1390s. Fifteen years before, when Peter of Candia composed his commentary on the *Sentences* in Paris, the views of Scotus and Ockham were discussed at large. Ockham's theory of ideas was also quoted in *De universalibus* by John Wyclif, written in England in 1373 or 1374, in the commentary on the *Sentences* by Peter of Ailly, and in the *Notulae* by Jean Gerson, written around 1400.[94]

est omnimode immutabiles, quia in Deo. Nonam, quod sunt *principales*, quia quodlibet duplex potest habere esse: formale quod est dependens, et virtuale sive principale, quia illud est a quo dependet. Decimam, quod omnibus rebus dependentibus *dant numerum* inquantum sunt earum efficientes MENSURAM, inquantum sunt formales earum. Non quod Plato voluerit quod essent verae formae informantes, sed quod iuxta earum repraesentationem Deus rebus daret formam et mensuram. Item, quod dant modum inquantum sunt finales causae. Dant enim singulis modum tendendi in finem. Sic enim et praecise eo modo res dependens naturaliter in Deum tendit quomodo idea secundum quam producta est sibi inidit. Undecimam, quod sunt verae *conditrices* sicut principia effectiva. Unde beatus Augustinus libro 83 Quaestionum quaestione <46>: 'Ratione alia conditus est homo et alia equus', non quod velit quod alia sit in se, sed in repraesentatione in ordine ad obiectum quod praenoscitur et ad extra producitur. Et ultimam sive duodecimam, quod sunt *notiones exemplares*, quia res productae in ordine ad earum repraesentationem producuntur. Haec et his similia secundum beatum Dionysium libro praedicto sumpta sunt ex imaginatione Platonis."

[92] See the references in n. 72 above. Cf. Marsilius, *Sent.*, I q. 1 a. 3, fol. 8va-9ra.

[93] Marsilius, *Sent.*, I q. 1, fol. 2va. Marsilius did not deal with the opinions of his *socii* (Heilmann of Wunnenberg and Johannes Holzadel), which is rather remarkable, as it is against the regulations for delevering a *principium* in Heidelberg. I have discussed this problem in my 'Neuplatonismus' (forthcoming).

[94] John Wyclif, *Tractatus de universalibus*, c. 15, ed. I.J. Mueller, Oxford 1985, 359 (for the dating, see ibid., xix-xxx); Peter of Ailly, *Quaestiones super libros Sententiarum*, I q. 6 a. 3, Strasbourg 1490, repr. Frankfurt am Main 1968, fol. 14rbT-<16>rbDD; Jean Gerson, *Notulae super quaedam verba Dionysii de Caelesti hierarchia*, as cited by A. Combes, *Jean Gerson*, 44 and 319 (for the dating, see ibid., 420). For Peter of Candia, see n. 69 above.

A significant point of difference between Peter of Candia and Marsilius of Inghen is the fact that the latter simply equated the views of Scotus and Ockham, whereas the former also detected a noticeable difference between them. According to Peter of Candia, the opinions of Scotus and Ockham converge to the extent that they both assume a plurality of ideas that are distinct from divine essence. They differ, however, in that Scotus's distinction between the ideas was based on the differences between quiddities, whereas Ockham's was based on the differences between the actually existing creatures.[95] According to Marsilius, on the other hand, both Scotus and Ockham believed that the idea is the creature known in God. Perhaps he was led to this conclusion by Ockham's remark, referred to above, that Scotus was right in his criticism of Henry of Ghent.[96]

Marsilius did, however, perceive a clear difference between the views of Scotus and Ockham, on the one hand, and those of Thomas Aquinas and Henry of Ghent, on the other. The latter two, he claimed, believed that the idea is the divine essence, whereas the former two held that that idea is the creature that can be produced by divine essence (*creatura producibilis*).[97]

It is curious that Marsilius meticulously indicated where these views of Thomas, Henry of Ghent, and Ockham could be found.[98] When quoting the opinions of other authors, he usually omitted such detailed references. A possible explanation of this unexpected precision would be that Marsilius had in his library two of the three works quoted, viz., the first part of Thomas Aquinas's *Summa Theologiae* and the *Quodlibeta* by Henry of Ghent.[99] Ockham's commentary on the *Sentences* is missing from his inventory of books. Yet this does not mean that Marsilius did not have first-hand knowledge of Ockham's position. His extensive discussion of it, which also included Ockham's reply to a series of objections, closely follows Ockham's own text, and we may thus gather that Marsilius had a copy of Ockham's work at hand. It was by no means unusual to use works that were not part of one's own library (bear in mind that few theologians had a library as large as Marsilius's). In the case of Marsilius we also know, for instance, that he repeatedly quoted from the commentary on the *Sentences* of Giles of Rome, although this work does not appear in his library's inventory either.

---

[95] See the text quoted by A. Combes, *Un inédit*, 59 (Paris, Bibl. Nat., lat., nouv. acq. 1467, fol. 99vb).
[96] Marsilius, *Sent.*, I q. 1 a. 1 (ed. Strasbourg 1501), fol. 2va. Cf. Ockham, *Scriptum*, I d. 35 q. 4 (OTh, 4), 467.
[97] Marsilius, *Sent.*, I q. 1 a. 1, fol. 2va.
[98] Ibid.
[99] *Die Rektorbücher der Universität Heidelberg*, 1/2, 476 (82) and 477 (89).

Marsilius's criticism of Ockham

According to Marsilius, the central moment in Ockham's view was his claim that Augustine's description of the ideas fits not divine essence but rather the known creatures. In his explication and quotations, Marsilius accurately captured Ockham's position in great detail. He did not fail to mention Ockham's contention that it is possible for a creature to be the idea of itself.

As for the rationale behind the position of Scotus and Ockham, Marsilius suggested that it might have been their view that the idea is the luminescence (*relucentia*) of the creature in God. In Ockham's case, this strikes us as incorrect: Ockham did not speak of *relucentia* with regard to the ideas. In the case of Scotus, however, notwithstanding the fact that he did not use the term either, Marsilius's suggestion seems to capture fairly well the essence of his position. It is interesting to note here that John of Ripa, in his estimate of the position of Scotus, used this very notion of *relucere*, which suggests that Marsilius may have been following John of Ripa.[100]

Ockham's view that the idea coincides with the creature was criticized by Marsilius on four points.[101] (Remember that Marsilius held that the ideas coincide with God's essence.) First, summarizing what he took to be the position of Augustine and pseudo-Dionysius, Marsilius stated that an idea is the ground of knowledge of a thing (*ratio cognoscendi rem*), or the example used in producing a thing (*exemplar producendi*). *Pace* Ockham, neither of these claims fits the produced thing (creature) itself. Therefore, the creature cannot be an idea of itself.

Second, if the Antichrist-to-be, (the being to be produced in the future) is the idea of his own producibility (*producibilitas*), then 'idea' is used as an ampliative term (*terminus ampliativus*), viz., as a term denoting not only present things (the standard meaning qua tense), but also future ones. The future Antichrist does not yet exist. Hence, the term 'idea' cannot denote a real (present) Antichrist, but only the Antichrist's exemplar in God. Therefore, idea and creature do not coincide.[102]

Third, when producing the creatures, God is looking at his essence, because the creatures are produced in its image. God's ideas of the creatures must therefore coincide with divine essence, and not with the creatures themselves.

Finally, on Ockham's view, Marsilius inferred, the idea of producing a

---

[100] Marsilius, *Sent.*, I q. 1 a. 1 (ed. Strasbourg 1501), fol. 2va: "(F)orte moventur ex hoc quod idea est relucentia creaturarum in Deo. Et huiusmodi relucentia non videtur esse nisi ipsae creaturae cognitae in ipso." Cf. Scotus, *Lectura*, I d. 35 q. u. n. 33 (ed. Vat., 17), 456; *Ordinatio*, I d. 36 q. u. n. 41 (ed. Vat., 6), 287. Compare John of Ripa, *Sent.*, I d. 35 a. 4 (Paris, Bibl. Nat., lat., 15.369), fol. 306ra, as cited by A. Combes, *Jean Gerson*, 620: "(D)icit (Scotus, *MH*) quod ydee sunt ipsemet creature secundum quod ipsemet obiectiue relucent in diuina mente (...)."

[101] *Sent.*, I q. 1 a. 1 (ed. Strasbourg 1501), fol. 3ra-rb.

[102] For Marsilius's use of ampliative terms, see E.P. Bos, *Marsilius of Inghen*, 100 and 213.

stone must either be identical with the stone itself, or with the stone insofar as it is known by God. If the former, then God must look beyond himself, which is in contradiction with the position of Augustine, quoted by Ockham himself. If the latter, then the idea of its production is not the stone itself, but rather God's foreknowledge of the stone.

This criticism of the theory of ideas shows that Marsilius disagreed with Ockham on an important aspect of the problem of divine knowledge. Although Ockham's theory of ideas was criticized by other theologians as well, for instance by John Wyclif, who also criticized the *discipuli istius opinionis*, there is no reason to suspect that Marsilius's criticism was simply common practice, or a mere echo of the criticism vented by Lutterell and the papal committee: he openly and publicly referred to Ockham's view as a *opinio valentis*.[103] Moreover, toward the end of the fourteenth century and at the beginning of the fifteenth century there was an atmosphere of distinct sympathy for Ockham's position among several theologians. His view was extensively quoted and largely adopted by Peter of Ailly, and Jean Gerson, in his early works, even hailed it as the unity to which most of the views on ideas could be reduced.[104]

The position of Marsilius

After delivering his criticism of Ockham, Marsilius proceeded to expound his own view, which again betrays the important though possibly indirect influence of pseudo-Dionysius.

Marsilius distinguished between three respects in which the ideas may be considered:

1. as forms of knowledge (*formae cognoscendi*),
2. as examples (*exemplaria*) used by the maker in producing the creatures,
3. as the maker's act of volition (*voluntates*) or decision (*electiones*) to produce something according to the idea.[105]

While the first two of these descriptions contain nothing new, the third does. Marsilius's outspoken and direct link between the idea and the will of God is lacking in most of the thirteenth- and fourteenth-century thinkers discussed above. Only Thomas Aquinas provides a clear example of a kindred

---

[103] *Sent.*, I q. 1 a. 1 (ed. Strasbourg 1501), fol. 2va. For Wyclif's criticism, see John Wyclif, *Tractatus de universalibus*, c. 15 (ed. Mueller), 359-71. Cf. V. Herold, 'Wyclifs Polemik gegen Ockhams Auffassung der platonischen Ideen und ihr Nachklang in der tschechischen hussitischen Philosophie', *From Ockham to Wyclif*, ed. A. Hudson and M. Wilks, Oxford 1987 (Studies in Church History, Subsidia, 5), 185-215. See also John Wyclif, *On universals (Tractatus de Universalibus)*, transl. A. Kenny, introd. P.V. Spade, Oxford 1985, vii-xlvii; A. Kenny, 'The Realism of the *De universalibus*', *Wyclif in his Times*, ed. A. Kenny, Oxford 1986, 17-29.

[104] Peter of Ailly, *Sent.*, I q. 6 a. 3 (ed. Strasbourg 1490), foll. 14rbT-<16>rbDD. For Gerson, see the texts cited by A. Combes, *Jean Gerson*, 202 n. 1.

[105] Marsilius, *Sent.*, I q. 1 a. 1 (ed. Strasbourg 1501), fol. 3vb.

association. The classical source for this link between idea and will is *De divinis nominibus* by pseudo-Dionysius, who called the ideas 'θελήματα', rendered as 'voluntates' in all medieval translations, which is also the term Marsilius used.[106]

Marsilius's reason, in light of his overall system of thought, for drawing this link between idea and will should probably be sought in his conviction that the ideas completely coincide with God's essence; being one with God's essence they must also coincide with his will. Interestingly, Peter of Ailly in his commentary on the *Sentences* called this point, viz., that the ideas coincide with God's essence, the one on which the *antiqui doctores* were in agreement.[107] If this view can be said to represent the common opinion at the end of the fourteenth century, this means that Marsilius's theory of ideas was probably viewed as 'ancient' by his contemporaries.

The ideas are neither really nor formally distinct

In creating, Marsilius believed, God is not looking at individual *exemplaria*, but rather at his essence. God's essence itself is the idea of every individual creature. As God has intuitive knowledge of his own essence, he can at once distinguish all the perfections it contains, without the slightest division in his act of knowledge. Marsilius used an example to illustrate this last point. The same intuitive act of knowledge by virtue of which Socrates is known, at once also includes knowledge of all his properties. This single act of knowledge is more perfect than the collection of acts by which the properties are known individually. Since God is perfect in every way, the act of knowledge by which he knows his essence must be as described.[108]

Marsilius briefly criticized two competing views in this connection: first, that the ideas in God are really distinct, and second, that they are intrinsically or formally distinct. The first of these views was held by Peter of Ailly, who like Ockham believed that the ideas of the creatures are the creatures themselves. As the creatures are really distinct, he argued, so must be the ideas in God.[109]

As for the second view, Marsilius's criticism was probably directed against John of Ripa, as may be gathered from the following considerations. When Marsilius speaks of ideas that are formally or intrinsically distinct, he means ideas that are different in such a way that the one is not the other, that is, the essence (*essentia*) of the one idea is not the same as that of the other. The terminology here is very close to that used by John of Ripa in his description of the distinction between divine ideas: they are formally distinct,

---

[106] *Dionysiaca*, I, 360. Cf. Thomas, *Sent.*, I d. 39 q. 1 a. 2 ad 1 (ed. Mandonnet, 1), 923.
[107] Peter of Ailly, *Sent.*, I q. 6 a. 3 (ed. Strasbourg 1490), fol. 14rbT.
[108] Marsilius, *Sent.*, I q. 1 a. 1 (ed. Strasbourg 1501), fol. 3va.
[109] Marsilius, *Sent.*, I q. 1 a. 1, fol. 3vb; Peter of Ailly, *Sent.*, I q. 6 a. 3 (ed. Strasbourg 1490), fol. <15>raY.

as he put it, in that they exist intrinsically in divine essence as distinct *rationes essentiales*. The conceptual correspondence to the position criticized by Marsilius is obvious. Moreover, we know that Marsilius was familiar with John of Ripa's commentary on the *Sentences*. Finally, Ripa's theory of ideas enjoyed considerable fame at the time (which for Marsilius may have been a reason to respond to it), as is testified by the fact that it was quoted by Peter of Candia and Jean Gerson.[110]

The ideas are extrinsece et obiectivaliter *distinct*

Although Marsilius was basically of the opinion that the ideas in God are identical and one, he also thought it proper to say that they are *extrinsece et obiectivaliter* distinct in the mind of God. Yet this difference between the ideas, and their concomitant plurality, is not due to any distinction within God's essence, which is ruled out by the unity of divine essence. Rather, it is a consequence of the differences between the creatures produced by God (which is why Marsilius spoke of an *extrinsece* distinction), and of the fact that they are known by him as different (hence: *obiectivaliter*). God knows that he is the cause of infinitely many differences between the creatures; that is why his mind contains infinitely many different ideas.[111]

It has been argued recently that with the above construction Marsilius placed the thoughts in God's mind at the level of *kinds*. This is by no means obvious, however. Marsilius nowhere addressed the problem from this angle, nor can it be "clearly inferred from his severe criticism of Ockham".[112] Marsilius did not criticize Ockham's view that God has ideas of the individuals. The fifth property in Marsilius's account of the ideas (that they are universal with regard to their causality) could be called upon in support of this claim, but the fact remains that Marsilius did not develop it into a criticism of Ockham. Of more importance in this connection seems to be Marsilius's view that the existence of ideas is bound up with divine causality, and that God is the cause of singular things. Seen in this light, we are inclined to argue rather the opposite, viz., that it probably was Marsilius's view that God *does* have ideas of singular things.[113]

---

[110] Marsilius, *Sent.*, I q. 1 a. 1, fol. 3vb. Cf. John of Ripa, *Conclusiones*, I d. 35 q. u. a. 1 nn. 1 and 3 (ed. Combes), 210f; A. Combes, *Un inédit*, 53-55. As for the quotations by Peter of Candia and Gerson, see Combes, *Un inédit*, 59f (Peter); *Jean Gerson*, 203 (Gerson).

[111] Ibid., fol. 4rb.

[112] E.P. Bos, 'Marsilius van Inghen en 'mogelijke werelden'', *Algemeen Nederlands Tijdschrift voor Wijsbegeerte* 75 (1983), 9.

[113] The opinion that God does not have ideas of singular things, even if it was not held by Marsilius, does occur in the work of other theologians of the second half of the fourteenth century. According to John of Ripa, e.g., God does not know the individual thing with an idea of its own, but only through the essential *rationes* of things (the ideas of universal essences). See John of Ripa, *Sent.*, I d. 38 q. 2 a. 3, as cited by H. Schwamm, *Magistri Ioannis de Ripa OFM doctrina de praescientia divina*, Rome 1930 (Analecta Gregoriana, 1), 36-38.

CHAPTER SIX

DIVINE FOREKNOWLEDGE AND FUTURE CONTINGENTS
FIRST PART: THE PERIOD 1250-1330

One of the most intriguing problems with regard to God's knowledge is the question of how God has knowledge of contingent events, and in particular how he has knowledge of man's free acts of will. This is also a most difficult question to answer. It has at least two troublesome aspects: on the one hand, the ontological status of the contingent, and on the other, the epistemological nature of divine knowledge.

The notion of a 'contingent thing' (*res contingens*), for medieval thinkers, covered both objects and events. We will follow medieval usage in this respect, except where the exposition demands otherwise. A common conceptual delineation of the contingent in the Middle Ages determined it as that which is neither impossible, like a square circle, nor necessary, like the existence of God. A contingent thing may or may not exist or happen (i.e., it is possible), but it does not necessarily exist or happen (i.e., its negation is not impossible). That the contingent is not necessarily the case precludes both that it necessarily exists *at all times*, as in the case of God, and that it necessarily exists *periodically* or *from time to time*, as in the case of the solar eclipse.[1]

Contingent things happen occasionally and are therefore by definition subject to change. As opposed to necessary things that happen periodically, such as the solar eclipse, the contingent is indeterminate and fortuitous. There are no causes from which the existence of a contingent being can be infallibly deduced. This indeterminacy and mutability has far-reaching consequences for the intelligiblity of the contingent. Conceptions of knowledge in the Middle Ages were still heavily constrained by the classical Platonic and Aristotelian idea that scientific knowledge can only treat of what is necessary and immutable (the universal). Against this background, the claim that God has knowledge of the contingent (the singular and the individual) was faced with tremendous difficulties.[2] Moreover, it was generally acknowledged that the contingent can only be known through the senses. Yet God does not possess any senses, for he is pure spirit. So how can he know the contingent? For some traditions, such as that of the classical Peripatetics (Alexander of

---

[1] For the medieval notion of contingency, see K. Jacobi, *Die Modalbegriffe in den logischen Schriften des Wilhelm von Shyreswood und in anderen Kompendien des 12. und 13. Jahrhunderts*, Leiden-Köln 1980 (STGM, 13), 71-95.

[2] The influence of this Platonic and Aristotelian idea of scientific knowledge is dealt with in C. Bérubé, *La connaissance*, 13-68.

Aphrodisias), this was reason enough to deny that the deity has knowledge of the contingent.

The various problems that beset the nature of divine knowledge in this context can best be illustrated by means of the following traditional example. How can the Antichrist's freedom to sin be reconciled with the special character of divine knowledge? God is omniscient and perfect. Therefore he must know each contingent thing, including the sinning of the Antichrist at some future moment t_F. Now, God's knowledge is also eternal and immutable. This means that God must know before moment t_F that the Antichrist will sin at t_F. But then it is no longer clear that the sinning of the Antichrist is still contingent. For if he sins contingently, this means that it is possible that he does not sin. Suppose now that in point of fact he does not sin at time t_F. Then God was wrong, which is impossible because of his perfection. Nor is it possible for God to correct his knowledge when moment t_F comes along, since his knowledge is immutable. In sum, then, it is impossible that the Antichrist should act otherwise than foreseen by God. The nature of God's knowledge seems to imply of necessity that what he knows will ineluctably happen.

From Antiquity, the conundrum of accomodating divine foreknowledge with the existence of the contingent, and with human freedom in particular, was seen as an extremely difficult and arduous problem. Cicero's musings on the subject in his *De fato* are well-known. As for the Middle Ages, Ockham's dark words may serve as emblematic: "No man is able to explain how God knows the contingent". Similar despairing remarks are found in such writers as Adam Wodeham, Gregory of Rimini, and Marsilius of Inghen. Many contemporary authors still are skeptical of finding a satisfactory solution to the problem.[3]

The problem of divine foreknowledge will be examined in the next two chapters. In this chapter we shall focus first on the period between 1250 and 1330. After presenting the main sources from Antiqiuity and early Middle Ages that set the scene for later discussion, we shall examine the positions of Thomas Aquinas, Duns Scotus, and William of Ockham, as well as the reception of their views. Characteristic of this period, which lasted until the early fourteenth century, was the treatment of the question of foreknowledge as simply one of the many problems pertaining to divine knowledge, without according it any special attention. This tended to change in the works that originated in England from ca. 1330 onward, and on the continent from ca. 1340 onward. In these newer works the issue of foreknowledge became the foremost problem with regard to divine knowledge generally, tending to

---

[3] Ockham, *Scriptum*, I d. 38 q. u. (OTh, 4), 583f. The views of Wodeham, Gregory of Rimini and Marsilius will be discussed in the next chapter. As for the skepticism of some contemporary authors, see A. Kenny, *The God of the Philosophers*, Oxford ²1986, 87; J.L. Walls, 'A Fable of Foreknowledge and Freedom', *Philosophy* 62 (1987), 67-75.

overshadow many other traditional questions. Leading thinkers in this period were Gregory of Rimini and Marsilius of Inghen, who will be the subject of our next chapter.

The main sources

A number of sources were responsible for the particular form the problem of divine foreknowledge assumed in the thirteenth and fourteenth centuries. Most important among them were Aristotle, Augustine, Boethius, Anselm, and the treatises on the fallacies. These sources played a role in the analysis of the problem, and contributed some of the answers that gained general acceptance. We shall briefly review some of the most relevant aspects of these analyses.

Aristotle

By far the best known of the sources, in particular with regard to the logical aspects of the problem, was Aristotle's *Perihermeneias*. In this work (c. 9) Aristotle distinguished between the truth conditions of singular judgments about the future on the one hand, and those of singular judgments about past or present on the other. If assertions about the future are true in the same manner as those about past or present, then everything happens by necessity and there can be no freedom. The argument proceeds by linking the truth of assertions with the factuality of events. For assertions about the *present* the following holds:

> If it is true that A is white, then it is necessary that A is white. For if A is not white, then 'A is white' is false.

Now, if this same rule is applied to assertions about the *future*, we get:

> If it has always been true that A will be white, then it is necessary that A will be white. For if A will not be white, then 'A will be white' has been false.

The conclusion would be that A's whiteness is necessary.[4]

Aristotle did not accept the conclusion that all things happen of necessity. To escape from the above argument, he attributed different truth conditions to judgments about the future from those applied to judgments about present or past. It is difficult to explain which truth conditions he had in mind in these

---

[4] For a discussion of Aristotle's reasoning, see the literature mentioned in W.L. Craig, *The Problem of Divine Foreknowledge*, 281-283. See also G. Fine, 'Truth and Necessity in De interpretatione 9', *History of Philosophy Quarterly* 1 (1984), 23-47; J. van Eck, 'Another Interpretation of Aristotle's De interpretatione IX. A Support for the so-called second oldest or 'mediaeval' interpretation', *Vivarium* 26 (1988), 19-38.

texts, partly because of their brevity, partly because of the fact that he lacked a clear technical vocabulary. Modern secondary literature is still divided on the issue, particularly with regard to the question of whether Aristotle relinquished the principle of bivalence (every proposition P is either true or false) and that of the excluded middle (of every pair of contradictory propositions, precisely one is true) with regard to singular contingent propositions.

J.L. Ackrill has distinguished between two interpretations that are equally supported by Aristotle's text.[5] According to the first interpretation, Aristotle accepted the principle of the excluded middle for assertions about the future: necessarily, either P or not-P is true. Unlike assertions about present or past, however, a judgement P about the future is neither necessarily true (if true), nor necessarily false (if false). Assertions about the future have truth values, but these are still indeterminate. It is not known beforehand whether P is true or false. Now, the future would indeed be necessary if P had a predetermined truth value. But P's truth value is indeterminate, so this does not follow. This is the interpretation of Aristotle that was favored by Thomas Aquinas. Notice that expressions such as 'determinate' and 'indeterminate' truth values were not used by Aristotle himself. They are found in the commentaries on the *Perihermeneias* by Ammonius and Boethius, and were also used by Thomas in his explanation of Aristotle.[6]

According to the second interpretation mentioned by Ackrill, assertions about the future do not have truth values at all. If P is true, then what is described by P will necessarily happen. On this reading of Aristotle, truth values immediately imply necessity. The only escape from a wholly necessary future is to deny that assertions about the future have truth values. This was the explanation given by Peter Aureoli. He argued that Aristotle relinquished the principle of bivalence with regard to assertions about the future.[7] Notice, though, that there is a residual problem now, no matter which of the two interpretations we choose: if assertions about the future have either indeterminate truth values or none at all, then how can God possibly know them?

---

[5] J.L. Ackrill, *Aristotle's Categories and De interpretatione*, transl. with notes and glossary, Oxford [7]1979 (Clarendon Aristotle Series), 139-142.

[6] Thomas, *Expositio libri Peryermenias*, I lect. 15, editio altera retractata, ed. Leon., 1*/1, Rome-Paris 1989, 81b-82a. For other medieval advocates of this reading of Aristotle, see N. Rescher, *Essays in Philosophical Analysis*, Pittsburg 1969, 278f. The contribution of Ammonius and Boethius is discussed in R. Sorabji, *Necessity, Cause, and Blame. Perspectives on Aristotle's Theory*, London 1980, 93; M.F. Lowe, 'Aristotle on the Sea-Battle. A Clarification', *Analysis* 40 (1980), 55-59, esp. 58.

[7] See the text edited in Ph. Boehner, *Tractatus de praedestinatione et de praescientia Dei et de futuris contingentibus of William Ockham*, St. Bonaventure, New York 1945 (Franciscan Institute Publications, 2), 119.

A related issue on which Aristotle was regularly quoted was that of the necessity of the past. Aristotle had claimed that it is impossible even for God to undo the past (*Ethica Nicomachea*, VI c. 2, 1139b5-11). Philosophers in the thirteenth and fourteenth centuries tended to agree with him. They considered it contradictory that a thing that existed at some past moment t_p should later cease to have existed at t_p. Two contradictory assertions would then both be true, viz., 'X was at t_p' and 'X was not at t_p'. It is beyond God's power to realize such contradictions. The claim that the past can be undone is therefore simply absurd.[8]

There was a special application of this argument to divine knowledge. If God has foreknowledge, then his knowledge has the necessity of the past. God knew beforehand that A was going to happen. His knowledge of A is therefore an event in the past, and hence is necessary even before A actually takes place.[9]

A weaker claim that was discussed particularly in the fourteenth century was that after moment t_p, God may still be said to have the *possibility* to *not* make A happen at t_p. The question here is not whether the past can *actually* be undone, or more precisely, whether the past can be *redone* with reversed truth value, as discussed above, but rather whether the freedom God had before A took place is retained after t_p. Some fourteenth-century thinkers took the position that God's eternity precludes his losing the possibility to act otherwise than how he did act. All moments in time are to God's eternity as the present is to us. We human beings cannot change the past, but our actions in present and future are free. The freedom we have with regard to the present and the future is that which God has with regard to the past. Hence past and future are equally contingent to God, and God retains the possibility to act differently from the way he did even with regard to that which has already happened. This was the position of Bradwardine, Gregory of Rimini, and Peter of Ailly.[10]

This argument suggests that God's knowledge is as contingent as the future, in spite of the fact that it is eternal and immutable. The necessity of the past does not apply to God's knowledge. Though God knows from eternity that A will happen in the future, and even though his knowledge belongs (quasi) to the past, he still has the possibility to have foreknown a different future.

---

[8] This argument was used by, among others, Thomas Aquinas, *STheol.*, I q. 25 a. 4 (ed. Leon., 4), 295b-296a. On the necessity of the past, with references to Aristotle, see R. Sorabji, *Necessity*, 105; C.G. Normore, 'Divine Omniscience, Omnipotence, and Future Contingents', ed. T. Rudavsky, *Divine Omniscience*, 3-22, esp. 3-9. For the medieval view, cf. W.J. Courtenay, *Covenant and Causality in Medieval Thought*, London 1984 (Variorum Reprints), VIIIb, 165f.

[9] Thus for example in Thomas, *STheol.*, I q. 14 a. 13 ad 2, 186b.

[10] The relevant passages are referred to by W.J. Courtenay, *Covenant and Causality*, VIIIb,

Augustine

Philosophers in the Middle Ages saw in Augustine the paradigm of what a truly Christian view of divine foreknowledge should be like: accomodating *both* God's foreknowledge *and* man's freedom.[11] Augustine's example served as a permanent constraint on the theory of divine knowledge. Marsilius of Inghen spoke of a 'rein' (*frenum*) in this connection. It became something like a vow that was pledged at the outset of a discussion of divine knowledge, particularly in the second half of the fourteenth century. Philosophers such as Thomas of Strasbourg and Marsilius referred to Augustine's canon to make their purpose clear: man's freedom should not be sacrificed to the certainty of God's knowledge, nor vice versa.

Another important function of Augustine's work was that it communicated the views of Cicero and of the Stoics. The first became the representative of the position that God cannot have knowledge of the contingent because of human freedom. The view of the Stoics came to epitomize the opposite line of thought that from the certainty of God's knowledge it follows that everything happens of necessity.[12]

Finally, Augustine believed that man is not free *in spite of* God's foreknowledge but rather *because* of it. Man's acts are free because of his will. Now, if someone does not have full control of his will, then his will is no longer truly will, and he ceases to be free. So if God foreknows that someone *wills* something, this means that it is willed *freely*. The certainty of God's foreknowledge certifies that man will use his will, and thus that he is free. This argument was often used in connection with the transcendence of God's causality, as by Thomas Aquinas, who stated it as follows: God is the cause of all being, including contingent being. Therefore God is not an impediment for contingency, but rather a warrant that contingent events will indeed happen contingently.[13]

Boethius

In his commentary on the *Perihermeneias*, Boethius interpreted Aristotle as saying that assertions about past and present have determinate truth values, whereas the truth value of contingent assertions about the future is indeterminate. The truth value is determinate if factuality has made it irreversible.

149f (Bradwardine), 154-165 and 174a (Gregory), 162f n. 151 (Peter of Ailly). For the background of this view in Lombard, see id., *Capacity and Volition*, 53f.

[11] Augustine, *De civitate Dei*, V c. 9, Opera Pars 14/1, Turnhout 1955 (CCSL, 47), 138: "(E)t Deum dicimus omnia scire antequam fiant, et uoluntate nos facere, quidquid a nobis non nisi uolentibus fieri sentimus et novimus."

[12] Ibid., cc. 8-9, 130-140. Cf. Thomas of Strasbourg, *Sent.*, I d. 40 q. 1 a. 3 (ed. Venice 1564), fol. 110va-vb; Conrad of Soltau, *Sent.*, I (Stuttgart, Württ. Landesbibl., Cod. Theol. Fol., 118), fol. 48rb.

[13] Thomas, *Expositio libri Peryermenias*, I lect. 14 (ed. Leon., 1*/1), 78b-79a. Cf. Augus-

Assertions about the future are determinately true or false only in case their truth value has already been fixed.[14] This view was adopted by many philosophers of the thirteenth and fourteenth centuries, including Marsilius of Inghen.

Another important point in Boethius was that the human will is the basis of all forms of contingency. Even chance (*casus*) is not a natural phenomenon but the result of an interaction between nature and the human will. In nature itself everything happens of necessity. Some of these necessary events intervene in the life of man in unexpected ways, as when a falling stone hits a person who happens to be passing by. Had that person not decided to take this particular road, then the stone would not have hit him. The stone fell necessarily, but that it hit the man was a coincidence. A similarly strict use of terms like 'coincidence' and 'contingency' to refer only to human acts of will and their consequences can be found in many fourteenth-century philosophers, including Ockham, Francis of Marchia (OFM, † after 1344), and the author of the commentary on the *Physics* that was printed under the name of Marsilius.[15]

In *De consolatione*, Boethius devoted an entire book to questions of providence and divine foreknowledge (Lib. V). His account there was to be of enormous influence, as was the entire work. We shall briefly review four the points he made that are particularly important for our theme.[16]

1. The known is known in the way of the knower. The lower forms of knowledge are contained in the higher forms of knowledge, but not vice versa. Whatever is known by the lower faculties of knowledge is also known by the higher ones. God is the supreme faculty of knowledge. Through these Neoplatonic considerations, Boethius wanted to make two things clear. First, that man is unable to grasp how God has knowledge of the contingent; he must focus on God's simplicity, for God's form of knowledge is higher than his.

---

tine, *De civitate Dei*, V c. 9, 138; id., *De libero arbitrio*, III, iii.8 n. 34, (CCSL, 29), 280. For a discussion of Augustine's view, see W.L. Rowe, 'Augustine on Foreknowledge and Free Will', *The Review of Metaphysics* 18 (1964), 356-363; J. Hopkins, 'Augustine on Foreknowledge and Free Will', *International Journal for Philosophy of Religion* 8 (1977), 111-126.

[14] Boethius, *Commentarii in librum Aristotelis Perihermeneias*, I, I c. 9, and II, III c. 9, ed. C. Meiser, Leipzig 1877-1880, 122f and 249f. For a discussion, see N. Kretzmann, '"Nos ipsi principia sumus": Boethius and the Basic of Contingency', ed. T. Rudavsky, *Divine Omniscience*, 24-27; Kretzmann, 'Boethius and the Truth about Tomorrow's Sea Battle', *Logos and Pragma*, ed. L.-M. de Rijk and H.A.G. Braakhuis, Nijmegen 1987 (Artistarium Supplementa, 3), 83.

[15] For Boethius and Ockham, see N. Kretzmann, "Nos ipsi", 33-39 and 48 n. 62. For the other authors mentioned, see A. Maier, *Die Vorläufer Galileis im 14. Jahrhundert*, Rome 1949 (Studien zur Naturphilosophie der Spätscholastik), 219-250, esp. 241-243 and 249. On the authenticity of the commentary printed under the name of Marsilius, see the forthcoming article of Th. Dewender, 'Einige Bemerkungen'.

[16] The influence of Boethius on the Middle Ages is discussed by N.M. Häring, *Lexikon des Mittelalters*, s.v. 'Boethius, Anicius Manlius Severinus'.

Second, that God's knowledge does not depend upon the mutable way of being of its object; he knows the mutable in his own immutable way.[17]

2. Knowledge does not change the nature of what is known. God can see at one glance both the necessary (the rising of the sun) and the contingent (the raising of an arm), without the modality of the contingent being changed. This is true even of human knowledge, so why should it be different in God?[18] In the thirteenth and fourteenth centuries, this idea was very common. It was highlighted in the 1330s and 1340s by such philosophers as Adam Wodeham and Gregory of Rimini, in their discussion of the causality of divine knowledge.

3. God has knowledge of the contingent because his knowledge is eternal. Eternity was described by Boethius as the complete and perfect possession of unbounded life, the pure presence of everything. He distinguished eternity in this sense from eternal duration, which was conceived of as the infinite extension of time into past and future. Because all things are present to eternity, God sees things that for man are still hidden in the uncertain future. Hence, for God the indeterminacy of the future does not mean that it cannot be known with certainty.[19] As we shall see, the interpretation of God's eternity with regard to his foreknowledge was a frequent subject of debate in the late Middle Ages, particularly in connection with the view of Thomas Aquinas.

4. Boethius distinguished between two forms of necessity, unconditional necessity (such a the necessary mortality of man), and conditional necessity (for instance, if we know that someone is walking, then it is necessary that someone is walking). The two forms of necessity are completely separate from one another. Unlike unconditional necessity, conditional necessity does not flow from the nature of a thing, but from the condition under which it is considered. Boethius applied his distinction to the things that are known by God. If a contingent thing is considered insofar as it is known by God, then it is necessary. God's knowledge is infallible, so if God knows that something exists, then it is necessary that it exists. On the other hand, if a contingent thing is considered in itself, and according to its own nature, then it is contingent and independent.[20]

Anselm

The views of Anselm of Canterbury concurred with those of Boethius in several important respects. In *De concordia*, Anselm referred to God's

---

[17] Boethius, *Philosophiae consolatio*, V p. 4 nn. 24-30, and p. 5 n. 12, ed. L. Bieler, Opera Pars 1, Turnhout 1984 (CCSL, 94), 97f and 101. Cf. J. Gruber, *Kommentar zu Boethius De consolatione philosophiae*, Berlin-New York 1978 (Texte und Kommentare, 9), 403-405.
[18] Boethius, *Philosophiae consolatio*, V p. 6 nn. 18-24, 103f.
[19] Ibid., nn. 4-14, 102f.
[20] Ibid., nn. 27-29 and n. 31, 104f.

eternity as the solution to the problem of how God can know the contingent. The immutable presence of eternity he compared to the immutability of the past.[21]

Anselm distinguished between *necessitas praecedens* and *necessitas sequens*. This distinction played a central part in his account of foreknowledge. It partly resembles the fourteenth-century distinction between *necessitas consequentis* and *necessitas conseqentiae*, which was used among others by Robert Holcot, who pointed to Anselm as his source. *Necessitas praecedens* bears the character of a cause. It causes something to exist. It was also described as the kind of necessity a thing has when there are no causes to prevent its being.[22] Marsilius used this description in his definition of 'determinate truth value'.

The second kind of necessity is not that of a cause but of an effect. It is a form of logical necessity based on the principle of identity and non-contradiction: if something is the case, it cannot not be the case. Events from the past are necessary in this sense, as are future events inasmuch as they are known by God. This second kind of necessity does not interfere with human freedom. Only the first kind of necessity is incompatible with contingency.[23]

The literature on the fallacies

The distinction between *sensus compositionis* and *sensus divisionis*, as it occurred in the literature on the fallacies, played a role of some importance, particularly with regard to the semantic problems in relation to divine foreknowledge. This distinction, which is also known as that between meaning *de dicto* and *de re*, originally derived from Aristotle's *Sophistici elenchi* (166a22-30). Aristotle showed there that the meaning of a sentence changes according to the way its parts are either taken together or considered in isolation. For instance, the sentence 'Someone who is sitting can walk' is false if the predicates 'sitting' and 'walking' are taken together and considered to be simultaneously applicable. The same sentence is true if its predicates are considered in isolation, and as not being applicable at the same time: someone who is now sitting may at some other moment be walking. The distinction was standardly included in medieval textbooks on logic that were used at the faculties of arts, as for instance in the well-known *Tractatus* of

---

[21] Anselm, *De concordia praescientiae et praedestinationis et gratiae Dei cum libero arbitrio*, I cc. 40-45, ed. F.S. Schmitt, Rome 1940, repr. Stuttgart-Bad Cannstatt 1968 (Opera Omnia, 2), 252-5. For a commentary on this passage, see P.A. Streveler, 'Anselm on Future Contingencies. A Critical Analysis of the Argument of the 'De concordia'', *Anselm Studies. An Occasional Journal* 1 (1983), 165-173, esp. 169f.

[22] On these two kinds of necessity, see D.P. Henry, *The Logic of Saint Anselm*, Oxford 1967, 172-180; C.G. Normore, 'Future Contingents', 360f. For Holcot, see Streveler, 'Anselm', 171 n. 3.

[23] Anselm, *Cur Deus homo*, II c. 17, ed. F.S. Schmitt, Rome 1940, repr. Stuttgart-Bad Cannstatt 1968 (Opera Omnia, 2), 125.

Peter of Spain. It was applied by many authors in the analysis of such sentences as 'What God knows is necessary', and 'God can know something that he does not know'.[24]

THOMAS AQUINAS

In his commentaries on Aristotle, Thomas distinguished between three forms of contingency: freedom of choice (*contingens ad utrumlibet*), things that happen by chance (*contingens ut in paucioribus*), and natural phenomena that usually behave in a regular way, but in which exceptions may occur (*contingens ut in pluribus*). The first kind is a consequence of human freedom of will, which is impartial and indifferent with regard to the finite things it strives for. Whatever is caused by the will could as well have been otherwise. The other two kinds of contingency are not the result of a single cause, but rather of the unexpected coincidence of several causes, as when two people meet by accident (chance), or when the wood we expected to catch fire fails to do so because it is damp (exception to a rule of nature). This threefold distinction is also found in the commentaries on the *Sentences* by the Dominican theologians Jacob of Metz, first version written 1302-1303, and Durand of St. Pourçain, first version written between 1304 and 1307-1308.[25]

The way Thomas related the forms of contingency to their intelligibility is important for our understanding of the various reactions with which his view was met. He argued that contingent effects that are caused by free will cannot possibly be known beforehand when they are still contained in their causes. This sets them apart from necessary effects that can indeed be known in their causes. The intelligibility of a thing, according to Thomas, follows the nature of its being. What is as yet indeterminate in its being can only be known in an indeterminate way. We do not know beforehand whether John will be walking, but we do know that he will be either walking or not. This uncertainty with regard to future contingents caused by the will is absolute. According to Thomas, this applies to human knowledge as well as to God. The

---

[24] The history of the distinction is delineated in A. Maierù, *Terminologia logica della tarda scolastica*, Rome 1972 (Lessico intellettuale Europeo, 8), 499-600; N. Kretzmann, 'Sensus compositus, sensus divisus and Propositional Attitudes', *Medioevo* 7 (1981), 195-229; S. Knuuttila, 'Modal Logic', *The Cambridge History of Later Mediaeval Philosophy*, ed. N. Kretzmann, A. Kenny, and J. Pinborg, Cambridge 1982, 347f. For the medieval literature on the fallacies, see L.–M. de Rijk, *Logica Modernorum*, Vol. 1, Assen 1962 (Wijsgerige Teksten en Studies, 6); J. Pinborg, *Logik und Semantik im Mittelalter*, Stuttgart-Bad Cannstatt 1972 (Problemata, 10), 66-69. For Peter of Spain, see *Tractatus*, VII nn. 57-76 (ed. de Rijk), 115-127.

[25] For Thomas's view on contingency, see K. Jacobi, 'Kontingente Naturgeschehnisse', *Studia Mediewistyczne* 18 (1977), 3-70, with references to the relevant places in Thomas. On Jacob of Metz and Durand, see B. Decker, *Die Gotteslehre*, 172f (Jacob of Metz., *Sent.*, I d. 38 q. 1, first version), 187 (Durand, *Sent.*, I d. 38 q. 3, first version). The dating of these commentaries is according to Decker, *Die Gotteslehre*, 107f.

effect of a free act of will can only be known with certainty once it has actually been realized. Its being has then become determinate, and even necessary (a prerequisite for scientific knowledge), for that which is cannot not be. As a determinate being it has lost its mutability, and can be an object of intellectual knowledge.[26]

In order to fit the requirements for scientific knowledge, Thomas brought eternity into his account of God's knowledge, as we have seen earlier in Boethius. Following Boethius, Thomas distinguished between eternity proper and eternal duration. God's knowledge is determined by eternity, which encompasses all times. All temporal beings are present to God's knowledge, exactly as they are present at some moment in time. This means that contingent things are known to God in their own determinate being, and not only in their indeterminate causes.[27]

Although Thomas claimed elsewhere that the domain of God's causality also encompasses man's free acts of will, remarkably enough he did not use God's causality in his account of foreknowledge. This marks a clear difference between his explanation of God's knowledge in general, where he did use arguments from causality, as we have seen in chapters 2 and 4, and of his knowledge of the free acts of man.[28]

With regard to the second and third forms of contingency, uncertainty is not absolute, but relative to the level of knowledge involved. The fact that two people happen to meet in the street is a coincidence for someone who is ignorant of what their plans were, but inevitable for someone who knew. The fact that the wood fails to burn is inexplicable for someone who is unaware that it is damp, but can be predicted by someone who knows. The knowledge of these forms of contingency depends upon the knowledge of the causes. Unlike effects of will, these events can be deduced from their causes; hence they can be known by God with absolute certainty, for he knows their causes through his knowledge of himself (the line of Avicenna).[29]

Thomas's views of God's knowledge of the contingent were often criticized, by Franciscan as well as Dominican writers. Three points in particular

---

[26] *Expositio libri Peryermenias*, I lect. 13 (ed. Leon., 1*/1), 69a; *Sent.*, I d. 38 q. 1 a. 5 c. (ed. Mandonnet, 1), 910; *De veritate*, q. 2 a. 12 c. (ed. Leon., 22/1), 83b. For a discussion of Aristotle's view on the necessity of the present, which was Thomas's source here, see Ch. Kirwan, 'Aristotle on the Necessity of the Present', *Oxford Studies in Ancient Philosophy* 6 (1986), 167-187, esp. 177-187.

[27] *Sent.*, I d. 38 q. 1 a. 5 c., 910f; *STheol.*, I q. 14 a. 13 c. (ed. Leon., 4), 186b. For a discussion, see J.F. Wippel, 'Divine Knowledge, Divine Power, and Human Freedom in Thomas Aquinas and Henry of Ghent', ed. T. Rudavsky, *Divine Omniscience*, 213-241, esp. 213-221; W.L. Craig, *The Problem of Divine Foreknowledge*, 103-107.

[28] On God's causality in Thomas, see Wippel, 'Divine Knowledge', 221-226, with further bibliographical references.

[29] *Expositio libri Peryermenias*, I lect. 14 (ed. Leon., 1*/1), 76b; *In octo libros Physicorum Aristotelis expositio*, II lect. 10 n. 238, ed. M. Maggiòlo, Turin-Rome 1954, 115a; *ScG*, I c. 67 n. 559 (ed. Pera, 2), 78b; *STheol.*, I q. 22 a. 2 ad 1 (ed. Leon., 4), 265a-b.

168   CHAPTER SIX

were up for discussion: first, that the free acts of will cannot be known in their causes; second, that all things are present to God in his eternity; and third, that God knows the contingent in its own being. We shall address these points in order.

The first point was criticized by William de la Mare for the following reason. If it is impossible to know the free acts of will in their causes, then how could the prophets have had knowledge of what they were foretelling? Obviously, they did not have knowledge of the future events themselves, for these did not yet exist. Therefore they must have known them in their causes. This is even more true of the sacred angels who foresaw future events with certainty in God.[30]

Criticism of a more philosophical nature was given by Jacob of Metz and Durand of St. Pourçain, who unlike Thomas did not distinguish between the various grades of intelligibility of contingent events. According to Jacob of Metz, certain knowledge of all future effects, including free acts of will, is possible for someone who knows everything there is to know about a cause: what makes it a cause, what makes it exist, and what may prevent if from acting. The same argument was used by Durand, who in addition drew attention to the causality of divine essence. God knows all things through his essence which, being the cause of all things, can serve as the medium through which God knows the contingent. The same claim was made by four of the five writers of the so-called *Correctoria corruptorii*, who unlike Jacob and Durand expressly sought to defend Thomas. They added that if it is said that some contingent events cannot be known in their causes, this is because only the most proximal cause (*causa proxima*) has been taken into account, and not the total constellation of causes. Only the *Correctorium corruptorii 'Circa'*, written by John of Paris, stated that God cannot have certain knowledge of the contingent through his knowledge of the causes.[31]

In the fourteenth century, the deployment of divine causality in explanations of foreknowledge of the contingent was typical in particular of Scoticizing Franciscans. In the sixteenth and seventeenth centuries, it became influential in Spanish Dominican theology as well, through the work of Bañez. According to Bañez, it was not eternity that was central in Thomas, but rather causality. Even if the contingent would not be present to God in his eternity, then he would still be able to know it with certainty.[32] As should be clear from

---

[30] *Le Correctorium corruptorii 'Quare'*, a. 3 (ed. Glorieux), 20 (William de la Mare).
[31] B. Decker, *Die Gotteslehre*, 176 (Jacob of Metz, *Sent.*, I d. 38 q. 1, second version, written 1304/5-06), 187 (Durand, *Sent.*, I d. 38 q. 3, first version); *Le Correctorium corruptorii 'Quare'*, a. 3 (ed. Glorieux), 23f; *Le Correctorium corruptorii 'Sciendum'*, a. 3 (ed. Glorieux), 43f; *Le Correctorium corruptorii 'Quaestione'*, a. 3 (ed. Muller), 23; Rambert of Bologna, *Apologeticum veritatis contra Corruptorium*, ed. J.-P. Muller, Vatican City 1943 (Studi e testi, 108), a. 3, 31; *Le Correctorium corruptorii 'Circa' de Jean Quidort de Paris*, ed. J.-P. Muller, Rome 1941 (Studia Anselmiana, 12-13), a. 3, 31.
[32] For Bañez's reading of Thomas and its influence, see Fr. Schmitt, *Die Lehre des hl.*

the above, these later interpretations of Thomas's position were prepared by earlier Dominican efforts in the thirteenth and fourteenth centuries, most notably the *Correctoria corruptorii* and the works of Jacob of Metz and Durand of St. Pourçain.

We now come to the second point, Thomas's view that all things are present to God in his eternity. The first to criticize this view were William de la Mare and the Dominican writers Peter of Auvergne († 1304), Jacob of Metz, Durand of St. Pourçain, and William Peter of Godin († 1336). The criticism gained much influence, and can be found throughout the fourteenth century. From the texts it is clear that the Dominican philosophers felt the influence of William de la Mare on this point. De la Mare took it that by 'presence' Thomas meant *real* presence. He objected that this would mean that the things that are known by God have eternal existence, an implication he found erroneous. He submitted, rather, that God knows the things *as if* (*ac si*) they were present, viz., through his knowledge of causal concepts and ideas. For what does not yet exist, cannot itself be present to eternity.[33]

In 1283, the view that God knows future things not by means of the ideas but in their own nature was denounced in the so-called *Littera septem siggilorum*, a list of twenty-two theses drafted by seven Franciscan theologians, among them Richard of Middleton, at the request of the Franciscan Minister-General Bonagratia, and directed against Peter of John Olivi (OFM, † 1298). As a direct consequence of this, the view that God knows the things only 'as if' they were present (held by Bonaventure and De la Mare) assumed a more or less official authority for Franciscans of the time. A significant detail here was that the libel also stated that the criticized view, viz., that God knows the things themselves, should not be called heretical, as De la Mare had done.[34] Bonagratia probably wanted to evade an official discussion of the orthodoxy of Thomas's view.

The *Lectura thomasina* by the Dominican William Peter of Godin, written 1296-1300, makes reference to the criticism by De la Mare. The author spoke of adversaries who criticized the view of Thomas as being erroneous. To the allegation that the view of Thomas was contrary to faith, he replied that eternity coexists with all moments in time, while the reverse does not hold. From this fact he also inferred that two different moments t_1 and t_2, while both present to eternity, do not coexist with each other. The objection Godin was trying to meet here, viz., that all things that are present to eternity must also

---

Thomas von Aquin vom göttlichen Wissen des zukünftig Kontingenten bei seinen grossen Kommentatoren, Nijmegen 1950 (Diss.), 111-114 and 198f.

[33] *Le Correctorium corruptorii 'Quare'*, a. 3 (ed. Glorieux), 18f (William de la Mare).

[34] Cf. G. Fussenegger, "Littera septem siggilorum' contra doctrinam Petri Iohannis Olivi edita', *Archivum franciscanum historicum* 47 (1954), 45-53, esp. 51 n. 5. On this letter and on the condemnation of Peter of John Olivi, see J. Koch, *Kleine Schriften*, II, 191-274, esp. 209-211. As for Bonaventure, see *Sent.*, I d. 36 a. 1 q. 1 c. (Opera Theologica Selecta, 1), 493b.

be present to each other, is one that is frequently raised against Thomas, even by present-day writers on the subject.[35]

To De la Mare's objection that the future is not yet real and therefore cannot be present, Godin replied that a thing considered in itself is present to eternity only as long as it exists, but that God can see it from eternity. For with respect to God there is eternal *praesentialitas cogniti*. Godin rejected the eternal *praesentialitas rei*, thus following the criticism of De la Mare. The same line was followed in the *Quodlibeta* of Peter of Auvergne (*Quodl*. IV q. 2, originated in 1299) and in the commentaries on the *Sentences* of Hervaeus Natalis and Durand of St. Pourçain. Jacob of Metz, however, interpreted Thomas as meaning real presence. He explicitly responded to the competing interpretation, which he claimed did not agree with the words of Thomas (a similar remark had been made by De la Mare). As his own view, Jacob submitted that the things are not really present in God's eternity, but have only an 'as if' presence.[36]

The interpretation of Thomas given by Jacob of Metz was criticized in the *Correctorium* addressed against him by Hervaeus Natalis, written 1302-1307 or ca. 1310. Hervaeus did not take issue with Jacob's view of a merely 'as if' presence (which he actually shared), but rather with his reluctance to accept this view as the correct interpretation of Thomas. The interpretation of Thomas given by William de la Mare and Jacob of Metz is also found in the Franciscans Duns Scotus and James of Ascoli.[37]

This brings us to the third issue mentioned above, the question of whether Thomas believed that God knows future contingents in their own being outside God, or through the ideas. In the *Summa theologiae*, Thomas had stated that all things are present to God, not only because he has knowledge of their concepts, but also because his knowledge is aimed at the things insofar as they exist in their own presence. This remark led De la Mare to surmise, in keeping with his general interpretation of Thomas, that Thomas

---

[35] See B. Decker, *Die Gotteslehre*, 183f, with references to the relevant places in the *Lectura thomasina*. For the dating of this work, see p. 44. Cf. the criticism on Thomas by A. Kenny, *The God of the Philosophers*, 38f.

[36] Decker, *Die Gotteslehre*, 184 (Peter of Godin), 184f (Peter of Auvergne), 186f (Hervaeus), 188 (Durand), 177 and 183 (Jacob of Metz). For William de la Mare, see *Le Correctorium corruptorii 'Quare'*, a. 3 (ed. Glorieux), 18 and 20.

[37] Decker, *Die Gotteslehre*, 186f (Hervaeus); Scotus, *Lectura*, I d. 39 qq. 1-5 n. 23 (ed. Vat., 17), 486; James of Ascoli, as edited in H. Schwamm, *Robert Cowton OFM über das göttliche Vorherwissen*, Innsbruck 1931 (Philosophie und Grenzwissenschaften, 3/5), 50 (430). For the *Correctorium* of Hervaeus, see F. Roensch, *Early Thomistic School*, Dubuque, Iowa 1964, 107 and 115, and Decker, *Die Gotteslehre*, 22. Also in recent times, there is no consensus regarding the correct interpretation of Thomas on this issue. According to J. de Finance, 'La présence des choses à l' éternité d'après les scolastiques', *Archives de Philosophie* 19 (1956), 24-62, esp. 25-35, Thomas meant real presence. By contrast, M.Th. Liske, 'Was meint Thomas von Aquin mit 'Gott weiss das Künftige als gegenwärtig'?', *Theologie und Philosophie* 60 (1985), 520-537, esp. 526f, reads Thomas as meaning only 'as if' presence.

believed that God is somehow the recipient of knowledge from the things, which would be repugnant to his nature as pure act. If there is an alternative source for God's knowledge, other than concepts and ideas, then this source must lie outside of him. In sum, De la Mare charged Thomas with presenting two modes of divine knowledge, one of which he accepted (knowledge through ideas), while rejecting the other (knowledge of things in their own presence).[38]

The view De la Mare did not quarrel with, viz., that God knows the existence of contingent things by means of the ideas, was put forward by Thomas in his commentary on the *Sentences*. The practical ideas in God's mind, he claimed, are not only the cause of form but also of matter, hence also of the existence of each thing. Therefore knowledge of the ideas is sufficient for God to know all there is to know about a thing. The critical passage in Thomas's *Sentences* commentary was commonly known at the time, as is clear from the fact that it was quoted, albeit anonymously, by Duns Scotus and Robert Cowton.[39]

If we look at the reactions to De la Mare's criticism in the *Correctoria corruptorii*, we see that some of them, notably '*Quare*' and '*Quaestione*', interpreted Thomas's disputed view in the light of the above passage from the commentary on the *Sentences*. In all five of the *Correctoria* the idea that Thomas believed that God receives his knowledge from outside is rejected as absurd. According to the *Correctorium corruptorii 'Quare'*, which was probably the first reaction to De la Mare, God knows all things in their presence through the intelligible forms, just like man has knowledge of the existence of things in the past by means of the intelligible forms. In the *Correctorium corruptorii 'Quaestione'* the emphasis was placed on the fact that God has knowledge of future things because he is the creator of everything, including matter and being. Because his knowledge is atemporal, God sees at a glance *both* the concept in his mind comprehending form as well as matter and being, *and* the future thing for which the concept stands. The latter is what Thomas meant by the presence of things, so the author of *'Quaestione'* contended, while the former is what is meant by knowledge of concepts.[40]

A different interpretation was proffered by John of Paris in the *Correctorium corruptorii 'Circa'*. Knowledge of concepts can only yield knowledge of the essence of a thing, not of its existence. In addition, therefore, God has to know

---

[38] *STheol.*, I q. 14 a. 13 c. (ed. Leon., 4), 186b; *Le Correctorium corruptorii 'Quare'*, a. 3 (ed. Glorieux), 20f (William de la Mare).

[39] Thomas, *Sent.*, I d. 38 q. 1 a. 3 ad 1 (ed. Mandonnet, 1), 904. For the quotations of this passage by Scotus and Cowton, see my 'A propos de Lectura I d. 39. Un passage dissimulé de Thomas d'Aquin chez Duns Scot?', *AHDLMA* 52 (1985), 231-236.

[40] *Le Correctorium corruptorii 'Quare'*, a. 3 (ed. Glorieux), 24; *Le Correctorium corruptorii 'Quaestione'*, a. 3 (ed. Muller), 20.

future things in their presence, or else his knowledge would not be complete. This additional knowledge is supplied through God's eternity. In his commentary on the *Sentences*, John of Paris attributed to the 'moderni' the view that concepts alone suffice for God to have knowledge of the existence of future things. His own view he concisely summarized as follows: Even if God would not have ideas but yet be eternal, future things would still be present to him. In *'Circa'*, this view was attributed to Thomas.[41]

SEMANTIC ASPECTS

As stated at the beginning of this chapter, semantic analysis played an important role in the account of divine foreknowledge. Thomas used it with regard to two questions in particular: first, with regard to the *necessity* of God's knowledge, and second, with regard to the *immutability* of God's knowledge. We shall deal with both issues in turn.

The necessity of God's knowledge

Thomas affirmed the necessity of God's knowledge, including that of future contingents. This necessity he derived from the nature of divine knowledge and the manner in which things are the object of God's knowledge. His position in this respect is a clear example of Aristotelian-Boethian epistemological subjectivism, according to which the mode of knowledge depends entirely on the subject and not on the object of knowledge. Thomas explained this subjectivism in terms of linguistic analysis. The that-clause in sentences like 'I say that Socrates is walking' does not have signficative power. It functions only as the material object of the activity expressed by the verb 'to say'. Therefore the truth value and the modality of the sentence as a whole are not affected by the verb contained in the that-clause. Even if Socrates is not walking, the sentence 'I say that Socrates is walking' can be true. When this principle is applied to divine knowledge, we find that the modality and truth of what is known depend upon God's knowledge. Thomas thus rejected the position of Robert Grosseteste and Bonaventure, who argued that God's knowledge is contingent because what is known is contingent, a view that had many supporters in the fourteenth century, including Marsilius of Inghen.[42]

That God's knowledge is necessary, Thomas inferred from the necessity of the past. If God has foreknowledge, then his knowledge must somehow be

---

[41] John of Paris, *Sent.*, I q. 116 (ed. Muller), 353f; *Le Correctorium corruptorii 'Circa'*, a. 3 (ed. Muller), 27 and 31.

[42] Thomas, *Sent.*, I d. 38 q. 1 a. 5 ad 4 (ed. Mandonnet, 1), 913; *De veritate*, q. 2 a. 12 a. 7 (ed. Leon., 22/1), 85a-86b; *STheol.*, I q. 14 a. 13 ad 2 (ed. Leon, 4), 186b-187a; Grosseteste, *De libero arbitrio*, c. 7, edited in: L. Baur, *Die philosophische Werke des Robert Grosseteste, Bischofs von Lincoln*, Münster 1912 (BGPhThMA, 9), 176; Bonaventure, *Sent.*, I d. 38 a. 2 q. 2 (Opera Theologica Selecta, 1), 540a. For an interesting discussion of Thomas's position, see A.N. Prior, *Papers on Time and Tense*, 34f. On Marsilius, see the next chapter.

like a past event, notwithstanding the fact that he does not exist in time. Thomas took issue with the view that God retains the possibility *not* to have known, because his knowledge is beyond time. Although there is no outside force to constrain him, Thomas argued, God's immutability implies that it is impossible for him to presently know more or less than he would have known previously.[43]

Thus equipped, Thomas turned to the conditional sentence 'If God knew that A will happen, then A will happen', of which he gave the following analysis. The antecendent is necessary because God's knowledge is necessary. Because the antecendent is about God's act of knowledge, A must be taken as a known in the consequent as well, this time not as a material object but as present to eternity. Now, God knows contingent things if they exist. What exists cannot not-exist. Hence, considered with respect to God's knowledge, A is necessary. Therefore, the consequent ('A will happen') is necessary.[44]

Considered in relation to God's knowledge, the known is necessary. From this it does not follow, however, that it is necessary in itself, or that it is produced by a necessary cause. Thomas explained himself here by invoking the distinction between *de dicto* and *de re*. The assertion, 'Whatever God knows is necessary', is true when taken *de dicto*. Taken in this sense, it states the necessary truth that whatever God knows exists. This necessity does not affect the contingency of what is known, but merely expresses the fact that all things are present to God. Taken *de re*, however, the same assertion means that everything that is known by God is a necessary being. In this sense it is false, for there actually are contingent things (God has made causes that work contingently) which are known by God in his omniscience.[45]

The immutability of God's knowledge

Thomas believed not only that God's knowledge is necessary, but also that it is immutable. The question here is whether this means that God is unable to know something other than what he does know. A succint illustration of the problem can be given in terms of Nelson Pike's doctrine of essential predication.[46] Pike defines a property P as being an *essential predicate* of an

---

[43] Thomas, *Sent.*, I d. 38 q. 1 a. 5 ad 4, 913.
[44] *De veritate*, q. 2 a. 12 ad 7 (ed. Leon., 22/1), 86a. This analysis has often been critically discussed in the secondary literature on the subject. See A.N. Prior, *Papers on Time and Tense*, 31-44; A. Kenny, 'Divine Foreknowledge and Human Freedom', *A Collection of Critical Essays*, ed. A. Kenny, London-Melbourne 1969, 260f; J.F. Wippel, 'Divine Knowledge', 216-218. See also B.E. Nwigwe, *Die Lehre von der göttlichen Vorsehung und menschlichen Freiheit bei Thomas von Aquin und ihre zeitlogische Kritik durch A.N. Prior and P.T. Geach*, Münster, Westfalen 1985 (Diss.).
[45] *STheol.*, I q. 14 a. 13 ad 3 (ed. Leon., 4), 187b. See also Thomas, *Sent.*, I d. 38 q. 1 a. 5 ad 5 (ed. Mandonnet, 1), 914; *De veritate*, q. 2 a. 12 ad 4, 84b-85a.
[46] N. Pike, *God and Timelessness*, 17-28.

individual G iff without P, G would loose its identity. Now, according to Thomas, God has knowledge of all possible things (by the knowledge of his essence) as well as of all actual things (by his eternity). The first type of knowledge he called *scientia simplicis intelligentiae*, the second type *scientia visionis*.[47] We formalize this as follows. Let pE be the property of God (G) wherein he has knowledge of all possible things pA, pB, pC, ... (where 'pE' means: 'God knows pA, pB, pC, ...'). Let E be the property of God wherein he knows all actual things A, B, C, ... (where 'E' means: 'God knows A, B, C, ...'). Our question now reads as follows: does God's immutability imply that he would no longer be God if he did not have properties pE or E? Furthermore, assuming that God had created a different world, containing not the objects A, B, C, ..., but different objects A', B', C', ..., his knowledge would be different: not E but E'. Is this possibility ruled out by his immutability?

Because God's knowledge is perfect, and because it is impossible for there to be other things than those that are possible, Thomas concluded that God's *scientia simplicis intelligentiae* is indeed immutable. In Pike's terminology, this means that pE is an essential predicate. If God did not know all that is possible, he would not know his essence, which is contradicted by his perfection.[48]

With regard to E and E', the question is more complicated. God's perfection requires that he must always know everything that exists. Yet he might have created different things, for he is free. Should we perhaps say that both E and E' are essential predicates? But this would be impossible, for if God knows both E and E', and yet has created only A, B, C, ..., then his knowledge would be imperfect: he would know the existence of A', B', C', ..., even while these objects do not exist. Nor can we say that God knows A', B', C', ... *after* he knows A, B, C, ..., for his knowledge is eternal; whatever he knows, he always knows. To solve this problem Thomas again turned to the distinction *de dicto/de re*. There are two ways to understand the assertion, 'God can know something that he does not know': either with (*de dicto*) or without (*de re*) the supposition that God already has knowledge of something. Taken in the first sense, the assertion is false, for God's knowledge is eternal and immutable; taken in the second sense, it is true, for God is free and can know whatever he makes. This can be explained as follows. Starting from the case that God does not know anything yet, he can know either A, B, C, ... or A', B', C', ... If he already knows A, B, C, ..., however, he can no longer know A', B', C', ... Similarly, if he already knows A', B', C', ..., he can no longer know A, B, C, ... God's perfection implies that if there are things, he

---

[47] Thomas, *Sent.*, I d. 39 q. 1 a. 2 c. (ed. Mandonnet. 1), 922; *ScG*, I c. 61 nn. 550f and c. 69 n. 590 (ed. Pera, 2), 77b and 82a.
[48] *Sent.*, I d. 39 q. 1 a. 2 c., 922.

necessarily knows them eternally and immutably. Therefore either E is an essential predicate or E' is, but not both. From this Thomas concluded that it is false to say that God can know more than he does, because 'to know more' carries with it the presupposition that he already knows something, which means that the assertion must be taken *de dicto*, or, as it was also called, *in sensu composito*.[49]

Duns Scotus

Duns Scotus offered an approach that is clearly different from that of Thomas. In his *Reportata Parisiensia*, Scotus remarked that all *doctores* were in agreement *that* God has knowledge of future contingents, but that they differed on the question *how* this is so.[50] Scotus took issue with the Boethian view adopted by Thomas Aquinas, which was well-known at the time, and chose instead a line of thought that had emerged toward the end of the thirteenth century through the work of Henry of Ghent, viz., that God knows the contingent through the infallible causality of his will. This view was to develop into one of the three major strands that dominated the fourteenth century. Although its source was Henry of Ghent, and in spite of the fact that most philosophers, most notably William of Alnwick, did not endorse the modifications added by Scotus but rather returned to Henry's original version, it was with the name of Scotus that the view was generally associated. The only exception was Alexander of Alessandria, a contemporary of Scotus, who remarked that the position was not a new one but had been held before by certain *antiqui*, by which he probably meant Henry of Ghent.[51] Based as it was on divine causality, the view had an obviously Avicennian background, although both Henry of Ghent and Scotus criticized Avicenna's necessitarianism.

Scotus took issue with the following two elements: first, that God knows the future by means of the ideas, and second, that God knows the future because all things are present to his eternity (the line of Boethius). In the next paragraphs we will examine Scotus's criticism of these views.[52]

God does not know future contingents by means of ideas

The first aspect criticized by Scotus can be found in the commentaries on the *Sentences* of Bonaventure and Thomas Aquinas. Earlier in this chapter we have seen that it was identified as the view of Thomas by the authors of the

---

[49] Ibid., 923; *De veritate*, q. 2 a. 13 ad 5 (ed. Leon., 22/1), 90a.
[50] Scotus, *Reportata Parisiensia*, I d. 38 q. 2 n. 2 (ed. Wadding, 11/1), fol. 218a.
[51] See H. Schwamm, *Das göttliche Vorherwissen*, 106-108 and 138f.
[52] For a discussion of Scotus's criticism, see also K. Bannach, *Die Lehre*, 166f; W.L. Craig, *The Problem of Divine Foreknowledge*, 127-133, also published in *FcS* 47 (1987), 98-122, esp. 99-106.

Correctoria 'Quare' and *'Quaestione'*. From De la Mare's *Correctorium* and from the *Littera septem siggilorum*, we know that it was also adumbrated, or at least not criticized, by Franciscan philosophers at the end of the thirteenth century. We have established elsewhere that Scotus's criticism was directed most probably against the version of this view as we find it in Thomas's commentary on the *Sentences*, and not against Bonaventure, as is often claimed.[53]

Scotus's criticism was as follows. Ideas are known before God wills the existence of something. Hence, what ideas represent must be independent of existence and nonexistence. Existents are represented in the same fashion as things that are possible but never will exist. Therefore, knowledge of the ideas does not supply knowledge of existence. Moreover, what is represented by ideas, is represented necessarily, eternally, and immutably. Assuming that contingent events are known by means of ideas, God would know them as necessary and immutable, which is contradicted by their being contingent. Also, if the idea were to give knowledge of both alternatives of a contingent event (being and not-being), then for each event God would know contradictory propositions as being both eternally true, which is impossible.[54] This criticism was closely related to Scotus's own theory of ideas, which differed substantially from that of Thomas: the ideas are the quiddities God knows by immediate knowledge of his essence. On this account, if ideas were to represent existence, this existence would be completely tied to the quiddities, and hence would be necessary.

God does not know the contingent through his eternity

Scotus's other point of criticism concerned the Boethian stance Thomas took with regard to presence to eternity. His objections closely followed those of William de la Mare, interpreting presence as *real* presence instead of presence *as if*. Scotus pressed four points, three of which are also found in De la Mare's *Correctorium*. In the first place, and most importantly, he objected that what does not yet exist cannot be present to eternity. Here we see that Scotus obviously interpreted Thomas's 'presence' as 'real presence'. Secondly, if future things are present to eternity in the way of their actual existence, then they cannot be created any more. For to be present in the way of actual existence means to have already been created. Thus interpreted, Thomas's view jeopardized the notion of creation from nothing. Thirdly, God is perfectly able to know the future in its causes, because he knows the creatures he is later going to create. Hence it is not necessary to assume that God knows the future as present to him in his eternity. Finally, if by his

---

[53] See my 'A propos de Lectura I d. 39', 231-233 and 235f, with references to the relevant places in Thomas and Bonaventure.

[54] *Lectura*, I d. 39 qq. 1-5, nn. 21f (ed. Vat., 17), 485.

eternity (*aeternitas*) all things are present to God, then by eternal duration (*aevum*) all things must be present to the angels. For eternal duration is indivisible as well, Thomas claimed (according to Scotus), hence equal to all time. But angels do not have knowledge in this way; therefore neither does God.[55]

Scotus's criticism of the above two views made its way into the works of many Franciscans in the fourteenth century. It was adopted in almost its original form in the commentaries on the *Sentences* of Francis of Mayronnes and Peter of Aquila, and figured in the works of many other Scotists, such as William of Alnwick, Johannes de Bassolis, Landulph Caracciolo, Francis of Marchia, and Hugh of Novocastro.[56]

The position of Scotus

Scotus believed that God knows all future contingents by knowing what his will is going to produce. God's will is the cause of all created being, and there is nothing that can interfere with it. Therefore, God's knowledge of the creatures as gained from the will is infallible.

Scotus distinguished between two interpretations of the phrase 'knowledge gained from the will': first, that the intellect sees the determination of the will itself, and second, that it sees not the determination itself, but its representation in the essence. We shall consider these options in turn.

First interpretation

On the first interpretation of 'knowledge gained from the will', the process of knowledge proceeds as follows:[57]

> 1. First God knows all possible events in his essence in a 'neutral' way, so to speak; that is to say, he does not yet know them as something to be caused (*non ut facienda*).
> 2. Then out of each pair of contradictory events the will chooses one, and determines when it will take place.
> 3. Then the intellect sees the determination of the will (*determinatio voluntatis*), and sees that there is nothing to stop the will from realizing its determination.
> 4. Finally, the intellect knows with unfailing certainty that the future event will take place, and when it will take place.

---

[55] Ibid., nn. 27-30, 487f. Cf. *Le Correctorium corruptorii 'Quare'*, a. 3 (ed. Glorieux), 18-20 (William de la Mare). Only the last point is absent in William de la Mare.

[56] Francis of Mayronnes, *Sent.*, I dd. 38-39 q. 1 a. 4 (ed. Venice 1520), fol. 113rbH-113vaI-K; Peter of Aquila, *Sent.*, I d. 38 q. 2 a. 2 (ed. Speyer 1480), coll. 1f. For the other authors mentioned, see the texts cited by H. Schwamm, *Das göttliche Vorherwissen*, 168f (William of Alnwick), 207 (Johannes de Bassolis), 230 (Hugh of Novocastro), 242 (Francis of Marchia), 280 (Landulph Caracciolo).

[57] *Lectura*, I d. 39 qq. 1-5 n. 64 (ed. Vat., 17), 500f. Scotus's view is also discussed in D.C. Langston, *God's Willing Knowledge. The Influence of Scotus' Analysis of Omniscience*, University Park-London 1986, 9-52; W.L. Craig, *The Problem of Divine Foreknowledge*, 136-139; A.B. Wolter, *The Philosophical Theology*, 285-333.

This is essentially an account of the view of Henry of Ghent. He held that God has immutable knowledge of the existence of mutable, contingent things in that God's intellect sees the determination (*determinatio*) of the will that is completely immutable. Scotus detected a flaw in this explanation, however. He argued that it implied a certain degree of discursiveness that does not sit well with the intuitiveness of God's knowledge. In order to know of something that it will happen, God would have to bring two things into connection: the determination of divine will and its immutability. In the *Reportata Parisiensia*, Scotus added a second and more weighty objection: if God has knowledge by seeing the determination of the will, then the intellect would be moved by the will as well as by the essence. But only the essence can move God's knowledge, as Scotus had previously established.[58]

Second interpretation

It was precisely on this latter point that the second interpretation corrected the first one, which makes it rather curious that this point was mentioned only in the *Reportata Parisiensia* and not in the *Lectura*. Scotus preferred the second interpretation, which went as follows:[59]

> "It is perhaps more correct to say that when the will has decided to choose one of the two contradictory alternatives, the thing has the form of the makeable and the producible (*illud habet rationem factibilis et producibilis*). And then the intellect sees the event (*complexio*) not because it sees the determination of the will, but because his essence is for him the immediate form (*ratio*) that represents the event."

The two interpretations and the first Scotists

From Hermann Schwamm's study of the reception of Scotus's views on God's knowledge of the contingent, we know that quite a number of Scotists of the first half of the fourteenth century mentioned only the first of the two interpretations, which they also endorsed for themselves: that God knows the will's determination itself. This was the case with Francis of Mayronnes, Hugh of Novocastro, Landulph Caracciolo, and Peter of Aquila.[60] These early Scotists were thus all following to some extent the line of Henry of Ghent, without giving clear reasons why they did not take over Scotus's correction of it.

Explicit criticism of Scotus's correction was given by William of Alnwick, who like the authors just mentioned opted for the first interpretation. Alnwick

---

[58] Henry of Ghent, *Quodlibeta*, VIII q. 2 (ed. Paris 1518), fol. 301vH-I; Scotus, *Lectura*, I d. 39 qq. 1-5 n. 64, 501; *Reportata Parisiensia*, I d. 38 q. 2 n. 4 (ed. Wadding, 11/1), fol. 218b. See also the parallel text from the *Reportatio* I A, d. 38 (Wien, Oesterr. Nationalbibl., CVP, 1453), fol. 114rb, quoted by Wolter, *The Philosophical Theology*, 291 n. 18.

[59] *Lectura*, I d. 39 qq. 1-5 n. 65, 501.

[60] H. Schwamm, *Das göttliche Vorherwissen*, 166 (Francis of Mayronnes), 232 (Hugh of

had two objections. First, divine essence represents everything as necessary by nature. Hence it is unfit to serve as the medium of knowledge for the free determination of the will. Moreover, divine essence has ontological precedence over the will. The superior cannot receive from the inferior. Therefore the essence cannot receive a representational form from the will. Thus it cannot serve as the medium of knowledge for the determination of the will.[61]

The second interpretation, which Scotus had preferred, was taken over by James of Ascoli, who on the other hand did not mention the first one.[62]

The mixed position of Antonius Andreas and Robert Cowton

The position of Thomas Aquinas and that of Duns Scotus seem particularly hard to combine at first sight. Yet an attempt was made by two writers of the beginning of the fourteenth century, Antonius Andreas (OFM, † ca. 1320) and Robert Cowton.

According to Antonius Andreas, God has infallible knowledge of the contingent because he sees in his essence all things and everything that can happen to them. Because all things are present to him in his eternity, God also sees their actual existence. Up to this point, Andreas's position resembled that of Thomas. With regard to the question of how the certainty of God's knowledge can be combined with the contingency of its object, however, Andreas clearly took Scotus's side. He argued that divine will contingently determines what will happen. What has been determined contingently will also happen contingently. Hence God has knowledge not only of what he knows as necessary in his essence, but of contingents as well.[63]

Exactly *why* Andreas wanted to merge the views of Thomas and Scotus on this point does not become clear from his account. This is different in the case of Robert Cowton, who wrote his commentary on the *Sentences* at Oxford in 1309-1311. He explicitly sought to give a foundation for his combined view. Cowton held that God's will determines what will be the case (compare Scotus), and that in his eternity God contemplates its existence (compare Thomas). This last point he explained with reference to Boethius, like Thomas. As his reason for wanting to combine the two views, Cowton submitted that he considered it impossible, even for God, to know a contingent event by its cause before it has actually taken place. This point had also been made by Thomas Aquinas, but had been criticized by Scotus and various Scotists. For Cowton, it meant that the determination of God's will alone is not sufficient: God must also know the event itself, which is why his eternity is brought in. Divine will and eternity are in perfect harmony in this respect:

Novocastro), 280 (Landulph Caracciolo), and 290 (Peter of Aquila).

[61] See the texts cited by Schwamm, *Das göttliche Vorherwissen*, 173.

[62] Città del Vaticano, Bibl. Apost., Vat. lat., 1012, foll. 91va-92va, as edited by H. Schwamm, *Robert Cowton*, (433) 53 and (439f) 59f.

[63] The relevant passages are cited in Schwamm, *Das göttliche Vorherwissen*, 145f.

if God wills an event to happen in the future, it is at once present to eternity as a real event.[64]

Cowton's attempted synthesis was criticized by James of Ascoli, who did not believe that the views of Thomas and Scotus could be united at this point. In particular, he took offence at the realistic interpretation of presence to eternity which Cowton (allegedly) gave of Thomas. His objection was in part an argument Scotus had given against knowledge of contingents by means of ideas: if all things are present to God, then the members of a contradiction will be simultaneously true.[65]

To better understand the conditions and motives from which such views as those of Antonius Andreas and Robert Cowton emerged, two important observations should be noted. First, Scotistic writers who objected to Thomas's real presence, usually themselves advocated a presence 'as if'. According to William of Alnwick, for instance, the future is present (*praesens*) to God in the determination of the divine act of will, not in itself. The Franciscan Alexander of Alessandria said the same: the real existence of a thing is present (*praesens*) to God, not in itself, but as something that is willed by him (*in esse volito*).[66] It is not inconceivable that this 'as if' presence was the bridge between Thomas and Scotus that inspired Andreas and Cowton. Earlier in this chapter, we saw that Thomas's position was interpreted in terms of the 'as if' theory by several philosophers around 1300. This interpretation must have had a certain currency, and also concurred with the Scoticizing view of William of Alnwick and Alexander of Alessandria regarding the contingent's presence in God.

Secondly, Henry of Ghent had defended not only the view that was later adopted by Scotus, but also maintained the view of Thomas. All things are present to God, he claimed, not only because God knows the determination of his will, but also because God sees all things in his eternity. Henry did not believe that knowledge of the contingent in its cause (that is, in the determination of the will) is sufficient for knowing that it exists. For existence, that kind of knowledge is merely conjectural. Therefore God must also have knowledge by which he can know the existence of the contingent, analogous to the sensory knowledge by which man infallibly knows when something exists.[67] It should be clear that there is a similarity here between Henry's view and that of Robert Cowton. Presumably, Cowton's combination of Thomas

---

[64] Robert Cowton, *Sent.*, I dd. 38-39, as cited in Schwamm, *Robert Cowton*, (390f) 10f and (399) 19; and in id., *Das göttliche Vorherwissen*, 132. The dating of Robert's *Sentences* commentary is according to H. Theissing, *Glaube und Theologie bei Robert Cowton OFM*, Münster 1969 (BGPhThMA, 42/3), 12.

[65] Città del Vaticano, Bibl. Apost., Vat. lat., 1012, foll. 91va-92va, as edited by H. Schwamm, *Robert Cowton*, (428) 48.

[66] The germane passages are cited by H. Schwamm, *Das göttliche Vorherwissen*, 137 (Alexander of Alessandria) and 181 (Alnwick).

[67] Henry of Ghent, *Quodlibeta*, VIII q. 2 (ed. Paris 1518), fol 303rM.

and Scotus should be seen as a reverberation of the original framing of the problem by Henry of Ghent. This suggestion also fits in with Cowton's general outlook, of which we know that it was close to Henry of Ghent in many respects.[68]

The contingency of God's knowledge according to Scotus

In contrast with Thomas Aquinas, Scotus held that God's knowledge of contingents is itself contingent and not necessary. It follows the modality of the objects of knowledge. That God has knowledge is necessary, but that he has knowledge of a contingent object is not necessary; similarly, it is necessary that man is a living being, but not that he is a *white* living being.[69] In the *Lectura*, this point was not elaborated any further. In the *Reportata Parisiensia*, however, Scotus gave the following explanation of it, using the example of the 'soul of the Antichrist'. If two things coincide in their truth (*convertuntur*), then it is not possible that one is necessary and the other contingent. 'To will that the Antichrist's soul will exist', and 'to know that the Antichrist's soul will exist' coincide as to their truth, for the existence of this soul is knowable only insofar as it is willed by God. Yet this will is not necessary, for the Antichrist's soul is willed by God as a contingent thing. Therefore, God's knowledge of its existence must also be contingent.[70]

The gist of the argument is not difficult to understand, and is obviously in keeping with what has been discussed above. God's will acts in a contingent way and the intellect knows what has been determined by the will. The contingent things known by the intellect might as well have been not-made by the will. Hence they might have been not-known. This view, together with its characteristic inference from contingency of will to contingency of knowledge, was later adopted by many Scotists, including Johannes de Bassolis, Hugh of Novocastro, William of Rubione, and Peter of Aquila.[71]

Scotus's view on this point fell in with the Franciscan tradition of Robert Grosseteste and Bonaventure, who had claimed that God's knowledge of the contingent is itself contingent, though they did not argue this position from the contingency of the will. According to Grosseteste, what is true of the antecedent is also true of the consequent, provided the second follows upon the first. Now, let the antecedent be, 'The Antichrist will not be', which is contingent. Then the consequent, 'God knows from eternity that the Antichrist will not be', will also be contingent. Bonaventure's position was that with regard to assertions of the form 'God knows that A will be', we should distinguish, on the one hand, the divine act of knowledge (as the *principale*

---

[68] Cf. H. Theissing, *Glaube und Theologie*, 14f, with further bibliographical references.
[69] *Lectura*, I d. 39 qq. 1-5 n. 80 (ed. Vat., 17), 505f.
[70] *Reportata Parisiensia*, I q. 40 q. u. n. 12 (ed. Wadding, 11/1), fol. 222a.
[71] H. Schwamm, *Das göttliche Vorherwissen*, 213 (Johannes de Bassolis), 234 (Hugh of Novocastro), 256f (William of Rubione), and 293 (Peter of Aquila).

significatum), and on the other hand, the relation of the future contingent to this act (as the *connotatum*). The divine act of knowledge itself is necessary, for it coincides with God. Because the *connotatum* is contingent, however, the assertion 'God knows that A will be' will also be contingent, taken as a whole.[72]

Contingency and certainty

That future contingents are known contingently, Scotus warned, should not be taken to mean that God could somehow be mistaken about them. The known might have been different, yet God knows exactly what it is going to be, for he himself is its cause. That the known *can* be different does not make God's knowledge fallible; it would only be so if the known actually *were* different from what God knows it to be. According to Scotus, the assertion 'God knows that A is' is perfectly compatible with 'It is *possible* that A is not', though not with 'A *is* not'.[73]

There was a marked difference between Thomas and Scotus with regard to the relation between contingency and certainty. Thomas believed that the known is contingent only *outside* of God's knowledge, inasmuch as it was produced by contingently working causes. *Inside* God's knowledge it is necessary, because it exists forever in God's eternity (the necessity of present and past: that which is cannot not-be). Contingency and certainty are located in distinct modes of being (inside/ouside knowledge); they do not threaten each other, because the necessity of knowledge does not affect the modality of what is known. Scotus, on the other hand, believed that the reason for their compatibility lies in the fact that God's will is responsible both for the certainty of knowledge and for the contingency of what is known. It is the *prima radix contingentiae*: all worldly contingency rests on the contingency of divine will. Instead of precluding the certainty of the intellect, the fact that it derives from the will insures that it is congruent with contingency.[74] Whereas Thomas thought distinct levels of being were needed to keep the two apart, Scotus located them both at the one level of divine knowledge.

The position that God's will is the root of all contingency acquired much influence. It was taken over by all Scotists, particularly William of Alnwick.[75] Several non-Scotists subscribed to it as well, most notably Marsilius of Inghen.

---

[72] For Grosseste and Bonaventure, see the references in n. 42 above. This was also the view of Richard of Middleton, *Sent.*, I d. 38 a. 1 q. 6 ad 7 (ed. Brescia 1591), fol. 342a.
[73] *Lectura*, Sent., I d. 39 qq. 1-5 nn. 71f (ed. Vat., 17), 503f.
[74] Ibid., n. 61, 500.
[75] H. Schwamm, *Das göttliche Vorherwissen*, 332.

Contingency and immutability

Thomas and Scotus also differed on the relation between contingency and immutability. From the belief that God is an immutable being, Thomas inferred that his knowledge must be necessary. Scotus, however, made a sharp distinction between these two. God's knowledge is immutable because it is non-successive, which does not imply necessity, but can go with contingency. With this unlinking of immutability and necessity, Scotus subscribed to a distinctly non-Aristotelian notion of contingency, as has been demonstrated in particular by Simo Knuuttila.[76] Scotus took issue with the Aristotelian-Boethian reading of the rule 'omne quod est quando est necesse est esse', as given by Thomas. He believed that at the instant something *is*, it is not necessary but can still not-be.

To further demonstrate this, Scotus distinguished between the rule's *sensus compositionis* and its *sensus divisionis*. Taken in the first sense, he took it to be a true categorical assertion, meaning: 'Necessarily, everything is if it is'. This is simply a case of the Anselmian *necessitas sequens* or *necessitas consequentiae*, discussed earlier in this chapter: if something is, it cannot at the same time not-be. Interpreted in *sensus compositionis*, this necessity does not affect the modality of being. This is different if the rule is interpreted in *sensus divisionis*. According to Scotus, on this reading it turns into a hypothetical assertion, meaning: 'Everything that is exists of necessity, if it exists'. Scotus took this assertion to be false. For a contingent thing is not necessary if it exists; it still *can* be different even the moment it exists, though of course it is not *actually* different.[77]

The distinctive trait of Scotus's interpretation was precisely the fact that he wanted to preserve the possibility of not-being even at the instant t_i at which a thing comes into being. Thomas, on the other hand, located the possibility in the indeterminacy of the thing's cause *prior to* t_i. At t_i itself the possibility disappears. This idea is particularly clear from the way Thomas complied with the classical requirement that the object of scientific knowledge should be necessary, in that he understood the object as being present to God (and hence as necessary). For Scotus, the object retains its contingency even when it is immutably known in its factuality.

The coexistence of being and possible-non-being was criticized by William of Ockham. One of the objections he raised against this view was that a possibility that cannot be realized is not a possibility. If something *is* at time

---

[76] Scotus, *Lectura*, I d. 39 qq. 1-5 n. 77 (ed. Vat., 17), 505; *Reportata Parisiensia*, I d. 40 q. u. n. 14 (ed. Wadding, 11/1), fol. 222a; S. Knuuttila, 'Time and Modality in Scholasticism', *Reforging the Great Chain of Being. Studies in the History of Modal Theory*, ed. S. Knuuttila, Dordrecht 1981 (Synthese Historical Library, 20), 163-257, esp. 217-234; id., 'Duns Scotus' Criticism of the 'Statistical' Interpretation of Modality', *Sprache und Erkenntnis im Mittelalter*, Vol. 1, ed. W. Kluxen et al., Berlin-New York 1981 (MM, 13/1), 441-450.

[77] *Lectura*, I d. 39 qq. 1-5 n. 58, 499.

t_1, the possibility of its not-being cannot be realized any more at t_1. Hence at t_1 there no longer is the possibility of not-being. A similar objection was raised in the *Liber propugnatorius*. In a discussion of Scotus's view of contingency in Johannes Baconis's commentary on the *Sentences*, this criticism, which Baconis attributed to Thomas Wilton, was quoted extensively. Thomas Wilton in his criticism followed the traditional line we have seen in Aquinas: that which is or was, cannot not-be. Therefore, God's knowledge is not contingent but necessary.[78] From these and other reactions, it is clear that Scotus's view of contingency was well-known to non-Scotistic philosophers at the beginning of the fourteenth century, even if not endorsed by them.

WILLIAM OF OCKHAM

Ockham is famous for his position that God knows all future contingents in a certain and evident fashion (*certitudinaliter et evidenter*), and that man is unable to explain how this is possible.[79] In the period that is the subject of our study (1250-1400), Ockham was the first to state so explicitly that an explanation is beyond our reach. The general philosophical landscape in which his pessimism was set, and from which it can be understood, was formed by the climate of critical thought at early fourteenth-century Oxford, and by the criticism that had coalesced with regard to the main positions at the time, notably those of Thomas and Scotus.[80] The same attitude of reluctance can also be found in later writers such as Adam Wodeham, Gregory of Rimini, and Marsilius of Inghen. They were doubtless inspired in part by Ockham, whom Adam Wodeham indeed expressly cited on this topic. Thus, we now turn to Ockham.

Setting the problem

As Ockham saw it, the main problem with God's foreknowledge of future contingents was this: how can something be known if it does not yet exist, and hence does not have truth? He referred to Aristotle's discussion of the truth

---

[78] For Ockham, see M. McCord Adams, *William Ockham*, II, 1131f. *Liber propugnatorius*, I d. 39 q. 5 (ed. Venice 1523), fol. 121vb; Johannes Baconis, *Sent.*, I d. 40 q. u. a. 2 par. 2 (ed. Cremona 1618), foll. 386b-387a (opinion of Scotus) and parr. 3-5, foll. 387b-389b (criticism by Wilton).

[79] Ockham, *Scriptum*, I d. 38 q. u. (OTh, 4), 583f; id., *Tractatus de praedestinatione et de praescientia Dei respectu futurorum contingentium*, q. 1, ed. Ph. Boehner and S. Brown, St. Bonaventure, New York 1978 (OPh, 2), 516f. For a discussion of Ockham's view, see M. McCord Adams, *Willam Ockham*, II, 1143-1148; W.L. Craig, *The Problem of Divine Foreknowledge*, 146-168, with further bibliographical references on pp. 288f; D. Perler, *Prädestination, Zeit und Kontingenz*, Amsterdam 1988 (Bochumer Studien zur Philosophie, 12). The influence of Ockhams *Tractatus* in Oxford in the second half of the 1320s is documented by a question of Arnold of Strelley, see H.G. Gelber, 'Ockham's Early Influence: A Question About Predestination and Foreknowledge by Arnold of Strelley, OP', *AHDLMA* 63 (1988), 255-289.

[80] Cf. L. Honnefelder, 'Das Verhältnis von Theologie und Philosophie als veränderndes

value of contingent propositions about the future in *Perihermeneias* (c. 9).[81] In his reading of Aristotle, he followed the line of Boethius we saw earlier in this chapter. Even though, of each contradictory pair of singular contingent propositions about the future, necessarily one is true and the other false, their truth values are as yet indeterminate, and hence cannot be known with certainty. Another basic aspect of Ockham's approach, and again one in which he was following Boethius, was the fact that he restricted contingency to the effects of free will. Things that are *not* caused by free will but by means of natural causes, as for instance the rising of the sun, can be known beforehand because natural causes work in determinate ways and can produce only one kind of effect.[82]

That God knows what the future is going to be, Ockham believed to be totally incomprehensible to natural reason. Our only access to it is by means of *auctoritates* from the Scipture and from the saints. From a philosophical point of view, all we can say is that divine essence is one intuitive act of knowledge, both of itself and of all other things, and that it is so perfect and clear that it has evident knowledge of all past, present, and future events.[83]

By 'evident knowledge', Ockham meant knowledge of true propositions based on intuitive knowledge of the terms. Man has evident knowledge of contingent propositions (such as, 'Socrates is white') if he has intuitive knowledge of the terms, that is, if he knows that Socrates and whiteness exist at the same time and are true of the same thing. In like fashion God has evident knowledge, Ockham claimed, not only of the necessary and contingent truths of the present, but of those of past and future as well. He knows the existence of all things; hence he knows exactly when they will be, which propositions are true and which are false.[84]

Ockham's criticism of other views

Ockham rejected the view of Thomas and of many Thomists that God knows the contingent because all things are present to his eternity. He did not spell out his objections to this view, but we may gather (for reasons that will become clear) that they were probably the same as those raised by De la Mare and Scotus: that which does not yet exist cannot be present to God. Ockham

---

Moment in der Entwicklung des Selbstverständnisses der Philosophie', *Thomas von Aquin im philosophischen Gespräch*, ed. W. Kluxen, München 1975 (Alber-Broschur Philosophie), 212-215; K. Flasch, *Das philosophische Denken im Mittelalter. Von Augustin zu Machiavelli*, Stuttgart 1986, 426-430.

[81] *Scriptum*, I d. 38 q. u. (OTh, 4), 584; *Tractatus*, q. 1 (OPh, 2), 516; *Summa logicae*, III/3 c. 32, ed. Ph. Boehner, G. Gál, and S. Brown, St. Bonaventure, New York 1974 (OPh, 1), 710.

[82] Ockham, *Expositio in librum Perihermenias Aristotelis*, I c. 6 par. 14f, ed. A. Gambatese and S. Brown, St. Bonaventure, New York 1978 (OPh, 2), 421f; *Scriptum*, I d. 38 q. u., 584.

[83] *Scriptum*, I d. 38 q. u. (OTh, 4), 585.

[84] Ibid. For Ockham's view on evident knowledge, see K. Tachau. *Vision and Certitude*, 122.

also rejected the view that God knows the contingent by means of ideas functioning as forms of knowledge (*rationes cognoscendi*). Again, he did not provide detailed arguments, but presumably his general criticism of ideas as forms of knowledge was applicable here. Finally, Ockham took issue with the position of Scotus, the only position he criticized extensively, which bears witness to the great interest taken in Scotus's view at Oxford at the time.[85]

Ockham raised four arguments against the position of Scotus, which we shall review in order.[86] His first and most important objection, which was later used against Scotus by Adam Wodeham and Gregory of Rimini, was that the will cannot determine God's knowledge: for even if God would not act as a cause, then he would still have evident knowledge of the future by virtue of his essence. Ockham did not deny that God is the cause of contingents, nor that God's will (in part) determines what will happen and when, but merely that the will serves as the medium through which God has knowledge. According to Ockham, God's will determines the truth of contingents but not God's knowledge of them.[87]

Second, Ockham criticized Scotus's idea that knowledge is certain in virtue of the will. If the will's determination of a future event is contingent, that is, if it could be other than it is, then also God's knowledge could be other than it is. Hence, knowledge in virtue of the will cannot be certain.

Ockham's third objection highlighted the freedom of human action. If the determination of God's will is such that man must necessarily act as God has ordained, then the certainty of God's knowledge is bought at the price of man's responsibility for his own actions. Assuming on the other hand that man is free, then more is required than God's knowledge of his own act of will: if his knowledge is to be certain, then in addition he must know man's act of will, which determines what man is going to do. But this knowledge cannot be eternal, since man does not exist from eternity. (Here we see that Ockham rejected the view that future things are present to God's eternity.)

Finally, Ockham took issue with Scotus's theory of stages in God. He argued that there can be no succession in God, therefore also no consecutive stages. Moreover, if God's knowledge proceeds in stages then a contradiction is implied, for God would (first) know an event neutrally and (then) determinately. This means that one and the same thing is known both without and with truth, which is a contradiction. Also, stages in God would imply a certain imperfection, as God would have to receive the perfection of his knowledge of the future from something else, that is, from the will.

---

[85] For the influence of Scotus at Oxford, see J.I. Catto, 'Theology and Theologians', 509-512. Cf. C. Bérubé, 'La première école scotiste', *Logique, ontologie et théologie au XIVe siècle. Preuve et raisons à l'université de Paris*, ed. Z. Kaluza and P. Vignaux, Paris 1984, 9-24.

[86] *Scriptum*, I d. 38 q. u. (OTh, 4), 582f and 585.

[87] Ibid., 585. On the role of God's will, see Ph. Boehner, *The Tractatus*, 55.

Similar objections were raised against Scotus in the *Liber propugnatorius* and in the commentary on the *Sentences* of Peter Aureoli. In the *Liber propugnatorius*, it was argued that Scotus's line of reasoning was valid only on the assumption that God's will is the total cause of all contingent being. For only then can his knowledge be certain in virtue of the will. But God is *not* the total cause of all contingent being, for sins are caused by man and not by God. The phrasing of this objection differed from that of Ockham, who did not mention sin, but it was nonetheless essentially the same as Ockham's third argument. Like Ockham, the author of the *Liber propugnatorius* criticized the theory of stages, arguing that it implies a degree of imperfection in God's intellect, which must receive something from the will. Moreover, the theory is inconsistent. If the intellect in the first instance knows something *without* determination, and in a next instance knows it *with* a determination, then it must already know in the first instance that this determination is forthcoming. The determination is known as something of the future, hence also the future existence of the things that are going to be is thus determined by the will. But this means that the intellect can know future things without the determination of the will itself, which contradicts the theory's original assumption.[88]

Similar problems were detected by Peter Aureoli. God does not have knowledge of all future things by virtue of the determination of will, for he is not the cause of man's free acts of will, and in particular not the cause of sin. Also, the idea that God is determined by the will impugns his necessity. It is impossible, Aureoli argued, that God receive something from a medium of knowledge.[89]

Veritas determinata in contingent propositions about the future

Ockham believed that God knows the truth of contingent propositions about the future. But according to Aristotle, natural reason incarnate, future propositions do not have determinate and knowable truth values. To solve this quandary, Ockham reinterpreted the notion of 'determinate truth value' (*veritas determinata*) in the following way.[90] A contingent proposition about the future has determinate truth value iff it is either true such that it is not false, or false such that it is not true.[91] The truth or falsity of this proposition, according to Ockham, is not determined by something previous, but by the future fact itself. Let this fact occur at t_F (a moment in the future), then proposition p is true such that it is not false at all times $t_{i<F}$ (defined as all moments in time preceding t_F). If the Antichrist will come, then p, 'The Antichrist will come', is true and not false. On the other hand, if the fact does

---

[88] *Liber propugnatorius*, I d. 39 q. 2 (ed. Venice 1523), fol. 119rb-va.
[89] Aureoli, *Sent.*, I d. 38 a. 1 (ed. Rome 1596), fol. 876bD-E.
[90] Cf. (still useful) Ph. Boehner, *The Tractatus*, 48; M. McCord Adams, *William Ockham*, II, 1137-1143.
[91] Cf. *Scriptum*, I d. 38 q. u. (OTh, 4), 587.

not happen at t_F, then proposition p is false and not true at $t_{i<F}$. On this reading, the truth of p is as contingent as the future fact itself. Because p is true before t_F, it can be known at $t_{i<F}$.

Typical of this reading of determinate truth is the fact that it blocks the implication of there being a cause at $t_{i<F}$ that is causally (hence necessarily) responsible for the occurrence of the t_F event. This is accomplished by reversing the usual perspective on the course of events (from past to future), starting rather from the future fact occurring at t_F and looking back from there into the past. The change of perspective allowed Ockham to break the connection between necessity and immutability. During the interval $t_{i<F}$, the truth value of p cannot be changed, for it is not determined by events in $t_{i<F}$ but by the t_F event. Yet p is not necessary, its immutability notwithstanding: the event at t_F, the coming of the Antichrist, is contingent and not necessary, as it is not determined by causes at $t_{i<F}$, but by the free will of God. Ockham was thus able to claim that propositions about future contingents have determinate and immutable truth values, while the events themselves remain utterly contingent. Hence, contingency, *veritas determinata* and immutability can go together.

The above analysis also holds good for propositions that materially are about the future, but in which the verbs are set in past or present tense. Examples are: 'God *knows* that the Antichrist will come' and 'God *knew* that the Antichrist will come'. Propositions like these are contingent, because the coming of the Antichrist is itself a contingent event, and because God only knows/knew that the Antichrist will be coming if he *will* be coming. Because of their dependency upon the future, these propositions do not fall under the necessity of past and present, but under the contingency of the future.

In his discussion of the *suppositiones* (presuppositions) in the *Tractatus de praedestinatione*, Ockham cited this view, viz., that some propositions with verbs in present or past tense are not necessary, as a kind of second rule, a complement to the well-known rule that to every true proposition about the present there is a corresponding necessary proposition about the past (if p is true, then henceforth necessarily 'It was true that p').[92]

The same position on present and past propositions about the future also occurred in the *Notabilia de contingencia et presciencia dei* by Richard Campsall, a probably elder contemporary of Ockham, who read on the *Sentences* at Oxford not later than 1316-1317, as well as in the commentaries on the *Sentences* of Robert Holcot, Adam Wodeham, Gregory of Rimini, and Marsilius of Inghen. The only known manuscript of Campsall's *Notabilia*, London, British Museum, Harleian Mss., 3243, fol. 78 (88), contains two marginal remarks inserted by the copyist or by a fourteenth-century reader,

---

[92] *Tractatus*, q. 1 sup. 3 (OPh, 2), 515. See also *Summa logicae*, III/3 c. 32 (OPh, 1), 712f. Cf. C.G. Normore, 'Future Contingents', 371; M. McCord Adams, *William Ockham*, II, 1142f.

pointing out the use of the additional (new?) rule, from which we may gather that it enjoyed special interest.⁹³

The view that propositions about the future have determinate truth value was criticized in the commentary on the *Sentences* of Peter Aureoli. Ockham did not take notice of this criticism, but reactions to it are found in later commentaries on the *Sentences* by Gregory of Rimini, Alfonsus Vargas, and Peter of Ailly. Aureoli based himself on Aristotle's view that the truth or falsity of a proposition depends upon the existence of the fact referred to. If the fact does not yet exist, the proposition has no truth value; it is neither true nor false. Once the fact is there, the proposition has truth value. Conversely, if a proposition about the future has truth value, then the corresponding fact must already have been fixed and will necessarily be realized. Aureoli believed that the principle of bivalence is not valid with regard to contingent propositions about the future.⁹⁴

Aureoli also believed that the notions of immutability and necessity are inseparably linked. What is immutable cannot fail to be necessary, that is, it cannot be contingent, because the two notions are defined in the same way: what cannot possibly be different is necessary, and what cannot possibly change is immutable. Considering that 'to change' means 'to be different from before (*prius*)', whatever is immutable must also be necessary. According to Aureoli this equivalence applies to propositions as well. Assuming that proposition p ('The Antichrist will come at t_F') is immutably true at $t_{i<F}$, then p is true of necessity and not contingent; likewise, the coming of the Antichrist at t_F is necessary. The truth value we assumed for p cannot be changed during the interval $t_{i<F}$, for it is determined by the Antichrist's coming at t_F, therefore during $t_{i<F}$, p is necessarily true. At t_F, the event described by p will necessarily happen, for otherwise p would not have been true at $t_{i<F}$.⁹⁵

Contingency and (im)mutability of God's knowledge

With regard to the modality of God's knowledge Ockham followed the general Franciscan line as set out by Robert Grosseteste, Bonaventure, and Duns Scotus: God's knowledge of the contingent is contingent itself. This contingency of knowledge should not, however, be taken to imply contin-

---

⁹³ Richard Campsall, *Notabilia de contingencia et presciencia dei*, IX n. 17 and XIV n. 22, ed. E.A. Synan, Toronto 1982 (The Works of Richard of Campsall, 2), 41f; Robert Holcot, *In quatuor libros Sententiarum quaestiones*, II q. 2, Lyon 1518, repr. Frankfurt a/M 1967, fol. hiiira; Adam Wodeham, *Lectura Oxoniensis*, III q. 3 (Paris, Bibl. Maz., 915), fol. 179rb-va; Gregory of Rimini, *Lectura*, I d. 38 q. 2 and dd. 40-41 q. 1 (ed. Trapp-Marcolino, 3), 302f and 350. The view of Marsilius will be discussed in the next chapter. As for the two *marginalia* mentioned, see F. Hoffmann, *Die theologische Methode des Oxforder Dominikanerlehrers Robert Holcot*, Münster 1972 (BGPhThMA NF, 5), 371f nn. 9 and 14. On Campsall's biography, see K.H. Tachau, *Vision and Certitude*, 159f, with futher bibliographical references.

gency in God himself. Like Bonaventure, Ockham made a distinction between the knowledge by which God knows the contingents and the manner in which these are known to him. God's knowledge itself is necessary and immutable, as it coincides with divine essence. Yet the manner in which God has knowledge is contingent: what is known is contingent, hence it could as well have not been known.[96]

Closely related to the problem of the contingency of divine knowledge is that of its (im)mutability. On this point, in the *Scriptum* Ockham discussed both the question whether God's knowledge can be increased and whether it can be changed. The two questions are by no means the same: mutability does not necessarily imply growth, yet growth implies change. In this context he distinguished between two senses of knowledge, one broad (*cognoscere*), the other strict (*scire*). In the broad sense of the term, God literally knows all things: complex as well as non-complex things (propositions and terms), necessary as well as contingent things, true as well as false things, possible as well as impossible things. In the strict sense of the term he only knows what is true, that is: propositions, for according to Ockham only propositions are true.[97]

Ockham claimed that God's knowledge in the broad sense (*cognoscere*) cannot be increased and that it is immutable. It cannot be added to because God already knows all things, and it is impossible to know more. It is immutable because God always knows all things by virtue of his perfection.[98]

God's knowledge in the strict sense (*scire*) cannot be increased either. This was argued as follows. The number of true propositions is always the same, for of each pair of contradictory propositions (p or not-p) always one is true. If Socrates is walking, then proposition p ('Socrates is walking') is true and not-p ('Socrates is not walking') is false. If he is not walking, then p is false and not-p is true. The truth values of those propositions may be subject to change, yet one of them is always true, and that is the one that is known by God.[99]

Knowledge in the strict sense of the word, Ockham submitted, is a predicate that is attributed to God by man when God knows something true. God knows all true propositions. As the world changes, some of these

---

[94] Aureoli, *Sent.*, I d. 38 a. 3, as edited by Ph. Boehner, *The Tractatus*, 122f. Cf. C.G. Normore, 'Future Contingents', 370. The criticism of Gregory of Rimini, Alfonsus Vargas, and Peter of Ailly will be dealt with in the next chapter.

[95] The relevant passages are referred to by Normore, 'Future Contingents', 369 n. 28.

[96] *Scriptum*, I d. 38 q. u. (OTh, 4), 587; *Tractatus*, q. 2 (OPh, 2), 529f.

[97] *Scriptum*, I d. 39 q. u., 589; *Tractatus*, q. 1, 518. Ockham's distinction was referred to in the *Quodlibeta* of Robert Holcot, see the text in W.J. Courtenay, 'A Revised Text of Robert Holcot's Quodlibetal Dispute on Whether God is Able to Know More Than He Knows', *Archiv für Geschichte der Philosophie* 53 (1971), 1-21, esp. 8.

[98] *Scriptum*, I d. 39 q. u., 589.

[99] Ibid., 589f; *Tractatus*, q. 2 (OPh, 2), 526.

propositions become true and others become false. Of the true propositions man can claim that they are known by God in the strict sense: if God knows them (as he does because he knows everything), then he knows something that is true. According to Ockham, this does not mean that God is subject to change if he first knows one true proposition, and then another; all that changes is that which causes the propositions to switch truth values: creation itself. He explained this by means of an example. Suppose you falsely believe the proposition 'Socrates is sitting' to be true. Now, if Socrates actually sits down the act of knowledge in your intellect remains the same, but the proposition 'Socrates is sitting' changes from false to true. Hence also your not-knowledge changes into knowledge, even though absolutely nothing in you has changed. This is analogous, Ockham claimed, to the way we can say of God that he comes to know something he did not know before (or conversely). It does not mean that God has changed, but merely that the proposition known by God has changed its truth value. God himself remains immutably the same.[100]

Ockham's belief that the number of propositions known by God is fixed was criticized by Robert Holcot in one of his *quaestiones quodlibetales*, who accused Ockham of inconsistency on this point. Assuming that true propositions form the object of God's knowledge in the strict sense, then the number of things known by God can be increased and decreased, and can even become zero, depending on the number of propositions that are true.

Moreover, Holcot argued, it is not true that there necessarily are just as many true propositions as there are false ones. For if of a pair of contradictory propositions the false one is not spoken or thought of, and is not written down, then it is not false but simply nonexistent: only propositions that exist can be true or false. If the true proposition is spoken or thought of, or if it has been written down, then it exists. It follows that there can be more true propositions than false ones, and conversely.[101]

Obviously, Holcot subscribed to a *token* view of propositions as the ones that are actually pronounced, thought of, or written down. Of one event E there can be many true and false token propositions. If one thousand people form in their minds a true proposition about E, then there are one thousand true token propositions about E. If there are five hundred people who do the same, then there are only five hundred true tokens: God's knowledge of these propositions has become less. If *nobody* forms a true proposition about E, then God does not know a true proposition about E either. Yet, according to

---

[100] *Scriptum*, I d. 39 q. u., 590f; *Tractatus*, q. 2, 524f and 531.
[101] See the edition by W.J. Courtenay, A Revised Text', 9f and 15. For a discussion of Holcot's view, see E.A. Moody, 'A Quodlibetal Question of Robert Holcot OP on the Problem of the Object of Knowledge and of Belief', *Speculum* 39 (1964), 53-74; J. Pinborg, *Logik und Semantik*, 148-153; G. Nuchelmans, *Theories of the Proposition*, 205f; M. McCord Adams, *William Ockham*, II, 1085-1114.

Holcot, this does not imply that God knows nothing. He distinguished between things and truths (propositions). Through his essence God knows all things. But if there are no propositions, for instance if there were no human beings, then God would not have knowledge of truths, for only propositions can be true.[102]

Ockham, on the other hand, in arguing that God cannot know more than he does, based himself on *type* propositions rather than tokens. Type propositions can be shared by different people: the tokens thought (spoken, written) by different people may actually belong to the same type. In this view the number of propositions is independent of their being spoken, thought, or written down. Marilyn McCord Adams has correctly pointed out the connection between this position of Ockham and his early view on the ontological status of concepts and propositions, viz., that they are only objects of knowledge and do not have qualitative being as really existing mental acts. Seen in this light, propositions cannot be construed as tokens, because the self-same proposition can be the object of different acts of knowledge.[103]

Rules on the (im)mutability of God's knowledge in the strict sense

Following his exposition on the (im)mutability of God's knowledge, Ockham gave a number of logico-semantic rules which systematically list the possible conditions under which the truth values of propositions, and hence God's knowledge in the strict sense, can be said to change. His rules are as follows.[104]

> 1. Propositions about the present can change from falsity to truth and from truth to falsity. God can know these propositions after not having known them, and not-know after having known them. For instance, let proposition p be: 'Socrates is sitting'. God only comes to know p the moment Socrates is sitting down, and not before. If Socrates stands up again, God ceases to know p.
> 2.1 Affirmative propositions about the future are immutably true until the facts they describe are realized. Before that moment comes by, nothing can change the truth value of those propositions. The propositions are immutably known by God until their corresponding facts are realized. As soon as that happens, they turn false. ('Socrates will be sitting at t_i' is false at t_i itself as well as after t_i.)
> 2.2 Of affirmative propositions about the future it cannot be said that God knows them after not having known them before (for they are immutably true before the fact), though it can be said that he no longer knows them after having known them (for after the fact they are no longer true).
> 3.1 Some propositions about the future are true without ever having become true (in the past), although they can become false (in the future). For instance,

---

[102] M. McCord Adams, *William Ockham*, II, 1093, which includes references to the germane passages.
[103] Ibid., 1099f. For this definition of *type* propositions, see W. and M. Kneale, *The Development of Logic*, Oxford ⁷1978, 49 and 53.
[104] *Tractatus*, q. 2 (OPh, 2), 524-526.

let proposition p be: 'Socrates will be sitting at t_i'. God's knowledge of p has no beginning, but it does come to an end (at t_j).

3.2 Some propositions about the future are false without ever having become false in the past, although they can become true in the future. For instance, proposition not-p: 'Socrates will not be sitting at t_i'. After t_i not-p is always true. Hence God's knowledge of not-p has a beginning (notably at time t_j), but does not end.

Similar rules can be found in the writings of Walter Chatton, Richard Campsall, John of Rodington, Robert Holcot, and Adam Wodeham. The rules of Campsall and Rodington were quoted in the anonymous commentary on the *Sentences,* Città del Vaticano, Bibl. Apost., Vat. lat., 986 (fol. 28va-b).[105] As far as we have been able to ascertain, no rules of this kind were mentioned by Parisian theologians of the beginning of the fourteenth century. There they did not occur until in the 1340s, in the commentaries on the *Sentences* of Gregory of Rimini and John of Mirecourt.[106] Later, they were also used by Marsilius of Inghen. Their origin must therefore be located in England (Oxford), in such thinkers as Walter Chatton, Richard Campsall, and William of Ockham. We shall return to these rules, which are a clear example of the application of logico-semantic techniques in the context of divine knowledge, in the next chapter.

---

[105] Chatton, *Reportatio,* I d. 38, as cited by H. Schwamm, *Das göttliche Vorherwissen,* 318; Campsall, *Notabilia* (ed. Synan, 2), 38-43; Rodington, *Sent.,* I d. 38, as cited by K.H. Tachau, 'The Influence of Richard Campsall on Fourteenth-Century Oxford Thought', *From Ockham to Wyclif,* ed. A. Hudson and M. Wilks, Oxford 1987 (Studies in Church History, Subsidia, 5), 116f n. 27 (Rodington delivered his lectures on the *Sentences* probably 1328-29); Holcot, *Sent.,* II q. 2 a. 7, as cited by F. Hoffmann, *Die theologische Methode,* 309f n. 48 (see also the forthcoming edition by P.A Streveler et al., *Seeing the Future Clearly. Quodlibetal Questions on Future Contingents by Robert Holcot*); Adam Wodeham, *Lectura Oxoniensis,* III q. 2 (Paris, Bibl. Maz., 915), foll. 175va-176rb. As for the quotation in the anonymous *Sentences* commentary (Città del Vaticano, Bibl. Apost., Vat. lat., 986), see K.H. Tachau, 'The Influence', 116f, and id., *Vision and Certitude,* 217 n. 32.

[106] Gregory, *Lectura,* I dd. 35-36 q. 1 additio 148c (ed. Trapp-Marcolino, 3), 231f; Mirecourt, *Lectura in primum Sententiarum,* I d. 35 (Bologna, Bibl. Com. dell' Archiginnasio, A 921), fol. 47va-vb. Mirecourt used as his source the views cited in Thomas Bradwardine's *De futuris contingentibus.* Cf. J.–F. Genest, 'Le *De futuris contingentibus* de Thomas Bradwardine', *Recherches Augustiniennes* 14 (1974), 271f; J.–F. Genest and P. Vignaux, 'La bibliothèque anglaise de Jean de Mirecourt: *subtilitas* ou plagiat?', *Die Philosophie im 14. und 15. Jahrhundert. In memoriam Konstanty Michalski (1879-1947),* ed. O. Pluta, Amsterdam 1988 (Bochumer Studien zur Philosophie, 10), 275-301, esp. 293. Most probably, Bradwardine's question *De futuris contingentibus* was part of his commentary on the *Sentences,* delivered 1332-1333. See J.–F. Genest and K.H. Tachau, 'La Lecture de Thomas Bradwardine sur les Sentences', *AHDLMA* 65 (1990), 301-306.

CHAPTER SEVEN

DIVINE FOREKNOWLEDGE AND FUTURE CONTINGENTS
SECOND PART: THE PERIOD 1330-1400

Many of the commentaries on the *Sentences* that originated in England from 1330 onward, and on the continent from 1340 onward, show a remarkable tendency to focus their discussion of divine knowledge on the problem of God's foreknowledge and related issues. By comparison, the more traditional problems of the late thirteenth and early fourteenth century (such as, does God need rational relations in order to know the creatures, or: does he know creation by means of ideas?) were scarcely raised any more. This is true of the various redactions of Adam Wodeham's commentary on the *Sentences*, of that of Robert Holcot, and of those of Gregory of Rimini, John of Mirecourt (who read on the *Sentences* at Paris in 1344-1345), Alfonsus Vargas, Hugolin of Orvieto, and Peter of Ailly.[1] The commentaries of John of Mirecourt and Peter of Ailly even go so far as to devote themselves exclusively to foreknowledge at this point. This does not rule out the possibility that in their actual lectures on Lombard they were still addressing these older problems as well. The commentaries were not transcripts of the lectures themselves, but *ordinationes* compiled later.

A common characteristic of the continental commentaries of this period is that they were heavily influenced by the work of English theologians such as William of Ockham, Richard Campsall, and Adam Wodeham.[2] One of the first authors whose work clearly shows this influence was Gregory of Rimini. It was through his work in particular that the logico-semantic account of certain knowledge of contingent events, as it had been developed in England, became known in Paris. The first part of this chapter will be devoted to Gregory's view of divine foreknowledge. We shall consider the extent to which he payed tribute to the English theologians mentioned above, and review his response to Aureoli's argument that God does *not* have knowledge of future contingents — a response that was picked up by Alfonsus Vargas and Peter of Ailly. Another aspect which shall concern us here is Gregory's discussion of the views of Thomas Aquinas and Duns Scotus. Finally, in the second part of this chapter, we shall discuss at length the position of Marsilius of Inghen.

---

[1] For the dating of Mirecourt's commentary, see W.J. Courtenay, *Covenant and Causality*, VIIIa, 226.
[2] Cf. Courtenay, 'The Role of English Thought', 115-137.

Gregory of Rimini

Following his division of objects of divine knowledge (see chapter 4), Gregory divided future things into those that can be signified noncomplexly (*res futurae*) and those that can only be signified complexly (*enuntiabilia futura*). Remarkably, Gregory stated that things of the first category (*res futurae*) are not only *possible* in the future, but that they *will actually exist* in the future. Hence, what *can* exist but *will not* exist in the future is not a *res futura* in Gregory's sense of the word. His reason for this restricted use of the expression was probably that the addition of 'futura' in 'res futura' is an implicit stipulation of the fact that the *res* will exist in the future. A similar restriction was also made with regard to the *enuntiabilia futura*. According to Gregory, all *enuntiabilia futura* can be expressed by true assertions about the future. This means that they all are about facts or events that will actually be realized in the future.

That God knows the *res futurae* Gregory inferred from the general claim, established earlier, that God knows all things. By contrast, his proof that God knows the *enuntiabilia futura* was much more complex. It consisted of two steps. The first step starts from God's knowledge of himself, and is reminiscent of Scotus. God has perfect knowledge of himself. Hence he also knows that of which he wills that it shall exist. Now, because God knows that nothing can interfere with his will, he also knows that what he wills shall exist.

The argument is not yet complete, however. According to Gregory, the first step shows us only that God has foreknowledge of *many* future things, not necessarily of *all*. A second step is needed, which runs as follows: God has foreknowledge of many *enuntiabilia*, therefore he has foreknowledge of all of them. For if it is possible that God knows some of them, then he also knows them all.[3]

Some obvious questions spring to mind with regard to this stepwise approach. The second step seems entirely redundant. Why was the first step itself not sufficient to prove that God knows all future *enuntiabilia*? Perhaps this was an echo of the critical reaction to Scotus as found in the *Liber propugnatorius* and the commentary on the *Sentences* of Peter Aureoli. If God knows *everything* through his will, then God and not man is the cause of evil and of sin.[4] Elsewhere we find that Gregory considered sin to be a *complexe significabile*, and that he criticized the view that God is the cause or the supporter of these *complexe significabilia*.[5] By splitting up his proof into two distinct steps, he was able to show that God knows all future things without necessarily implying that he is also the cause of all things.

---

[3] *Lectura*, I d. 38 q. 2 a. 1 (ed. Trapp-Marcolino, 3), 274-276, and a. 3, 285.

[4] Cf. *Liber propugnatorius*, I d. 39 q. 2 (ed. Venice 1523), fol. 119rb; Aureoli, *Sent.*, I. d. 38 a. 1 (ed. Rome 1596), fol. 875bE-F and fol. 876bD.

[5] *Lectura*, II dd. 34-37 q. 1 a. 2 (ed. Trapp-Marcolino, 6), 235, and a. 3, 272.

The view that God knows the future was criticized by Peter Aureoli. It was his opinion that assertions like 'God knows that the Antichrist will come' are false, because they falsely presuppose that God can know the future as a secondary object. The future does not yet exist, therefore it cannot be known.[6] This position obviously agrees with Aureoli's denial that contingent propositions about the future have truth values (see above, p. 189). Having no truth value, such propositions cannot be known; if God would know them, the corresponding future events would happen of necessity.

Aureoli believed that God's knowledge abstracts away from all created aspects of time, and that it is concerned only with his essence which contains all being. That is why God knows the actuality of all things in a kind of timelessness vis-a-vis himself: no creature is past or future with respect to God's knowledge. Although Aureoli made reference to Boethius's *De consolatione* (Lib. V pros. 6), it would be a mistake to put his view on a par with that of Thomas Aquinas (God sees all future things as present to him in his eternity). Thomas's position was explicitly rejected by Aureoli, as it apparently implied that God's knowledge is directed at something other than his essence.[7]

Aureoli's position was criticized in the commentaries on the *Sentences* of Gregory of Rimini, Alfonsus Vargas, and Peter of Ailly. The basis of Aureoli's position, as we have just seen, was that assertions such as 'God knows that the Antichrist will come' are false. This claim was denied by Gregory of Rimini: contingent propositions about the future have determinate truth values (*veritas determinata*), hence they are either true or false, and therefore they can be known. Yet this does not mean that the future is necessary, for everything expressed by a contingent proposition about the future still can not-be. Gregory subscribed to Ockham's view that the truth value depends upon the future fact, and hence shares in the fact's contingency. The same position was taken by John of Mirecourt.[8]

Alfonsus Vargas reacted in a similar vein, arguing that propositions about the future must have determinate truth value, otherwise certain prophecies contained in the Scripture, such as 'The dead will rise again' and 'The Antichrist will come', would be false. His proof started from the claim that knowledge is always about something true, and never about something indeterminate (thus reversing Aureoli's own argument). Proposition p, 'The Antichrist will come', can be known, for it is known by God who knows all future things. Therefore it must be true. The same goes for other propositions

---

[6] Aureoli, *Sent.*, I d. 39 a. 1 (ed. Rome 1596), fol. 892aE-F.
[7] Ibid., d. 38 a. 1, fol. 877bC-D and fol. 880aA-E; also a. 2, fol. 882aE.
[8] Gregory, *Lectura*, I d. 38 q. 1 a. 2 (ed. Trapp-Marcolino, 3), 254f, and q. 2 a. 1, 277; John of Mirecourt, *Lectura in primum Sententiarum*, I d. 35 q. 1 (Bologna, Bibl. Com. dell' Archiginnasio, A 921), fol. 47va.

about the future. Therefore they must all be true.[9]

The criticism of Peter of Ailly was again similar to that of Gregory, whom he quoted literally on this issue (though without mentioning his name). Propositions about the future have determinate truth value and are known by God as either true or false. The contrary opinion of Aureoli he called dangerous (*pericolosa*) and against faith (*contraria fidei*).[10] We see here that not only philosophical motives played a role in the debate, but also scriptural testimony of divine omniscience. Such criticism can also be found in Gregory and Alfonsus Vargas, though it was not as articulate there as in Peter of Ailly.

Criticism of other positions

Like Scotus before him, Gregory rejected the view that God knows the future by means of ideas. His objection was that it would require a medium between knower and known. But God knows all creatures intuitively and without medium. Hence there cannot be ideas in God.[11] Gregory's criticism was aimed not so much at the question of whether ideas can represent the existence of creatures, but rather at the doctrine of ideas in general. His criticism is clearly different in nature from that of Scotus. Gregory rejected outright the notion of a theory of ideas, whereas Scotus said that ideas are not capable of representing the contingency of creatures, since they represent in a natural way. Gregory consistently did not discuss the ideas anywhere else in his commentary on the *Sentences*, unlike Scotus.

Gregory did not have knowledge of the source of the view that God knows the contingent by means of ideas. He quoted it *verbatim* from the commentary on the *Sentences* of Peter Aureoli where it was also discussed and criticized. Aureoli in his turn did not mention his source, but it is not inconceivable that he came to know the view through the work of Scotus, whom he frequently quoted. This position was also criticized by Adam Wodeham.[12]

The same point made by Gregory, that God does not need ideas in order to know the creatures because his knowledge works without medium, had already been made before by Johannes Baconis. Contrary to Gregory, however, Baconis did not reject ideas as such. Following the line of Scotus, he identified them with the creatures known by God. The creatures are known without medium, intuitively and directly. Apart from the fact that Johannes

---

[9] Alfonsus Vargas, *Sent.*, I d. 38 aa. 3-4 (ed. Venice 1490), col. 615. Unlike Vargas, John of Mirecourt disconnected divine knowledge and propositional truth, claiming that even if God would not know which proposition is true and which is false, the one would still be true and the other false. See John of Mirecourt, *Lectura*, I d. 35 q. 1 (Napoli, Bibl. Naz., VII C 28), as cited by H. Schwamm, *Das göttliche Vorherwissen*, 324.

[10] Peter of Ailly, *Sent.*, I q. 11 (ed. Strasbourg 1490), fol. <q6>rbM-vaM.

[11] Gregory, *Lectura*, I d. 38 q. 2 (ed. Trapp-Marcolino, 3), 280f.

[12] Aureoli, *Sent.*, I d. 38 a. 1 (ed. Rome 1596), fol. 875bC-D (presentation of the anonymous opinion that God knows the future by means of ideas) and fol. 876bE-877bB (criticism); Adam Wodeham, *Lectura Oxoniensis*, III q. 3 (Paris, Bibl. Maz., 915), fol. 178vb-179va.

Baconis spoke of the known creatures as ideas, whereas Gregory of Rimini spoke only of known creatures, we see that their views were virtually identical.[13]

The issue of God's unmediated knowledge of the creatures also recurred in the form of an objection against Scotus. Remarkably, Gregory (like Ockham) mentioned *both* solutions given by Scotus instead of only one of them, as most Franciscan theologians did (see above, p. 178). He argued that both solutions are deficient as they both assume a medium of knowledge in God, viz., the determination of God's will. Gregory's further criticism was obviously influenced by Ockham, and he took over some of Ockham's objections against Scotus. First, the more general claim that there can be no consecutive stages in God. Scotus's theory of stages was criticized in other passages as well, where *verbatim* quotations again demonstrate the fact that Gregory based himself on Ockham.[14]

Secondly, he objected that there cannot be a stage or instance (viz., Scotus's first instance) at which propositions about the future are 'neutral', as this would require a third truth value next to truth and falsity. We have already seen that according to Gregory every proposition about the future is either true or false.

Third, knowledge of the determination of divine will is not sufficient to know all future things with certainty. Because man is free, his actions do not follow of necessity from the determination of divine will, for otherwise he would act as an ordinary natural cause. In order to have certain knowledge of man's actions, then, God must know the free decisions of the human will in addition to the determination of his own will. Gregory provided a *verbatim* quotation from Ockham at this point.[15]

Finally, Gregory cited Ockham's objection that God cannot have certain knowledge of the future because the determination of the will is contingent and not necessary. He criticized this objection, however, for its lack of cogency. Although the determination of the will is indeed contingent, he argued, God can still have certain knowledge in virtue of it. Assuming there is a determination and an effect that follows upon it at some time in the future, and assuming that there is perfect knowledge of the fact that the effect will follow upon the determination, then nothing further is required in order to have certain knowledge of the future effect. Hence God can know with certainty what will happen. He has knowledge of everything he wills, either by himself or together with man. And whatever is willed by God will happen the way he wills it. In this criticism, Gregory took up an objection that had also

---

[13] Johannes Baconis, *Sent.*, I d. 39 q. 1 a. 2 (ed. Cremona 1618), fol. 382bA.
[14] *Lectura*, I d. 39 q. 2 a. 2 (ed. Trapp-Marcolino, 3), 281. See also I d. 9 q. 1 a. 2 (ed. Trapp-Marcolino, 2), 151-155, with references to Ockham.
[15] Ibid., d. 38 q. 2 a. 2 (ed. Trapp-Marcolino, 3), 282.

been raised against Ockham by John of Mirecourt: though the determination of the will is contingent and might have been other than it is, once God has determined that an event will happen at a certain moment he can have certain knowledge of it.[16]

Two general comments on Gregory's criticism of Scotus are in order. First, it is curious that Gregory criticized the last objection quoted from Ockham and not the third, in spite of the fact that they are obviously closely related. Regarding the last objection, he stated that God knows everything that is willed either by him alone or together with man. This fits in well with a claim he made elsewhere, viz., that God is the immediate cause of each effect that is produced, even of the effects that are produced by the free will of man.[17] Why did Gregory not apply these observations to the third objection quoted from Ockham? Gregory had no compunction about saying that God is the immediate cause of all effects and yet that man's actions are free.[18] From this angle, Ockham's claim that God's knowledge of his own will alone is not enough (the third objection) can hardly have made an impression on Gregory. For he believed that God's knowledge includes the effects he will cause in co-operation with man; therefore, God can foreknow the effects of man's free acts of will.

To understand Gregory's reticence with regard to the third objection, we should perhaps again turn to the criticism of Scotus by the *Liber propugnatorius* and by Peter Aureoli, referred to in the previous section. It is highly probable that Gregory was reluctant to state expressly that God is the cause of all human actions in the context of his discussion of Scotus, because he wanted to avoid being exposed to the objections that were raised against Scotus on this point by the author of the *Liber propugnatorius* and Peter Aureoli, viz., that it involved a denial of human freedom. Another explanation might be that Gregory somehow had a foreboding of the condemnations of 1347. In that year a number of theses taken from the commentary on the *Sentences* of John of Mirecourt were censored by a group of *magistri* at the University of Paris (the so-called *articuli novelli*). Among the condemned theses were the views that divine will is the cause of all things (*cujuslibet rei ad extra, qualitercumque ipsa sit vel fiat ab aliquo*), and that God has willed someone to sin.[19]

---

[16] Ibid.; John of Mirecourt, *Lectura*, I d. 35 (Bologna, Bibl. Com. dell' Archiginnasio, A 921), fol. 48ra (octavo, mentioning of Ockham's argument) and fol. 48rb.

[17] Gregory, *Lectura*, I d. 45 q. 1 (ed. Trapp-Marcolino, 3), 487.

[18] Cf. ibid., dd. 35-36 q. 1, 218f.

[19] *Chartularium Universitatis Parisiensis*, Vol. 2, ed. H. Denifle and E. Chatelain, Paris 1891, repr. Brussels 1964, n. 1147, 610 (propp. 9 and 10). The censored propositions (propp. 9 and 10) were taken from Mirecourt's *Lectura*, I q. 39 concl. 2 ad 1 no. 2 and I q. 40 concl. 2 ad 3, respectively. See F. Stegmüller, 'Die zwei Apologien des Jean de Mirecourt', *RThAM* 5 (1933), 193f n. c and a. On this condemnation, see recently W.J. Courtenay, 'John of Mirecourt's Condemnation. Its Original Form', *RThAM* 53 (1986), 190f, with further bibliographical references. According to A.D. Trapp, 'Peter Ceffons of Clairvaux', *RThAM* 24

This brings us to our second comment, which concerns the role of divine will. In spite of his criticism of Scotus, it was Ockham's belief that divine will determines which of a pair of contradictory propositions (p or not-p) will be true. On the other hand, he also criticized the view of Scotus that God knows future contingents through his will: even if God were not in any way the cause of contingent effects, he would still be able to know them. The same position was taken by Adam Wodeham: God co-operates with the causes of all contingent events, but even if this were not the case, he would still know exactly what happens in past, present, and future. Gregory of Rimini also subscribed to this view. We have seen that God, according to Gregory, knows a large part of the *enuntiabilia futura* because he knows what will be produced by his will. Yet he also believed that even lacking a will, God would still be able to know all things.[20]

This double valuation of divine will (as determining what will be, while at the same time being irrelevant for the process of knowledge) may be due to the fact that both Ockham, Adam Wodeham, and Gregory of Rimini rejected the interposition of a medium between divine knowledge and the known, even if that position would be taken by divine will. As a result of this, the functions of divine omnicausality and divine omniscience remained juxtaposed to one another instead of being assimilated, as in Henry of Ghent and Duns Scotus.

The double valuation is all the more remarkable if we bear in mind that both Ockham and Gregory strongly pressed the identity between God's will and his intellect. They concurred in the view that there is no distinction *ex natura rei* between God's will and his intellect.[21] In principle, one would therefore expect them to find no difficulty at all in claims like 'God knows all things through his will'. Yet the opposite was true. Apparently the rejection of a medium of knowledge weighed more heavily than the identity of intellect and will.

The position of Gregory of Rimini

Not only in his criticism, but also in the construction of his own position, Gregory payed tribute to Ockham. The debt included his basic conviction: how divine wisdom is able to know all future things is beyond the scope of human comprehension and explanation (*incomprehensibilis*). Like Ockham,

---

(1957), 147-154, Gregory played an active and decisive role in the condemnation of 1347. This thesis, which in the context of our discussion is very challenging, has rightly been criticized, as not yet verified, by W.J. Courtenay, *Covenant and Causality*, VIIIb, 156f.

[20] Ockham, *Scriptum*, I d. 38 q. u. (OTh, 4), 585; *Tractatus*, q. 1 (OPh, 2), 516-518; Adam Wodeham, *Lectura Oxoniensis*, III q. 2 (Paris, Bibl. Maz., 915), fol. 175rb; Gregory, *Lectura*, I d. 38 q. 2 a. 2 (ed. Trapp-Marcolino, 3), 282.

[21] As for Gregory, see *Lectura*, I d. 8 q. 1 a. 2 (ed. Trapp-Marcolino, 2), 32, and d. 13 q. 1, 198.

he added that we can still say something on the subject. On the basis of experience and through reflection on the nature of his own intuitive knowledge, man can gain some insight into the way God has intuitive knowledge, and into the way he sees all things with his intellectual and eternal eye (*oculus intellectualis aeternusque*). Human beings have intuitive vision of the things that are present to them. In virtue of this intuition, we have certain knowledge of contingent truths, infallibly knowing where (*ubi*) and how (*qualiter*) a contingent thing exists. This is also the way God sees all things. His eye is an incomprehensible intuition (*intuitio incomprehensibilis*) which immediately and instantly sees all possible and actual things at a glance. That is why God has distinct, true, and certain judgments about each of the things that exist, existed, or will exist. Because intuition and judgment are not distinct in God, divine intuition is an immeasurable judgment (*immensum iudicium*) which judges all contingent things in a single act.[22]

Gregory's view of intuitive knowledge differed from that of Ockham in ways that need not concern us here, as they did not affect the question at hand. Aside from this fact, however, it is interesting to note that Gregory used two notions that do not occur in Ockham, viz., that of the 'intellectual eye' and the 'immeasurable judgment'. They were not notions of Gregory's own invention, however, having been used by Adam Wodeham in his *Lectura Oxoniensis*. Wodeham also adopted Ockham's pessimistic position that man in this life is incapable of explaining how God can have certain knowledge of future contingents. According to Wodeham, all we can say is that God knows the future because his knowledge is unbounded and immeasurable, like the eye from which nothing remains hidden (*oculus a quo nihil absconditur*). In the same connection, Wodeham also used the notion of an 'immeasurable judgment' (*immensum iudicium*). God's knowledge is an immeasurable judgment; therefore nothing remains hidden for him, and he judges everything.[23] The fact that Gregory used these two notions again underlines the fact that important aspects of Ockham's thought were assimilated by Gregory via the interpretation of Adam Wodeham.

Certainty and contingency
The logico-semantic approach

We now turn to the logico-semantic approach as it was applied by Gregory. With regard to question of how the certainty of God's foreknowledge can be accomodated with the contingency of the known, there is a significant difference between the accounts given by Thomas Aquinas and Duns Scotus on the one hand, and that of William of Ockham on the other. According to

---

[22] Ibid., d. 38 q. 2 a. 2 (ed. Trapp-Marcolino, 3), 283.
[23] Adam Wodeham, *Lectura Oxoniensis*, III q. 2 (Paris, Bibl. Maz., 915), fol. 175ra-rb.

Thomas, God has certain knowledge because the known is present to him in his eternity. The known remains contingent because its modality of being does not depend on the manner in which it is known but only on the cause by which it is produced. If the cause acts contingently, then the effect is contingent, even if it is known of necessity in God's eternity. Scotus solved the problem by relating the contingency of the known to the contingent causality of God's will. Because God knows all contingents through his will, of which he has certain knowledge, contingency and certainty are like two sides of the same coin. What Thomas and Scotus have in common here, is the fact that they argued their respective positions by means of what we may call material *metaphysical* arguments. Thomas based himself on the ontology of divine eternity and contingent causality of creation, while Scotus appealed to the ontology of divine omnicausality.

By contrast, Ockham's approach to the same question was very different. Here we see the first intimations of an altogether new, *logico-semantic* style of argumentation. Ockham took issue with the views of Thomas and Scotus, arguing that the combination of certainty and contingency does not admit of a material explanation. He solved the problem by combining the following two claims: first, that a true contingent proposition about the future can be false, and second, that God knows all true propositions. The first claim insures that the certainty of God's knowledge is respected, while the second warrants the contingency of the known.[24] In this 'extrinsic' or 'formal' approach, the problem was brought back to its bare essentials: the two fundamental tenets around which the problem hinges, viz., omniscience and contingency, were logically identified and presented in a manageable and orderly way. Incidentally, it should be noted that this new approach was not due to a lack of interest in more material metaphysical speculations. It should be understood rather from the inexplicability of God's foreknowledge stressed by Ockham, and from the growing interest in the possibilities of applying analytical methods to theology and philosophy.[25]

The new type of approach was also advocated by Gregory. Instead of giving a material explanation, he showed by means of propositional analysis that the certainty of God's knowledge can be combined with the contingency of the known. He chose the following three theses as his starting point:[26]

> 1. The contingency of a future event E resides in the fact that it can exist in the future *and* can not-exist in the future ($Poss(E)$ & $Poss(\text{not-}E)$), *not* in the fact

---

[24] Cf. Ockham, *Tractatus*, q. 2 a. 2 (OPh, 2), 522-524.

[25] On the applications of analytical methods in theology and philosophy, see W.J. Courtenay, *Schools and Scholars*, 258-306; A. de Libera, 'Le développement de nouveaux instruments conceptuels et leur utilisation dans la philosophie de la nature au XIVe siècle', *Knowledge and the Sciences in Medieval Philosophy*, Vol. 1, ed. M. Asztalos, J.E. Murdoch, and I. Niiniluoto, Helsinki 1990 (Acta Philosophica Fennica, 48), 158-197.

[26] *Lectura*, I d. 38 q. 2 a. 3 (ed. Trapp-Marcolino, 3), 285.

that it can exist *or* not-exist in the future ($Poss(E)$ v $Poss(\text{not-}E)$). For the latter is true of all things, even of necessary ones. Characteristic of a future contingent is that if the proposition p, 'E will be at t_i', is true, then the following propositions are true as well: $Poss(p)$ ('E will possibly be at t_i'), and $Poss(\text{not-}p)$ ('E will possibly not-be at t_i')

2. God knows all future things, both of the first (*res futurae*) and of the second category (*enuntiabilia futura*).

3. God's foreknowledge, and in particular his judgment about future *enuntiabilia*, cannot possibly be false.

Gregory's proof that certainty and contingency can be combined can now be summarized as follows, using his own example, viz., the fact that Peter will sin at some future time t_i. Suppose that Peter will sin at t_i. Because this is a contingent event, the first thesis implies that propositions $Poss(p)$, 'Peter will possibly sin at t_i', and $Poss(\text{not-}p)$, 'Peter will possibly not-sin at t_i', are both true. Moreover, because we assume that Peter will sin at t_i, proposition p is also true: 'Peter will sin at t_i'. It follows that p, $Poss(p)$, and $Poss(\text{not-}p)$ are all true. Now, the second and third theses imply that God knows all future things and that his judgment is always true. This means that God knows the fact expressed by proposition p. If p is true, then so is $Know(p)$, 'God knows that Peter will sin at t_i'. Knowledge does not affect the modality of the known: therefore if p and $Know(p)$ go together, so do $Poss(p)$ and $Know(p)$. Gregory concluded that God knows that Peter will sin at t_i, and yet Peter will sin contingently and not of necessity. Thus the certainty of God's foreknowledge can be combined with the contingency of the known. Gregory's logico-semantic analysis was later also used by Hugolin of Orvieto and Marsilius of Inghen.[27]

As an additional proof Gregory submitted an argument that had also been used by Thomas Aquinas. By virtue of his perfection, God knows future things exactly as they will happen in the future. Things that happen contingently will therefore be foreknown by God as contingent things. Far from precluding the contingency of the known, the perfection and certainty of God's knowledge imply that he knows the contingent as such. The same argument recurred in Adam Wodeham. Divine knowledge being immeasurable, nothing remains hidden for it. Future things that happen contingently are known by God as contingent things. Therefore the certainty of divine knowledge is not opposed to the contingency of the known.[28]

Criticism of Thomas Aquinas

Gregory extensively discussed the point made by Thomas that the known is necessary with respect to God's knowledge, while being contingent in itself.

---

[27] Gregory, *Lectura*, I d. 38 q. 2 a. 3, 287; Hugolin, *Sent.*, I d. 40 q. 2 a. 2 (ed. Eckermann, 2), 332f. As for Marsilius, see below.

[28] Gregory, *Lectura*, I d. 38 q. 2 a. 3, 289; Adam Wodeham, *Lectura Oxoniensis*, III q. 3

A critical assessment of this claim was also given by Scotus and (more elaborately) by Adam Wodeham. Gregory's discussion was clearly inspired by that of Wodeham, with the interesting difference that Wodeham attributed the view to Thomas and his *sequaces*, whereas Gregory did not speak of *sequaces* but mentioned Giles of Rome, with a precise reference to the latter's commentary on the *Sentences*.[29]

Gregory distinguished between three possible interpretations of the disputed view of Thomas and Giles. The first is that an event E is necessary as well as contingent, where the necessity derives from the first cause (God) and the contingency from E's proximal (created) cause. By the second interpretation, the following two propositions are true of E: 'E will happen of necessity in virtue of the first cause and divine knowledge', and 'E will happen contingently in virtue of its proximal cause and E's essence'. The difference between these two interpretations is that the first one attributes contrary predicates ('necessary' and 'contingent') to event E itself, whereas the second one is speaking *about* E at two different levels. By way of example, Gregory gave the following two propositions: 'This future thing is known by God', and 'This future thing is *not* known by its proximal cause'. These can be true at the same time. 'Known by God' and 'not known by the proximal cause' are not contradictory predicates, for the first one is about the knowledge of God and the second one about the knowledge of the proximal cause. *Without* these qualifications, however, 'known' and 'not known' are indeed contradictory. The case is the same with 'necessary because of the first cause' and 'contingent because of the proximal cause': these are *not* contradictory predicates, even though 'contingent' and 'necessary' are.

Gregory's third interpretation was that event E is necessarily future with regard to God's knowledge, but contingent when considered in itself. According to Gregory, this reading agrees least of all with the literal meaning (the *proprietas sermonis*) of the position of Thomas and Giles. Yet he argued that their view is tenable only when taken in this third and least literal sense. Both the first and the second interpretations contain contradictions and falsehoods. In the first interpretation contradictory predicates are attributed to E, which is impossible. Nothing can be both necessary and contingent, for that which is necessary cannot not-be. The second interpretation, by contrast, makes all future things happen of necessity. As all things are necessary effects of the first cause, the contingent causality of their proximal causes is of no consequence (an objection that had also been raised by Scotus). Moreover, on this view the things that are produced by the first cause without the aid of

---

(Paris, Bibl. Maz., 915), fol. 176vb.
[29] Gregory, *Lectura*, I d. 38 q. 2 a. 3, 295 (ad primum, with reference to Giles of Rome); Scotus, *Lectura*, I d. 39 qq. 1-5 nn. 32-37 (ed. Vat., 17), 488-490; Adam Wodeham, *Lectura Oxoniensis*, III q. 3, fol. 178ra-178va. Again we see that Gregory was well acquainted with the work of Giles of Rome.

secondary causes, such as the world and the souls of human beings, would be absolutely necessary (*simpliciter necessario*). But this is false, because God produces all things contingently and in freedom (again a point that had also been made by Scotus).[30]

Adam Wodeham and Gottschalk of Nepomuk, who quoted literally from Wodeham, remarked that the second interpretation violated the ban on necessitarianism contained in the Paris condemnations of 1277 (prop. 21). It is no coincidence that Wodeham, Gregory, and Gottschalk of Nepomuk came to speak of divine causality in this second interpretation. In his commentary on the *Sentences* as well as in the *Summa theologiae*, Thomas himself had compared the necessity of divine knowledge to that of a necessary and immutable effective cause.[31]

All this leaves the third interpretation, which according to Gregory is the only one that is defensible. For the necessity it is dealing with is not of the absolute kind (*necessitas simplex*) but only conditional necessity (*necessitas condicionalis*). By 'conditional necessity' Gregory meant what Thomas had called *necessitas ex suppositione*. If God knows that event E will happen, then it is necessary that E will happen, for God's knowledge is infallible. This necessity does not reflect upon E itself, but concerns only the conditional necessity, deriving from God's perfection, that if $Know(p)$, 'God knows that E will happen', then also p, 'E will happen' (and vice versa).[32]

In addition to the discussion related above, Gregory also dwelt extensively on Thomas's claim that the antecedent and the consequent of the following conditional proposition c(p) are both necessary: 'If God knew that E will to happen, then E will happen'. By contrast, Gregory claimed that antecedent and consequent are both contingent here. We shall follow his argument in some detail.

With regard to the antecedent, 'God knew that E will happen', Gregory did not believe that all propositions which are about the past are therefore also necessary. In the wake of Richard Campsall, Ockham, Adam Wodeham and others, he distinguished between two kinds of propositions about the past: those whose truth value depends upon a fact in the past, and those that depend upon a fact in the future. Propositions of this second kind are not necessary: they are as contingent as the future fact itself. According to Gregory, it is simply pointless to speak of God's foreknowledge as being necessary, except in the sense of knowledge by virtue of which (*qua*) God knows everything.

---

[30] Gregory, *Lectura*, I d. 38 q. 2 a. 3, 295-297. Cf. Scotus, *Lectura*, I d. 39 qq. 1-5 n. 35 and n. 37, 489f.

[31] Adam Wodeham, *Lectura Oxoniensis*, III q. 3 (Paris, Bibl. Maz., 915), fol. 178rb; Gottschalk of Nepomuk, *Sent.*, I dd. 35-40 (Kraków, Bibl. Jag., 1499), fol. 45vb. Cf. Thomas Aquinas, *Sent.*, I d. 38 q. 1 a. 5 c. (ed. Mandonnet, 1), 909f; *STheol.*, I q. 14 a. 13 ad 1 (ed. Leon., 4), 186b.

[32] Gregory, *Lectura*, I d. 38 q. 2 (ed. Trapp-Marcolino, 3), 298f.

That kind of knowledge coincides with divine essence and is therefore as necessary as the essence itself. Gregory again endorsed here a position also held by Ockham.[33]

Alfonsus Vargas associated the contingency of the antecedent with the position of the *doctores moderni*, by which he meant contemporary theologians. Interestingly, he remarked that this view was not conceived by the *moderni* themselves but could already be found in the works of Peter Lombard and Peter of Tarantasia (the future Innocence V, † 1276). This remark should probably be seen as a critical reaction to the manner in which his contemporaries presented the view. Some of them apparently seemed to believe that it was quite new, or at least presented it as such. Thomas Bradwardine may serve as an example of this attitude, as we shall see below.[34]

As we saw in the previous chapter, Thomas was of the opinion that the consequent, 'E will happen', falls under the scope of God's knowledge in the conditional proposition c(p). If the antecedent is about an act of knowledge, then the consequent must not be considered in itself, but rather in accordance with the knower's mode of being. God knows all things in their presence (*praesentalitas*) as existing things. Whatever exists is necessary when it exists, according to the well-known rule of Aristotle. Therefore the consequent is necessary.

Gregory raised several objections against this view, two of which we shall briefly consider here. First, he drew attention to an ambiguity contained in the notion of *praesentialitas*, a point that had been important in the interpretation of Thomas before, particularly toward the end of thirteenth and at the beginning of the fourteenth century, and that was later discussed by theologians such as Michael Aiguani (commentary on the *Sentences* at Paris, 1362-1363) and Gottschalk of Nepomuk. Did the 'presence' refer to the things themselves or only to God's knowledge? If Thomas meant the first, Gregory argued, then his view was simply false. For the created things that are known by God are not eternal, hence they cannot be eternally present to God. Moreover, eternal presence in this sense would lead to contradictions: future things would be future and not-future (viz., present) at the same time, and things that are yet to be created would have been created already from eternity. On the other hand, if Thomas's notion of 'presence' is taken in the second sense, then his view is correct. God's knowledge is beyond all time: it has neither future nor past, but is a single present act. Therefore all things are truly known by God as present in this sense. This view of the presence of divine knowledge later recurred in Hugolin of Orvieto and Michael Aiguani.[35]

---

[33] Ibid., 302f.

[34] Alfonsus Vargas, *Sent.*, I dd. 38-39 aa. 3-4 (ed. Venice 1490), col. 623f. and 625. For Peter of Tarantasia, see P. Mikat, *LThK*, s.v. 'Innozenz V' (with further bibliographical references).

[35] Gregory, *Lectura*, I d. 38 q. 2 (ed. Trapp-Marcolino, 3), 301f; Michael Aiguani, *Sent.*, I

Second, Gregory took issue with Thomas's contention that the consequent must follow the mode of being of the knower mentioned in the antecedent. As a counterexample he gave the following conditional proposition: 'If the soul knows (*vere intelligit*) that the stone is material and extended, then the stone is material and extended'. Now, taking the stone of the consequent in accordance with the mode of being of the human soul, we would be led to the absurd conclusion that the stone is immaterial and non-extended. From extensive quotations by Johannes Baconis in his commentary on the *Sentences*, we learn that similar objections were raised by Thomas Wilton (Master of theology at Paris, 1312-1322). Wilton called Thomas's position *contra communem logicam*.[36]

THE INFLUENCE OF MAN ON DIVINE KNOWLEDGE

In his discussion of the question of whether God has foreknowledge, Gregory considered the (anonymous) argument that if God would have foreknowledge, everything would happen of necessity. The same argument was mentioned by John of Mirecourt, who adopted it from the commentary on the *Sentences* of Robert of Halifax (written between ca. 1335 and 1340).[37] It is based on the following three premises.

> 1. If a true consequent necessarily follows from a true antecedent, and if the consequent cannot interfere (*impedire*) with the truth of the antecedent, then the consequent cannot but be true. Otherwise it would be possible that a false consequent necessarily follows from a true antecedent. But this impossible (etc.).
> 2. From the antecedent p, 'God knew that Peter will sin at t_i', necessarily follows the consequent q, 'Peter will sin at t_i'. For God only knows true things and his knowledge is infallible. Hence, if he foreknew that Peter will sin, then Peter will actually sin.
> 3. Peter cannot stop antecedent p ('God knew that Peter will sin at t_i') from being true. For divine foreknowledge coincides with divine essence; hence it is necessary. Moreover, the antecedent p is immutable; it is true from eternity, and whatever is eternal is also immutable.

Based on these theses, the following argument can be made. If Peter cannot interfere with the truth of antecedent p, then it is also impossible for him to

---

(Kraków, Bibl. Jag., 1459), fol. 56rb-va; Gottschalk of Nepomuk, *Sent.*, II d. 1 q. 2 (Kraków, Bibl. Jag., 1499), fol. 56rb-vb; Hugolin, *Sent.*, I d. 40 q. 2 a. 1 (ed. Eckermann, 2), 328.

[36] Gregory, *Lectura*, I d. 38 q. 2, 302; Johannes Baconis, *Sent.*, I d. 40 q. 1 a. 2 par. 1 (ed. Cremona 1618), fol. 386aE-bA (Thomas Wilton). As far as we know, Wilton's own commentary on the *Sentences* has not been preserved. On Wilton, see W. Senko, *LThK*, s.v. 'Thomas Wilton (Wylton)'.

[37] *Lectura*, I d. 38 q. 2 (ed. Trapp-Marcolino, 3), 272f. Cf. John of Mirecourt, *Lectura*, I d. 35 (Bologna, Bibl. Com. dell' Archiginnasio, A 921), foll. 47vb-48ra (<contra conclusionem secundam> tertio sic). As for the source (Halifax) used by Mirecourt, see J.-F. Genest and P.

stop consequent q ('Peter will sin at t_i') from being true. Therefore he will sin of necessity.

Gregory did not agree with this line of reasoning. By the nature of his criticism we can clearly see that his position with regard to the contingency of God's foreknowledge and the role of human freedom therein was very close to the English tradition of thinkers such as Richard Campsall and Adam Wodeham. First, he took offense at the alleged necessity of antecedent p. It is a contingent fact that Peter will sin, so 'God knew that Peter will sin' is contingent too. More important for his affinity with the English tradition, however, was Gregory's second contention, viz., that it is within Peter's power (*in potestate Petri*) to change the antecedent p such that it is not true and never has been true. Peter can make it happen (*facere*) that God foreknows something different. For it is within his power to abstain from sinning at t_i, that is: he can make the opposite of consequent q true, 'Peter will not sin at t_i'. Now, if not-q is true, then God cannot have foreknown that Peter will sin at t_i. Hence antecedent p is false.[38]

In support of his view, Gregory referred to texts from Augustine, Boethius, Hugo of St. Victor, and Peter Lombard. This fact is not without significance. It sounds harsh to claim that man can change God's foreknowledge. Taken at face value, this seems to state outright that man has power over God. Some thinkers of the fourteenth century actually interpreted it in this way, as may be gathered from the later reaction of Marsilius of Inghen, who was very cautious on this point. Seen in this light, the appeal to generally acknowledged *auctoritates* was much needed indeed.

Although the *auctoritates* could not be omitted at Paris in 1343-1344, the situation at Oxford was different. There the view in question had been common for some time, which appears to have softened much of its harsh tone. This can be gathered from the works of Richard Campsall, Adam Wodeham, and Robert Holcot, all of whom took the position that God's knowledge is contingent, and that man is able to make it happen (*facere*) that God foreknows something different. That this view was common at Oxford at the time, and that it initially was typically English, is corroborated by a remark of Thomas Bradwardine in his *De causa dei* (1338-1344), describing it as *communior et famosior apud moderniores philosophos, atque theologos, et praecipue apud nostrates, et quasi sola ab eis concorditer approbata*. Bradwardine himself, however, took offense at the alleged Pelagian implications of the view. He objected that man's actions must of necessity follow the decisions of divine will.[39]

Vignaux, 'La bibliothèque anglaise', 284 and 293. The dating of Halifax's commentary is according to W.J. Courtenay, *Schools and Scholars*, 272.

[38] Gregory, *Lectura*, I d. 38 q. 2, 303f.

[39] Richard Campsall, *Notabilia*, VII n. 12 (ed. Synan, 2), 40; Adam Wodeham, *Lectura Oxoniensis*, III q. 2 (Paris, Bibl. Maz., 915), fol. 175vb; Robert Holcot, *Quodl.*, as edited in

The above facts concerning the view that man can influence God's knowledge make a new and important contribution to our understanding of what William J. Courtenay has called the *theologia anglicana*: the theology that developed in England in particular in the 1330s.[40] The influence in Paris of the view in question was not confined to Gregory of Rimini, but included John of Mirecourt and later also Michael Aiguani.[41]

In order to get a better understanding of the background of Gregory's position we shall briefly pause here to look at Wodeham, whose position Gregory was certainly familiar with. Our reason for focusing on Wodeham is the fact that his influence at this point was particularly significant, as we know from the critical discussion of his position by Marsilius of Inghen.

According to Wodeham, God's foreknowledge and judgment of a future event E depends upon two things: first, the being (*entitas*) of God's immense knowledge and of his infinite judgment, and second, the future fact E. The assumption that the being of God's immense knowledge and of his infinite judgment is dependent upon E is needed because the *entitas* itself is by its nature indifferent with respect to the question of whether E will or will not be. In no way (*in nullo*) does it follow from God's knowledge *that* E will be the case. Rather the opposite is true: *if* E will be the case, then God knows this by his immense knowledge, and only then does he judge *that* E will be. From these considerations, Wodeham inferred that if E is contingent, then so are God's foreknowledge and his judgment.[42]

The claim that foreknowledge depends on man's freedom was urged even more perspicuously in three so-called *conclusiones* (theses). These claims of Wodeham bear a striking resemblance to certain theses in Richard Campsall's *Notabilia*.[43] The arguments also show the characteristic use of antecedent and consequent we saw earlier in Gregory.

1. With regard to future contingents E whose existence depends upon the freedom of created will, man can make it happen (*facere*) that God knew from

---

W.J. Courtenay, 'A Revised Text', 13; Thomas Bradwardine, *De causa Dei contra Pelagium*, III c. 26, London 1618, repr. Frankfurt a/M 1964, fol. 703A-D. The dating of *De causa Dei* is according to W.J. Courtenay, *Schools and Scholars*, 136. For a discussion of Bradwardine's view, see H.A. Oberman, *Archbischop Thomas Bradwardine. A Fourteenth Century Augustinian. A Study of His Theology in Its Historical Context*, Utrecht 1957; G. Leff, *Bradwardine and the Pelagians. A Study of His 'De causa Dei' and Its Opponents*, Cambridge 1957 (Cambridge Studies in Medieval Life and Thought, New Series, 5). See also recently W.J. Courtenay, *Capacity and Volition*, 155-157.

[40] W.J. Courtenay, 'The Role of English Thought', 111-115; *Schools and Scholars*, 250-306.

[41] John of Mirecourt, *Lectura*, I d. 35 (Bologna, Bibl. Com. dell' Archiginnasio, A 921), fol. 48rb; Michael Aiguani, *Sent.*, I (Kraków, Bibl. Jag., 1459), fol. 61rb.

[42] Adam Wodeham, *Lectura Oxoniensis*, III q. 2 (Paris, Bibl. Maz., 915), foll. 174va-vb and 175va.

[43] Ibid., 175vb (octava conclusio; nono sequitur; decima conclusio). Cf. Richard Campsall, *Notabilia*, VII n. 12f and VIII n. 14f (ed. Synan, 2), 40f.

eternity that E will be. Alternatively, it is also within his power (*potestas*) to make it happen that God never knew that E would take place. For by virtue of his free will man can make it happen that E will be or that E will not be. If the first, then God knew from eternity that E will happen; if the second, then he knew from eternity that E will not happen. The truth of the antecedent ('E will be' or 'E will not be') depends upon the free will of man, therefore also the truth of the consequent ('God knew that E will be' or 'God knew that E will not be').

2. Man can make it happen (*facere*) that God has always foreknown what he never foreknew, and that he has never foreknown what he always foreknew. The fact that God foreknows everything from eternity does not preclude that man acts in freedom and that he can influence what is foreknown by God.

3. Man can make it happen (*facere*) that propositions which have always been true have never been true, and conversely. Even though he will make E happen at time t_i, he still has the possibility *not* to make E happen at t_i. Because he makes E happen at t_i, proposition p has always been true in the past: 'E will happen at t_i'. If he would *not* make E happen at t_i, then not-p would always have been true, 'E will not happen at t_i'.

It is no coincidence that Wodeham dealt first with God's knowledge (second thesis) before turning to the truth of propositions (third thesis). As we have seen in chapter 4, he believed that propositions about creation can be true even before the fact, because their truth is then based on divine knowledge. God's knowledge is eternal, whereas creation is not. Because God knows exactly what will happen, his knowledge insures that propositions have truth values even before creation exists; yet these truth values remain indeterminate until the corresponding states of affairs occur.

In a *dubium*, Wodeham pressed his position. Taking Lombard's *Sentences* (I d. 38 c. 1) as his lead, he addressed the question of whether divine foreknowledge is the cause of the future thing's existence, or whether rather the opposite holds, that the thing is the cause of the foreknowledge. First, he argued that the existence of a contingent thing cannot be the cause of God's knowledge as such, any more than it can be the cause of God himself. Yet, together with the infinity of God's knowledge it can be a necessary causal prerequisite (*concausa necessario requisita*) for there to be any *fore*knowledge at all. The notion of foreknowledge itself requires that the existence of something in the *future* is known. But this future thing does not exist because God has foreknowledge of it; rather, God has foreknowledge because he knows something that will exist in the future. Moreover, Wodeham believed that it is the existence of the future thing which causes divine knowledge to be true. For existence precedes the knowledge of existence. Things do not exist because God has true knowledge, but God has true knowledge because things exist. This claim accords well with the three theses mentioned above.

Finally, Wodeham determined that divine knowledge is a cause only if considered in conjunction with God's satisfaction with the known (*beneplacitum*). Without this qualification, God's knowledge is not practical but purely speculative (here Wodeham was following the line of Lombard).[44]

Let us now return to Gregory of Rimini, who like Wodeham devoted a separate *dubium* to the question of causality. He also took over the use of typical notions such as 'infinite' and 'immense', which in this context are quite characteristic of Wodeham's approach. Apart from these more formal points of agreement, Gregory also concurred materially in Wodeham's view. First, he also believed that divine foreknowledge cannot be the cause of the known, unless this knowledge includes God's satisfaction and is seen as being one with God's essence and his will. True propositions and true speculative knowledge are only signs (*signa*) of what will happen, and not its cause.

Secondly, Gregory distinguished between two ways of reading the conditional proposition c(p), 'God has foreknowledge of future things because they happen in the future'. If c(p) is taken to mean that future things are the cause of God's foreknowledge itself, then it is false. For what is eternal (i.e., God's knowledge) cannot be caused by what is temporal (i.e., future things). On the other hand, if c(p) is taken to mean that God has foreknowledge because he has knowledge about the *future*, then the proposition is true. For without future events God does not have foreknowledge. Understood in this particular sense, then, future things can indeed be seen as the cause, or more precisely, as the associate cause (*causa vel potius concausa*) of God's foreknowledge: together with the immense perfection of divine knowledge it causes God to have *fore*knowledge, yet without being the cause of God's knowledge itself. To reinforce this last point, Gregory submitted an analogy that was also used by Ockham. Suppose that while Peter is standing up proposition p, 'Peter is sitting', is formed. Obviously, p is false. Now, if Peter subsequently sits down proposition p becomes true. Peter's sitting down is the cause of p's being true, yet not the cause of p itself, for the proposition already existed before Peter sat down. In a similar fashion, future things are the cause of God's having foreknowledge, yet without causing God's knowledge itself.[45]

The (im)mutability of divine knowledge

Closely related to these problems is the question of whether and in what sense God's knowledge is immutable. Here Gregory took a rather sophisticated position. His reasoning involved several layers of distinctions, chief among which was that between the knowledge of complex things (propositions) and

---

[44] Adam Wodeham, *Lectura Oxoniensis*, III q. 3, foll. 176vb-177ra. Cf. Peter Lombard, *Sententiae*, I d. 38 c. 1 n. 8 (editio tertia), 277.

[45] Gregory, *Lectura*, I d. 38 q. 2 (ed. Trapp-Marcolino, 3), 307f.

the knowledge of non-complex things (concepts), which we have already seen. His general point of departure was quite simple, however: taken as identical with divine essence, divine knowledge is simply immutable, while if taken as knowledge of the existence of creatures, it is mutable. In the following paragraphs, we shall follow Gregory's discussion of this (im)mutability of divine knowledge.

God's knowledge of incomplex things (*res*) is immutable when taken as *scientia simplicis notitiae*. It cannot be increased or decreased, for it is typical of this kind of knowledge that God *always* knows *all* possible things. When taken as *scientia visionis* (knowledge of existence), however, God's knowledge of incomplex *res* is mutable. In this sense God can know more things or less things, for contingent things that will exist at t_i might as well not exist at t_i.[46]

Propositions about the mutability of God's *scientia visionis* are true when taken in *sensus divisus* and false in *sensus compositus*, for otherwise it would follow that God can know and not know something at the same time. Gregory made an exception for propositions about not foreknowing what was foreknown, as for instance: 'It is possible that God does not foreknow what he foreknew' (*Deus potest aliquam rem non praescire quam praescivit*). These are also true *in sensu composito*. Event E at t_E is foreknown by God *until* t_E, but not *after* t_E. It is perfectly possible that God ceases to foreknow event E, hence that he foreknew more than he foreknows now.[47]

A point of some historical interest is the way in which Gregory applied the traditional distinction between *sensus compositus* and *sensus divisus*. He no longer used it as an instrument for reading the same proposition in two different ways, as Thomas and even Ockham had done, but rather as identifying two different, syntactically distinct propositions. Propositions which have the object in first position and the modal operator (*potest*) after both object and subject, Gregory claimed, are syntactically (*de virtute sermonis*) always in *sensus divisus*. An example: 'Aliquam rem, quam Deus non scit, potest scire'. According to Gregory, this proposition is true because it does not imply that God can simultaneously know and not know one and the same *res*, but only that he can know something different from what he knows. On the other hand, ambiguity occurs in propositions which have the subject in first position, followed by modal operator and object. These allow a *sensus compositus* reading, as for instance, 'Deus potest aliquam rem nescire quam scit'. According to Gregory, the syntax of this proposition is such that it implies that God can both know and not know the same thing, which makes it false *de virtute sermonis*.[48]

---

[46] Ibid., d. 39 q. 1 a. 1, 313-315.
[47] Ibid., 315f.
[48] Ibid., 315.

Norman Kretzmann has shown that the new syntactical approach was developed in England, in particular by William Heytesbury († 1372/1373) in his *De sensu composito et diviso*, written not long before 1335. Gregory of Rimini, as we know, was acquainted with the new English works on logic by Richard Kilvington († 1361) and William Heytesbury, and applied their approach in his commentary on the *Sentences*. Later, it was also adopted by Marsilius of Inghen. That it was not commonly accepted in Paris in ca. 1343-1344 is clear from a remark made by Gregory, who informs us that not everyone agreed (*non omnes advertunt*) that differences in syntax imply differences in meaning.[49]

With regard to God's knowledge of complex things (*enuntiabilia*), Gregory believed that it is immutable when taken in the sense of *simplex apprehensio*. It cannot be increased or decreased, because in this mode God has knowledge of all possible *enuntiabilia*. His judgmental knowledge, by contrast, is mutable. Because the truth values of the *enuntiabilia* are subject to change, so are God's judgments about them, for judgment follows truth value. Hence *sensus divisus* propositions about the mutability of God's jugment are always true.[50]

Also true are some *sensus compositus* propositions about the mutability of God's judgmental knowledge, viz., those propositions that mention both the knowing and what is known. For example, 'God can know an *enuntiabile* that he did not know'. According to Gregory this proposition is true because an *enuntiabile* that is true now can have been false before.

Finally, God's judgmental knowledge of *enuntiabilia* may be mutable, as we have just seen, but it cannot be increased or decreased. Of each pair of contradictory *enuntiabilia* always one side is true, so that the number of known *enuntiabilia* always remains the same. God may come to know different *enuntiabilia*, but the total number of what he knows is always the same. This point was also made by Gottschalk of Nepomuk.[51]

To summarize the results of this discussion, we find that Gregory's position on the mutability of divine knowledge was quite on a par with that of Ockham, except for the fact that he deployed the notion of *enuntiabilia*. It is not difficult to see why this notion did not make any difference here. Qua truth value, Gregory's *enuntiabilia* correspond completely to Ockham's type propositions: the truth value of the first in fact derives from that of the second. Possible changes in God's knowledge are linked to changes in the truth of *enuntiabilia* (Gregory) or type propositions (Ockham), respectively, so that the outcome is the same for either approach.

---

[49] Ibid. Cf. N. Kretzman, '*Sensus compositus*', 195-229. Quotations from the logical works of Kilvington and Heytesbury in Gregory's *Lectura* are referred to by W.J. Courtenay, 'The Role of English Thought', 126 and 156 n. 84. For Marsilius, see below.

[50] Gregory, *Lectura*, I d. 38 q. 2, 317f.

[51] Ibid., 318f; Gottschalk of Nepomuk, *Sent.*, I dd. 35-40 (Kraków, Bibl. Jag., 1499), fol. 45vb (conclusio 3).

Marsilius of Inghen

Introduction

In previous chapters, we have seen that Marsilius believed that natural reason can prove that God has knowledge, and that he has knowledge of creatures in particular. The same conclusions on both points can be reached equally by natural reason and by faith. In practice, this meant that Marsilius argued his position almost exclusively by means of philosophical arguments.

With regard to God's knowledge of future contingents, however, the situation was quite different. Here Marsilius primarily based himself on Scripture, instead of natural reason. His reasons for doing so were twofold. First, the problem proved extremely difficult to resolve. Marsilius spoke here of a *quaestio difficillissima*. In the second place, and in connection with the first, Marsilius was anxious not to be led astray from Scripture and tradition, which he considered a very real danger in this context, dealing with logical and philosophical arguments of an all too subtle nature. To illustrate this, we shall cite three examplary responses to such questions, which we shall discuss in more detail below.[52]

Our first example concerns the view that all things happen of necessity and that man is hence not free. According to Marsilius, this is a view that no true believer (*fidelis*) should ever advocate, not even when he finds himself unable to refute the arguments of his adversaries, be it as philosopher or as theologian. Here the authority of Scripture is greater and more certain than that of human ingenuity (*perspicacitas*). For Scripture was revealed to man by the Holy Spirit, which is the spirit of truth and not of error (*est spiritus veritatis et non erroris*).

Another instance involves the question of whether God is the cause of evil. Marsilius urged that it be handled with great caution and without too much logical subtility, lest one should be led to strange and obnoxious conclusions. Theology, he added, is not the science of logicizing superstition (*superstitio logicalis*); it is a reverent science (*scientia pietalis*), the task of which it is not to destroy but to build (*aedificare*). Logical subtlety may only be used to prevent the spreading of erroneous views (*ad cautelam*).

As a last example we mention Marsilius's attitude with regard to the question of whether man's freedom can be reconciled with the certainty of divine foreknowledge. Marsilius expressed great hesitation as to whether man can answer this question. Although the same cautious attitude was also taken by Ockham, Wodeham, and Gregory of Rimini (by whom Marsilius was certainly influenced here), he showed much more compunction than any of them. He found the issue to be incomprehensible, in point of fact

---

[52] Marsilius, *Sent.*, II q. 16 a. 3 (ed. Strasbourg 1501), foll. 279vb-280ra; also I q. 20 a. 2 and q. 45 a. 2, foll. 84rb and 191vb; and I q. 40 (ed. Hoenen), 71f, 73 and 92, respectively.

inexplicable (*incomprehensibile et penitus inexplicabile*), so that it was only waveringly (*balbutiendo*) and with the utmost reservation that he chanced to say anything about it (*ponamus frena nostrae inquisitioni*). That man is free, and that God foreknows the free acts of man, were the tenets he wanted to defend. To argue either that man is not free or that God's knowledge is not certain, he considered to be mere sophistry. Before entering into his discussion, Marsilius declared that if he were inattentively to swerve from faith, he would make a public denouncement of his view. This declaration of intent was repeated in the course of his further discussion.

These examples suffice to show that Marsilius was acutely aware of what he saw as the boundaries of human ingenuity. Particularly where future contingents are concerned, he urged theologians to be prudent in their use of logical instruments. That his idea of these boundaries was fairly articulate is underlined by the fact that he did not show similar reluctance with regard to other questions. On the other hand, it would be a mistake to think that this self-imposed philosophical prudency of Marsilius implied that he had nothing philosophical to say about God's knowledge of future contingents and related issues. In the remainder of this chapter, we shall see that quite the opposite is true.

Definition of God's foreknowledge

As a nominal definition (*quid nominis*) of 'foreknowledge' Marsilius gave the following locution: 'to know something before it exists, and to know at which moment in the future it will exist'. Similar definitions were given by other theologians such as Gregory of Rimini and Henry of Oyta. Gregory's definition, which, compared to Marsilius's, was more concise but otherwise identical in content, employed the notion of 'evident knowledge'. Where Gregory spoke of 'evident', Marsilius used the more arduous 'to know at which moment in the future it will exist'. A third definition, that of Henry of Oyta, is interesting because he remarked that the notion of 'foreknowledge' as such cannot refer to creatures, because otherwise God could not have foreknowledge from eternity. According to Henry, to have foreknowledge means that one knows that something will be in time, or that something is future in time (*esse futurum in tempore*).[53]

If God has *fore*knowledge, Marsilius contended, this does not mean that his knowledge itself is in time. God is eternal and immutable, and he sees all things at once. The prefix 'fore' indicates merely that, as seen in time, things

---

[53] Marsilius, *Sent.*, I q. 40 a. 1 (ed. Hoenen), 73; Gregory, *Lectura*, I d. 38 q. 2 a. 1 (ed. Trapp-Marcolino, 3), 275; Henry of Oyta, *Lectura textualis*, I d. 38 (München, Bayer. Staatsbibl., CLM, 5590), fol. 99r. According to Marsilius a nominal definition conveys *what, how* and *in which way* a term signifies. See Marsilius, *Quaestiones super librum posteriorum* (Toledo, Bibl. del Cab., 95-5), as cited by E.P. Bos, *Marsilius of Inghen*, 196.

are known by God before they exist. Marsilius referred here to the well-known passage in Boethius's *De consolatione* (Lib. V pros. 6), where it is said that it is more correct to speak of *providentia* instead of *praevidentia*.[54]

That God has foreknowledge Marsilius inferred from two considerations: first, that God has knowledge of all things (which had been established earlier), and second, that God is perfect. Because God has knowledge of all things, it follows that he also has knowledge of future things; because future things do not yet exist, it follows that God has foreknowledge of them (first part of the definition, 'to know something before it exists'). Now, because God is perfect, he must know the time at which future things will exist (second part of definition). For if God knew only *that* something will exist but not *when*, his knowledge would be imperfect, which is contrary to divine perfection.[55]

The object of God's foreknowledge

According to Marsilius, the objects of God's foreknowledge are *complexe enuntiabilia*, that is, facts or states of affairs as they can be expressed by propositions. The fact that Marsilius used the notion of *complexe enuntiabile* in this context does not mean that he somehow wanted to associate himself with the position of Gregory of Rimini, which he criticized elsewhere. His use of the notion nowhere carried the ontological and epistemological weight attached to it by Gregory. He used it only to highlight the fact that there is a composition of 'thing' and 'existence' in the object of knowledge. God's foreknowledge is about the contingent *existence* of future things, not about future things considered as *things*, apart from their existence.[56]

Marsilius sharply distinguished between these two modes of knowledge, the knowledge of *things* and that of *existents*. God's knowledge of things (*scientia simplicis notitiae*) is necessary in character. In virtue of its perfection, God's essence represents all possible perfections in a natural way. Hence, if God knows his essence he also of necessity knows all possible things. By contrast, God's knowledge of the existence of things (*scientia visionis*) is contingent, for what he knows in this manner is itself contingent. Moreover, this mode of knowledge consists in judgments that something exists or does not exist. Finally, because God's knowledge is perfect, his judgement about existence must always be true and evident.[57]

Marsilius did not believe that God's knowledge of contingents meets the classical Aristotelian requirements of scientific knowledge (true and evident knowledge of that which could not have been other than it is). The reason for

---

[54] Marsilius, *Sent.*, I q. 40 a. 2, 97f.
[55] Ibid., a. 1, 73.
[56] Ibid., 74.
[57] Ibid., 74, and a. 2, 83.

this was very simple. According to Marsilius, future things can not-be. It is even possible that there are no future things at all, a view that is also found in the commentary on the *Sentences* of Gregory of Rimini and the *Quaestiones Sententiarum* of Henry of Oyta, two works Marsilius knew. On the other hand, however, this mutability on the side of the object does not rule out that God can have certain and infallible knowledge of future contingents. God's *immensitas* insures that he knows exactly what will exist, as well as when and how it will exist (a point we shall presently come back to).[58]

The contingency of the future

That there are future things which will happen contingently is a claim that Marsilius discussed in several places, in different contexts. In his commentaries on the *Perihermeneias* and the *Metaphysics*, he defended it against the opposing view that the future happens of necessity, a view he attributed to Plato and Bradwardine. In his commentary on the *Sentences*, he defended it against the anonymous view that human beings are not free, and that they do not sin out of their own free will. We shall first take a look at the discussion in Marsilius's commentaries on Aristotle, returning to the *Sentences* later.

The commentaries on Aristotle: Marsilius's criticism of Plato and Bradwardine

The necessitarianism which Marsilius attributed to Plato and Bradwardine was based on the following two premises:

> 1. Nothing is produced unless by sufficient causes (*causae sufficientes*) that are not obstructed in their efficacy.
> 2. If there are sufficient causes, the effect is produced immediately, and it cannot not be produced.

In other words, each effect has one or more causes; if these causes exist, then their effect exists of necessity. The argument seems to be a stylized version of the view that there are no accidental causes, a position criticized by Aristotle in the *Metaphysics*.

The presentation of the argument and its attribution to Plato were based on Buridan's commentary on the *Metaphysics*, as we learn from the *verbatim* quotations in Marsilius's commentaries on *Perihermeneias* and *Metaphysics*. An interesting detail here is that the quotations from Buridan were much more

---

[58] Ibid., a. 1, 74, and a. 2, 86 and 96; Gregory, *Lectura*, I dd. 42-44 q. 1 a. 2 (ed. Trapp-Marcolino, 3), 377; Henry of Oyta, *Quaestiones Sententiarum,* I (München, Bayer. Staatsbibl., CLM, 8867), fol. 168ra.

[59] Marsilius, *Quaestiones super librum Metaphysicorum*, VI q. 5 (Wien, Oesterr. Nationalbibl., CVP, 5297), fol. 74ra; id., *Quaestiones veteris artis, Perih.*, I (Wien, Oesterr. Nationalbibl., CVP, 5159), fol. 140vb. Cf. Buridan, *Metaphysik*, VI q. 5 (ed. Paris 1518), fol. 35vb.

lengthy in the commentary on *Perihermeneias* than in that on the *Metaphysics*, a tendency that can also be found elsewhere.[59]

It is not quite clear on what grounds Marsilius and Buridan attributed the argument to Plato. His name was not mentioned in the relevant passage from Aristotle's *Metaphysics*, nor was the argument attributed to him in the commentaries that had been important for the reception of classical sources and that were still used in the fourteenth century. Thus, for instance, in Thomas Aquinas's commentary on the *Metaphysics* (which was often quoted by Buridan, and of which Marsilius had a copy in his library) the view was ascribed to Avicenna. In his commentary on the *Perihermeneias*, Thomas attributed it to the Stoics, based on information he had found in Boethius's second commentary on *Perihermeneias*, which was still used in the fourteenth century. Albert the Great's commentary on the *Metaphysics*, which also contained much material on older sources, did not point to Plato either. It could be that the source for the attribution to Plato must be sought in one of the Greek commentaries on Aristotle that where known at the time, or in the Latin *Timaeus* or one of its commentaries.[60]

Much easier to explain is why Marsilius attributed the argument to Bradwardine. Several theologians explicitly credited Bradwardine with the view that all things happen of necessity, as for instance Francis of Perugia in his commentary on the *Sentences* and Henry of Oyta in his *Quaestiones Sententiarum* (of which Marsilius possessed a copy).[61] Whether this attribution was correct is a question that falls beyond the scope of our present inquiry. The second premise did in fact occur in Bradwardine's *De causa Dei* in more or less the same words as quoted by Marsilius. Bradwardine spoke of *necessitas naturaliter praecedens*, which he believed was universal and

---

[60] Thomas, *In Metaphysicam*, VI lect. 3 nn. 1192f (ed. Cathala), 362b-363a; *Expositio libri Peryermenias*, I lect. 14 (ed. Leon., 1*/1), 74b. As for Marsilius's library, see *Die Rektorbücher der Universität Heidelberg*, 1/2, 501 (303): "Item (468) Thomam super methaphysicam in pergameno." The view of Avicenna is dealt with by A. Maier, *Die Vorläufer Galileis*, 231. Thomas's attribution to the Stoics was based on Boethius, *In Perihermeneias*, II, III c. 9 (ed. Meiser), 217. For the Latin *Timaeus* and its commentaries as a possibile source, see R. Klibansky, *The Continuity of the Platonic Tradition During the Middle Ages. With a New Preface and Four Supplementary Chapters*, Millwood, New York 1982, 74f (a listing of commentaries on the Latin *Timeaus* is provided on p. 52).

[61] Marsilius, *Quaestiones super librum Metaphysicorum*, VI q. 5 (Wien, Oesterr. Nationalbibl., CVP, 5297), fol. 74ra. Cf. Buridan, *Metaphysik*, VI q. 5 (ed. Paris 1518), fol. 36ra. Buridan only spoke of 'Plato et alii plurimi', to which Marsilius added, 'sicut Bradwardinus'. For theologians who attributed this view to Bradwardine, see Francis of Perugia, *Sent.*, II dd. 27-29 a. 2, as cited by H. Schwamm, *Magistri Iohannis de Ripa*, 193; Henry of Oyta, *Quaestiones Sententiarum*, I (München, Bayer. Staatsbibl., CLM, 8867), fol. 167rb. For Henry's commentary in Marsilius's library, see *Die Rektorbücher der Universität Heidelberg*, 1/2, 475 (63). Other thinkers who ascribed this view to Bradwardine include Johannes Baconis and Richard Kilvington, see J.-F. Genest, 'Le *De futuris contingentibus*', 267f; W.J. Courtenay, *Capacity and Volition*, 167 n. 49. See also C. du Plessis d'Argentre, *Collectio judiciorum de novis erroribus*, Vol. 1, Paris 1724, anno 1330: Errores Thomae Bradwardini, 323b-330a.

governed both natural causes and the free will of man.⁶² It was precisely this passage from *De causa Dei* that was quoted in John of Ripa's commentary on the *Sentences* and in the *Quaestiones Sententiarum* of Henry of Oyta. Hence, it must surely have been known to Marsilius.⁶³

According to Marsilius, the position of Plato and Bradwardine was false and heretical (*falsa et haeretica*), yet difficult to refute. He had no problem with the first premise, which he believed was true, but rather with the second, which he believed was valid only for natural causes, and not for free causes like God or man. Marsilius was following Buridan here. They both formed part of an originally Boethian line of thought that had been emerging since the beginning of the fourteenth century in the work of a number of theologians and philosophers. According to them, contingency applies only to the domain of free will, while everything in the domain of natural causes happens of necessity.⁶⁴

A different response to Bradwardine was that of Henry of Oyta. He also challenged the alleged universality of the second premise, but unlike other critics he rejected it for *all* causes (*quaelibet causa secunda*). God freely cooperates with all created causes. Therefore, if God so wishes, each cause can also not produce its effect, notwithstanding the fact that the cause is predisposed to produce the effect. It appears that Henry of Oyta was raising a point that had been made earlier by Scotus in the *Lectura*, viz., that divine causality permeates the inner being of all creatures. Because God's causality is contingent, so is that of each created cause. Henry did not refer to Scotus here, yet we know that he was acquainted with his work.⁶⁵

Marsilius based his arguments for freedom and contingency on Aristotle, most notably his *Perihermeneias* (I c. 9, 18a28-19b4), and on experience

---

⁶² Bradwardine, *De causa Dei*, III c. 2 (ed. London 1618), fol. 646E. For a discussion of Bradwardine's view, see B.R. de la Torre, *Thomas Buckingham and the Contingency of Futures*, Notre Dame 1987 (Publications in Medieval Studies, 25), 91-101; W.J. Courtenay, *Capacity and Volition*, 155-158. Bradwardine's biography is provided by J.-F. Genest, 'Le *De futuris contingentibus*', 251-253.

⁶³ John of Ripa, *Sent.*, I d. 39 a. 4, as cited by H. Schwamm, *Magistri Iohannis de Ripa*, 97 and 112; Henry of Oyta, *Quaestiones Sententiarum*, I (München, Bayer. Staatsbibl., CLM, 8867), 167rb. This passage from *De causa Dei* was also quoted by Thomas Buckingham in his *Sentences* commentary (delivered probably 1337-1338) and in his *Ostensio meriti liberae actionis*. See J.-F. Genest, 'Le *De futuris contingentibus*', 267f n. 83 and B.R. de la Torre, *Thomas Buckingham*, 130 and 159 (contains on pp. 149-379 an edition of the *Ostensio*, q. 1). The dating of Buckingham's *Sentences* commentary is according to W.J. Courtenay, *Capacity and Volition*, 169f n. 62.

⁶⁴ Marsilius, *Quaestiones super librum Metaphysicorum*, VI q. 5 (Wien, Oesterr. Nationalbibl., CVP, 5297), fol. 75ra-rb; *Quaestiones veteris artis, Perih.*, I (Wien, Oesterr. Nationalbibl., CVP, 5159), fol. 143vb. Cf. Buridan, *Metaphysik*, VI q. 5 (ed. Paris 1518), fol. 36vb. For a historical description of the view that contingency only applies to the domain of free will, see A. Maier, *Die Vorläufer Galileis*, 241ff.

⁶⁵ Henry of Oyta, *Quaestiones Sententiarum*, I (München, Bayer. Staatsbibl., CLM, 8867), fol. 167va. Cf. Scotus, *Lectura*, I d. 39 qq. 1-5 nn. 35f and 41 (ed. Vat., 17), 489f and 492. Henry's view is discussed by A. Lang, *Heinrich von Oyta*, 211.

(*experientia*). The appeal to experience is particularly interesting. Marsilius argued that everyone experiences himself as being free, and as being able to act or not-act at will. Of this fact of experience no further reasoned account (*rationes efficaces*) can be given. This is not a shortcoming, however. Rather, it is intrinsic to the fact that freedom is a datum of experience. There is no further proof of reason, no more than there is for the fact that fire is hot. Marsilius was following the line of Scotus and Ockham here, who also believed that freedom cannot be proved by means of arguments, but that it is evidently known to us in experience. Such experiential proofs of free will were also used by Buridan and Gregory of Rimini.[66]

Other questions were still left open, such as whether God is free, and what faith has to say on future contingents. Marsilius remarked that it would not be expedient to broach such matters in the course of his lectures on Aristotle, as it was not allowed at that time to use (*recitari*) loci from Scripture. These and similar questions he therefore relegated to theology. Marsilius was probably referring to university regulations concerning the material that was to be used in lectures on the work of Aristotle. A similar reference can be found in Buridan's commentary on the *Physics*, and thus we may conclude that it was not uncommon at the time.[67]

The commentary on the Sentences: *contingency and God as the cause of sin*

The arguments based on Aristotle and experience were also used by Marsilius in his commentary on the *Sentences*. To these he added what might be called a more typically 'theological' argument, which was based on the Scripture. In the future the Antichrist will sin, as we know from the Scripture. But the Antichrist will be committing a sin only on the assumption that he does so contingently; for if he would sin of necessity, he would not sin at all. Hence it follows from the Scripture that there are contingent events.[68]

Marsilius discussed two objections (*responsiones*) to this argument, which were raised by what he called the *tenentes oppositam viam*: first, the Antichrist does not sin, for he necessarily rises against God, and second, the Antichrist does sin, but he does so of necessity. Marsilius took issue with both

---

[66] Marsilius, *Quaestiones super librum Metaphysicorum*, VI q. 5 (Wien, Oesterr. Nationalbibl., CVP, 5297), fol. 75ra-rb; *Quaestiones veteris artis, Perih.*, I (Wien, Oesterr. Nationalbibl., CVP, 5159), fol. 143va; Ockham, *Quodlibeta*, I q. 16 (OTh, 9), 88; Buridan, *Super decem libros Ethicorum*, III q. 1, Paris 1513, repr. Frankfurt a/M 1968, fol. 37va; Gregory, *Lectura*, II dd. 24-25 q. 1 (ed. Trapp-Marcolino, 6), 2. As for Scotus, see A.B. Wolter, *The Philosophical Theology*, 298f.

[67] Marsilius, *Quaestiones super librum Metaphysicorum*, VI q. 5, fol. 75ra; *Quaestiones veteris artis, Perih.*, I, fol. 143rb-va. As for the germane passages in the university regulations, see B. Michael, *Johannes Buridan*, Vol. I, 166f (with references to Parisian statutes and to Buridan). As for the oldest statutes of the Arts Faculty at Heidelberg, where Marsilius commented on the *Metaphysics*, see *Urkundenbuch der Universitaet Heidelberg*, ed. E. Winkelmann, Vol 1, Heidelberg 1886, n. 23, 31-44.

[68] Marsilius, *Sent.*, I q. 40 a. 2 (ed. Hoenen), 75 and 77f.

objections. Against the first he argued that it would imply that God is unjust. According to the Scripture, the Antichrist was damned by God. But if he was damned without sinning, then God would be unjust. Against the second objection, Marsilius argued that it would imply that God is the cause of sin (*principalis actor, causa peccati*, and *per se causa mali*). For if God creates a person of whom he knows that it will be impossible for him not to sin, then it is really God who commits the sin. Hence, God would no longer be 'God', that is, the most perfect being.[69]

We do not know what kind of *tenentes oppositam viam* Marsilius had in mind here. Was he thinking of the respondents in a disputation who were assigned to defend these counterarguments by way of practical exercise? Or was he thinking of theologians whose views were generally renowned to include or to imply the above position? There is something to be said for the first possibility. It was not unusual for theologians to use parts of the disputations in which they had been engaged as students in the *ordinatio* of their commentary on the *Sentences*. There are several examples of this, so it is not inconceivable that Marsilius did the same.[70] More particularly, we know that the view that God wills sin was defended by some theologians in their disputations *grata exercitii*. Examples are found in the commentaries on the *Sentences* of Thomas Buckingham and Peter Ceffons (originated at Paris, 1348-1349).[71]

As regards the second objection, which was taken to imply that God is the cause of sin, Marsilius may have been thinking of the theses that were censored by Paris theologians in 1347 (as well as after), and that were generally known in the second half of the fourteenth century. One of these, which in point of fact derived from the work of John of Mirecourt, was that God is the cause of sin as such (*causa et auctor peccati ut peccatum*). The notions of *causa* and *auctor* were also used by Marsilius.[72]

Of the censored theses, particulary those positing God as being the cause of evil were generally known, as can be gathered from the commentaries on the *Sentences* of Peter Ceffons and Gottschalk of Nepomuk. The latter's work was written in Paris at the time Marsilius was a student of theology there.

---

[69] Ibid., 75-77.

[70] See for instance the citations from the *Sentences* commentary of Hartmanus (Kraków, Bibl. Jag., 1276, fol. 17r) in K. Michalski, *La philosophie au XIVe siècle*, ed. K. Flasch, Frankfurt 1969 (Opuscula Philosophica, 1), 154f. Cf. A.D. Trapp, 'Augustinian Theology', 146-274.

[71] As for Buckingham and Ceffons, see the passages cited by K. Michalski, *La philosophie*, 13 (Paris, Bibl. Nat., lat., 16400, fol. 96rb) and 409 (Troyes, Bibl. Munic., 62, fol. 78v), respectively. For the dating of Ceffon's commentary, see W.J. Courtenay, *Adam Wodeham*, 135.

[72] CUP, II, n. 1147, 612 (prop. 34). For similar propositions, see 610f (propp. 10 and 14). The censored proposition (prop. 34) is taken from Mirecourt's *Lectura*, II q. 2 concl. 3 prob. 2. See F. Stegmüller, 'Die zwei Apologien', 202 n. e.

Similar theses were cited in other works as well. Thus, John of Ripa referred to a *quidam doctor modernus* who allegedly was against the view that God does not will sin. In the *Collectorium super Magnificat* (1427-1428), Jean Gerson mentioned the views 'quod Deus erat causa peccati, quod Deus facit hominem peccare, quod Deus vult hominem peccare dum peccat', which he attributed to Thomas Bradwardine.[73]

Another source for Marsilius's presentation of the second objection may have been Robert Holcot's commentary on the *Sentences*. Marsilius had a copy of this work in his library. Elsewhere in his *Sentences* commentary he attributed the view that God is the cause of evil to Robert Holcot. Moreover, in Holcot's commentary we find expressions that are strongly reminiscent of the implication which Marsilius found in the second objection, viz., that 'Deus est principalior causa peccati'.[74]

Holcot based his view on the following two premises: first, God co-operates with every action in the created world, and second, sin is a thing (*res*), for it is an act of the will. If these premises are both true, Holcot argued, then it follows of necessity that God is the immediate cause of sin. Marsilius firmly rejected this view: although the premises are both true, the conclusion is invidious and should be banned from the schools (*in scholis*). Marsilius himself followed what he called the opinion of the *doctores nostri*, that God is only the cause of the act of will, not of its movement away from the good. This was the view of Gregory of Rimini, whom Marsilius elsewhere called *doctor noster*, and of John of Ripa. Both were well-known theologians in the second half of the fourteenth century, which may have been the reason why Marsilius spoke of *doctores nostri*.[75]

Veritas (in)determinata in propositions about the future

Because future contingents can happen as well as not happen, true contingent propositions about the future are never true determinately (*determinate*), but only indeterminately so (*indeterminate*). For a proposition p to be determinately true means that there is no power to keep p from being true given moment t_p. If p is indeterminately true, this means that it can also be false at t_p. Marsilius's description of determinate and indeterminate truth differed from that of

---

[73] Peter Ceffons, as edited in K. Michalski, *La philosophie*, 409; Gottschalk of Nepomuk, *Sent.*, I (Kraków, Bibl. Jag., 1499), fol. 52vb; John of Ripa, as cited by H. Schwamm, *Magistri Iohannis de Ripa*, 131; Gerson as referred to by Z. Kaluza, *Les querelles*, 71 n. 31 (with reference to the germane passages in Bradwardine). For the dating of the *Collectorium*, see Kaluza, *Les querelles*, 36.

[74] Marsilius, *Sent.*, I q. 45 a. 2 (ed. Strasbourg 1501), fol. 191va-vb; Robert Holcot, *Sent.*, II q. 1 (ed. Lyon 1518), fol. <gvi>bEE-FF. For a discussion of Holcot's teachings on God's causality concerning evil, see F. Hoffmann, *Die theologische Methode*, 40-44.

[75] Marsilius, *Sent.*, I q. 45 a. 2, fol. 191va-vb. Cf. Gregory, *Lectura*, I d. 45 q. 1 (ed. Trapp-Marcolino, 3), 499; H. Schwamm, *Magistri Iohannis de Ripa*, 132 (with references to the relevant places in John of Ripa).

Ockham, who called a proposition determinately true iff it is true such that it is not false. Unlike the definition Marsilius used, Ockham's did not carry with it the connotation of 'necessary truth'. He was thus able to claim that all contingent propositions about the future are determinately true. This was not possible for Marsilius, however: by his definition, this would mean that all things happen of necessity.[76]

Ockham's notion of *determinate verum* can also be found in the commentary on the *Sentences* of Henry of Oyta, which means that it was still in use toward the end of the fourteenth century. Marsilius's use of the notion, however, seems to derive rather from Buridan or Albert of Saxony, who in their commentaries on *Perihermeneias* also associated it with necessity. They consequently believed that contingent propositions about the future cannot be determinately true, but only indeterminately so, a view also found in the commentary on the *Sentences* of Thomas of Strasbourg.[77]

According to Marsilius, true propositions about present or past are always determinately true, except when their truth depends on something in the future. Their truth value has been immutably fixed, hence they are necessarily true. For once they exist or have existed, the things referred to can no longer not exist. Marsilius here rejected the view that God can undo the past. The position endorsed by Marsilius with regard to the necessity of propositions about the past had been called that of *multi moderni* by Gregory of Rimini.[78]

How does God know future contingents?

On the question of how God has certain and infallible knowledge of contingents, Marsilius subscribed to a line of thought that we may call the '*immensitas* approach': God knows all future contingents through his *immensitas*, knowing what, how, and when they will be. An important aspect of this view is that the contingency of the future is safeguarded. For what happens in the future is independent of God's foreknowledge: contingent event E does not happen at t_E because God has foreknowledge, but God has foreknowledge because E happens at t_E.[79]

The *immensitas* view came to be generally known in the second half of the

---

[76] Marsilius, *Quaestiones veteris artis, Perih.*, I (Wien, Oesterr. Nationalbibl., CVP, 5159), fol. 138va; *Sent.*, I q. 40 (ed. Hoenen), 103f. For Ockham, see Ph. Boehner, *The Tractatus*, 48.

[77] Henry of Oyta, *Quaestiones Sententiarum*, I q. 10 a. 1 concl. 2, as cited by A. Lang, *Heinrich von Oyta*, 189f; Buridan, *Questiones longe super librum Perihermeneias*, I q. 10, ed. R. van der Lecq, Nijmegen 1983 (Artistarium, 4), 47 and 49; Albert of Saxony, *Quaestio de futuris contingentibus*, published in William of Ockham, *Expositio aurea*, Bologna 1496, repr. Ridgewood, New Jersey 1964, fol. <ti>b-tiia; Thomas of Strasbourg, *Sent.*, I d. 40 q. 1 a. 3 (ed. Venice 1564), fol. 111va.

[78] Marsilius, *Quaestiones veteris artis, Perih.*, I (Wien, Oesterr. Nationalbibl., CVP, 5159), fol. 138ra-rb; id., *Sent.*, I q. 40 a. 2 (ed. Hoenen), 100; Gregory, *Lectura*, I dd. 42-44 q. 1 a. 2 additio 155 (ed. Trapp-Marcolino, 3), 364.

[79] *Sent.*, I q. 40 a. 1, 74, and a. 2, 96, 99 and 109.

fourteenth century through the works of Adam Wodeham and their reception in Gregory of Rimini's commentary on the *Sentences*. This is illustrated in a number of texts. The approach was discussed by John of Ripa in his commentary on the *Sentences*, where it was called the view of *multorum doctorum modernorum*. Peter of Candia referred to it as the view that *communiter tenetur*. To explain its popularity, he noted that it was such an easy position (*facilis*). In the commentary on the *Sentences* of John Hiltalingen of Basel, who read on the *Sentences* at Paris in 1365-1366, when Marsilius was a student of theology there, as well as in the *Sentences* commentary of Henry of Oyta, the view was associated with the names of Adam Wodeham and Gregory of Rimini.[80]

Although the notion of *immensitas* was central to Marsilius's theory, he did not give an explanation of its meaning in the context of divine foreknowledge, nor did he refer to Wodeham or Gregory on this point. Elsewhere in his commentary on the *Sentences*, however, he discussed the immensity of divine spiritual quantity (*immensitas quantitatis spiritualis*). From this discussion we can get some idea of what he meant by God's 'immensity'. He wanted to express the radical *difference* between attributes of God and of creatures. In the next paragraphs, we shall take a closer look at this notion.[81]

The concept of an 'immense spiritual quantity' had its origin in the doctrine of Trinity. It was used by many theologians, including Bonaventure, Thomas Aquinas, Giles of Rome, and Marsilius of Inghen, in their discussion of the identity between the three divine persons. They took their lead from Aristotle's dictum that things are the same if they have the same quantity, and that they are different if they have different quantities. Usually the quantity was distinguished into three different aspects of sameness or difference between things: duration, extension, and power. Two things are different if, for instance, one is older, bigger, or more powerful than the other. According to Marsilius, these three aspects exhaust the concept of quantity: any form of sameness or difference can be reduced to one or more of these aspects.

Now, the three aspects of quantity were designed to fit corporeal, extended quantities. Therefore, they could not automatically be applied to God, for his quantity is spiritual rather than corporeal. The aspects thus had to be adapted first. Giles of Rome and Marsilius of Inghen accordingly changed the corporeal aspect of 'duration' into the spiritual aspect of 'eternity', 'extension' they replaced with 'perfection', and 'corporeal power' with 'spiritual power'. Marsilius again claimed that the three new aspects are exhaustive of

---

[80] The relevant passages from the *Sentences* commentaries of John of Ripa, Peter of Candia, and John Hiltalingen of Basel are cited by H. Schwamm, *Magistri Iohannis de Ripa*, 26 and 204f, 206, 206f respectively; Henry of Oyta, *Quaestiones Sententiarum*, I (München, Bayer. Staatsbibl., CLM, 8867), foll. 184va-vb and 185rb.

[81] The sources mentioned in following two paragraphs are referred to in my 'Der Sentenzenkommentar', 122-125.

the concept of spiritual quantity: the three divine persons are the same in each of the three respects, hence they are completely the same. Moreover, Marsilius believed that the three aspects coincide with divine essence, which means that they are indistinguishably *one* in God. If God is different in one quantitative respect, then he must also be different in the other two. From these considerations Marsilius drew the conclusion that whatever is different from divine essence (which goes for all creatures), must necessarily be different in duration, perfection, and power.

If we combine this conclusion with Marsilius's claim that each perfection in the created world can be substituted by a more perfect one, we find that divine perfection must be such that it cannot be perfected in any way whatsoever.[82] Because created perfection is always of finite quantity, the quantity of God's essence must be altogether infinite. The same must be true of God's knowledge, considering that it coincides with his essence. God's knowledge must be altogether infinite; unlike the knowledge of man, it cannot be perfected in any way whatsoever.

The heart of Marsilius's notion of immensity is the radical difference between God's knowledge and that of the creatures. Human knowledge is mutable, fallible, and finite. Divine knowledge could not be more different: it is eternal in 'duration', hence immutable, it is perfect in 'extension', and infinite in 'power'. This is why God has knowledge of all things, including, in particular, the future contingents that man is unable to know because of his threefold imperfection.[83]

As a final corollary, we should draw attention to the fact that on the above analysis God's eternity is only one aspect of his immense spiritual quantity. This explains why Marsilius did not resort to the notion of eternity in solving the question of divine knowledge (except for one occasion, to which we will shortly turn), but preferred the more comprehensive notion of immensity.

Unlike Scotus, Marsilius did not derive the certainty of God's knowledge from the causality of his will. Yet he did not deny that all contingent actions directly involve divine causality. Marsilius believed that God is the immediate cause of everything that exists, cooperating with all causes, including those that act freely. Like Scotus he supported this view by appealing to the first thesis of the *Liber de causis*, which says that the first cause has more influence on the effect than the second cause has.[84] He also complied with

---

[82] Cf. *Sent.*, I q. 43 a. 2 (ed. Strasbourg 1501), fol. 184ra-rb.

[83] This interpretation is also supported by the fact that Marsilius, *Sent.*, I q. 40 a. 2 (ed. Hoenen), 95, derived the immensity of divine goodness from exactly the same kind of opposition, viz., that between the bounded power of created will and the unbounded power of God.

[84] Marsilius, *Sent.*, II q. 16 a. 2 (ed. Strasbourg 1501), fol. 276rb, and a. 3, fol. 277rb; also I q. 40 (ed. Hoenen), 72, and a. 2, 94f. Cf. Scotus, *Lectura*, I d. 39 qq. 1-5 n. 36 (ed. Vat., 17), 489f; *Liber de causis*, prop. 1 n. 1, ed. A. Pattin, *Tijdschrift voor Filosofie* 28 (1966), 90-203, esp. 134.

Scotus in holding that God is the cause of contingency in the creatures, the *causa omnis contingentiae futurae radicalis et originalis*, an expression that calls to mind Francis of Mayronnes, Adam Wodeham, and Henry of Oyta.[85] In sum, we find in Marsilius the same double valuation of the role of divine will that we saw earlier in Ockham, Gregory of Rimini, and Adam Wodeham. On the one hand, God is the universal cause of all things, while on the other hand, he is not the cause of his knowledge of things. What God foreknows depends on future events, and not on his act of will.

Contingency and certainty: the semantic approach

We now come to the question of how the contingency of the future can be combined with the certainty of God's knowledge. Again, we find that Marsilius's position was clearly influenced by logical views of English origin, as they had spread to the continent particularly through the work of Gregory of Rimini and later also that of Hugolin of Orvieto. Philosophical reflection tended to be based no longer on traditional metaphysics, but rather on logico-semantic analysis.

That Marsilius took over this 'extrinsic' approach seems to be more than a coincidence, particularly with respect to the integration of contingency and certainty. As we have seen, Marsilius started from the observation *that* contingency and certainty go together; the problem was only to explain *how* this is possible. Also, he professed that man would never be able to solve the problem in its own terms. Obviously, this is perfectly congruent with the logico-semantic approach by which the question is reduced to the analysis of two mutually consistent 'axioms', contingency and certainty.

Marsilius's analysis of the problem was basically the same as that of Gregory of Rimini. It consisted of the following three steps.

> 1. If proposition p is true, 'The Antichrist will sin at t_i', then *Poss*(not-p) is true as well, 'The Antichrist can not-sin at t_i'. Since the sinning of the Antichrist is a contingent event, it must be possible for him not to sin.
> 2. If proposition p is true, then *Know*(p) is true as well, 'God knows that the Antichrist will sin at t_i'. If the Antichrist sins, then God must know it from eternity, since his knowledge is infallible and perfect.
> 3. Because *Know*(p) follows from p, and p goes with *Poss*(not-p), *Know*(p) also goes with *Poss*(not-p). For in every true conditional the proposition that goes with the antecedent must also go with the consequent.

---

[85] Marsilius, *Sent.*, I q. 40, 72, and a. 2, 98; id., *Quaestiones super librum Metaphysicorum*, VI q. 5 (Wien, Oesterr. Nationalbibl., CVP, 5297), fol. 76va; Francis of Mayronnes, *Sent.*, I dd. 38-39 q. 1 a. 2 (ed. Venice 1520), fol. 112vbP-Q; Adam Wodeham, *Lectura Oxoniensis*, III q. 3 (Paris, Bibl. Maz., 915), fol. 177rb; Henry of Oyta, *Quaestiones Sententiarum*, I (München, Bayer. Staatsbibl., CLM, 8867), fol. 168ra (see also A. Lang, *Heinrich von Oyta*, 190f). Cf. Scotus, *Lectura*, I d. 39 qq. 1-5 n. 41, 492.

Marsilius inferred that the certainty of God's foreknowledge is consistent with the contingency of what is known: God knows with certainty that the Antichrist will sin at t_i, and yet the Antichrist's sinning at t_i will be contingent.[86]

MODALITY AND (IM)MUTABILITY OF GOD'S FOREKNOWLEDGE

Like many other fourteenth-century theologians, Marsilius held that the modality of God's knowledge follows that of the known. Since the future is contingent, God's knowledge of the future is contingent too. Underlying this claim was the hypothesis that God knows things exactly as they are: if they can not-be, then God must know they can not-be. Thus he knows them contingently. Propositions such as p, 'God knew that E will be', although containing a verb in past tense, are no exception to this rule. Proposition p may be true from eternity, but according to Marsilius this does not mean that it is necessarily true, for its truth depends on future event E, which is contingent. This view was adopted by many other theologians of the fourteenth century, particularly in response to Thomas Aquinas.[87]

Although future events are contingently known by God, this does not mean that his foreknowledge itself is contingent. Marsilius explained that foreknowledge coincides with God, and that therefore it is necessary. In this context, he distinguished between God's foreknowledge *as such* (which is necessary) and his foreknowledge *of* some future event (which is contingent). John of Ripa associated this distinction, which was also made by Adam Wodeham and Gregory of Rimini, with the view of *quorundam modernorum* on the influence of the contingent on God's knowledge.[88] We shall presently return to this point.

Marsilius drew a parallel distinction between foreknowledge as immutable and as mutable. God's foreknowledge *as such* is immutable (*immutabilis*), for God is immutable himself. His foreknowledge-*of* is mutable, however, since future things are known in mutable manner (*mutabiliter*). Yet this does not mean that God's knowledge is somehow fallible. That would require him to first foreknow that something will happen (E), and later foreknow that it will not happen (not-E), a possibility Marsilius rejected because of God's perfection. If E will happen in the future, then God knows it from eternity. The same is the case if E will not happen. Contingency and mutability do not entail that divine foreknowledge is somehow mutable itself, but rather that the object of foreknowledge can be different from what it actually is.[89]

---

[86] *Sent.*, I q. 40 a. 2, 79f.
[87] Ibid., 82 and 107; *Quaestiones super librum Metaphysicorum*, VI q. 5 (Wien, Oesterr. Nationalbibl., CVP, 5297), fol. 76rb.
[88] *Sent.*, I q. 40 a. 2, 102. For John of Ripa, see H. Schwamm, *Magistri Iohannis de Ripa*, 60 and 204.

To explain how God can mutably know something without being mutable himself, Marsilius invoked the notion of divine eternity. In God's eternity there is no past or future but only an everlasting presence. All things are present to God like the things at t_i are present to man at t_i. Hence, it is impossible for God to first know that something will be, and then that it will not be, for there is no 'before' and 'after' in God. Further, God's foreknowledge does not share in the necessity of the past, since there is no past in God. According to Marsilius, it is only because of our limited imagination that we tend to think of God's knowledge as somehow taking place in time, first knowing this and then knowing that, and as being subject to the necessity of the past.[90]

In the same way, Marsilius explained how God, whose will is eternal, can will (*velle*) something that he did not will (*voluit*), or how he can not will what he has willed. All things are always present to God. Now, just like a person at t_i is free to will either E or not-E without this possibility changing his will at t_i, so also can God in his eternity freely will E or not-E without changing himself. Whatever God willed from eternity, he is still (and always will be) able to not-will, without having to change his will.[91]

The appeal to divine eternity in this particular context is found in several theologians of the fourteenth century, such as Adam Wodeham, Gregory of Rimini, Michael Aiguani, and Henry of Oyta. They all refer back to Peter Lombard's *Sentences* at this point, where it was stated that the original capacities of God's will and God's knowledge always remain the same and are never diminished. If from eternity God could once have known something different, then he still can. And the same is true for his will. In neither case is God himself changed.[92]

The authority of Lombard notwithstanding, the view in question had not always been commonly accepted. As early as the thirteenth century, lists were circulated containing theses from the *Sentences* that were criticized by anonymous theologians (*quas non sustinent doctores*). One such thesis was precisely that God is still able to do (*potest*) what he was able to do (*potuit*). Considering the fact that Marsilius and the other theologians did not mention any such lists in this context, simply following Lombard instead, we may

---

[89] Marsilius, *Sent.*, I q. 40 a. 2, 105-107 and 111; *Quaestiones veteris artis, Perih.*, I (Wien, Oesterr. Nationalbibl., CVP, 5159), fol. 145rb.

[90] *Sent.*, I q. 40 a. 2, 97; *Quaestiones super librum Metaphysicorum*, VI q. 5 (Wien, Oesterr. Nationalbibl., CVP, 5297), fol. 76va.

[91] *Abbreviationes super octo libros Physicorum*, VIII (ed. Venice 1521), fol. 35va-vb.

[92] Adam Wodeham, *Lectura Oxoniensis*, III q. 2 (Paris. Bibl. Maz., 915), fol. 175va-vb; Gregory, *Lectura*, I dd. 42-44 q. 1 additio 155 (ed. Trapp-Marcolino, 3), 362; Michael Aiguani, *Sent.*, I (Kraków, Bibl. Jag., 1459), fol. 71vb; Henry of Oyta, *Lectura textualis*, I d. 44 (München, Bayer. Staatsbibl., CLM, 5590), fol. 109v. Cf. Peter Lombard, *Sententiae*, I d. 44 c. 2 n. 2 and n. 4 (ed. tertia), 305f. For Lombard and early adherents of his view, cf. W.J. Courtenay, *Capacity and Volition*, 53f and 65-68.

infer that the lists had lost a good deal of their authority, at least from the 1330s onward.[93]

Propositions about the (im)mutability of knower and known

With respect to the topic of the modality of knower (God) and known (future contingent), Marsilius gave an inventory of propositions that are true as *propositio composita* and *propositio divisa*, respectively, similar to the distinction we saw earlier in Gregory of Rimini. The distinction between composite and divided propositions was essentially parallel to that between *sensus compositus* and *sensus divisus* which we have already seen. Marsilius apparently considered the two to be interchangeable. While in the commentary on the *Sentences* he spoke only of *propositio composita* and *divisa*, in the corresponding passage in the *Consequentiae* (which formed part of the *Parva logicalia*) he spoke of *sensus compositus* and *divisus*. Moreover, the definition of *sensus compositus* and *divisus* in the *Consequentiae* perfectly fits the two sets of propositions, composite and divided, described in the commentary on the *Sentences*, and also matches the definition of composite and divided propositions given by Buridan.[94]

The only difference between the two pairs of concepts seems to be that the first implies that differences in meaning go with differences in syntax, while the second says only that differences in meaning relate to an ambiguity in the original proposition. Thus, the first distinction is between two different *propositions* (*propositio composita* and *propositio divisa*), whereas the second distinction is between two *senses* (*sensus*) of one and the same proposition. The distinction between *propositio composita* and *divisa* developed in the course of the fourteenth century, parallel to, and partly in place of, the older distinction between *sensus compositus* and *sensus divisus*.[95]

The newer distinction was also used by John Buridan. He believed that it is the position of the modal operator (*modus*) that determines whether a proposition is composite or divided. If the *modus* is placed either at the beginning or at the end of a proposition, then it is a *propositio composita*. An example: 'That someone is walking is possible', or 'It is possible that someone is walking'. In cases like these, the *modus* is the predicate and the *dictum* ('that someone is walking') is the subject, or conversely. In a *propositio divisa*, on the other hand, the *modus* is contained inside the *dictum*,

---

[93] For these listings, cf. E.A. Synan, 'Nineteen Less Probable Opinions of Peter Lombard', *Med. Stud.* 27 (1965), 340-344, esp. 343 (London, British Museum, Harleian Mss, 3243, fol. 88v). A similar list, with only slight modifications, can be found in Città del Vaticano, Bibl. Apost., Vat. lat., 3088, fol. 36va (not mentioned by Synan).

[94] *Sent.*, I q. 40 a. 2 (ed. Hoenen), 84-86; *Consequentiae* (Uppsala, Universitetsbiblioteket, C 640), fol. 8r-v, cited in E.P. Bos, *Marsilius of Inghen*, 218f. For Buridan, see n. 96 below.

[95] N. Kretzmann, '*Sensus compositus*', 196f. Cf. the syntactical approach of Gregory of Rimini discussed above, p. 213.

dividing it into predicate and subject. In this case, the *modus* acts as (or in combination with) the copula, as for instance in 'Someone can be walking'.[96]

In Buridan's analysis we see that the distinction between *propositio composita* and *propositio divisa* reflects a difference in syntactical structure. Applying this to the examples given by Marsilius, we find that they fit Buridan's analysis perfectly. In propositions that are called *composita*, the *modus* (if any) is placed at the beginning of the proposition, while in those that are called *divisa* it is contained inside the *dictum*.

According to Marsilius, the following propositions (1-4) are true when taken as composite. Their truth is based on two axioms: first, if E will be, then God knows that E will be, and second, if God knows that E will be, then E will be.

> 1. Necessarily, if E is foreknown by God, then E will be (*necesse est, si aliquid Deus praescit, id esse futurum*).
> 2. God foreknows that E will be, therefore E will be (*Deus praescit A fore, ergo A erit*).
> 3. It is impossible that something happens which is not foreknown by God (*impossibile est aliquid fieri quod Deus non praescit*).
> 4. It cannot be that God foresees something in one way and that it happens in some other way (*non stat quod Deus uno modo praeviderit et aliter eveniat*).

Propositions 5-8, on the other hand, Marsilius believed to be true as *divisa*. Their truth is based on two axioms: first, it is not impossible that E will be, and second, it is not necessary that E will be.

> 5. Something that is foreseen by God can still fail to happen (*aliquid quod Deus praevidit possibile est non evenire*).
> 6. Though God knows that E will happen, E can still fail to happen (*quamvis scit A fore, tamen A potest non fore*).
> 7. Something that God does not foreknow can still happen (*aliquid quod Deus non praescit potest fieri*).
> 8. Differently from the way foreseen by God, it is possible for something to happen (*aliter quam Deus praevidit possibile est evenire*).

MAN'S INFLUENCE ON DIVINE KNOWLEDGE

Marsilius subscribed to the view that man can determine what God foreknows, which in the 1340s had become known in Paris through the reception of the work of English theologians such as Adam Wodeham and Robert

---

[96] Buridan, *Questiones longe super librum Perihermeneias*, II q. 7 (ed. van der Lecq), 77f; Buridan, *Tractatus de consequentiis*, II c. 2, ed. H. Hubien, Louvain-Paris 1976 (Philosophes médiévaux, 16), 56f. For a discussion, see R. van der Lecq, 'Buridan on Modal Propositions', *English Logic and Semantics from the End of the Twelfth Century to the Time of Ockham and Burleigh*, ed. H.A.G. Braakhuis, C.H. Kneepkens, and L.M. de Rijk, Nijmegen 1981 (Artistarium Supplementa, 1), 427-442.

Holcot. Marsilius, however, was very cautious in enunciating his position. He denied that God's knowledge depends on (*dependet a*) the free will of man, for God does not depend on anything. Nor did he think it proper to say that man can make it happen (*potest facere*) that God foreknows what he will do, except at the propositional level. For to make it happen that God foreknows something is to make God to be (*esse facere Deum*), which is impossible.[97]

The causality of human will: response to Adam Wodeham

Marsilius was very anxious to avoid the implication that God's foreknowledge is somehow dependent upon man. In his discussion with Adam Wodeham on the causality of human will, he complained that the latter had not been emphatic enough on this point. Marsilius wanted to make his own view as lucid as possible. He therefore distinguished between two different ways of seeing human causality in relation to divine knowledge. On the one hand, one might claim that man may act in such a way as to change God's foreknowledge itself (*agere circa providentiam*). Quite different, on the other hand, is the claim that whichever way man acts, the act is also foreknown by God from eternity (*facere aliquid ad quod sequitur Deum ab aeterno praescire*). According to Marsilius, only the second interpretation can be admitted. God in his *immensitas* has knowledge of what man will do, without depending on man in any way whatsoever. This probably also explains why Marsilius, unlike Adam Wodeham and Gregory of Rimini, never stated that man's action can be seen as the *concausa* of God's knowledge.[98]

At the propositional level, by contrast, Marsilius had no compunction about speaking of *facere*. For if we take a proposition p, such as 'God knows that Socrates will sin tomorrow', we see that it is within the power of Socrates to make p either true or false. Sins are committed in freedom, so depending on whether man chooses to sin or not, the corresponding proposition p about God's foreknowledge is made either true or false. What is changed by man is not God's knowledge itself (the *significatum* of p), but only the truth value of p *about* God's knowledge (i.e., the *significans*).[99]

According to John of Ripa, the view that man can make it happen that God foreknows something was advocated by many theologians (*hoc dicunt multi reputati probabiles et famosi*). He nonetheless chose to disagree with it, finding it totally absurd (*nimis absurdum*), and a view to be despised and derided by every theologian and philosopher. How could what is eternal and immutable ever fall under the power of what is created and mutable? Although created will is able to act, it is not within its province to make this act be known and willed by God.[100]

---

[97] *Sent.*, I q. 40 a. 2 (ed. Hoenen), 88f.
[98] Ibid., 89-91.
[99] Ibid., 108f.

John of Ripa vaguely referred to "certain *moderni*", but from remarks of John Hiltalingen of Basel we may gather that his criticism was directed against Gregory of Rimini in particular. While not endorsing Gregory's view himself, Hiltalingen nonetheless undertook to defend it against Ripa's objections. Historically, his defense holds great interest. It anticipated Marsilius's distinction between two senses of *facere*: according to John Hiltalingen, what Gregory had meant was not that man is the *causa factiva* of God's foreknowledge, but only its *causa illativa*.[101]

Considering that John of Ripa's commentary on the *Sentences* was known in Paris at the time Marsilius was studying theology there, and considering further that Hiltalingen's response also dates precisely from that period, it is not inconceivable that Marsilius was influenced by the two theologians: by John of Ripa through his harsh criticism, and by Hiltalingen through his restatement of the position of Gregory of Rimini.

---

[100] John of Ripa, *Sent.*, I d. 39 a. 1, as cited by H. Schwamm, *Magistri Iohannis de Ripa*, 60-62 and 64.

[101] John Hiltalingen of Basel, *Sent.*, I q. 30 (München, Bayer. Staatsbibl., CLM, 26711), fol. 135vb, as cited by Schwamm, *Magistri Iohannis de Ripa*, 210.

CHAPTER EIGHT

SYNTHESIS AND EVALUATION

In the preceding chapters we discussed the various developments that the views on divine knowledge went through in the period 1250-1400. Our purpose has been to assemble the tools for historically and systematically situating Marsilius of Inghen's philosophical and theological views on divine knowledge. As noted in the introduction (chapter 1), the problem of divine knowledge finds itself at the intersection of important questions in several domains, including logic, metaphysics, and ethics. This made it a particularly apt angle from which to study the developments that took place in philosophy and theology in the late Middle Ages. Thus, we have been able not only to situate Marsilius's view on divine knowledge among those of his contemporaries, but also to place it in the context of developments of a more general nature.

In the fourteenth century, as well as after, the views of Thomas Aquinas, Duns Scotus, and William of Ockham were generally acknowledged as the three basic positions with regard to divine knowledge. It was particularly Ockham's view that influenced Marsilius on several important issues, an influence that was largely indirect, being mediated by the commentaries on the *Sentences* of Adam Wodeham and Gregory of Rimini. Gregory's work is of great historical significance. His commentary on the *Sentences* was one of the first in Paris to include a discussion of the views of English theologians of ca. 1317-1340, most notably those of Ockham and Adam Wodeham. Earlier, their position was virtually unknown in Paris. It was partly through Gregory's commentary that the application of semantic analysis to the question of how the certainty of God's knowledge can be combined with the contingency of the known (the creature), which had been used in England for some time already, came to be generally known in Paris.

In this book, we did not confine ourselves solely to Marsilius of Inghen. A substantial part of it was devoted to Thomas Aquinas, Duns Scotus, William of Ockham, and Gregory of Rimini. We presented their views on the various aspects of the problem of divine knowledge, and tried to bring out the ambiguities and problems inherent in them, particularly insofar as they were also appreciated by contemporary thinkers at that time. As we saw in the preceding chapters, the more ambiguities and inconsistencies a view contained, the more variegated its reception tended to become. In one particular case, this effect was so strong that the positions of Thomas Aquinas and Duns Scotus with regard to God's knowledge of contingents were seen as mutually consistent by one theologian (Robert Cowton), while radically opposed according to another (James of Ascoli).

A historically adequate understanding of the complex network of thirteenth- and fourteenth-century interpretations of the views of the theologians mentioned above — a network that Marsilius knew very well because of his prolonged stay in Paris and Heidelberg, and of which he himself was very much a part — requires us to discuss not only the primary views themselves, but also the various interpretations and classifications to which they were subjected by others in the thirteenth and fourteenth century. Basing ourselves each time on the main relevant contemporary sources, we have tried to observe this requirement as strictly as possible.

Theological and philosophical framework

The question of divine knowledge has a distinctly religious and theological dimension, viz., that of God's care for man. In virtue of his perfect knowledge and his insight in the course of worldly events, God may come to man's help. For man, correspondingly, this means that he may have confidence in the help of God. Expressed in a more abstract and more philosophical way, basically the same conviction is present in the idea that God's knowledge is causally responsible for the order of the world. Apparently, this insight of religious and philosophical man is as ancient as it is pervasive. On the one hand, creation narratives have always played an important role in otherwise very different religions, while, on the other, a spiritual principle of order was proposed by philosophers as early as Anaxagoras, Diogenes of Apollonia, and Plato.

Particularly the more abstract aspect of divine knowledge has remained an object of speculation in philosophy and philosophical theology to this very day. Its core concept is 'intellectuality' rather than 'care'. Corresponding to the order and differentiation of real being, an isomorphous intellectual structure in the thought of the first principle is assumed. This intellectual structure, and the (self-)knowledge the first principle has of it, are the true cause of the order inherent in reality. The history of the entwinement of order and intellectuality stretches from Plato's theory of ideas to the thinkers discussed in this study, and beyond.

From the explanation of order in terms of the act of knowledge of an intellectual first principle also follows the essential intelligibility of reality. Although man may not *actually* be able to know everything, all things are *essentially* intelligible, as they ultimately go back to the act of knowledge of the first principle. Considered from a different angle, this also means that philosophy, defined as the intellectual reflection on the structure of reality, is given a foundation and a *raison d'être*: every part of reality can be an object of reflection, as all being is intelligible. There is little doubt in our mind that philosophical and theological reflections on divine knowledge, from the late Middle Ages onward, through the work of thinkers such as Theodoric of Freiberg and Heymericus a Campo, helped to clear the way for a new vision of the human mind and its relation to reality, thus creating a bridge to the modern era.

Ever since Parmenides, the relation between mind and being has been one of the most fascinating issues in Western philosophy. The reflections on divine knowledge in the late Middle Ages constituted an important link in the history of this theme. Before turning to an evaluation of our findings here, we shall first briefly recapitulate the principal stages of development the problem of divine knowledge underwent between 1250 and 1400.

Developments between 1250 and 1400

As is well-known, periodization is generally a precarious project. It often happens that the characteristics of one period are also found in others, both earlier and later, thus spoiling the search for neat divisions. Unfortunately, the history of the problem of divine knowledge is no exception. Yet, we feel that the historian of philosophy should not be discouraged by this problem. He must investigate which issues were of importance during a given period of time, which developments took place, what they consisted in, and what were their causes. For the historian, this is the only available access to an understanding of the background of past discussions. Discussions in the late Middle Ages resemble their counterparts in modern philosophy, in that they were periodically dominated by certain fashionable issues, with an undercurrent of more traditional problems that never quite lost their interest. The historian of philosophy must carefully take stock of the various problems and interests that were topical during a given period of time. Close observation of the order in which the issues came into view and faded away again may enable him to put the individual thinkers of the period in a broader historical perspective.

Philosophy and theology between 1250 and 1400 were marked, first of all, by a *characteristic method*, which is an important help for its division into periods. Almost without exception, the texts that have come down to us were products of the educational system. This applies to the theological commentaries on the *Sentences* of Peter Lombard, as well as to the philosophical commentaries on Aristotle. What is more, some of these commentaries were composed as parts of obligatory disputations on older or contemporary views. This characteristic feature is responsible for the fact that the texts under consideration show a double aspect, one of *continuity*, and one of *variation*.

As for the aspect of continuity, it is not difficult to identify the texts that are most relevant here. Throughout the years 1250-1400, the *Sentences* of

Peter Lombard and the works of Aristotle were obligatory subjects of tuition. As such, they permeated the thought of generations of readers and commentators. To an extent that can hardly be overestimated, the themes addressed by Lombard and Aristotle, and the problems they drew attention to, determined the discussions carried on during the period. A telling example is one of the questions raised in the twelfth book of Aristotle's *Metaphysics*, viz., whether God can know something different from himself. Although this question enjoyed particular interest between 1255 and 1290, it was raised by many philosophers and theologians throughout the late Middle Ages.

Another notable aspect of continuity is afforded by the continuous influence of introductory textbooks such as the *Tractatus* of Peter of Spain and other logical works. The educational system ensured that philosophers and theologians of the time shared a background in logical analysis. Thus, certain issues in connection with divine knowledge could easily be identified as types of semantic problems, and be solved accordingly. An example of this kind is the appeal to the distinction between *sensus divisus* and *sensus compositus* in solving questions such as whether, necessarily, if God foreknows that A, it will happen that A.

Finally, among the texts that had a lasting influence during the years 1250-1400, we should also include a number of other works that were widely read and often cited, such as those of Augustine (particularly his theory of ideas), Boethius, pseudo-Dionysius, Avicenna, Averroes, and Anselm of Canterbury, as well as those of contemporary writers such as Thomas Aquinas, Scotus, and Ockham.

The obvious continuity with regard to the subjects that were discussed, and the works that were read, does not entail that the reactions to them were always the same, however. For example, the interpretations of the passage from Aristotle referred to above were extremely varied. Another example is the fact that the influence of Lombard was not always the same. From ca. 1330 onward, as we have seen, the English commentaries on the *Sentences* tended to treat Lombard's framework in a much less rigid fashion than contemporary commentaries from Paris did. As was also noted, there even were lists of theses from Lombard that were expressly rejected by certain *magistri*.

This brings us to the second aspect, that of variation. Due to the form of tuition, which consisted in part of obligatory disputations, and because of the fact that many philosophical and theological commentaries were composed of *quaestiones*, the familiar 'classical' views, as well as many contemporary ones, were constantly subjected to relentless discussion. Time and again, eager students and dapper commentators scrutinized the underlying assumptions of a growing number of positions. As a direct consequence of this procedure, the weaknesses as well as the strong points of any given position were discovered relatively quickly. Moreover, from the disputations of any given view flowed a variety of interpretations. This accounts for the fact that in the course of mere decennia many competing interpretations of the views of Thomas and Scotus emerged and were defended. Moreover, the peculiar character of tuition largely explains the sudden emergence, in many works at a time, of identical problems and new methods of argumentation. We mention two examples here. Around 1280, many theologians suddenly started to ask the question of how the unity of God's essence can be combined with a plurality of known creatures. The explanation for this phenomenon, as we have seen, lies in the discussion of the views of Henry of Ghent, which were based on those of Avicenna. Secondly, suddenly around 1340, various Parisian theologians began to apply the semantic approach to the question of divine foreknowledge. The phenomenon was caused by the fact that during the 1340s the works of English theologians, such as Adam Wodeham, became known in Paris, and with them the new methods of argumentation they used.

Obviously, the periodization of an era must account for such changes and developments. The historian must identify the works, views, or events that were principally responsible for the developments that took place. Change, however, is only one aspect of the complex reality of historical processes. It needs to be complemented by its counterpart of continuity. The differences between two periods of an era can never be absolute. In the context of the subject of our study, they were the result of theological and philosophical discussions of, first, a given body of texts, and second, a series of 'classical' or contemporary interpretations of these texts. This means that certain themes recurred time and again, and that our partitioning of the period, no matter how sophisticated its definition, can never be watertight. In more than one respect, the complex reality of history resembles a game of chess. The board, the pieces, and the rules of the game are like the continuity in history, while the indefinite variety of games that can be played with them gives us a sense of the wealth of events. In each single game of chess the aspect of continuity is of fundamental importance, but it is only through the aspect of variation that differences between the individual games may show up, and that we may speak of *developments* in the game.

1. Does God know creation? Reaction to Aristotle and Averroes, ca. 1255-1290.

From 1255 onward, virtually all of Aristotle's works, including the *libri naturales* and the *Metaphysics*, were officially read at the faculty of arts in Paris. Aristotle's work were known before, of course. There had even been several interdictions against his work in Paris in 1210, 1215, 1231, and 1245. The year 1255, however, constituted a landmark. It was of fundamental importance for the development of the problem of divine knowledge. From this time on, all prospective philosophers were introduced, in the course of their education, to the brief and ambiguous expositions on divine knowledge in Aristotle's *Metaphysics* and in Averroes's commentary on it. While a clear awareness of the fact that there is a problem with regard to God's knowledge of creation had been lacking in the first half of the thirteenth century, this dramatically changed after 1255. Accordingly, we take this year as the beginning of a new period.

One of the questions now officially facing philosophers and theologians, was whether it is compatible with divine perfection that God knows something other than his own essence. On the one hand, the commentary of Averroes seemed to rule out this possibility. Here it was argued that God does not have knowledge of his creatures, neither singularly nor universally, and that he only has knowledge of the being of his own essence. On the other hand, it was traditionally believed that God does have knowledge of the creatures. The confrontation between these opposing claims was the beginning of a new period of reflection on the status of God's knowledge of the creatures.

One of the first elaborate reactions to the views of Aristotle and Averroes, from a theological point of view, was that of Thomas Aquinas, e.g., in his commentary on the *Sentences* (1252-1256). In the years that followed, the views of Aristotle and Averroes were discussed by almost all theologians, partly in connection with the work of Thomas. The discussion came to a head around the 1270s, as can be gathered from the Paris censures of 1270 and 1277, and from Giles of Rome's *De erroribus philosophorum*. From the 1290s onward, the discussion seems to have lost much of its original acuity. In this connection it is significant that the views of Aristotle and Averroes were not discussed in Scotus's Oxford and Paris commentaries on the *Sentences*. Even more telling is the fact that, ten years later, thinkers such as Peter Aureoli and Johannes Baconis believed that Aristotle's and Averroes's views on divine knowledge were identical to those of Augustine, who was then held in authority on this issue. A change of context had taken place. From the beginning of the fourteenth century, the question of whether God can have knowledge of the creatures, and the question of what were the views of Aristotle and Averroes on this matter, increasingly tended to be put in terms of *provability*. The question now became: can it be *proved*, according to Aristotle and Averroes, that God has knowledge of his creatures?

The historical impact of the reaction to Aristotle and Averroes, with its ensuing reflection on the status of God's knowledge of the creatures, was tremendous. Insights and problems developed in those years effectively determined the discussion on divine knowledge until well into the fourteenth century.

Finally, we draw attention to the fact that there was never a general consensus, between 1250 and 1400, on what the correct reading of Aristotle and Averroes should be. Far from converging on a single interpretation, theologians and philosophers of the time proposed widely differing readings. As a thirteenth-century example, we mention the opposing interpretations of Aristotle suggested by Thomas Aquinas and Bonaventure; a century later, the same pattern was exemplified by Johannes Baconis and Gregory of Rimini.[1]

2. Unity vs. plurality. Influence of Henry of Ghent, ca. 1280-1332/43

Toward the end of the thirteenth century, many philosophers and theologians closely attended to the thought of Avicenna. This is exemplified by the works of Henry of Ghent and Duns Scotus, as well as by the annotation of Avicenna's *Metaphysics* by Godfrey of Fontaines. The reflection on Avicenna was of great significance for the problem of divine attributes, and for that of the relation between divine essence and the known creature. It decisively influenced later discussions of these subjects.

A central theme in this context was the relation between unity and plurality: how can something that is one (i.e., God's essence) have many properties (i.e., attributes) and represent many things (viz., creatures)? The question was initiated by Avicenna's Neoplatonic view that something which is one cannot itself be the immediate cause of many different things. In the Latin West, an important contribution was made by Henry of Ghent. In several of his *Quodlibeta*, he raised the issue of unity and plurality in the context of divine attributes and of God's knowledge of the creatures. The first emphatic occurrence of this theme is in Henry's fifth *Quodlibet*, which took place in 1280 or 1281.

Although the question of unity and plurality had been raised earlier, also in connection with divine knowledge, it was not until 1280 that it assumed more or less universal interest, in Paris as well as in Oxford. This may be gathered from the subjects of the disputations held at Oxford in the 1280s and 90s.[2] We take this year, 1280, to mark the beginning of a global reorientation with regard to the problem of divine knowledge.

Henry of Ghent's view on divine attributes and God's knowledge of the creatures, as well as the specific problems raised by him in this context, were discussed by many theologians, including Godfrey of Fontaines, Thomas Sutton, Duns Scotus, Henry of Harclay, and William of Ockham. Thus, it was in a reaction to Henry of Ghent that Scotus took up the famous concept of formal distinction. For some time, Henry's view served as a framework for the discussion of divine attributes, and of God's knowledge of the creatures. Generally speaking, however, he had more critics than followers. After 1300,

---

[1] See chapter 4 above. As for Bonaventure, who denied that, according to Aristotle, God has knowledge of creatures, see his *Collationes in Hexaëmeron*, I, col. 3 § 1 nn. 2f, ed. F. Delorme, Florence 1934 (BFSMA, 8), 91.

[2] Cf. A.G. Little and F. Pelster, *Oxford Theology and Theologians c. A.D. 1282-1302*, 3 vols, Oxford 1934 (Oxford Historical Society, 96), 383a, s.v. 'Deus'.

this was partly under the influence of the fundamental objections raised by such writers as Duns Scotus. Yet, there were also thinkers who, having initially endorsed Scotus's criticism, later returned to the position of Henry of Ghent. This applies, for example, to Henry of Harclay. It appears from his texts that he eventually preferred Henry's view to that of Scotus. Apparently, the latter's fundamental criticism did not immediately spell the end for the problem of unity and plurality, as reintroduced by Henry of Ghent.

It is difficult to say with any precision when the influence of Henry of Ghent's treatment of the problem came to an end. His views were quoted by Scotus and Ockham in their commentaries on the *Sentences*, both of which, and particularly that of Scotus, were much-used source books in the fourteenth century. This makes it difficult to decide whether a fourteenth-century discussion of the position of Henry of Ghent reflects a genuine interest in this position itself, or is a mere echo of the quotations in Scotus and Ockham. However this may be, in the course of the first half of the fourteenth century, the problem of unity and plurality gradually gave way to the related problem of the formal distinction, proposed by Scotus as an alternative to Henry's theory of the attributes. In Oxford, this shift of attention took place from ca. 1332 onward; it is found, for example in the *Lectura Oxoniensis* of Adam Wodeham, which later became highly influential. In Paris, the shift took place some ten years later, from ca. 1343 onward. There it is found, for example, in the commentary on the *Sentences* of Gregory of Rimini. The years 1332 (Oxford) and 1343 (Paris) may therefore be taken to mark the end of this period.

3. Renewed reflection on the status of science, from ca. 1298

From the beginning of the twelfth century, theology and philosophy in the intellectual West had been involved in a process of increasing rationalization. Rational scientific methods gained more and more ground, while the reflection on religious points no longer served only to secure the blessing of the good, but also to fathom the contents of faith in a purely rational vein.

The process was fostered by developments in the field of logic and semantics, in particular by the study of Aristotle's *Prior* and *Posterior analytics*. These works contain discussions of the syllogism (*Prior analytics*), and of the status and nature of knowledge, science, and demonstration (*Posterior analytics*). A new notion of scientificity developed, which was granted universal, supra-disciplinary application. As a result of these developments, the thirteenth century saw the rise of theological works that used the same standards of scientificity, and the same methods of argumentation, as were applied outside the field of theology. In particular, this was the case with commentaries on the *Sentences* of the second half of the thirteenth century.

Around 1300, a new and important element was introduced into this process, which also affected the domain of divine knowledge. While scientific theology had traditionally been confined to the explanation of the *contents* of faith, it now tended to address also the manner in which these contents were discussed. Reflection reached beyond the matter of discussion to its form, and often indeed confined itself to the latter. From the beginning of the fourteenth century, views were increasingly often criticized for the *manner* in which they were reached, rather than for the *content* they conveyed. A typical example is a remark in the *Liber propugnatorius* against some view of Scotus: 'Although this view is correct, Scotus's line of reasoning is insufficient.'[3]

An important consequence of the new mode of reflection on theology was that a distinction was made between what could be proved and what could not be proved. It was found that some of the traditional points concerning divine knowledge admitted of a strict demonstration, while other points, though no less true than the first, could only be made plausible by means of probable arguments. Although thinkers tended to disagree about which points on divine knowledge could be proved, the shift of attention toward provability constituted a qualitative change as compared to the thirteenth century. Earlier thinkers, such as Thomas Aquinas, Giles of Rome, Godfrey of Fontaines, and Henry of Ghent, confined their reflection almost exclusively to the level of content, and hardly ever ventured onto the meta-level of demonstration.

Scotus was one of the first to give evidence of this new development. In the prologues to his commentaries on the *Sentences*, he discussed at length the scientific status of theology. For the first time, he made a clear distinction between what can and what cannot be proved scientifically in regard of God's knowledge. In his commentary on the *Sentences*, he criticized the views and argumentations of earlier theologians in this connection, including Thomas Aquinas and, in particular, Henry of Ghent. The year 1298, in which Scotus gave his first lectures on the *Sentences* at Oxford, may be taken as the starting point of this period.

It was particularly in the first twenty-five years of the fourteenth century that the formal mode of reflection developed. In Paris, it seems to have been initiated largely by the lectures Scotus gave there. The centre of the formal movement was in England, however. Next to Scotus, various other writers contributed to it, including the author of the *Liber propugnatorius*, Peter Aureoli, William of Ockham, and Walter Chatton.

As with the earlier periods, it is difficult to say when this development ended. Several of the new points that were highlighted at the beginning of the fourteenth century had a lasting influence on subsequent periods. The question of demonstrability, e.g., was raised throughout the fourteenth

---

[3] *Liber propugnatorius*, I d. 2 q. 3 (ed. Venice 1523), fol. 22va.

century. It became connected with the older question of what the position of Aristotle and Averroes had been, partly because many philosophers and theologians took them as a model for man's natural thought. Considering the fact that Aristotle's work was an obligatory part of philosophical education in the fourteenth century, we can understand that the associated question of demonstrability enjoyed a more or less enduring interest.

From ca. 1315-1325 onward, the reflection on method and argumentation gradually engraved itself on the structure of the commentaries on the *Sentences*, both in England and in Paris. It became fashionable to frame *quaestiones* in terms of *suppositiones* and *conclusiones*, thus emphasizing the logical structure of the argument. This method of design was adopted by almost all fourteenth-century commentaries originating after 1315-25. Moreover, next to criticism of a view's content, formal criticism continued to be important throughout the fourteenth century. In light of these facts, we should conclude that the critical-formal aspect, developed in England at the beginning of the fourteenth century, had a permanent, structural influence on the theology and philosophy of the fourteenth century, in particular because of its influence on the structure of most commentaries on the *Sentences*.

4. Logico-semantic approach, from ca. 1317 (England) and ca. 1343 (Paris)

As is well-known, logical tuition was part of the arts program at the *studia* of the orders, as well as at the faculties of arts of the universities. If we bear in mind that all prospective theologians were required to take a degree in the arts, it is hardly surprising that many works on theology contain logical expositions and analyses. Trained in the logical branch of the arts, theologians were able to recognize and analyze ambiguities in the meaning of propositions. A typical example is the use of the distinction between *sensus compositus* and *sensus divisus* in the analysis of ambiguous propositions on God's foreknowledge. Also important for the problem of divine knowledge were the theory of the *proprietates terminorum*, the study of syncategorematic terms (such as 'all', in 'Does God know all numbers?'), and the analysis of the various kinds of fallacy, discussed in *sophismata* and other logical treatises. In addition, several 'classical' works, such as Boethius's widely read *De consolatione* and Anselm's *De concordia*, contained logico-semantic considerations with regard to the problem of divine knowledge. It is against this more or less common background, determined by the educational system and by some much-read texts, that we should understand the use of semantic analysis by Thomas Aquinas and other thirteenth-century theologians.

Around 1317, however, a new and important development made its appearance, at first in Oxford and London. The logico-semantic approach to divine knowledge, which had been lingering in the background for some time, suddenly came to dominate the field, producing treatises that were devoted exclusively to the semantic analysis of propositions about God's (fore)knowledge. Also the commentaries on the *Perihermeneias* and on the *Sentences* were increasingly concerned with semantic analyses of the problem. As far as we know, the first signs of this new development appear in the *Notabilia* of Richard Campsall, written in 1317 or shortly after, in several works of Ockham, and in the commentary on the *Sentences* of Walter Chatton. Subsequently, the movement carried over into the work of theologians such as John of Rodington, Adam Wodeham, and Robert Holcot. Although the exact date of origin of Richard Campsall's *Notabilia* has still not been established, it is safe to assume that the new development in England took place around 1317, or anyway not long after.[4]

Two causes were responsible for the change. One factor was the reflection on method and argumentation in theology, as it had developed in England from ca. 1298. As a result of this reflection, there was a growing interest, also within the field of theology, in the logical and formal status of propositions, and in the factors that determine their truth values. Typical questions in this context included: 'Which propositions can be true simultaneously', 'How does the change in truth value of one proposition affect that of the other', and 'What is the difference between a proposition being true and its being necessarily true?'

Secondly, the views of Thomas and Scotus, commonly acknowledged as the most fundamental contributions to the issue, had been the subject of meticulous discussion for a considerable period of time. Through the years, there had come to be a growing awareness of a number of problems associated with these views. The discovery of these problems, most notably that of certainty and contingency, and the lack of a satisfactory, alternative material solution, were felt as a scientific deadlock by many theologians. Some of them, including Ockham, observed in this context that a material solution is beyond the reach of human understanding. Yet, at the same time, these thinkers allowed for philosophical reflection on divine foreknowledge at a formal level, i.e., at the level of the truth value of propositions. With regard to the question of certainty and contingency, this was an important problem shift: the focus of attention was no longer the *content* of foreknowledge, but rather its *extrinsic* and *formal* aspects.

The development with regard to divine knowledge formed part of a broad reorientation that took place in England in the 1320s and 1330s. Traditional

---

[4] For the dating of Campsall's *Notabilia* (1317, or shortly after), see K.H. Tachau, *Vision and Certitude*, 159. This dating is not disputed in her most recent publication on Campsall, 'Richard Campsall as a Theologian: New Evidence', *Historia Philosophiae Medii Aevi. Studien zur Geschichte der Philosophie des Mittelalters*, ed. B. Mojsisch and O. Pluta, Vol. 2, Amsterdam-Philadelphia 1991, 979-1002.

questions in various domains of theology and philosophy were gradually displaced by questions of a more formal and analytical nature. The two factors that specifically changed the outlook on divine knowledge doubtless contributed to this general change (among other things, through the customary analysis of current opinions and of fictitious casus in the disputations).

In the commentaries on the *Sentences* that originated in Paris, the semantic approach to foreknowledge did not occur before the 1340s. When in due course it made its appearance there, this was under the influence of views deriving from the works of English theologians like Ockham and Wodeham. The commentary on the *Sentences* of Gregory of Rimini (1343-4) was one of the first works in which the new English approach was adopted. In this sense, the year 1343 marks the beginning of the period in Paris.

Under the influence of theologians such as Gregory of Rimini and Hugolin of Orvieto, whose works remained popular for a considerable period, the semantic approach to divine knowledge spread on the continent, and eventually became more or less generally accepted.[5] In his commentary on the *Sentences*, Marsilius of Inghen opted for the 'extrinsic', semantic approach as an alternative to more material lines of reasoning with regard to the question of certainty and contingency. Toward the end of the fourteenth century, the semantic approach was evidently still a viable choice.

The work of Marsilius bears the marks of each of the four aspects of development discussed here, with the exception of the second one — his remarks on the problem of unity and plurality derived from a different background, notably his discussion with John of Ripa. Most prominent in Marsilius are the third and fourth aspect: his reflection on the status of knowledge, and his application of the logico-semantic approach. In these respects, he was typically a fourteenth-century thinker.

MARSILIUS AND THE DEVELOPMENT OF THE MAIN VIEWS ON DIVINE KNOWLEDGE

We now turn to an evaluation of the results of our study. In this final section, we shall try to situate Marsilius in the context of late medieval thought. We do so, first, by reviewing the points on which he was following the three dominant views on divine knowledge of his time, viz., those of Thomas Aquinas, Duns Scotus, and William of Ockham. Subsequently, we shall examine which other thinkers influenced Marsilius, and consider the extent to which his view concurred with, or diverged from, the positions that were

---

[5] For the influence of Gregory, see M. Schulze, '*Via Gregorii* in Forschung und Quellen', *Gregor von Rimini. Werk und Wirkung bis zur Reformation*, ed. H.A. Oberman, Berlin-New York 1981 (Spätmittelalter und Reformation, 20), 1-126. The influence of Hugolin is discussed by V. Marcolino, 'Die Resonanz des Sentenzenkommentars Hugolins von Orvieto bis zur Reformationszeit', *Schwerpunkte und Wirkungen des Sentenzenkommentars Hugolins von Orvieto OESA*, ed. W. Eckermann, Würzburg 1990 (Cassiciacum, 42), 297-321.

taken to be characteristic of the *moderni* (Adam Wodeham and Gregory of Rimini) in the second half of the fourteenth century.

Thomas Aquinas and Marsilius of Inghen

As we have seen, several of the views and arguments used by Thomas were common in the fourteenth century. This calls for great prudence when considering a possible connection between Thomas and Marsilius. If their views appear to be similar, this does not necessarily mean that Marsilius was directly dependent on Thomas. Direct dependency should be surmised only when no other explanation of the similarity is available, that is to say, when it cannot be accounted for in terms of the views and assumptions that were more or less common in the fourteenth century, nor in terms of the views defended by other authors known to Marsilius. And finally, of course, there is strong evidence *in favour* of direct dependence when Marsilius himself explicitly associated his view with that of Thomas.

With regard to divine knowledge, there is only one place where Marsilius mentioned Thomas as holding a view similar to the one he himself endorsed, viz., in the first *principium* of his commentary on the *Sentences*, in connection with the claim that the ideas really coincide with God's essence. Yet, from the fact that Marsilius, in the same context, also quoted two other opinions according to which the ideas coincide with God's essence, and because he did not draw upon Thomas anywhere else in his theory of ideas, we may conclude that Thomas's view was only one among several others positions that were all similar to the view defended by Marsilius. With regard to the theory of ideas, there is no distinct connection between Thomas and Marsilius — which is not to deny, of course, that Thomas and Marsilius each defended a view that toward the end of the fourteenth century was seen as characteristic of the selfsame, older tradition.

Much the same pattern of connection seems to apply to other issues as well. The similarities between Thomas and Marsilius derived from views that were commonly accepted in the fourteenth century: thus, there is no apparent need for assuming a direct connection between Thomas and Marsilius. We list the following three points.

1. *Proofs of God's knowledge: arguments from perfection and from causality.* As we have noted, the arguments from perfection and from causality were used by almost all theologians of the late thirteenth and fourteenth century, in one form or another. Hence, they were far too common to warrant a direct connection between Thomas and Marsilius. Moreover, the argument from causality was used by Marsilius in its typical fourteenth-century form, which it had assumed from ca. 1320, particularly in the works of Adam Wodeham, Francis of Mayronnes, William of Rubione, and Gregory of Rimini. This version of the argument was based on the singularity of the

effect, instead of the universal nature of the cause, as in Thomas and Scotus.

2. *Eternity.* As we saw in the previous chapter, Marsilius appealed to the notion of divine eternity in his account of foreknowledge. Although, generally speaking, this is a clear indication that the author was dependent on Thomas, the particular case of Marsilius is an exception to this rule. Marsilius's use of the notion of eternity did not go back to Thomas, but rather to Peter Lombard, whose view on eternity in the *Sentences* received a great deal of attention from several influential fourteenth-century theologians, including Adam Wodeham, Gregory of Rimini, and Henry of Oyta.

Moreover, we noted that philosophers and theologians of the thirteenth and fourteenth century widely disagreed about what the correct interpretation of Thomas's view on God's eternity should be, and what, according to Thomas, is the ontological status of the object that is known as 'present' to this eternity. According to one faction, what Thomas meant was *real* presence: things have real existence in God's eternity. This was the interpretation given by the Dominican theologian Jacob of Metz, as well as that of the Franciscans William de la Mare, Duns Scotus, and James of Ascoli. Others defended the view that Thomas's 'presence' should be read as presence *as if*: in virtue of his knowledge of their causes and their ideas, God knows the creatures 'as if' they are present to him. This was the interpretation given by William Peter of Godin in the *Lectura thomasina*, as well as that of Peter of Auvergne, Hervaeus Natalis, and Durand of St. Pourçain.

The fact that there were several mutually inconsistent readings of Thomas makes it extremely difficult to establish a direct influence from Thomas. This applies in particular to Marsilius, who did not expressly base himself either on Thomas or on any of his interpreters. Moreover, we know that his view on a closely related issue, viz., the problem of eternity and contingency in relation to divine knowledge, was radically opposed to that of Thomas. According to the latter, the eternity of God's knowledge implies that God's knowledge is necessary. This was denied by Marsilius, who followed the line of argument developed by Adam Wodeham and Gregory of Rimini at this point.

3. *Divine attributes.* As we saw in chapter 3, Marsilius's theory of the attributes was clearly different from that of Thomas in his commentary on the *Sentences*, where he claimed that the rational differences between the attributes correspond to rational differences within God. There is a similarity, however, between Marsilius's position and that of Thomas in the *Summa theologiae*: the difference between the divine attributes exists only in the human mind (not in God), and is caused by the difference between the finiteness of the human mind and the infinity of God's perfection. Yet, Marsilius apparently did not derive his view directly from Thomas, but rather from intermediate sources. The distinction between, on the one hand, the

(finite) attributional notion in the human mind, and, on the other, the (infinite) attributional perfection of God came to Marsilius through the work of Adam Wodeham and Gregory of Rimini. The opinion that the attributes in the human mind are different because of the limited powers of the human understanding, which is unable to express God's infinity by means of a single concept, probably reached Marsilius through the Augustinian tradition of Thomas of Strasbourg.

Duns Scotus and Marsilius of Inghen

There is no evidence for the claim that Marsilius's views on divine knowledge were based directly on those of Scotus. Yet, on several points there was indirect influence of a more general nature, viz., with regard to those of Scotus's views that were framed at the beginning of the fourteenth century and were incorporated in the common philosophical wisdom of the fourteenth century. We shall first take a look at the points on which Marsilius sympathized with views that were also held by Scotus.

1. *The role of divine will*. Marsilius believed that God is the immediate cause of all things because he cooperates with every cause. His manner of argumentation for this position resembled that of Scotus, inasmuch as they both referred to the *Liber de causis*. Also like Scotus, Marsilius was of the opinion that God is the cause of contingency in the created world. It does not follow, however, that Marsilius depended directly on Scotus here. Similar views were held by several other theologians, including Adam Wodeham and Gregory of Rimini, with whose work Marsilius was well acquainted.

Interestingly, Marsilius, like Wodeham and Gregory, on the one hand affirmed that God is the cooperating cause of future things, while on the other hand refusing to explain the certainty of God's foreknowledge in terms of God's causality. In the case of Gregory and Marsilius, the reason for this was their reluctance to make divine will the cause of sin.

2. *The separation of immutability and necessity*. Marsilius believed that what is immutable and eternal need not be necessary in every respect. Although typical of Scotus, this view probably came to Marsilius through the discussion about Lombard's view of eternity, mentioned earlier.

3. *Contingency of God's knowledge*. The view that God's knowledge is contingent had become widely known through Scotus's criticism of Thomas, in particular. However, considering that almost all theologians of the fourteenth century believed that God's knowledge of contingents is contingent, it is again difficult to establish a direct connection between Scotus and Marsilius.

In addition to points of indirect agreement, there were also two issues on which Marsilius clearly took distance from Scotus and the Scotists.

1. *Formal distinction*. Marsilius's main point of criticism, which had been

raised by many others as well, was that the notion of a formal distinction collapses into that of a real distinction, thus seriously compromising the unity of God. Because this objection was quite common at the time, it by itself carries little information about the philosophical background of the person who used it — except that he was obviously not a Scotist. In this particular case, however, we can say something more. From several *verbatim* quotations, we can be reasonably sure that Marsilius based himself on the work of Adam Wodeham. From Wodeham he also adopted the enumeration of expressions that Scotus and others used for the formal distinction and for things that are formally distinct — *distinctae formalitates, distinctae perfectiones, diversae rationes formales, modi reales eiusdem rei inter se et a parte rei distincti, distinctae cognoscibilitates vel quidditates*. Apparently, it had not escaped notice that, even to Scotus and the Scotists themselves, the notion of the formal distinction was far from clear and less than uncontroversial.

2. *Theory of ideas*. Marsilius discussed Scotus's theory of ideas together with that of Ockham, as he believed their positions to be essentially the same. According to Marsilius, both of them claimed that the idea is the thing known. His own position, by contrast, was that the idea coincides with God's essence, and hence cannot be the thing known.

Probably, the peculiar history of Scotus's theory of ideas at the beginning of the fourteenth century was responsible for Marsilius's identification of the views of Scotus and Ockham. Alternatively, his interpretation may have been suggested by the fact that Ockham sympathized with Scotus's criticism of Henry of Ghent, viz., that God can have direct knowledge of the creatures, unaided by *relationes ideales*. Marsilius probably did not have first-hand knowledge of the view of Scotus. This may be gathered from the fact that he gave the exact reference for the theory of ideas in the work of Ockham, but failed to do so in the case of Scotus.

Other theologians of the second half of the fourteenth century did not identify the views of Scotus and Ockham in this connection. According to Peter of Candia, for example, the view of Scotus is about the quiddity, while that of Ockham is about the (known) thing or creature.

William of Ockham and Marsilius of Inghen

Although Marsilius had knowledge of the sources of Ockham's view on divine knowledge, as is clear from his largely literal rendering of Ockham's theory of ideas, on their points of agreement he was influenced not so much by Ockham himself, but rather by 'Ockhamist' views in the work of Adam Wodeham and Gregory of Rimini. We shall first look at those aspects of Marsilius's position that were clearly in sympathy with that of Ockham.

1. *Divine attributes*. With regard to the question of divine attributes, Marsilius, like Ockham, made a sharp distinction between the level of concepts in the human mind, and that of the reality of God's essence. They both believed that the differences between the attributes exist only at the conceptual level, and not at that of reality. Furthermore, and again like Ockham, Marsilius criticized the formal distinction of Scotus and the Scotists. Both his theory of the attributes and his criticism of the formal distinction drew from the commentaries on the *Sentences* of Adam Wodeham and Gregory of Rimini. This may be deduced from the literal quotations Marsilius adopted from these works, and from the fact that he referred to Gregory of Rimini in this connection.

The fact that the 'Ockhamist' views came to Marsilius through the work of Adam Wodeham and Gregory of Rimini, means that the philosophical kinship between Marsilius and Ockham should be understood in terms of the reception of English theology in Paris in the 1340s and after.

2. *Semantic approach*. Much the same is true of the semantic approach to the problem of how the contingency of the future combines with the certainty of God's foreknowledge. Again, the 'Ockhamist' aspect of Marsilius's position did not come directly from Ockham, but was embedded in the more general context of the reception of English theology. This pattern of influence may be educed from two facts. First, the logico-semantic approach that Marsilius used was, broadly speaking, the same as that of Gregory of Rimini. Second, Marsilius discussed the question of whether man has influence on God's foreknowledge, that is, whether he can make it happen (*facere*) that God foreknows something different. This question was not addressed by Ockham, but reached Marsilius through the work of Adam Wodeham. Like Gregory of Rimini, Marsilius thought it proper to say that man can influence God's knowledge, though only when considered at the propositional level.

The extrinsic approach was widely associated with Ockham's claim that man is unable to explain the combination of certainty and contingency in intrinsic terms. In addition, it was sometimes associated further with a critique of the solutions given by Thomas Aquinas and Duns Scotus, largely corresponding to Ockham's criticism of their position. It should be noted, however, that in spite of their shared semantic outlook, the authors in question did not agree on all aspects of divine knowledge, in particular not with regard to more intrinsic issues. This is clear from distinct differences between Gregory of Rimini and William of Ockham, as well as between Marsilius and Ockham. It is to these differences that we now turn.

1. *Provability*. In contrast with Ockham, Marsilius believed that it can be proved that God has knowledge, and in particular that he has knowledge of the creatures. According to him, there is not the slightest difference between the teachings of faith and the findings of natural reason. What is more,

Marsilius rejected certain fundamental assumptions in Ockham's criticism of Thomas. He believed that it can be proved that God is the cause of all things, and that it is possible to derive intuitive knowledge of one thing (i.e., the creatures) from intuitive knowledge of the other (i.e., God's essence).

2. *Theory of ideas*. Marsilius criticized Ockham's view that the idea is the thing as known. From the history of the reception of Ockham's theory of ideas in the second half of the fourteenth century, it may be concluded (as established in chapter 5) that Marsilius's objections were not merely standard procedure, but should be seen as substantial philosophical criticism.

Other influences

No account of Marsilius's position with regard to divine knowledge could be expected to be adequate if it confined itself to a consideration of the three dominant views alone. It has been shown in this study that several other lines meet in Marsilius as well, deriving most notably from Thomas of Strasbourg's commentary on the *Sentences*, and from Buridan's commentaries on Aristotle. These other positions exerted a distinct influence on Marsilius with regard to divine knowledge and related issues. As for Thomas of Strasbourg, we noted earlier that he was probably the source for Marsilius's view on the differences between divine attributes in the human mind. His influence is clearly felt in Marsilius's reply to the claim, made by Peter Aureoli, that there is no distinction between the primary and secondary object of God's knowledge. Other examples in which his influence can be shown include Marsilius's treatment of the problem of God's knowledge of evil, and that of the distribution of divine powers. The influence of Buridan is obvious from the many quotations Marsilius adopted *verbatim* from his work, in particular with regard to the interpretation of Aristotle and Averroes on divine knowledge, causality, and finality, and with regard to his treatment of perfections and the modes of divine knowledge. Finally, we found distinct traces of Neoplatonic and hermetical writings in Marsilius, particularly in his proofs of God's knowledge and in his account of divine ideas.

It appears that, on the matter of divine knowledge, two quite different, and at first sight even incompatible, traditions were brought together in the work of Marsilius, viz., the critical and semantic tradition of the fourteenth century, and the speculative, metaphysical tradition of Neoplatonism. This was doubtless the result of the variegated philosophical atmosphere that exuded from the university of Paris at the time Marsilius was studying theology there, and was presumably preparing part of his commentary on the *Sentences*. As we have seen, in the years 1360-1370, the Neoplatonic views of John of Ripa were subject of discussion at the university of Paris, as well as the views of English theologians such as Ockham and Adam Wodeham.

Marsilius as modernus

From remarks by his contemporaries in the second half of the fourteenth century, we know that several of the views defended by Marsilius were seen as being related to views held by Ockham, Adam Wodeham, and Gregory of Rimini. They were accordingly called 'modern', a term then used for views that developed after ca. 1310. With regard to divine attributes, for example, we find that Marsilius followed a line of thought which Peter of Candia identified as that of Ockham and his *sequaces*, among whom he mentioned Adam Wodeham and Gregory of Rimini. Another example is Marsilius's claim that God knows the contingent in virtue of his *immensitas*, which was called the view of the *moderni* by John of Ripa. In the same connection, John Hiltalingen of Basel and Henry of Oyta mentioned Adam Wodeham and Gregory of Rimini. As a final example, we mention Marsilius's view that God is always able to produce ever greater effects, which Peter of Candia referred to as the received view of the *moderni*.

These facts are of considerable historical importance. We learn from them that Marsilius, in his own time, was seen as a representative of the 'modern' line of thought, and that he was placed in the tradition of Ockham. Moreover, we have seen that, on several important issues, Marsilius was decisively influenced by Buridan, who at the beginning of the fifteenth century was placed in the Ockhamist tradition. If we further bear in mind Marsilius's reputation as a logician who denied the existence of universals outside the human mind, we can understand why in later days, during the era of the *Wegestreit*, Marsilius could be chronicled as an *antesignanus nominalistarum*. Yet, with all these facts, we have not exhausted what can be said about Marsilius's historical image. As we have seen, his position was determined not only by writers such as Ockham, Wodeham, Gregory of Rimini, and John Buridan, but also by influences from quite different directions. Thus, his theory of divine ideas was identified as that of the *antiqui doctores* by his contemporaries. Marsilius defended this 'ancient view' in the opening lecture of his commentary on the *Sentences*, which was attended by all members of the faculty of theology at Heidelberg. The fact that he chose this special occasion for defending the 'old' view, and for simultaneously criticizing the then common Ockhamist view, makes it clear that Marsilius, despite his points of contact with Ockham, Wodeham, Gregory of Rimini, and Buridan, was not a mere *modernus* or a simple *sequax*.

BIBLIOGRAPHY

Reference Works

Acta facultatis artium universitatis Vindobonensis 1385-1416, ed. P. Uiblein, Graz 1968 (Publikationen des Instituts für Oesterreichische Geschichtsforschung, 6/2).

Catalogus translationum et commentariorum: Mediaeval and Renaissance Latin Translations and Commentaries. Annotated Lists and Guides, 6 vols to date, ed. P.O. Kristeller, Washington, D.C. 1960ff (Union académique internationale).

Chartularium Universitatis Parisiensis, 4 vols, ed. H. Denifle and E. Chatelain, Paris 1889-1897, repr. Brussels 1964.

Constitutiones Concilii quarti Lateranensis una cum Commentariis glossatorum, ed. A. García y García, Vatican City 1981 (Monumenta iuris canonici, A/2).

Dictionnaire de spiritualité, ascétique et mystique, ed. M. Viller and A. Rayez, Paris 1937ff.

Die Rektorbücher der Universität Heidelberg, 1 vol. to date, ed. J. Miethke, Heidelberg 1986ff (Die Amtsbücher der Universität Heidelberg, A).

Historisches Wörterbuch der Philosophie, ed. J. Ritter and K. Gründer, Darmstadt 1971ff.

Lexikon des Mittelalters, ed. R.-H. Bautier, München-Zürich 1980ff.

Lexikon für Theologie und Kirche, 2th edition, ed. J. Höfer and K. Rahner, Freiburg 1957, repr. Freiburg 1986.

Lohr, Ch.H., 'Medieval Latin Aristotle Commentaries. Authors: Johannes de Kanthi-Myngodus', *Traditio* 27 (1971), 251-351.

Markowski, M., 'Katalog dziel Marsyliusza z Inghen z ewidencja rekopisow', *Studia Mediewistyczne* 25/2 (1988), 39-132.

Plessis d'Argentre, C. du, *Collectio judiciorum de novis erroribus*, Vol. 1, Paris 1724.

Ravizza, M., 'Bibliography', *God, Foreknowledge, and Freedom*, ed. J.M. Fischer, Stanford, California 1989 (Stanford Series in Philosophy), 329-338.

Rekeningen der stad Nijmegen 1382-1543. Vol. I: 1382-1427, ed. H.D.J. van Schevichaven and J.C.J. Kleijntjes, Nijmegen 1910.

Theologisches Wörterbuch zum Neuen Testament, ed. G. Kittel, Stuttgart 1933ff.

Urkundenbuch der Universitaet Heidelberg, ed. E. Winkelmann, 2 vols, Heidelberg 1886.

Wainwright, W.J., *Philosophy of Religion. An Annotated Bibliography of Twentieth-Century Writings in English*, New York-London 1978.

Primary Sources

1. Manuscripts

Adam Wodeham, *Lectura Oxoniensis*, in: Paris, Bibl. Maz., 915; Paris, Bibl. de l'Univ., 193.

Conrad of Soltau, *In libros Sententiarum*, in: Stuttgart, Württ. Landesbibl., Cod. Theol. Fol. 118.

Gottschalk of Nepomuk, *In libros Sententiarum*, in: Kraków, Bibl. Jag., 1499.

Henry of Oyta, *Lectura textualis*, in: München, Bayer. Staatsbibl., CLM 5590.

——, *Quaestiones Sententiarum*, in: München, Bayer. Staatsbibl., CLM, 8867.

John Duns Scotus, *Reportatio I A*, in: Wien, Oesterr. Nationalbibl., CVP, 1453.

John of Mirecourt, *Lectura in primum Sententiarum*, in: Bologna, Bibl. Com. dell' Archiginnasio, A 921; Napoli, Bibl. Naz., VII C 28.

Marsilius of Inghen (?), *Quaestiones libri Physicorum*, in: Cuyk en St. Agatha, Kruisherenklooster, C 12 II.

Marsilius of Inghen, *Consequentiae*, in: Uppsala, Universitetsbiblioteket, C 640.

——, *Quaestiones super librum Metaphysicorum*, in: Wien, Oesterr. Nationalbibl., CVP, 5297.

——, *Quaestiones super librum posteriorum*, in: Toledo, Bibl. del Cab., 95-5.

——, *Quaestiones veteris artis*, in: Wien, Oesterr. Nationalbibl., CVP, 5159.
Michael Aiguani, *In libros Sententiarum*, in: Kraków, Bibl. Jag., 1459.
Thomas de Strampino, *Principia I-IV*, in Kraków, Bibl. Jag., 1199.

2. Printed sources

Achard of St. Victor, L'*unité de Dieu et la pluralité des créatures (De unitate <Dei> et pluralitate creaturarum*. Texte Latin inédit du manuscrit de Padoue (Antoniana, Scaff. V, 89), établi, traduit et présenté par E. Martineau, Authentica 1987.
Adam Wodeham, *Lectura secunda in librum primum Sententiarum*, ed. R. Wood and G. Gál, 3 vols, St. Bonaventure, New York 1990.
——, *Super quattuor libros Sententiarum*, Paris 1512 (abbreviated by Henry of Oyta).
——, *Tractatus de Indivisibilibus*, ed. R. Wood, Dordrecht 1988 (Synthese Historical Library, 31).
Al-Gazali, *Tahafut al-falasifah <Incoherence of the Philosophers>*, trans. S.A. Kamali, Lahore ²1963 (Pakistan Philosophical Congress Publications, 3).
Alan of Lille, *Anticlaudianus*, ed. R. Bossuat, Paris 1955 (Textes philosophiques du Moyen Age, 1).
——, [See also the section on secondary literature s.v. Häring].
Albert of Saxony, *Quaestio de futuris contingentibus*, published in: William of Ockham, *Expositio aurea*, Bologna 1496, repr. Ridgewood, New Jersey 1964.
Albert the Great, *Ethicorum libri X*, ed. A. Borgnet, Vol. 7, Paris 1891.
——, *Super Dionysium De divinis nominibus*, ed. P. Simon, Münster 1972 (Opera omnia, 37/1).
Alfonsus Vargas of Toledo, *In primum Sententiarum*, Venice 1490, repr. The Meriden Gravure Co. 1952 (Cassiciacum, American Series, 2).
Anselm of Canterbury, *Cur Deus homo*, ed. F.S. Schmitt, Rome 1940, repr. Stuttgart-Bad Cannstatt 1968 (Opera omnia, 2).
——, *De concordia praescientiae et praedestinationis et gratiae Dei cum libero arbitrio*, ed. F.S. Schmitt, Rome 1940, repr. Stuttgart-Bad Cannstatt 1968 (Opera omnia, 2).
——, *De processione spiritus sancti*, ed. F.S. Schmitt, Rome 1940, repr. Stuttgart-Bad Cannstatt 1968 (Opera omnia, 2).
Aristotle, *Opera*, ed. I. Bekker, Berlin 1831, repr. Berlin 1970.
Auctoritates Aristotelis, [see the section on secondary literature s.v. Hamesse].
Augustine, *De civitate Dei*, Opera Pars 14/1-2, Turnhout 1955 (CCSL, 47-48).
——, *De diversis quaestionibus octoginta tribus*, ed. A. Mutzenbecher, Opera Pars 12/2, Turnhout 1975 (CCSL, 44A).
——, *De libero arbitrio*, ed. W.H. Green, Opera Pars 2/2, Turnhout 1970 (CCSL, 29).
Averroes, *Die Epitome der Metaphysik des Averroes*, übersetzt und mit einer Einleitung und Erläuterungen versehen von S. van den Bergh, Leiden 1924 (Veröffentlichungen der 'De Goeje-Stiftung, 7).
——, *Ibn Rushd's Metaphysics. A Translation with Introduction of Ibn Rushd's Commentary on Aristotle's Metaphysics, Book Lam*, by Ch. Genequand, Leiden 1984 (Islamic Philosophy and Theology, 1).
——, *In De coelo*, Venice 1562, repr. Frankfurt a/M 1962 (ed. Iuntina, 5).
——, *In Ethicam*, Venice 1562, repr. Frankfurt a/M 1962 (ed. Iuntina, 3).
——, *In Metaphysicam*, Venice 1562, repr. Frankfurt a/Main 1962 (ed. Iuntina, 8).
——, *In Physicam*, Venice 1562, repr. Frankfurt a/M 1962 (ed. Iuntina, 4).
——, *Tahafut al-Tahafut (The Incoherence of the Incoherence)*, 2 vols, transl. with introd. and notes by S. van den Bergh, London 1954 (Unesco Collection of Great Works, Arabic Series).
Averroïsme Bolonais au XIVe siècle. Editions des textes, ed. Z. Kuksewicz, Wroclaw 1965 (Institut de philosophie et de sociologie de l'academie polonaise des sciences).
Avicenna, *Liber de philosophia prima sive scientia divina*, I-IV and V-X, ed. S. van Riet, Louvain-Leiden 1977-1980 (Avicenna Latinus).
Bartholomew of Usingen, *Exercitium physicorum*, Erfurt 1507.
Baumgarten, A.G., *Metaphysica*, editio VII, Halle 1779, repr. Hildesheim 1963.

Boethius, *Commentarii in librum Aristotelis Perihermeneias*, I and II, ed. C. Meiser, Leipzig 1877-1880.
——, *Philosophiae consolatio*, ed. L. Bieler, Opera Pars 1, Turnhout 1984 (CCSL, 94).
Bonaventura, *Commentaria in IV libros Sententiarum*, Florence 1934 (Opera Theologica Selecta, 1-4).
——, *Collationes in Hexaëmeron*, ed. F. Delorme, Florence 1934 (BFSMA, 8).
Dionysiaca. Recueil donnant l'ensemble des traductions latines des ouvrages attribués au Denys de l'Aréopage, 2 vols, Desclée de Brouwer et Cie 1937.
Durand of St. Pourçain, *In Sententias commentariorum libri IIII*, Venice 1571, repr. Ridgewood, New Jersey 1964.
Eustratius, *The Greek Commentaries on the Nicomachean Ethics of Aristotle in the Latin Translation of Robert Grosseteste Bishop of Lincoln († 1253), Vol. I, Eustratius on Book I and the anonymous scholia on books II, III, and IV*, ed. H.P.F. Mercken, Leiden 1973 (Corpus latinum commentariorum in Aristotelem graecorum, 6/1).
Francis of Mayronnes and Pierre Roger, *Disputatio (1320-1321)*, ed. J. Barbet, Paris 1961 (Textes philosophiques du Moyen Age, 10).
Francis of Mayronnes, *In libros Sententiarum*, Venice 1520, repr. Frankfurt a/Main 1966.
Gabriel Biel, *Collectorium circa quattuor libros Sententiarum*, ed. W. Werbeck and U. Hofmann, 5 vols, Tübingen 1973-1984.
Geert Groote, *Epistolae*, ed. W. Mulder, Antwerp 1933 (Tekstuitgaven van Ons Geestelijk Erf, 3).
Giles of Rome, *Errores philosophorum*, critical text with notes and Introd. by J. Koch. English transl. by J.O. Riedl, Milwaukee, Wisc. 1944.
——, *In primum librum Sententiarum*, Venice 1521, repr. Frankfurt a/Main 1968.
Godfrey of Fontaines, *Les quatre premièrs Quodlibets*, ed. M. de Wulf and A. Pelzer, Louvain 1904 (Les Philosophes Belges, 2).
——, *Les Quodlibet cinq, six et sept*, ed. M. de Wulf and J. Hoffmans, Louvain 1914 (Les philosophes Belges, 3).
Gregory of Rimini, *Lectura super primum et secundum Sententiarum*, ed. A.D. Trapp and V. Marcolino, 7 vols, Berlin 1979-1987 (Spätmittelalter und Reformation, 6-12).
Henry of Ghent, *Quodlibet* I, ed. R. Macken, Leuven-Leiden 1979 (Opera omnia, 5).
——, *Quodlibet* VII, ed. G.A. Wilson, Leuven 1991 (Opera omnia, 11).
——, *Quodlibet* IX, ed. R. Macken, Leuven 1983 (Opera omnia, 13).
——, *Quodlibeta*, Paris 1518, repr. Louvain 1961.
——, *Summae quaestionum ordinarium*, Paris 1520, repr. Louvain-Paderborn 1953 (Franciscan Institute Publications, Text Series, 5).
Henry of Harclay, [See the section on secondary literature s.v. Maurer].
Hervaeus Natalis, *In quatuor libros Sententiarum commentaria*, Paris 1647, repr. Westmead Farnborough 1966.
——, *Quodlibeta*, Venice 1513, repr. Ridgewood, New Jersey 1966.
Hugolin of Orvieto, *Commentarius in quattuor libros Sententiarum*, ed. W. Eckermann and V. Marcolino, 4 vols, Würzburg 1980-1988 (Cassiciacum, Supplementband, 8-11).
James of Ascoli, [See the section on secondary literature s.v. Yokoyama].
Jan Brugman, *Verspreide Sermoenen*, ed. Am. van Dijk, Antwerp 1948 (Klassieke galerij, 41).
Johannes Baconis, *Quaestiones in quatuor libros Sententiarum*, Cremona 1618, repr. Westmead, Farnborough 1969.
Johannes Capreolus, *Defensiones theologiae divi Thomae Aquinatis*, 7 vols, ed. C. Paban and Th. Pèques, Tours 1900-1908.
John Buridan, *Kommentar zur Aristotelischen Metaphysik*, Paris 1518, repr. Frankfurt a/Main 1964.
——, *Kommentar zur Aristotelischen Physik*, Paris 1509, repr. Frankfurt a/M 1964.
——, *Questiones longe super librum Perihermeneias*, ed. R. van der Lecq, Nijmegen 1983 (Artistarium, 4).
——, *Super decem libros Ethicorum*, Paris 1513, repr. Frankfurt a/M 1968.
——, *Tractatus de consequentiis*, ed. H. Hubien, Louvain-Paris 1976, (Philosophes médiévaux, 16).

John Duns Scotus, *De primo principio*, ed. W. Kluxen, Darmstadt 1974 (Texte zur Forschung, 20).
——, *Lectura*, Vatican City 1960ff (ed. Vat. 16ff).
——, *Ordinatio*, Lyon 1639, repr. Hildesheim 1968 (ed. Wadding, 5-10).
——, *Ordinatio*, Vatican City 1950ff (ed. Vat. 1ff).
——, *Reportata Parisiensia*, Lyon 1639, repr. Hildesheim 1969 (ed. Wadding, 11).
John Lutterell, *Libellus contra doctrinam G. Occam*, in: F. Hoffmann, *Die Schriften des Oxforder Kanzlers Iohannes Lutterell*, Leipzig 1959 (Erfurter theologische Studien, 6).
John of Jandun, *Quaestiones in duodecim libros Metaphysicae*, Venice 1553, repr. Frankfurt a/M 1966.
John of Paris, *Commentaire sur les Sentences, Reportation*, ed. J.-P. Muller, 2 vols, Rome 1961-1964 (Studia Anselmiana, 47, 52).
John of Ripa, *Conclusiones*, ed. A. Combes, Paris 1957 (Etudes de philosophie médiévale, 44).
——, *Determinationes*, ed. A. Combes, Paris 1957 (Textes philosophiques du Moyen Age, 4).
John Wyclif, *On universals (Tractatus de universalibus)*, transl. A. Kenny, introd. P.V. Spade, Oxford 1985.
——, *Tractatus de universalibus*, ed. I.J. Mueller, Oxford 1985.
Le Correctorium corruptorii 'Circa' de Jean Quidort de Paris, ed. J.-P. Muller, Rome 1941 (Studia Anselmiana, 12-13).
Le Correctorium corruptorii 'Quaestione'. Texte anonyme du ms. Merton 267, ed. J.-P. Muller, Rome 1954 (Studia Anselmiana, 35).
Le Correctorium corruptorii 'Quare'. Les premières polémiques Thomistes, Vol. I, ed. P. Glorieux, Le Saulchoir, Kain 1927 (Bibliothèque Thomiste, 9).
Le Correctorium corruptorii 'Sciendum'. Les premières polémiques Thomistes, Vol. II, ed. P. Glorieux, Paris 1956, (Bibliothèque Thomiste, 31).
Le livre des XXIV philosophes, Latin edition and French translation by F. Hudry, Grenoble 1989 (Collection Krisis).
Leibniz, G.W., *Essais de Théodicée*, ed. C.I. Gerhardt, Berlin 1885, Repr. Hildesheim 1961 (Die philosophischen Schriften, 1).
Liber de Causis, ed. A. Pattin, *Tijdschrift voor Filosofie* 28 (1966), 90-203.
Liber propugnatorius super primum Sententiarum contra Johannem Scotum, Venice 1523, repr. Frankfurt a/Main 1966.
Marsilius of Inghen, *Abbreviationes super octo libros Physicorum Aristotelis*, Venice 1521.
——, *Quaestiones super quattuor libros Sententiarum*, Strasbourg 1501, repr. Frankfurt a/M 1966.
——, [See also the section on secondary literature s.v. E.P. Bos; Hoenen].
Molina, Luis de, [See the section on secondary literature s.v. Stegmüller].
Peter Aureoli, *Commentarium in primum librum Sententiarum pars secunda*, Rome 1596.
Peter de Falco, *Questions disputées ordinaires*, ed. A.-J. Gondras, Louvain-Paris 1968 (Analecta Mediaevalia Namurcensia, 22).
Peter Lombard, *Sententiae in IV libris distinctae*, editio tertia, 2 vols, Grottaferrata 1971-1981 (Spicilegium Bonaventurianum, 4-5).
Peter of Ailly, *Quaestiones super libros Sententiarum*, Strasbourg 1490, repr. Frankfurt am Main 1968.
Peter of Aquila, *Quaestiones in 4 libros Sententiarum*, Speyer 1480, repr. Frankfurt am Main 1967.
Peter of Spain, *Tractatus called afterwards Summule logicales*, ed. L.M. de Rijk, Assen 1972 (Philosophical Texts and Studies, 22).
Pomponazzi, P., *Libri quinque de fato, de libero arbitrio et de praedestinatione*, ed. R. Lemay, Lucani 1957 (Thesaurus mundi. Bibliotheca scriptorum latinorum mediae et recentioris aetatis).
Proclus Diadochus, *Tria opuscula*, ed. H. Boese, Berlin 1960 (Quellen und Studien zur Geschichte der Philosophie, 1).
Rambert of Bologna, *Apologeticum veritatis contra Corruptorium*, ed. J.-P. Muller, Vatican City 1943 (Studi e testi, 108).
Richard Campsall, *The Works of Richard of Campsall*, ed. E.A. Synan, 2 vols, Toronto 1968-

1982 (Studies and Texts, 17, 58).
Richard Knapwell, *Quaestio disputata de unitate formae*, ed. F.E. Kelly, Paris 1982 (Bibliothèque Thomiste, 44).
Richard of Middleton, *Super quatuor libros Sententiarum*, Brescia 1591, repr. Frankfurt a/ Main 1963.
Richard of St. Victor, *De Trinitate*, ed. Jean Ribaillier, Paris 1958 (Textes philosophiques du Moyen Age, 6).
Robert Grosseteste, [See the section on secondary literature s.v. Baur]
Robert Holcot, *In quatuor libros Sententiarum quaestiones*, Lyon 1518, repr. Frankfurt a/M 1967.
——, [See also the section on secondary literature s.v. Courtenay; Gelber; Moody; Streveler].
Robert of Orford, *Reprobationes dictorum a fratre Egidio in primum Sententiarum. Les premières polémiques Thomistes*, ed. A.P. Vella, Paris 1968 (Bibliothèque Thomiste, 38).
Roger Marston, *Quodlibeta quattuor*, ed. G.F. Etzkorn and I.G. Brady, Florence 1968 (BFSMA, 26).
Some 14th Century Tracts on the Probationes Terminorum. Martin of Alnwick OFM, Richard Billingham, Edward Upton, and Others, ed. L.M. de Rijk, Nijmegen 1982 (Artistarium, 3).
Spinoza, B. de, *Korte verhandeling van God, de mensch en des zelfswelstand*, ed. C. Gebhardt, Heidelberg 1925, repr. 1972 (Opera, 1).
Themistius, *In Aristotelis Metaphysicorum librum lambda paraphrasis hebraice et latine*, ed. S. Landauer, Berlin 1903 (Commentaria in Aristotelem Graeca, 5).
Thomas Aquinas, *De substantiis separatis*, Rome 1969 (ed. Leon., 40).
——, *De veritate*, Rome 1975 (ed. Leon., 22/1).
——, *Expositio libri Peryermenias*, Rome-Paris 1989 (ed. Leon., 1*/1).
——, *In Metaphysicam Aristotelis commentaria*, ed. M.-R. Cathala, Turin 1926.
——, *In octo libros Physicorum Aristotelis expositio*, ed. M. Maggiòlo, Turin-Rome 1954.
——, *Liber de veritate catholicae fidei contra errores infidelium seu 'Summa contra gentiles'*, ed. C. Pera, 3 vols, Turin-Rome 1961-1967.
——, *Quaestiones quodlibetales*, ed. Fr.R. Spiazzi, editio VIII revisa, Turin-Rome 1949.
——, *Scriptum super libros Sententiarum*, ed. P. Mandonnet and M.F. Roos, 5 vols, Paris 1929-1956.
——, *Summa theologiae*, Rome 1888-1906 (ed. Leon., 4-12).
Thomas Bradwardine, *De causa Dei contra Pelagium*, London 1618, repr. Frankfurt a/M 1964.
——, [See also the section on secondary literature s.v. Genest].
Thomas Buckingham, [See the section on secondary literature s.v. Torre].
Thomas of Strasbourg, *Commentaria in IIII libros Sententiarum*, Venice 1564, repr. Ridgewood, New Jersey 1965.
Thomas of Sutton, *Contra Quodlibet Iohannis Duns Scoti*, ed. J. Schneider, München 1978 (VKHUTMG, 7).
——, *Quaestiones ordinariae*, ed. J. Schneider, München 1977 (VKHUTMG, 3).
——, *Quodlibeta*, ed. M. Schmaus and M. González-Haba, München 1969 (VKHUTMG, 2).
Walter Chatton, *Reportatio et Lectura super Sententias: Collatio ad Librum Primum et Prologus*, ed. J.C. Wey, Toronto 1989 (Studies and Texts, 90).
William of Alnwick, *Quaestiones disputatae de esse intelligibili et de quolibet*, ed. A. Ledoux, Florence 1937 (BFSMA, 10).
William of Auxerre, *Summa aurea*, ed. J. Ribaillier, 5 vols, Paris-Grottaferrata 1980-1987 (Spicilegium Bonaventurianum, 16-20).
William of Ockham, *Expositio in librum Perihermenias Aristotelis*, ed. A. Gambatese and S. Brown, St. Bonaventure, New York 1978 (OPh, 2).
——, *Quaestiones in secundum librum Sententiarum (reportatio)*, ed. G. Gál and R. Wood, St. Bonaventure, New York 1981 (OTh, 5).
——, *Quodlibeta septem*, ed. J.C. Wey, St. Bonaventure, New York 1980 (OTh, 9).
——, *Quodlibetal Questions*, 2 vols, transl. by A.J. Freddoso and F.E. Kelly, New Haven-London 1991.

——, *Scriptum in librum primum Sententiarum. Ordinatio*, ed. G. Gál, S. Brown, G. Etzkorn, and F. Kelly, St. Bonaventure, New York 1967-1979 (OTh, 1-4).
——, *Summa logicae*, ed. Ph. Boehner, G. Gál, and S. Brown, St. Bonaventure, New York 1974 (OPh, 1).
——, *Tractatus de praedestinatione et de praescientia Dei respectu futurorum contingentium*, ed. Ph. Boehner and S. Brown, St. Bonaventure, New York 1978 (OPh, 2).
——, [See also the section on secondary literature s.v. Boehner].
William of Rubione, *In quattuor libros Sententiarum*, Paris 1518.

SECONDARY LITERATURE

Ackrill, J.L., *Aristotle's Categories and De interpretatione*, transl. with notes and glossary, Oxford [7]1979 (Clarendon Aristotle Series).
Anawati, G.C., 'Saint Thomas d'Aquin et la Métaphysique d'Avicenne', *St. Thomas Aquinas 1274-1974. Commemorative Studies*, Vol. 1, Toronto, Canada 1974, 449-465.
Ashworth, E.J., 'Traditional Logic', *The Cambridge History of Renaissance Philosophy*, ed. Ch.B. Schmitt et al., Cambridge 1988, 143-172.
——, review of *Marsilius of Inghen*, by E.P. Bos, *Vivarium* 24 (1986), 158-162.
Badawi, A., *Histoire de la philosophie en Islam*, 2 vols, Paris 1972 (Etudes de philosophie médiévale, 60).
Bannach, K., *Die Lehre von der doppelten Macht Gottes bei Wilhelm von Ockham. Problemgeschichtliche Voraussetzungen und Bedeutung*, Wiesbaden 1975 (Veröffentlichungen des Instituts für Europäische Geschichte Mainz, 75).
Barth, T.A., 'Being, Univocity, and Analogy According to Duns Scotus', *John Duns Scotus, 1265-1965*, ed. J.K. Ryan and B.M. Bonansea, Washington, D.C. 1965 (SPhHPh, 3), 210-262.
Baudry, L., *Lexique philosophique de Guillaume d'Ockham. Etude des notions fondamentales*, Paris 1958.
Baur, L., *Die philosophische Werke des Robert Grosseteste, Bischofs von Lincoln*, Münster 1912 (BGPhThMA, 9).
Beckmann, J.P., 'Der Ideentheoretische Grundansatz bei Thomas von Aquin, Duns Scotus und Wilhelm von Ockham', *Tommaso d'Aquino nella storia del pensiero*, Vol. 2, Naples 1976 (Tommaso d'Aquino nel suo settimo centenario), 286-296.
——, *HWdPh*, s.v. 'Idee'.
Beierwaltes, W., 'Pronoia und Freiheit in der Philosophie des Proklos', *FZPhTH* 24 (1977), 88-111.
Bérubé, C., 'La première école scotiste', *Logique, ontologie et théologie au XIVe siècle. Preuve et raisons à l'université de Paris*, ed. Z. Kaluza and P. Vignaux, Paris 1984, 9-24.
——, *La connaissance de l'individuel au Moyen Age*, Montréal-Paris 1964 (Université de Montréal, Institut d'Etudes Médiévales).
Boehner, Ph. and E. Gilson, *Christliche Philosophie von ihren Anfängen bis Nikolaus von Cues*, Paderborn [3]1954.
Boehner, Ph., *Tractatus de praedestinatione et de praescientia Dei et de futuris contingentibus of William Ockham*, St. Bonaventure, New York 1945 (Franciscan Institute Publications, 2).
Boler, J., 'Connotative Terms in Ockham', *History of Philosophy Quarterly* 2 (1985), 21-37.
Bos, A.P., 'Greek Philosophical Theology and the *De mundo*', *On and Off the Beaten Track. Studies in the History of Platonism*, ed. T.G. Sinnige, Nijmegen 1985, 1-30.
——, *Providentia divina. The Theme of Divine 'pronoia' in Plato and Aristotle*, Assen-Amsterdam 1976.
Bos, E.P. and P.A. Meijer, eds., *On Proclus and His Influence in Medieval Philosophy*, Leiden 1992 (Philosophia antiqua, 53).
Bos, E.P., 'A Note on an Unknown Manuscript Bearing Upon Marsilius of Inghen's Philosophy of Nature. Ms Cuyk and St. Agatha (The Netherlands), Kruisherenklooster C 12', *Vivarium* 17 (1979), 61-68.
——, 'Marsilius van Inghen en 'mogelijke werelden'', *Algemeen Nederlands Tijdschrift voor*

Wijsbegeerte 75 (1983), 4-12.
——, 'William of Ockham's Interpretation of the First Proposition of the *Liber de causis*', *On Proclus and His Influence in Medieval Philosophy*, ed. E.P Bos and P.A. Meijer, Leiden 1992 (Philosophia antiqua, 53), 171-189.
——, *Marsilius of Inghen. Treatises on the Properties of Terms. A First Critical Edition*, Dordrecht 1983 (Synthese Historical Library, 22).
Braakhuis, H.A.G. and M.J.F.M. Hoenen, 'Marsilius of Ighen. A Dutch Philosopher and Theologian', *Marsilius of Inghen. Acts of the International Marsilius of Inghen Symposium*, Nijmegen, 18-20 December 1986, ed. H.A.G. Braakhuis and M.J.F.M. Hoenen, Nijmegen 1992 (Artistarium Supplementa).
Brady, I., *LThK*, 2th ed., s.v. 'William v. Vorillon'.
Catto, J.I., 'Theology and Theologians 1220-1320', *The Early Oxford Schools*, ed. J.I. Catto, Oxford 1984 (The History of the University of Oxford, 1), 471-517.
Cherniss, H., *Aristotle's Criticism of Plato and the Academy*, New York 1962.
Colish, M.L., *The Stoic Tradition from Antiquity to the Early Middle Ages. I: Stoicism in Classical Latin Literature*, Leiden ²1990.
Combes, A., *Jean Gerson. Commentateur Dionysien. Pour l'histoire des courants doctrinaux à l'université de Paris à la fin du XIVe siècle*, Paris ²1973 (Etudes de philosophie médiévale, 30).
——, *Un inédit de Saint Anselme? Le traité 'De unitate divinae essentiae et pluralitate creaturarum' d'apres Jean de Ripa*, Paris 1944 (Etudes de philosophie médiévale, 34).
Courtenay, W.J., "Antiqui' and 'moderni' in Late Medieval Thought', *JHI* 48 (1987), 3-10.
——, 'A Revised Text of Robert Holcot's Quodlibetal Dispute on Whether God is Able to Know More Than He Knows', *Archiv für Geschichte der Philosophie* 53 (1971), 1-21.
——, 'Force of Words and Figures of Speech. The Crisis over 'virtus sermonis' in the Fourteenth Century', *FcS* 44 (1984), 107-128.
——, 'In Search of Nominalism. Two Centuries of Historical Debate', *Gli studi di filosofia medievale fra otto e novecento. Atti del convegno internazionale*, Roma, 21-23 settembre 1989, ed. R. Imbach and A. Maierù, Rome 1991 (Storia e letteratura, 179), 233-251.
——, 'John of Mirecourt's Condemnation. Its Original Form', *RThAM* 53 (1986), 190f.
——, 'Late Medieval Nominalism Revisited: 1972-1982', *JHI* 44 (1983), 159-164.
——, 'Marsilius von Inghen († 1396) als Heidelberger Theologe', *Heidelberger Jahrbücher* 32 (1988), 25-42.
——, 'The Reception of Ockham's Thought in Fourteenth-Century England', *From Ockham to Wyclif*, ed. A. Hudson and M. Wilks, Oxford 1987 (Studies in Church History, Subsidia 5), 89-107.
——, 'The Role of English Thought in the Transformation of University Education in the Late Middle Ages', *Rebirth, Reform, and Resilience. Universities in Transition 1300-1700*, ed. J.M. Kittelson and P.J. Transue, Columbus 1984, 103-162.
——, *Adam Wodeham. An Introduction to His Life and Writings*, Leiden 1978 (Studies in Medieval and Reformation Thought, 21).
——, *Capacity and Volition. A History of the Distinction of Absolute and Ordained Power*, Bergamo 1990 (Quodlibet, 8).
——, *Covenant and Causality in Medieval Thought*, London 1984 (Variorum Reprints).
——, *School and Scholars in Fourteenth-Century England*, Princeton 1987.
Craig, W.L., *The Problem of Divine Foreknowledge and Future Contingents from Aristotle to Suarez*, Leiden 1988, (Brill's Studies in Intellectual History, 7).
d'Alverny, M.Th., 'Achard de Saint-Victor. De Trinitate - De unitate et pluralitate creaturarum', *RThAM* 21 (1954), 299-306.
Decker, B., *Die Gotteslehre des Jacob von Metz. Untersuchungen zur Dominikanertheologie zu Beginn des 14. Jahrhunderts*, Münster 1967 (BGPhThMA, 42/1).
Dewender, Th., 'Einige Bemerkungen zur Authentizität der Physikkommentare, die Marsilius von Inghen zugeschrieben werden', *Acta Mediaevalia*, ed. S. Wielgus et al., Lublin 1992 (forthcoming).
Dörrie, H., 'Der Begriff 'Pronoia' in Stoa und Platonismus', *FZPhTh* 24 (1977), 60-87.
Ebbesen, S., 'The Dead Man is Alive', *Synthese* 40 (1979), 43-70.

Eck, J. van, 'Another Interpretation of Aristotle's De interpretatione IX. A Support for the so-called second oldest or 'mediaeval' interpretation', *Vivarium* 26 (1988), 19-38.
Ehrle, F., *Der Sentenzenkommentar Peters von Candia des Pisaner Papstes Alexander V. Ein Beitrag zur Scheidung der Schulen in der Scholastik des 14. Jahrhunderts und zur Geschichte des Wegestreites*, Münster 1925 (FzS Beihefte, 9).
Etzkorn, G.J., 'Codex Merton 284: Evidence of Ockham's Early Influence in Oxford', *From Ockham to Wyclif*, ed. A. Hudson and M. Wilks, Oxford 1987 (Studies in Church History, Subsidia 5), 31-42.
Faes de Mottoni, B., *Il 'Corpus Dionysiacum' nel Medioevo, Rassegna di studi: 1900-1972*, Società editrice il mulino 1977 (Pubblicazioni del centro di studio per la storia della storiografia filosofica 3).
Fakhry, M., *A History of Islamic Philosophy*, New York-London 1970 (Studies in Oriental Culture, 5).
Fattori, M. and L. Bianchi, eds., *Idea. VI Colloquio Internazionale Roma, 5-7 gennaio 1989. Atti*, Rome 1990 (Lessico Intellettuale Europeo, 51).
Finance, J. de, 'La présence des choses à l' éternité d'après les scolastiques', *Archives de Philosophie* 19 (1956), 24-62.
Fine, G., 'Truth and Necessity in De interpretatione 9', *History of Philosophy Quarterly* 1 (1984), 23-47
Flasch, F., *Das philosophische Denken im Mittelalter. Von Augustin zu Machiavelli*, Stuttgart 1986.
Fussenegger, G., ''Littera septem siggilorum' contra doctrinam Petri Iohannis Olivi edita', *Archivum franciscanum historicum* 47 (1954), 45-53.
Gabriel, A.L., ''Via antiqua' and 'via moderna' and the Migration of Paris Students and Masters to the German Universities in the Fifteenth Century', *Antiqui und Moderni. Traditionsbewußtsein und Fortschrittsbewußtsein im späten Mittelalter*, ed. A. Zimmermann, Berlin 1974 (MM, 9), 439-483.
Gál, G., 'Adam of Wodeham's Question on the 'complexe significabile' as the immediate object of scientific knowledge', *FcS* 37 (1977), 66-102.
Gardet, L., 'Thomas et ses prédécesseurs Arabes', *St. Thomas Aquinas 1274-1974. Commemorative Studies*, Vol. 1, Toronto, Canada 1974, 419-448.
——, *La pensée religieuse d'Avicenne (Ibn sina)*, Paris 1951 (Etudes de philosophie médiévale, 41).
Geiger, L.B., 'Les rédactions successives de Contra Gentiles, I, 53 d'après l'autographe', *Saint Thomas d'Aquin aujourd'hui*, Paris 1963 (Recherches de philosophie, 6), 211-240.
Gelber, H.G., 'Ockham's Early Influence: A Question About Predestination and Foreknowledge by Arnold of Strelley, OP', *AHDLMA* 63 (1988), 255-289.
——, *Exploring the Bounderies of Reason. Three Questions on the Nature of God by Robert Holcot OP*, Toronto 1983 (Studies and Texts, 62).
——, *Logic and the Trinity: A Clash of Values in Scholastic Thought, 1300-1335*, Ann Arbor, Michigan 1981 (Ph.D. Thèsis 1974, University of Wisconsin).
Genest, J.-F., 'Le *De futuris contingentibus* de Thomas Bradwardine', *Recherches Augustiniennes* 14 (1974), 249-336.
Genest, J.-F. and K.H. Tachau, 'La Lecture de Thomas Bradwardine sur les Sentences', *AHDLMA* 65 (1990), 301-306.
Genest, J.-F. and P. Vignaux, 'La bibliothèque anglaise de Jean de Mirecourt: subtilitas ou plagiat?', *Die Philosophie im 14. und 15. Jahrhundert. In memoriam Konstanty Michalski (1879-1947)*, ed. O. Pluta, Amsterdam 1988 (Bochumer Studien zur Philosophie, 10), 275-301.
Gilbert, N.W., 'Comment', *JHI* 48 (1987), 41-50.
——, 'Ockham, Wyclif, and the 'via moderna'', *Antiqui und Moderni. Traditionsbewußtsein und Fortschrittsbewußtsein im späten Mittelalter*, ed. A. Zimmermann, Berlin 1974 (MM, 9), 85-125.
Gilson, E., 'Avicenne en Occident au Moyen Age', *AHDLMA* 44 (1969), 89-121.
——, *Jean Duns Scot. Introduction à ses positions fondamentales*, Paris 1952 (Etudes de philosophie médiévale, 42).

——, *Le thomisme. Introduction à la philosophie de Saint Thomas d'Aquin*, Paris ⁵1947 (Etudes de philosophie médiévale, 1).
Giocarinis, K., 'Eustratius of Nicaea's Defense of the Doctrine of Ideas', *FcS* 12 (1964), 159-204.
Goichon, A.-M., *La philosophie d'Avicenne et son influence en Europe médiévale*, Paris ²1951 (Forlong lectures 1940).
——, *The Encyclopaedia of Islam*, New Edition, s.v. 'Ibn Sina'.
Gruber, J., *Kommentar zu Boethius De consolatione philosophiae*, Berlin-New York 1978 (Texte und Kommentare, 9).
Guthrie, W.K.C., *Aristotle. An Encounter*, Cambridge 1981 (A History of Greek Philosophy, 6).
Hager, F.P., 'Proklos und Alexander von Aprodisias über ein Problem der Lehre von der Vorsehung', *Kephalaion. Studies in Greek Philosophy and its Continuation*, ed. J. Mansfeld and L.M. de Rijk, Assen 1975, 171-182.
Hamesse, J., *Auctoritates Aristotelis. Un florilège médiéval. Etude historique et édition critique*, Louvain-Paris 1974 (Philosophes Médiévaux, 17).
Häring, N.M., 'Magister Alanus de Insulis Regulae caelestis iuris', *AHDLMA* 48 (1981), 97-226.
——, *Lexikon des Mittelalters*, s.v. 'Boethius, Anicius Manlius Severinus'.
Hasker, W., *God, Time, and Knowledge*, Ithaca-London 1989 (CoSPhR).
Haubst, R., *Das Bild des Einen und Dreieinen Gottes in der Welt nach Nikolaus von Kues*, Trier 1952 (Trierer theologische Studien, 4).
Helm, P., *Eternal God. A Study of God without Time*, Oxford 1988.
Henninger, M., 'Henry of Harclay's Questions on Divine Prescience and Predestination', *FcS* 40 (1980), 167-243.
——, *Relations. Medieval Theories 1250-1325*, Oxford 1989.
Henry, D.P., *The Logic of Saint Anselm*, Oxford 1967.
Herold, V., 'Wyclifs Polemik gegen Ockhams Auffassung der platonischen Ideen und ihr Nachklang in der tschechischen hussitischen Philosophie', *From Ockham to Wyclif*, ed. A. Hudson and M. Wilks, Oxford 1987 (Studies in Church History, Subsidia, 5), 185-215.
Heynck, V., *LThK*, 2th ed., s.v. 'Nicolaus d'Orbellis (Dorbellus)'.
Hödl, L., 'Die philosophische Gotteslehre des Thomas von Aquin O.P. in der Diskussion der Schulen um die Wende des 13. zum 14. Jahrhundert', *Rivista di filosofia neo-scolastica* 70 (1978), 113-134.
Hoenen, M.J.F.M., 'A propos de Lectura I d. 39. Un passage dissimulé de Thomas d'Aquin chez Duns Scot?', *AHDLMA* 52 (1985), 231-236.
——, 'Can God be proved to act freely? Ockham's criticism of an argument in Thomas', *Ockham and Ockhamists*, Acts of the Symposium organized by the Dutch Society for Medieval Philosophy, Leiden, 10-12 September 1986, ed. E.P. Bos and H.A. Krop, Nijmegen 1987 (Artistarium Supplementa, 4), 15-23.
——, 'Der Sentenzenkommentar des Marsilius von Inghen. Aus dem Handschriftenbestand des Tübinger Wilhelmsstifts', *Theologische Quartalschrift* 171 (1991), 114-129.
——, 'Einige Notizen über die Handschriften und Drucke des Sentenzenkommentars von Marsilius von Inghen', *RThAM* 56 (1989), 117-163.
——, 'Hugolin von Orvietos Lehre von der scientia Dei im Rahmen der Lehrentwicklungen 1250-1350', *Augustiniana* 39 (1989), 483-501.
——, 'Marsilius von Inghen, Bibliographie. Appendix zu der geplanten Edition der wichtigsten Werke des Marsilius von Inghen', *BPhM* 31 (1989), 150-167.
——, 'Marsilius von Inghen, Bibliographie. Ergänzungen', *BPhM* 32 (1990), 191-195.
——, 'Neuplatonismus am Ende des 14. Jahrhunderts. Die Prinzipien zum Sentenzenkommentar des Marsilius von Inghen', *Acta Mediaevalia*, ed. S. Wielgus et al., Lublin 1992 (forthcoming).
——, *Marsilius van Inghen († 1396) over het goddelijke weten. Zijn plaats in de ontwikkeling van de opvattingen over het goddelijke weten ca. 1255-1396. Deel 1: Studie; Deel 2: Tekstuitgave van Marsilius van Inghen, Quaestiones super quattuor libros Sententiarum*,

Lib. I quaestt. 38 en 40, Nijmegen 1989 (Diss.).
Hoeres, W., 'Wesen und Dasein bei Heinrich von Gent und Duns Scotus', *FzS* 47 (1965), 122-186.
Hoffmann, F., *Die theologische Methode des Oxforder Dominikanerlehrers Robert Holcot*, Münster 1972 (BGPhThMA NF, 5).
——, [See also the section on sources s.v. John Lutterell].
Honnefelder, L., 'Das Verhältnis von Theologie und Philosophie als veränderndes Moment in der Entwicklung des Selbstverständnisses der Philosophie', *Thomas von Aquin im philosophischen Gespräch*, ed. W. Kluxen, München 1975 (Alber-Broschur Philosophie), 212-215.
Hopkins, J., 'Augustine on Foreknowledge and Free Will', *International Journal for Philosophy of Religion* 8 (1977), 111-126.
Imbach, R., 'Metaphysik, Theologie und Politik. Zur Diskussion zwischen Nikolaus von Straßburg und Dietrich von Freiberg über die Abtrennbarkeit der Akzidentien', *Theologie und Philosophie* 61 (1986), 359-395.
——, 'Philosophie und Eucharistie bei Wilhelm von Ockham. Ein vorläufiger Entwurf', *Ockham and Ockhamists*, ed. E.P. Bos and H. Krop, Nijmegen 1987 (Artistarium Supplementa, 4), 43-51.
——, *Deus est intelligere. Das Verhältnis von Sein und Denken in seiner Bedeutung für das Gottesverständnis bei Thomas von Aquin und in den Pariser Quaestionen Meister Eckharts*, Freiburg 1976 (Studia Friburgensia, NF 53).
Iserloh, E., 'Luthers Absage an den Humanismus. Der späte Erasmus', *Reformation, katholische Reform und Gegenreformation*, ed. H. Jedin, Freiburg 1967 (Handbuch der Kirchengeschichte, 4), 146-157.
Jacobi, K., 'Kontingente Naturgeschehnisse', *Studia Mediewistyczne* 18 (1977), 3-70.
——, *Die Modalbegriffe in den logischen Schriften des Wilhelm von Shyreswood und in anderen Kompendien des 12. und 13. Jahrhunderts*, Leiden-Köln 1980 (STGM, 13).
Jedin, H., 'Die erneuerte Scholastik: Michael Bajus und der Gnadenstreit', *Reformation, katholische Reform und Gegenreformation*, ed. H. Jedin, Freiburg 1967 (Handbuch der Kirchengeschichte, 4), 561-573.
Jordan, M., 'What's New in Ockham's Formal Distinction?', *FcS* 45 (1985), 97-110.
Kaluza, Z., 'La nature des écrits de Jean de Ripa', *Traditio* 43 (1987), 257-298.
——, *Les querelles doctrinales à Paris. Nominalistes et réalistes aux confins du XIVe et du XVe siècles*, Bergamo 1988 (Quodlibet, 2).
Kelly, F.E., 'Ockham: Avignon, before and after', *From Ockham to Wyclif*, ed. A. Hudson and M. Wilks, Oxford 1987 (Studies in Church History, Subsidia 5), 1-18.
Kenny, A., 'Divine Foreknowledge and Human Freedom', *A Collection of Critical Essays*, ed. A. Kenny, London-Melbourne 1969, 255-270.
——, 'The Realism of the *De universalibus*', *Wyclif in his Times*, ed. by A. Kenny, Oxford 1986, 17-29.
——, *The God of the Philosophers*, Oxford [2]1986.
Kirwan, Ch., 'Aristotle on the Necessity of the Present', *Oxford Studies in Ancient Philosophy* 6 (1986), 167-187.
Klibansky, R., *The Continuity of the Platonic Tradition During the Middle Ages. With a New Preface and Four Supplementary Chapters*, Millwood, New York 1982.
Kluxen, W., 'Maimonides and Latin Scholasticism', *Maimonides and Philosophy*, ed. S. Pines and Y. Yovel, Dordrecht 1986 (Archives internationales d'histoire des idées, 114), 224-232.
——, *HWdPh*, s.v. 'Idee'.
Kneepkens, C.H., 'The Mysterious Buser Again: William Buser of Heusden and the 'Obligationes' Tract *Ob rogatum*', *English Logic in Italy in the 14th and 15th Centuries. Acts of the 5th European Symposium on Medieval Logic and Semantics*, Rome, 10-14 November 1980, ed. A. Maierù, Napoli 1982, 147-166.
Knudsen, Chr., *HWdPh*, s.v. 'Idee'.
Knuuttila, S., 'Duns Scotus' Criticism of the 'Statistical' Interpretation of Modality', *Sprache und Erkenntnis im Mittelalter*, Vol. 1, ed. W. Kluxen et al., Berlin-New York 1981 (MM,

13/1), 441-450.

———, 'Modal Logic', *The Cambridge History of Later Medieval Philosophy from the Rediscovery of Aristotle to the Disintegration of Scholasticism 1100-1600*, ed. N. Kretzmann, A. Kenny, and J. Pinborg, Cambridge 1982, 342-357.

———, 'Time and Modality in Scholasticism', *Reforging the Great Chain of Being. Studies in the History of Modal Theory*, ed. S. Knuuttila, Dordrecht 1981 (Synthese Historical Library, 20), 163-257.

Knysh, G., 'Biographical Rectifications Concerning Ockham's Avignon Period', *FcS* 46 (1986), 61-91.

Koch, J., *Kleine Schriften*, II, Rome 1973 (Storia e letteratura, 128).

Kogan, B.S., 'Some Reflections on the Problem of Future Contingency in Alfarabi, Avicenna, and Averroes', ed. T. Rudavsky, *Divine Omniscience*, 95-101.

Kremer, K., *Die neuplatonische Seinsphilosophie und ihre Wirkung auf Thomas von Aquin*, Leiden 1966 (Studien zur Problemgeschichte der antiken und mittelalterlichen Philosophie, 1).

Kretzmann, N., '"Nos ipsi principia sumus": Boethius and the Basic of Contingency', ed. T. Rudavsky, *Divine Omniscience*, 25-30.

———, 'Boethius and the Truth about Tomorrow's Sea Battle', *Logos and Pragma*, ed. L.-M. de Rijk and H.A.G. Braakhuis, Nijmegen 1987 (Artistarium Supplementa, 3), 63-97.

———, '*Sensus compositus, sensus divisus* and Propositional Attitudes', *Medioevo* 7 (1981), 195-229.

Kretzmann, N., and E. Stump, 'Eternity', *The Journal of Philosophy* 78 (1981), 429-458.

Kürzinger, J., *Alfonsus Vargas Toletanus und seine theologische Einleitungslehre. Ein Beitrag zur Geschichte der Scholastik im 14. Jahrhundert*, Münster 1930 (BGPhThMA, 22/5-6).

Laks, A., *Diogène d'Apollonie. La dernière cosmologie présocratique*, Villeneuve d'Ascq 1983 (Cahiers de philologie, 9).

Lang, A., *Heinrich Totting von Oyta. Ein Beitrag zur Entstehungsgeschichte der ersten deutschen Universitäten und zur Problemgeschichte der Spätscholastik*, Münster 1937 (BGPhThMA, 33/4-5).

Langston, D.C., *God's Willing Knowledge. The Influence of Scotus' Analysis of Omniscience*, University Park-London 1986.

Leaman, O., *An Introduction to Medieval Islamic Philosophy*, Cambridge 1985.

Lechner, J., 'Franz von Perugia OFM und die Quästionen seines Sentenzenkommentars', *FzS* 25 (1938), 28-64.

Lecq, R. van der, 'Buridan on Modal Propositions', *English Logic and Semantics from the End of the Twelfth Century to the Time of Ockham and Burleigh*, ed. H.A.G. Braakhuis, C.H. Kneepkens, and L.M. de Rijk, Nijmegen 1981 (Artistarium Supplementa, 1), 427-442.

Leff, G., *Bradwardine and the Pelagians. A Study of His 'De causa Dei' and Its Opponents*, Cambridge 1957 (Cambridge Studies in Medieval Life and Thought, New Series, 5).

Lemaigre, B.M., 'Perfection de Dieu et multiplicité des attributs divins', *Revue des sciences philosophiques et théologiques* 50 (1966), 198-227.

Libera, A. de, 'Le développement de nouveaux instruments conceptuels et leur utilisation dans la philosophie de la nature au XIVe siècle', *Knowledge and the Sciences in Medieval Philosophy*, Vol. 1, ed. M. Asztalos, J.E. Murdoch, and I. Niiniluoto, Helsinki 1990 (Acta Philosophica Fennica, 48), 158-197.

Liske, M.Th., 'Was meint Thomas von Aquin mit 'Gott weiss das Künftige als gegenwärtig'?', *Theologie und Philosophie* 60 (1985), 520-537.

Little, A.G. and F. Pelster, *Oxford Theology and Theologians c. A.D. 1282-1302*, 3 vols, Oxford 1934 (Oxford Historical Society, 96).

Lloyd, A.C., 'The Aristotelianism of Eustratios of Nicaea', *Aristoteles. Werk und Wirkung*, Vol. 2, ed. J. Wiesner, Berlin-New York 1987, 341-351.

Lowe, M.F., 'Aristotle on the Sea-Battle. A Clarification', *Analysis* 40 (1980), 55-59.

Maier, A., *Ausgehendes Mittelalter II. Gesammelte Aufsätze zur Geistesgeschichte des 14. Jahrhunderts*, Rome 1967 (Storia e letteratura, 105).

———, *Die Vorläufer Galileis im 14. Jahrhundert*, Rome 1949 (Studien zur Naturphilosophie der Spätscholastik).

Maierù, A., *Terminologia logica della tarda scolastica*, Rome 1972 (Lessico intellettuale Europeo, 8).
Marcolino, V., 'Der Augustinertheologe an der Universität Paris', *Gregor von Rimini. Werk und Wirkung bis zur Reformation*, ed. H.A. Oberman, Berlin-New York 1981 (Spätmittelalter und Reformation, 20), 127-194.
——, 'Die Resonanz des Sentenzenkommentars Hugolins von Orvieto bis zur Reformationszeit', *Schwerpunkte und Wirkungen des Sentenzenkommentars Hugolins von Orvieto OESA*, ed. W. Eckermann, Würzburg 1990 (Cassiciacum, 42), 297-321.
Markoswki, M., 'Die handschriftliche Überlieferung der Werke des Marsilius von Inghen', *Marsilius of Inghen. Acts of the International Marsilius of Inghen Symposium*, Nijmegen, 18-20 December 1986, ed. H.A.G. Braakhuis and M.J.F.M. Hoenen, Nijmegen 1992 (Artistarium Supplementa).
——, 'Die neue Physik an der Krakauer Universität im XV. Jahrhundert', *Antiqui und Moderni. Traditionsbewußtsein und Fortschrittsbewußtsein im späten Mittelalter*, ed. A. Zimmermann, Berlin 1974 (MM, 9), 501-508.
Marmura, M., 'Divine Omniscience and Future Contingents in Alfarabi and Avicenna', ed. T. Rudavsky, *Divine Omniscience*, 81-94.
——, 'Some Aspects of Avicenna's Theory of God's Knowledge of Particulars', *Journal of the American Oriental Society* 82 (1961), 299-312.
Marrone, S.P., *Truth and Scientific Knowledge in the Thought of Henry of Ghent*, The Medieval Academy of America 1985 (Speculum Anniversary Monographs, 11).
Maurer, A.A., '*Ens Diminitum*. A Note on its Origin and Meaning', *Med. Stud.* 12 (1950), 216-222.
——, 'Henry of Harclay's Questions on the Divine Ideas', *Med. Stud.* 23 (1961), 163-193.
——, *Being and Knowing. Studies in Thomas Aquinas and Later Medieval Philosophers*, Toronto 1990 (Papers in Mediaeval Studies, 10).
——, *Medieval Philosophy*, Toronto ²1982 (The Gilson Series, 4).
McCord Adams, M., 'Ockham on Identity and Distinction', *FcS* 36 (1976), 5-74.
——, *William Ockham*, 2 vols, Notre Dame, Ind. 1987 (Publications in Medieval Studies, 26/1-2).
McEvoy, J., *The Philosophy of Robert Grosseteste*, Oxford 1982.
McInerny, R.M., *Being and Predication. Thomistic Interpretations*, Washington, D.C. 1986 (SPhHPh, 16).
Meier, L., 'Der Sentenzenkommentar des Johannes Bremer', *FzS* 15 (1928), 161-169.
Meier, S., 'Von der Koinzidenz zur *coincidentia oppositorum*. Zum philosophiehistorischen Hintergrund des Cusanischen Koinzidenzgedankens', *Die Philosophie im 14. Jahrhundert. In memoriam Konstanty Michalski* (1879-1947), ed. O. Pluta, Amsterdam 1988 (Bochumer Studien zur Philosophie, 10 Amsterdam 1988, 321-342.
Meuthen, E., *Die alte Universität*, Cologne-Vienna 1988 (Kölner Universitätsgeschichte, 1).
Michael, B., *Johannes Buridan: Studien zu seinem Leben, seinen Werken und zur Rezeption seiner Theorien im Europa des späten Mittelalters*, 2 vols, Berlin 1985 (Inaugural-Dissertation Berlin).
Michalski, K., *La philosophie au XIVe siècle*, ed. K. Flasch, Frankfurt 1969 (Opuscula Philosophica, 1).
Miethke, J., 'Marsilius von Inghen als Rektor der Universität Heidelberg', *Ruperto Carola* 76 (1987), 110-119.
——, *Ockhams Weg zur Sozialphilosophie*, Berlin 1969.
Mikat, P., *LThK*, 2th ed., s.v. 'Innozenz V'.
Möhler, W., *Die Trinitätslehre des Marsilius von Inghen. Ein Beitrag zur Geschichte der Theologie des Spätmittelalters*, Limburg/Lahn 1949.
Molland, A.G., 'Continuity and Measure in Medieval Natural Philosophy', *Mensura, Mass, Zahl, Zahlensymbolik im Mittelalter*, Vol. 1, ed. A. Zimmermann, Berlin-New York 1983 (MM, 16/1), 132-144.
Moody, E.A., 'A Quodlibetal Question of Robert Holcot OP on the Problem of the Object of Knowledge and of Belief', *Speculum* 39 (1964), 53-74.
Moraux, P., *d'Aristote à Bessarion. Trois exposés sur l'histoire et la transmission de*

l'Aristotélisme Grec, Les Presses de l'Université Laval 1970 (Les conférences Charles de Koninck).
Muralt, A. de, *L'enjeu de la philosophie médiévale. Etudes thomistes, scotistes, occamiennes et grégoriennes*, Leiden 1991, (STGM, 24).
Murdoch, J.E., 'Naissance et développement de l'atomisme au bas Moyen Age Latin', *La science de la natura. Théories et pratiques*, Montréal-Paris 1974 (Institut d'Etudes Médiévales, Université de Montréal, Cahiers d'études médiévales, 2), 11-32.
Normore, C., 'Divine Omniscience, Omnipotence, and Future Contingents', ed. T. Rudavsky, *Divine Omniscience*, 3-22.
——, 'Future Contingents', *The Cambridge History of Later Medieval Philosophy from the Rediscovery of Aristotle to the Disintegration of Scholasticism 1100-1600*, ed. N. Kretzmann, A. Kenny, and J. Pinborg, Cambridge 1982, 358-381.
Nuchelmans, G., *Theories of the Proposition. Ancient and Medieval Conceptions of the Bearers of Truth and Falsity*, Amsterdam-London 1973 (North-Holland Linguistic Series, 8).
Nwigwe, B.E., *Die Lehre von der göttlichen Vorsehung und menschlichen Freiheit bei Thomas von Aquin und ihre zeitlogische Kritik durch A.N. Prior and P.T. Geach*, Münster, Westfalen 1985 (Diss.).
Oberman, H.A., *Archbischop Thomas Bradwardine. A Fourteenth Century Augustinian. A Study of His Theology in Its Historical Context*, Utrecht 1957.
Pelster, F., 'Der Heidelberger Magister artium und Baccalarius theologiae Heilmann Wunnenberg als Lehrer des Marsilius von Inghen und Erklärer der Sentenzen', *Theologische Quartalschrift* 125 (1944), 83-86.
——, 'Zur ersten Polemik gegen Aureoli: Raymundus Bequini OP, seine Quästionen und sein Correctorium Petri Aureoli, das Quodlibet des Jacobus de Appamiis OESA', *FcS* 15 (1955), 30-47.
Perler, D., *Prädestination, Zeit und Kontingenz*, Amsterdam 1988 (Bochumer Studien zur Philosophie, 12).
——, *Satztheorien. Texte zur Sprachphilosophie und Wissenschaftstheorie im 14. Jahrhundert*, Darmstadt 1990 (Texte zur Forschung, 57).
Pike, N., *God and Timelessness*, London 1970.
Pinborg, J., *Logik und Semantik im Mittelalter*, Stuttgart-Bad Cannstatt 1972 (Problemata, 10).
Pines, S., 'Some Distinctive Metaphysical Conceptions in Themistius' Commentary on Book Lamba and Their Place in the History of Philosophy', *Aristoteles. Werk und Wirkung*, Vol. 2, ed. J. Wiesner, Berlin-New York 1987, 177-204.
Prior, A.N., 'The Formalities of Omniscience', *Philosophy* 37 (1962), 114-129.
——, *Papers on Time and Tense*, Oxford 1968.
Rad, G. von, *Weisheit in Israel*, Neukirchen-Vluyn ³1985.
Rengstorf, *ThWzNT*, s.v. 'διδασκαλος'.
Rescher, N., *Essays in Philosophical Analysis*, Pittsburg 1969.
Ribaillier, J., *DS*, s.v. 'Guillaume d'Auxerre'.
Rijk, L.M. de, *Logica Modernorum*, 3 vols, Assen 1962-1967 (Wijsgerige Teksten en Studies, 6, 16).
Ritter, G., *Studien zur Spätscholastik I: Marsilius von Inghen und die okkamistische Schule in Deutschland*, Heidelberg 1921 (Sitzungsberichte der Heidelberger Akademie der Wissenschaften, Philosophisch-historische Klasse, 1921/4).
Roensch, F., *Early Thomistic School*, Dubuque, Iowa 1964.
Ross, W.D., *Aristotle*, London ⁴1945.
Rossmann, H., 'Die Quodlibeta und verschiedene sonstige Schriften des Franz von Meyronnes OFM', *FzS* 54 (1972), 1-76.
——, 'Die Sentenzenkommentare des Franz von Meyronnes OFM', *FzS* 53 (1971), 129-227.
Rowe, W.L., 'Augustine on Foreknowledge and Free Will', *The Review of Metaphysics* 18 (1964), 356-363.
Rudavsky, T., ed., *Divine Omniscience and Omnipotence in Medieval Philosophy. Islamic, Jewish, and Christian Perspectives*, Dordrecht 1985 (Synthese Historical Libary, 25).
Ruello, F., 'La *divinorum nominum reseratio* selon Robert Grossetête et Albert le Grand',

AHDLMA 34 (1959), 99-197.

———, 'La notion 'thomiste' de 'ratio in divinis' dans la Disputatio de François de Meyronnes et de Pierre Roger (1320-1321)', *RThAM* 32 (1965), 54-75.

Salmon, P., *L'office divin au Moyen Age. Histoire de la formation du bréviaire du IXe au XVIe siècle*, Paris 1967 (Lex orandi, 43).

———, *L'office divin. Histoire de la formation du bréviaire*, Paris 1959 (Lex orandi, 27).

Scheffczyk, L., *Schöpfung und Vorsehung*, ed. M. Schmaus and A. Grillmeier, Freiburg 1963 (Handbuch der Dogmengeschichte, 2/2a).

Schmid, J., *LThK*, 2th ed., s.v. 'Vorsehung'.

Schmitt, Fr., *Die Lehre des hl. Thomas von Aquin vom göttlichen Wissen des zukünftig Kontingenten bei seinen grossen Kommentatoren*, Nijmegen 1950 (Diss.).

Schneider, Th., *Die Einheit des Menschen. Die anthropologische Formel 'anima forma corporis' im sogenannten Korrektorienstreit und bei Petrus Johannis Olivi*, Münster 1973 (BGPhThMA NF, 8).

Schnitker, Th.A. and D. v. Huebner, *Lexikon des Mittelalters*, s.v. 'Brevier'.

Schönberger, R., 'Realität und Differenz. Ockhams Kritik an der distinctio formalis', *Die Gegenwart Ockhams*, ed. W. Vossenkuhl and R. Schönberger, Weinheim 1990 (Acta humaniora), 97-122.

Schulze, M., '*Via Gregorii* in Forschung und Quellen', *Gregor von Rimini. Werk und Wirkung bis zur Reformation*, ed. H.A. Oberman, Berlin-New York 1981 (Spätmittelalter und Reformation, 20), 1-126.

Schwamm, H., *Das göttliche Vorherwissen bei Duns Scotus und seinen ersten Anhängern*, Innsbruck 1934 (Philosophie und Grenzwissenschaften, 5/1-4).

———, *Magistri Ioannis de Ripa OFM doctrina de praescientia divina*, Rome 1930 (Analecta Gregoriana, 1).

———, *Robert Cowton OFM über das göttliche Vorherwissen*, Innsbruck 1931 (Philosophie und Grenzwissenschaften, 3/5).

Senko, W., *LThK*, 2th ed., s.v. 'Thomas Wilton (Wylton)'.

Shank, M.H., *"Unless You believe, You Shall Not Understand": Logic, University, and Society in Late Medieval Vienna*, Princeton, New Jersey 1988.

Sharples, R.W., 'Alexander of Aphrodisias on Divine Providence: Two Problems', *The Classical Quarterly* 32 (1982), 198-211.

———, 'Alexander of Aphrodisias: Scholasticism and Innovation', *Aufstieg und Niedergang der römischen Welt*, Teil II Bd. 36/2, ed. W. Haase, Berlin 1987, S. 1176-1243.

Sorabji, R., *Necessity, Cause, and Blame. Perspectives on Aristotle's Theory*, London 1980.

Spade, P.V., 'Ockham's Distinctions between Absolute and Connotative Terms', *Vivarium* 13 (1975), 55-76.

Stegmüller, F., 'Die zwei Apologien des Jean de Mirecourt', *RThAM* 5 (1933), 40-78 and 192-204.

———, *Geschichte des Molinismus I: Neue Molinaschriften*, Münster 1935 (BGPhThMA, 32).

Streveler, P.A., 'Anselm on Future Contingencies. A Critical Analysis of the Argument of the 'De concordia'', *Anselm Studies. An Occasional Journal* 1 (1983), 165-173.

Streveler, P.A., et al., *Seeing the Future Clearly. Quodlibetal Questions on Future Contingents by Robert Holcot* (forthcoming).

Synan, E.A., 'Nineteen Less Probable Opinions of Peter Lombard', *Med. Stud.* 27 (1965), 340-344.

Tachau, K.H., 'French Theology in the Mid-Fourteenth Century: Vatican Latin 986 and Wroclaw, Milich F. 64', *AHDLMA* 51 (1984), 41-80.

———, 'Richard Campsall as a Theologian: New Evidence', *Historia Philosophiae Medii Aevi. Studien zur Geschichte der Philosophie des Mittelalters*, ed. B. Mojsisch and O. Pluta, Vol. 2, Amsterdam-Philadelphia 1991, 979-1002.

———, 'The Influence of Richard Campsall on Fourteenth-Century Oxford Thought', *From Ockham to Wyclif*, ed. A. Hudson and M. Wilks, Oxford 1987 (Studies in Church History, Subsidia, 5), 109-123.

———, 'Wodeham, Crathorn, and Holcot: the Development of the Complexe Significabile', *Logos and Pragma. Essays on the Philosophy of Language in Honour of Professor*

Gabriel Nuchelmans, ed. L.M. de Rijk and H.A.G. Braakhuis, Nijmegen 1987 (Artistarium supplementa, 3), 161-187.

——, *Vision and Certitude in the Age of Ockham. Optics, Epistemology, and the Foundations of Semantics 1250-1345*, Leiden 1988 (STGM, 22).

Tatarzynski, R., 'Le commentaire à la 'Metaphysique' d'Aristote attribué à Jean de Slupcza. La choix des questions relatives à la causalité', *MPhP* 24 (1979), 133-168.

Theissing, H., *Glaube und Theologie bei Robert Cowton OFM*, Münster 1969 (BGPhThMA, 42/3).

Thijssen, J.M.M.H., *Johannes Buridanus over het oneindige. Een onderzoek naar zijn theorie over het oneindige in het kader van zijn wetenschaps- en natuurfilosofie*. Deel 1: Studie; Deel 2: Teksten, Nijmegen 1988 (Diss.).

Torre, B.R. de la, *Thomas Buckingham and the Contingency of Futures*, Notre Dame 1987 (Publications in Medieval Studies, 25).

Trapp, A.D., 'Augustinian Theology of the 14th Century. Notes on Editions, Marginalia, Opinions and Book-Lore', *Augustiniana* 6 (1956), 146-274.

——, 'Peter Ceffons of Clairvaux', *RThAM* 24 (1957), 101-154.

——, *LThK*, 2th ed., s.v. 'Jacobus de Appamiis (Pamiers)'.

Trinkaus Zagzebski, L., *The Dilemma of Freedom and Foreknowledge*, New York-Oxford 1991.

Vansteenkiste, Cl., 'Das erste Buch der Nikomachischen Ethik bei Albertus Magnus', *Albertus Magnus doctor universalis 1280/1980*, ed. G. Meyer and A. Zimmermann, Mainz 1980 (Walberger Studien, Philosophische Reihe, 6), 373-384.

Vignaux, P., 'L'être comme perfection selon François de Meyronnes', *Etudes d'histoire littéraire et doctrinale*, Montréal-Paris 1962 (Université de Montréal, Publications de l'Institut d'Etudes Médiévales, 17), 259-318.

Viola, C., 'A propos de l''Inédit de Saint Anselme'', *BPhM* 33 (1991), 112-120.

Vossenkühl, W., 'Ockham on the cognition of non-existents', *FcS* 45 (1985), 33-45.

Walls, J.L., 'A Fable of Foreknowledge and Freedom', *Philosophy* 62 (1987), 67-75.

Wanke, O., *Die Kritik Wilhelms von Alnwick an der Ideenlehre des Johannes Duns Scotus*, Bonn 1965 (Inaugural-Diss. Bonn).

Weiler, A.G., *Heinrich von Gorkum († 1431). Seine Stellung in der Philosophie und der Theologie des Spätmittelalters*, Hilversum 1962.

Weisheipl, J.A., 'The Axiom 'Opus naturae est opus intelligentiae' and its Origin', *Albertus Magnus Doctor Universalis 1280/1980*, ed. G. Meyer and A. Zimmermann, Mainz 1980 (Walberger Studien, Philosophische Reihe, 6), 441-463.

Wetter, F., *Die Trinitätslehre des Johannes Duns Scotus*, Münster 1967 (BGPhThMA, 41/5).

Wierenga, E.R., *The Nature of God. An Inquiry into Divine Attributes*, Ithaca-London 1989 (CoSPhR).

Winkler, G.B., 'Das Psalmenargument des Erasmus im Streit um den freien Willen', *Histoire de l'exégèse au XVIe siècle. Textes du colloque international tenu a Genève en 1976*, comp. O. Fatio and P. Fraenkel, Genève 1978 (Etudes de philologie et d'histoire, 34), 95-117.

Wippel, J.F., 'Divine Knowledge, Divine Power, and Human Freedom in Thomas Aquinas and Henry of Ghent', ed. T. Rudavsky, *Divine Omniscience*, 213-241.

——, 'Thomas of Sutton on Divine Knowledge of Future Contingents', *Knowledge and the Sciences in Medieval Philosophy. Proceedings of the Eight International Congress of Medieval Philosophy*, Vol. 2, ed. S. Knuuttila, R. Työrinoja, and S. Ebbesen, Helsinki 1990 (Publications of the Luther-Agricola Society, B 19), 364-372.

——, *Metaphysical Themes in Thomas Aquinas*, Washington, D.C. 1984 (SPhHPh, 10).

——, *The Metaphysical Thought of Godfrey of Fontaines. A Study in Late Thirteenth-Century Philosophy*, Washington, D.C. 1981.

Wlodek, S (Z)., 'Quelques informations sur les commentaires médiévaux de la Métaphysique d'Aristote conservés dans les manuscrits de la Bibliothèque Jagellone à Cracovie', *Die Metaphysik im Mittelalter*, ed. P. Wilpert, Berlin 1963 (MM, 2), 767-774.

——, 'Zagadnienie *esse obiectivum* i intelektu u Jakuba z Ascoli', *Studia Mediewistyczne* 6 (1964), 3-18.

Wolfson, H.A., *The Philosophy of the Kalam*, Cambridge, Mass. 1976 (Structure and Growth of Philosophic Systems from Plato to Spinoza, 4).

Wolter, A.B., *The Philosophical Theology of John Duns Scotus*, ed. M. McCord Adams, Ithaca-London 1990.

——, *The Transcendentals and Their Function in the Metaphysics of Duns Scotus*, St. Bonaventure, New York 1946 (Franciscan Institute Publications Philosophy Series, 3).

Würsdörfer, J., *Erkennen und Wissen nach Gregor von Rimini. Ein Beitrag zur Geschichte der Erkenntnistheorie des Nominalismus*, Münster 1917 (BGPhThMA, 20/1).

Yokoyama, T., 'Zwei Quaestionen des Jacobus de Aesculo über das esse obiectivum', *Wahrheit und Verkündigung*, Vol. I, ed. L. Scheffczyk, W. Dettlof, and R. Heinzmann, München 1967, 31-74.

Zavalloni, R., *Richard de Mediavilla et la controverse sur la pluralité des formes*, Louvain 1951 (Philosophes médiévaux, 2).

Zumkeller, A., 'Die Augustinerschule des Mittelalters. Vertreter und philosophisch-theologische Lehre', *Analecta Augustiniana* 27 (1964), 167-262.

INDEX OF MANUSCRIPTS

Bologna, Bibl. Com. dell' Archiginnasio,
A 921:193n, 197n, 200n, 208n, 210n.
Brugge, Stadsbibliotheek, 491: 37n.
Cuyk en St. Agatha, Kruisherenklooster,
C 12 II: 110n-111n, 114n, 119n.
Erfurt, Wissenschaftl. Bibl.,
Cod. Amplon., Fol. 94: 120n.
Kraków, Bibl. Jagiellonska,
Cod. 1199: 144n, 148n.
Cod. 1276: 222n.
Cod. 1459: 115n, 208n, 210n, 229n.
Cod. 1499: 206n, 208n, 214n, 223n.
Cod. 1581: 20.
Cod. 2099: 17n.
London, British Museum,
Harleian Mss., 3243: 188, 230n.
München, Bayerische Staatsbibl.,
CLM, 5590: 112n, 216n, 229n.
CLM, 8718: 144n.
CLM, 8867: 218n-220n, 225n, 227n.
CLM, 26711: 233n.
Napoli, Bibl. Naz., VII C 28: 198n.
Oxford, Merton College, 284: 54n, 84.
Padova, Antoniana, Scaff. V, 89: 143&n.
Paris, Bibl. de l'Université, 193: 60n.
Paris, Bibl. Mazarine, 915: 29n-30n, 57n-60n, 97n, 103n-105n, 140n, 189n, 193n, 198, 201n-202n, 205n-206n, 209n-210n, 227n, 229n.
Paris, Bibl. Nationale,
lat., 15.369: 153n.
lat., 16.400: 222n.
lat., nouv. acq. 1.467: 152n.
Stuttgart, Württ. Landesbibl.,
Cod. Theol. Fol., 118: 114n, 142n, 162n.
Toledo, Bibl. del Cab., 95-5: 216n.
Troyes, Bibl. Munic., 62: 222n.
Uppsala, Universitetsbiblioteket, C 640: 230n.
Vaticano, Città del, Bibl. Apost.,
Borgh., 171: 50n, 79n, 86, 132, 133n, 135.
Pal. lat., 1805: 133n.
Vat. lat., 986: 193, 145n, 193n.
Vat. lat., 1012: 179n-180n.
Vat. lat., 3088: 230n.
Wien, Oesterr. Nationalbibl.,
CVP, 1453: 178n.
CVP, 5159: 218n, 220n-221n, 224n, 229n.
CVP, 5297: 30n-32n, 34n, 108n, 110n-111n, 114n, 148n, 218n-221n, 227n-229n.
Worcester, F. 3: 86, 95, 132.
Wroclaw, Bibl. Uniwersytecka, Mil. F. 64: 145n.

INDEX OF NAMES

Ancient, Medieval, and Early Modern Authors

Achard of St. Victor, 143&n.
Adam Wodeham, 1, 15, 20-21&n, 29-30, 57-58&n, 59, 60n, 97n, 99n, 103&n-104&n, 105, 115n, 119n, 139n, 140, 141&n, 158, 164, 184, 186, 188, 193, 195, 198, 201-202, 204-206, 209-212, 215, 222n, 225, 227-229, 231-232, 235, 239, 242, 245-253.
Agostino Nifo, 10.
Al-Farabi, 71&n.
Al-Gazali, 68, 69n.
Alan of Lille, 20, 146&n.
Albert of Saxony, 8, 118, 224.
Albert the Great, 28&n, 35, 65, 146, 147n, 148-150&n, 151, 219.
Alexander of Alessandria, 42n, 175, 180.
Alexander of Aphrodisias, 5&n, 6n, 71, 158.
Alexander of Hales, 35, 64.
Alexander of San Elpidio, 61n.
Alfonsus Vargas of Toledo, 61n, 99, 100-101, 118, 141, 189, 195, 197-198&n, 207.
Ammonius, 160.
Anaxagoras, 28, 236.
Anselm of Canterbury, 1, 25-26, 30, 57, 143n, 159, 164-165&n, 183, 238, 244.
Antonius Andreas, 179, 180.
Aristotle, 4n-5n, 6, 7n, 10&n, 12, 16-17n, 16, 26, 28, 31-32&n, 33, 38, 41, 43, 60, 63-66, 69, 71-72&n, 74, 78&n, 80, 88, 90, 93-94 102, 107n, 108, 114-117, 124n, 130, 135, 147&n-148, 157&n, 159&n-160&n, 161&n-162, 165-166, 167&n, 172, 183-185, 187, 189, 207, 217-221, 225, 237-241&n, 242, 244, 252.
Arnold of Strelley, 184n.
Augustine, 1, 20, 26, 30, 89, 112, 118, 121, 127&n, 135, 139-140, 142, 145, 147, 151n, 153-154, 159, 162, 163n, 185n, 209, 238, 240.
Averroes, 16, 27-28, 31&n-32, 60, 63, 65-66, 69&n, 71-72&n, 73-75, 78, 82, 88-91&n, 93-94, 99-100, 107n, 108&n-109&n, 110, 114-116&n, 117, 130, 135, 238-241, 244, 252.
Avicenna, 25&n, 38&n, 40-41&n, 63, 65-66&n, 67-69&n, 70, 71&n-72&n, 76, 94, 115, 145, 147, 167, 175, 219, 238, 241.

Bajus, Michael, 6n.
Bañez, Domingo, 6&n, 168.
Bartholomew of Usingen, 10, 33n.
Baumgarten, A.G., 6.
Bernard of Clairvaux, 20.
Bessarion, Cardinal, 5n.
Boethius, 26, 159, 160, 162-163&n, 164&n-165, 167, 172, 175-176, 179, 183, 185, 197, 209, 217, 219&n, 238, 244.
Bonagratia, 169.
Bonaventure, 20-21, 35, 39, 64, 66, 75, 78-79, 112, 123n, 146, 169, 172, 175-176&n, 181, 189-190, 225, 241&n.
Boniface IX, 9.

Calcidius, 146.
Cicero, 20, 26, 146, 158, 162.
Conrad of Soltau, 9, 21, 114, 142.

Diogenes of Apollonia, 4&n, 236.
Durand of St. Pourçain, 20-21, 48n, 53, 99, 139-140&n, 166, 168-170, 248.

Eckhardt, Meister, 64n.
Edward Upton, 118n.
Erasmus of Rotterdam, 6&n.
Eustratius, 148&n-150n, 151.

Francis of Marchia, 163, 177.
Francis of Mayronnes, 29, 42&n, 77&n-78, 84-85, 89&n, 132&n-133, 134&n, 142, 177-178, 227, 247.
Francis of Perugia, 144&n, 219&n.

Gabriel Biel, 11-12, 22, 144-145.
Galileo Galilei, 10, 163n, 210n.
Geert Groote, 8.
Gerard of Kalkar, 143&n-144.
Gerhardus Emelissa, 16.
Giles of Rom, 20, 26, 36, 37n, 61n, 65, 69&n-70, 73-74, 90, 103, 104, 109n, 115, 121, 125, 152, 205&n, 225, 240, 243, 249.
Giovanni Mariliani, 9.
Godfrey of Fontaines, 39-41&n, 42&n, 45,

INDEX OF NAMES

48n, 61, 78, 86, 124-125&n, 141, 241, 243.
Gottschalk of Nepomuk, 99, 105n, 206-207, 214, 222.
Gregory of Rimini, 1, 8, 12, 14-15, 17, 20-21, 28-31, 33&n, 57&n-59, 61&n, 63, 66, 73, 86, 93, 99-100&n, 101&n-103&n, 104-107&n, 108, 112, 115-116, 118-119, 158-159, 161, 164, 184, 186, 188-189, 193, 195-201&n, 202-205&n, 206-218, 221, 223-225, 227-229&n, 230, 232-233, 235, 241-242, 246&n-251, 253.

Hartmanus, 222n.
Heilmann of Wunnenberg, 9, 21&n, 151n.
Henry (?) de Lippia, 8.
Henry of Ghent, 17, 20, 22, 37n, 39-40&n, 41, 44-46, 49-50, 61n, 64, 75, 78&n-79&n, 80-81, 85-86, 96-97, 111, 121, 123-125&n, 126&n, 131&n-132, 134-135, 137, 142-143, 145, 151-152, 167n, 175, 178, 180-181, 201, 218, 239, 241-243, 250.
Henry of Gorkum, 13n.
Henry of Harclay, 50n, 78, 86&n, 95-96, 119n, 123, 125, 132-133&n, 135-136&n, 139&n, 241-242.
Henry of Oyta, 8, 21, 59n, 104&n, 112, 113n, 210n, 216, 219&n-220, 224&n-225, 227&n, 229, 248, 253.
Hermes Trismegistus, 30.
Hervaeus Natalis, 26, 37n, 48n, 64, 78, 85, 93, 121, 124-125, 170, 248.
Heymericus a Campo, 11, 237.
Hugh of Hervort, 8.
Hugh of Novocastro, 177-178, 181.
Hugo of St. Victor, 209.
Hugolin of Orvieto, 17, 20, 29, 57, 99-101&n, 107, 141, 195, 204, 207, 227, 246&n.

Jacob of Metz, 78&n, 79n, 166, 168-170, 248.
Jacob Wimpfeling, 10.
Jacobus de Appamiis, 101&n.
James of Ascoli, 48&n, 125, 132-133&n, 135, 139, 170, 179-180, 236, 248.
Jan Brugman, 8n.
Jean Gerson, 58&n, 151, 153n, 154, 156, 223.
Joachim of Fiore, 39n.
Jodocus Trutvetter, 10.
Johannes Aventinus, 12.
Johannes Baconis, 17, 66, 74, 76, 82, 85, 87-88, 90, 93, 135, 184, 198-199, 208, 219n, 240-241.
Johannes Bremer, 21&n.
Johannes Capreolus, 21, 29.
Johannes de Bassolis, 177, 181.
Johannes de Kanthi, 18n.
Johannes de Nova Domo, 11.
Johannes de Slupcza, 17&n.
Johannes Holzadel, 19, 21, 151n.
John Buridan, 8, 11-12, 16-18, 19n, 31, 34, 107, 109&n-110, 114-116, 118&n-119&n, 218-219&n, 220-221&n, 224, 230-231, 252-253.
John Duns Scotus, 2, 15, 17, 20-23, 25&n, 26-27, 29, 33, 37n, 39-40, 42&n-44&n, 45-46&n, 47-49, 58&n-59&n, 64, 75-89&n, 92-97, 107, 109-111, 117, 119n, 121&n, 123-125&n, 126&n, 130-131&n, 132-135, 138, 141-143, 146, 151-153&n, 158, 170-171&n, 175-177&n, 178-186&n, 187, 189, 195-196, 198-203, 205-206, 220-221, 226-227, 235, 238-243, 245-251, 253.
John Hiltalingen of Basel, 225, 233, 253.
John Lutterell, 52-53&n, 135&n, 139-140, 154.
John Major, 10.
John of Jandun, 17, 93.
John of Mirecourt, 193&n, 195&n, 197, 198n, 200&n, 208&n, 210, 222&n.
John of Naples, 140.
John of Paris, 25n, 36, 37n, 64, 69-70, 78, 124, 125, 168, 171-172.
John of Ripa, 20-21, 58, 143&n-144&n, 151, 153, 155-156&n, 220, 225n, 223&n, 225, 228&n, 232-233&n, 246, 252-253.
John of Rodington, 193&n, 245.
John Wyclif, 14n, 53fn, 151, 154&n, 193n.
John XXII, 53.

Landulph Caracciolo, 42n-43n, 177-178.
Leibniz, G.W., 6.
Leonardo da Vinci, 10.
Luther, Martin, 6&n.

Machiavelli, Niccolo, 185n.
Macrobius, 146.
Maimonides, 35&n-36.
Marsilius of Inghen, 1&n, 7&n-8, 9&n, 10&n-11&n, 12-16&n, 17-18&n, 19&n-20, 21&n-22, 23, 25, 29&n, 30-33&n, 34, 36, 56&n-57, 58-59&n, 60-61, 86, 99, 107&n-108, 109&n-110, 111&n-112, 113-116&n,

117-121, 141, 143-144&n, 145-147&n, 148-150&n, 151&n-151, 152-153&n, 154-156&n, 158-159, 162-163, 165, 172, 182, 184, 188, 193, 195, 204, 209, 210, 214-16&n, 217-219&n, 220-221&n, 222-226&n, 227-229&n, 230-233, 234-236, 246-253.
Martin of Alnwick, 118n.
Matheus de Eugebio, 66, 73.
Matthew of Krakau, 9-10.
Michael Aiguani, 115&n, 207, 210, 229.
Molina, Luis de, 6&n, 11.
Myngodus, 18n.

Nicholas d'Orbellis, 132&n.
Nicholas of Cusa, 3n, 146n.
Nicholas of Strasbourg, 124n.
Nicholas Oresme, 8.

Origen, 3&n.
Ovid, 20.

Parmenides, 237.
Peter Aureoli, 20-21, 26, 63, 66, 74, 76, 82, 86-88&n, 90, 97-99&n, 100-101&n, 117-119, 135, 160, 187, 195-198, 200, 240, 243, 252.
Peter Ceffons, 200n, 222&n.
Peter de Falco, 64-65, 69&n-70, 125.
Peter Lombard, 2, 19, 22, 35, 39n, 64, 103&n-104, 105n, 112-113, 141, 162n, 195, 207, 209, 211-212, 229&n, 237-238, 248-249.
Peter of Ailly, 10, 151, 154-155, 161, 189, 195, 197-198.
Peter of Aquila, 42&n, 77-78, 82, 88, 108, 132, 134, 141, 177-178, 181.
Peter of Auvergne, 169-170, 248.
Peter of Candia, 11n, 21, 58, 120&n, 143&n-144, 151-152, 156, 225, 250, 253.
Peter of John Olivi, 39, 69&n, 129n.
Peter of Spain, 118, 131, 166, 238.
Peter of Tarantasia (Innocence V), 37n, 207&n.
Peter of Trabibus, 39.
Peter Thomae, 79, 89.
Pierre Roger (Clemens VI), 42&n, 84.
Plato, 4&n, 20, 28, 35n, 78, 89, 145-147&n, 148-149, 154n, 157&n, 218-219&n, 220, 236.
Pomponazzi, Pietro, 22.
Porphyrius, 18.

Proclus, 5, 6n.
Protagoras, 28.
Pseudo-Dionysius, 25, 121, 146&n, 148-149, 150n, 153-155, 238.

Rambert of Bologna, 168n.
Raymundus Bequini, 101n.
Richard Billingham, 118&n.
Richard Campsall, 188, 189n, 193, 195, 206, 209-210, 245&n.
Richard Kilvington, 214&n, 219n.
Richard Knapwell, 129n.
Richard of Middleton, 64-65, 125, 129n, 132-133, 169, 182n.
Richard of St. Victor, 20, 30, 143.
Robert Cowton, 23, 37n, 46, 170n, 171&n, 179&n-180&n, 181, 236.
Robert Grosseteste, 69, 148n, 149&n, 172&n, 181.
Robert Holcot, 33&n, 54-55&n, 56, 102, 140, 141, 165, 188, 189n, 190n, 191&n-192, 193&n, 195, 209, 223&n, 231, 245-246.
Robert of Halifax, 208&n-209n.
Robert of Orford, 37n.
Roger Bacon, 66.
Roger Marston, 70, 71n.

Seneca, 20, 26.
Soto, Domingo de, 10-11.
Spinoza, B. de, 6, 35n.
Suárez, Francisco, 7n, 11.

Themistius, 28, 71-72&n, 82, 87.
Theodoric of Freiberg, 124n, 237.
Thomas Aquinas, 2, 20, 21n, 22-23, 25&n, 26-28, 33, 35-36&n, 37&n-38&n, 39-42&n, 44, 46, 51n, 53-54, 60, 63-64&n, 65-66, 69&n-70, 71n, 74-75&n, 77-78, 80, 89-92&n, 95, 99, 103, 105, 107, 109-110, 112, 121&n-130, 131n, 136-137, 139-140, 146&n, 148, 151-152, 154, 158, 160, 161n, 162, 164, 166-167&n, 168-169&n, 170&n-173&n, 174-175, 176&-177, 179-185, 195, 197, 202-208, 213, 210, 219n, 225, 228, 235, 238-241, 243-249, 252.
Thomas Bradwardine, 20, 161, 193n, 207, 209, 210n, 218-219&n, 220, 223&n
Thomas Bricot, 10.
Thomas Buckingham, 222, 210n.
Thomas de Strampino, 11, 144, 148.
Thomas of Strasbourg, 20-21&n, 29, 59,

INDEX OF NAMES

61&n, 112n, 107-108, 110, 112-115, 116n, 117-119, 141-143, 162, 224, 249, 252.
Thomas of Sutton, 37n, 39, 42n, 45-46&n, 47, 48n, 61, 78, 79n, 124, 241.
Thomas Wilton, 184, 208&n.

Urban V, 8.
Urban VI, 8.

Vitoria, Francisco de, 11.

Walter Burleigh, 131, 119n, 232n.
Walter Chatton, 43n, 51n, 119n, 193, 243, 245.
William Buser of Heusden, 8&n.
William Crathorn, 119n.
William de la Mare, 37n, 124&n, 128-129&n, 130, 138, 168-171, 176, 177n, 185, 248.
William Heytesbury, 214&n.
William of Alnwick, 25n, 42n-43n, 48, 88, 89n, 97, 119n, 132, 133n, 134, 138, 143-144, 175, 177-178, 180, 182.
William of Auvergne, 64, 103-104.
William of Auxerre, 64, 103&n-104&n.
William of Moerbeke, 6n.
William of Nottingham, 37n.
William of Ockham, 1-2, 6, 8, 11-12, 14&n-15, 17, 20, 22-23, 25, 29-29, 31-33, 35, 43n, 46&n-51&n, 52, 53&n-55&n, 56-59, 63-64, 73, 79, 84-85, 89-91&n, 92&n-93, 94-97&n, 102, 106n-107&n, 109-110, 115, 119n, 121&n, 124n, 125, 135&n-137, 137&n-138&n, 139-140&n, 141, 143, 145, 151-154&n, 155-156, 158, 160n, 163, 183-184&n, 185-188&n, 189-191&n, 192&n-193&n, 195, 197, 199-203, 206-207, 212-215, 221, 223-224&n, 227, 232n, 235, 238, 241-243, 245-246, 250-253.
William of Rubione, 29, 181, 247.
William of Sherwood, 157n.
William of Vaurouillon, 134&n.
William Peter of Godin, 169-170, 248.

Modern Authors

Ackrill, J.L., 160.
Anawati, G.C., 38n.
Ashworth, E.J., 10n.
Asztalos, M., 203n.

Badawi, A., 75n, 91n.
Bannach, K., 80n, 135n, 177n.
Barbet, J., 42n.
Barth, T.A., 44n.
Baudry, L. 137n.
Baur, L., 172n.
Beckmann, J.P., 121n, 125n, 134n.
Behm, 3n.
Beierwaltes, W., 6n.
Bergh, S. van den, 71n-72n.
Bérubé, C., 69n, 157n, 186n.
Bianchi, L., 121n.
Bieler, L., 164n.
Boehner, Ph., 3n, 22, 160n, 184n-187n, 190n, 224n.
Boese, H., 6n.
Boler, J., 138n.
Bonansea, B.M., 44n.
Borgnet, A. 146n.
Bos, A.P., 4n-5n.

Bos, E.P., 1, 6n, 10n, 16n, 92n, 94n, 111n, 124n, 153n, 156n, 216n, 230n.
Bossuat, R., 146n.
Braakhuis, H.A.G., 7n, 18n, 102n, 163n, 231n.
Brady, I.G., 70n, 134n.
Brown, S., 6n, 184n, 185n.

Cathala, M.-R., 27n.
Catto, J.I., 78n, 186n.
Chatelain, E., 200n.
Cherniss, H., 147n.
Colish, M.L., 5n.
Combes, A., 58n, 143n-144n, 151n-154n, 156n.
Courtenay, W.J., 9n, 13n, 14&n-15&n, 21n, 23n, 47n, 51n, 54-55n, 58n, 99n, 104n, 115n, 139n, 141&n, 161n, 190n-191n, 195n, 198n, 200n-202n, 209n-210&n, 214n, 219n-220n, 222n, 230n.
Craig, W.L., 7n, 159n, 167n, 177n, 184n.
d'Alverny, M.-Th., 30n, 143n.
Decker, B., 79n, 99n, 166n, 168n, 170n.
Delorme, F., 241n.
Denifle, H., 200n.
Dettlof, W., 48n.

Dewender, Th., 111n, 163n.
Dijk, Am. van, 8n.
Dörrie, H., 5n.

Ebbesen, S., 46n, 131n.
Eck, J. van, 159n.
Eckermann, W., 57n, 246n.
Ehrle, F., 11n, 13n, 58n, 120n, 143n-144n.
Etzkorn, G.F., 70n.
Etzkorn, G.J., 25n, 54n.

Faes de Mottoni, B., 150n.
Fakhry, M., 69n.
Fatio, O., 6n.
Fattori, M., 121n.
Finance, J. de, 170n.
Fine, G., 159n.
Fischer, J.M., 6n.
Flasch, K., 185n, 222n.
Fraenkel, P., 6n.
Freddoso, A.J., 52n.
Fussenegger, G., 169n.

Gabriel, A.L., 10n, 13n.
Gál, G., 103n, 185n.
Gambatese, A., 6n, 185n.
García y García, A., 39n.
Gardet, L., 71n, 75n.
Gebhardt, C., 6n.
Geiger, L.-B., 22n, 121n-122n.
Gelber, H.G., 37n, 42n-43&n, 51n, 55n, 184n.
Genequand, Ch., 72n.
Genest, J.-F., 193n, 208n, 219n-220n.
Gerhardt, C.I., 6n.
Gilbert, N.W., 14&n.
Gilson, E., 3n, 22. 50n, 66n, 125n.
Giocarinis, K., 148n.
Glorieux, P. 123n-124n.
Goichon, A.-M., 66n.
Gondras, A.-J., 64n.
González-Haba, M., 45n.
Grillmeier, A., 3n.
Gruber, J., 164n.
Guthrie, W.K.C., 147n.

Haase, W., 5n.
Hager, F.P., 6n.
Hamesse, J., 78n.
Häring, N.M., 146n, 163n.
Hasker, W., 7n.
Haubst, R., 146n.

Heinzmann, R., 48n.
Helm, P., 7n.
Henninger, M., 79n, 81n, 86n.
Henry, D.P., 165n.
Herold, V., 154n.
Heynck, V., 132n.
Hödl, L., 37n.
Hoenen, M.J.F.M., 1n, 7n, 11n, 18n-19n, 29n, 92n-94n, 101n, 114n, 120n, 151n, 171n, 176n.
Hoeres, W., 131n.
Hoffmann, F., 53n, 189n, 193n, 223n.
Hoffmans, J., 41n.
Hofmann, U., 144n.
Honnefelder, L., 184n.
Hopkins, J., 163n.
Hubien, H., 231n.
Hudson, A., 53n, 154n, 193n.
Huebner, D. von, 4n.

Imbach, R., 13n, 64, 66n, 124n.
Iserloh, E., 6n.

Jacobi, K., 157n, 166n.
Jedin, H., 6n
Jordan, M., 47n.

Kaluza, Z., 11n, 58n, 143n, 186n, 223n.
Kamali, S.A., 68n
Kelly, F.E., 25n, 52n-53n, 129n.
Kenny, A., 7n, 154n, 158n, 166n, 170n, 173n.
Kirwan, Ch., 167n.
Kittelson, J.M., 13n.
Kleijntjes, J.C.J., 9n.
Klibansky, R., 219n.
Kluxen, W., 26n, 35n, 121n, 183n, 185n.
Kneale, M., 192n.
Kneale, W., 192n.
Kneepkens, C.H., 8n, 231n.
Knudsen, Chr., 140n.
Knuuttila, S., 46n, 166n, 183.
Knysh, G., 53n.
Koch, J., 52n-53n, 54n, 65n, 140n, 169n.
Kogan, B.S., 70n-71n.
Koninck, Ch. de, 5n.
Kremer, K., 146n.
Kretzmann, N., 7&n, 163n, 166n, 214&n, 230n.
Kristeller, P.O., 30n.
Krop, H.A., 92n, 124n.
Kuksewicz, Z., 73n.

Kürzinger, J., 61n.

Laks, A., 4n.
Landauer, S., 72n.
Lang, A., 59n, 113n, 220n, 224n, 227n.
Langston, D.C., 177n.
Leaman, O., 69n, 71n.
Lechner, J., 144n.
Lecq, R. van der, 224n, 231n.
Ledoux, A., 48n, 133n.
Leff, G., 210n.
Lemaigre, B.M., 36n.
Lewis, B., 66n.
Libera, A. de, 203n.
Liske, M.Th., 170n.
Little, A.G., 241n.
Lloyd, A.C., 149n.
Lohr, Ch.H., 18n.
Lowe, M.F., 160n.

Macken, R., 40n, 79n, 123n.
Maggiòlo, M., 167n.
Maier, A., 1, 9&n, 163n, 219n-220n.
Maierù, A., 8n, 13n, 166n.
Mansfeld, J., 6n.
Marcolino, V., 28n, 101n, 144n, 245n.
Markowski, M., 1, 10n, 18n.
Marmura, M., 70n-71n.
Marrone, S.P., 131n.
Martineau, E., 143n.
Maurer, A.A., 50n, 79n, 86n, 94n, 125n, 130&n, 132n-136n, 138n.
McCord Adams, M., 22&n, 43n, 46n, 49n-50&n, 135n, 184n, 188n, 191n-192&n.
McEvoy, J., 149n.
McInerny, R.M., 36n.
Meier, G., 147n.
Meier, L., 21n.
Meijer, P.A., 6n, 94n.
Meiser, C., 163n.
Mercken, H.P.F., 148n.
Meuthen, E., 13n.
Meyer, G., 28n.
Meyer, S. 146n.
Michael, B., 19n, 221n.
Michalski, K., 193n, 222n.
Miethke, J., 9n, 20n, 53n, 140n.
Mikat, P., 207n.
Möhler, W., 1, 56&n, 109n.
Mojsisch, B., 245n.
Molland, A.G., 100n.

Moody, E.A., 191n.
Moraux, P., 5n.
Mueller, I.J., 151n.
Mulder, W., 8n.
Muller, J.-P., 25n, 139n, 168n.
Muralt, A. de, 130n, 135n.
Murdoch, J.E., 119n, 203n.
Mutzenbecher, A., 121n.

Niiniluoto, I., 203n.
Normore, C., 7n, 161n, 165n, 188n, 190n-191n.
Nuchelmans, G., 33n, 102n-103n, 104-105n.
Nwigwe, B.E., 173n.

Oberman, H.A., 101n, 210n, 245n.

Paban, C., 21n.
Pattin, A., 226n.
Pelster, F., 9, 101n, 241n.
Pelzer, A. 125n.
Pèques, Th., 21n.
Pera, C., 26n.
Perler, D., 102n, 184n.
Pike, N., 6, 7n, 173&n.
Pinborg, J., 7n, 35n, 72n, 166n, 191n.
Plessis d'Argentre, C. du, 219n.
Pluta, O., 146n, 193n, 245n.
Prior, A.N., 6&n, 172n-173n.

Rad, G. von, 3n.
Ravizza, M., 6n.
Raymundi, Fr., 160n.
Rengstorf, 145n.
Rescher, N., 160n.
Ribaillier, J., 103n-104n.
Riedl, J.O., 65n.
Riet, S. van, 25n.
Rijk, L.M. de, 6n, 102n, 118n, 163n, 166n, 231n.
Ritter, G., 1, 7n, 10n, 118n, 120n, 148n.
Roensch, F., 170n.
Ross, W.D., 147n.
Rossmann, H., 77n, 132n, 134n.
Rowe, W.L., 163n.
Rudavsky, T., 7n, 71n, 161n, 167n.
Ruello, F., 42n, 149n.
Ryan, J.K., 44n.

Salmon, P., 4n.
Scheffczyk, L., 3n, 48n.

Schevichaven, H.D.J. van, 9n.
Schmaus, M., 3n, 45n.
Schmid, J., 3n.
Schmitt, Ch.B., 10n.
Schmitt, F.S., 165n.
Schmitt, Fr., 168n.
Schneider, J., 46n.
Schneider, Th. 129n.
Schnitker, Th.A., 4n.
Schönberger, R., 46n, 48n.
Schulze, M., 246n.
Schwamm, H., 22, 29n, 156n, 170n, 177n, 178&n-182n, 193n, 200n, 219n-220n, 223n, 225n, 228n, 233n.
Senko, W., 208n.
Sharples, R.W., 5n.
Simon, P., 150n.
Sinnige, Th.G., 5n.
Sorabji, R., 160n-161n.
Spade, P.V., 138n, 154n.
Spiazzi, Fr.R., 123n.
Stegmüller, F., 6n, 200n, 222n.
Streveler, P.A., 55n, 165n, 193n.
Stump, E., 7&n.
Synan, E.A., 189n, 230n.
Tachau, K.H., 55n, 86&n, 88n, 91n, 98n, 102n, 107n, 145n, 185n, 189n, 193n, 245n.
Tatarzynski, R., 17n.
Theissing, H., 180n-181n.

Thijssen, J.M.M.H, 118n-119n.
Torre, B.R. de la, 220n.
Transue, P.J., 13n.
Trapp, A.D., 12n, 28n, 61n, 101n, 200n, 222n.
Trinkaus Zagzebski L., 7n.
Työrinoja, R., 46n.

Uiblein, P., 10n.

Vansteenkiste, Cl., 147n.
Vignaux, P., 89n, 134n, 186n, 193n, 209n.
Viola, C., 143n.
Vossenkuhl, W., 46n.
Vossenkühl, W., 91n.

Wadding, L., 25n.
Wainwright, W.J., 6n.
Walls, J.L., 158n.
Wanke, O., 89n, 134n.
Weiler, A.G., 13n.
Weisheipl, J.A., 28n.
Werbeck, W., 144n.
Wetter, F., 42n, 43&n.
Wey, J.C., 28n, 43n.
Wielgus, S., 19n, 111n.
Wierenga, E.R., 7n.
Wiesner, J., 72n. 149n.
Wilks, M., 53n, 154n, 193n.
Wilpert, P., 10n.
Winkelmann, E., 221n.
Winkler, G.B., 6n.
Wippel, J.F., 22, 36n, 41n, 46n, 125n, 131n, 167n, 173n.
Wlodek, S.(Z.), 10n, 133n.
Wolfson, H.A., 35-36.
Wolter, A.B., 22n, 25n, 44n, 177n-178n, 221n.
Wood, R., 119n.
Wulf, M. de, 41n, 125n.
Würsdörfer, J., 107n.
Würthwein, 3n.

Yokoyama, T., 48n, 133n, 135n.
Yovel, Y., 35n.

Zavalloni, R., 129n.
Zimmermann, A., 10n, 14n, 28n, 100n, 147n.
Zumkeller, A., 21n, 61n, 101n, 103n.

INDEX OF SUBJECTS AND PLACES

abstrahere, 93.
aedificare, 215.
aequipollenter, 87, 99.
aeternitas, 177.
aevum, 177.
agere circa providentiam, 232.
aliqui doctores, 59, 103.
analogy, 36, 111, 212.
animalitas, 45.
anonymi, 76.
Ansbach, 11.
Anselmian rule, 44, 57.
antesignani nominalistarum, 12, 253.
Antichrist, 24, 117-118, 158, 181, 187, 221.
antiqui, 15, 35, 52, 148, 175; *doctores*, 103, 155, 253; *nominales*, 7.
argumentation, methods of, 239.
Ars Meliduna, 104.
Articuli novelli, 200.
artistae, 11, 77, 108.
atomists, 119.
Avignon, 8, 52.

Basel, 10.
being, and possibile non-being, 183; and thought, 237; diminutive, 131, 134, 139; essential b. compared to existential b., 131-133; essential, 131-133; existential, 131-132; only two basic types of b., viz., rational and real, 46-48; real b. compared to rational b., 136; real b. vs. conceptual b., 91; real b. is more perfect than b.-as-known, 44; three basic types of b., viz., rational, real, and formal (Scotus), 48.
beneplacitum, 211.

casus, 163.
cátedra de nominales, 11-12.
catholici, 108.
causa, factiva, 233; *illativa*, 233; *peccati*, 222; *sufficiens*, 218; *c. vel potius concausa*, 212.
causality, natural, 99.
cause, accidental, 218; efficient 93-94, 145; two views of efficient causality, 94;

extrinsecal description of c., 95; final, 145; formal, 145; knowledge of the c. implies knowledge of the effect, 64; natural, 220; relational concept, 72; secondary, 129, 206, 220.
celestial bodies, 92-93, 115; depend upon God, 32.
chance, 5, 121, 157, 163, 166.
chimaera, 131.
Christology, 141.
cognitio, 82; *delectabilissima*, 33.
cognoscere, 190.
cognoscibilia complexe enuntiabilia, 102; *complexe significabilia*, 102; *cognoscibilia simplicia*, 102.
Cologne, 8, 11, 13.
communis opinio, 39, 137.
communitas in praedicando, 147.
complexe enuntiabile, 102-107, 196, 217; as object of God's knowledge, 102; division of, 104; truth value, 104.
complexe significabile, 33, 102.
composita, 134.
concausa necessario requisita, 211.
concepts, as objects of knowledge, 192; can exist without intellectual activity, 56; ontological status (Ockham), 52.
condemnation of, 1270: 65, 240; 1277: 65, 124, 206, 240; 1347: 200, 222.
connotare, 105.
connotatum, 182.
consecutive et resultative, 87.
contingency, 5, 248; three forms of, 166; and certainty, 167, 182, 202, 246; and immutability, 183; c. of the future, 218; defined by Gregory of Rimini, 203.
contingens ad utrumlibet, 166; *ut in paucioribus*, 166; *ut in pluribus*, 166.
contingent things, as cause of God's foreknowledge, 211-212; can only be known through the senses, 157; compared to necessary things, 157; medieval view of c., 157; ontological status, 157; their intelligibility, 157.
continuum, divisibility in the mind of God,

100; divisibility, 98, 100-101, 119.
contra sanctos nolo loqui, 142.
Correctoria corruptorii, 23, 123, 129, 137, 139, 168-169, 171, 176.
creation, dependent upon God, 75; difference from God, 88; distance between God and c., 116; from nothing, 176.

De mundo, 5.
de dicto/de re, 165, 173-175.
deformitates, 113.
Demiurg, 4.
demonstration, its logical structure, 137.
denominatio extrinseca, 104.
determinate and indeterminate truth, 160, 162, 165, 185, 187-189, 197-198, 211, 223-224; as defined by Marsilius, 223.
determinate verum, 224.
determinatio voluntatis, 177-178.
Deus, causa et auctor peccati ut peccatum, 222; *causa omnis contingentiae futurae radicalis et originalis*, 227.
Devotio moderna, 8.
dictum, 230-231.
differentia, secundum rationem quidditativam, 43; *secundum rationem*, 43; *virtualis*, 43.
disputations, 222, 237, 238, 245-246.
distinctae, cognoscibilitates vel quidditates, 250; *formalitates*, 250; *perfectiones*, 250.
distinctio secundum quid ex natura rei, 43.
distinction, *a parte rei*, 42, 59; between divine attributes, 56; between attributional concepts in the human mind, 57; between beings, 49; between real and rational being, 50, 56; between the divine persons, 49; every d. is a real d., 56; *ex natura rei* between divine attributes, 46; *ex natura rei*, 40, 42-43, 47, 142, 201.
distinction, four types of, 47; its being follows that of the things distinguished, 48; only two basic types of d., viz., rational and real, 46, 56; ontological status, 47; rational between attributes, 37, 52-53, 56; *secundum rationem, secundum considerationem*, 38; *simpliciter ex natura rei* vs. *secundum quid*, 48.
diversae rationes formales, 250.
divine attributes, 20, 35, 241, 242, 248, 251; are not in God, 55; are only distinct as attributional concepts, 60; are only one as attributional perfections, 60; are rationally distinguished, 36; as attributional perfection, 50-51, 55, 57, 249, 251, as predicates in the human mind, 50-52, 57, 248, 251; as terms in meta-language, 55; coincide with God's essence, 48, 59; compared to human attributes, 225; discussion about their epistomological and metaphysical status, 39; distinction between d. (Thomas), 36; distinctions between d. are distinctions between human concepts, 56; does their distinction depend on human knowledge of God?, 36; have no reality of their own, 36; have their foundation in the perfection of divine essence, 46; Islamic controversies, 36; mere products of the human mind?, 40; predicated of God in a proposition, 53; rationally distinct Thomas vs. Henry of Ghent, 40; rationally distinct, 40-41; their distinction is not constituted by divine or human knowledge, 44; their distinction reflects the different modes of human knowledge, 60; their multiplicity vs. God's unity, 36, 39, 40; their plurality exists only in the human mind, 51, 248, 251-252; their status, 39; d. vs. divine names, 35.
divine care of an infinity of individuals, 5.
divine causality, 156, 175; permeates all being, 220; medieval interpretation of Aristotle and Averroes, 252.
divine essence, as the foundation of ideal relations, 132; contains all perfections, 121.
divine eternity, 203, 229, 248.
divine finality, medieval interpretation of Aristotle and Averroes, 252.
divine foreknowledge, 11, 141, 163, 239; and certainty, 215; cannot be the causa of the known, 212; correspondance between medieval and modern views, 6; historical aspects, 7; impossibility, 6; logical aspects, 6, 159.
divine freedom, 76.
divine ideas, 22-23, 78-79, 84-85, 95, 113, 172-176, 236, 238, 250, 252-253; all i. are practical, 137; are *conditrices*, 150; are eternal, 139-140; are distinct, 155; are formally distinct, 155; are *illuminantes non illuminatae*, 150; are immutable, 139; are known by God in one single act, 146; are nothing, 138; are *per se stantes*, 150; are really distinct, 155; are *superstantes et*

supererectae, 150; are the *relucentia* of the creatures in God, 153; arguments for their existence, 121; as acts of volition, 154; as *creativae et productivae rerum*, 121, 136; as *creaturae producibiles*, 152; as *exemplaria*, 122, 133, 136-137, 154; as final cause of creation, 146; as forms of knowledge, 127, 135, 154; as grounds of knowledge, 153; as known creatures, 198-199; as known objects, 125, 127, 132, 134-136, 138, 140, 250, 252; as known quidditates, 126-127, 176; as *notiones exemplares*, 150; as practical i., 127; as principles of creation, 133, 146; as rational forms, 137; as *rationes* by which God knows and produces creation, 139; as *rationes*, 122, 137; as *relationes ideales*, 126, 127, 132; as *similitudines*, 135-136; coincide with creatures, 135, 152-153, 155; coincide with God's essence, 122, 134, 137-140, 146, 152-153, 155, 247, 250; compared to God's knowledge, 142-143; compared to God's productivity, 136, 142; d. do not represent existence, 176; exist of necessity, 136; follow upon God's knowledge of creation, 85; have no being, 135; have only *quid nominis*, 138-139; link between d. and divine volition, 154-155; of accidents, 124, 129-130; of all that can be produced separately, 138; of artificial beings, 134; of *composita*, 134; of forms, 129-130, 138; of *genera*, 129, 134, 138; of individuals, 124-125, 130, 133-134, 138; of matter; 124, 129-130, 134, 138; of natural beings, 134; of relations, 134; of species, 124, 133-134; of the conjunction of matter and form, 129; of the essences of creatures, 128; of the parts of *composita*, 134-138; of things that are produced in connection with something else, 127; of things that can be produced independently, 127; Platonic doctrine, 148; positive properties, 150; practical i. compared to speculative i., 125-126, 128, 137; practical i., 121, 123, 127-128, 141, 153; relation between thing and i., 123; speculative i., 123; their diversity compared to the diversity in the created world, 143; their existence denied, 142, 198; their function, 126; their ontological status, 121, 133-135, 138, 140; their plurality compared to God's unity, 122, 135, 137, 156; their properties, 145; what they are (Marsilius), 148; what they are not (Marsilius), 147-148.

divine intellect, attributes of, 6; is the measure of the thing known, 80-82; produces the known as *esse intelligibile*, 80-83.

divine knowledge, 121, 141, 235-237, 243, 245, 250; and human freedom, 3, 23; and logical and semantical questions, 3; and order of the world, 236; and truth-conditions of propositions, 24; argument from causality, 25, 27-28, 31, 247; argument from immateriality, 25, 29; argument from perfection, 25-27, 29; cannot be a priori proved, 27; epistemic-logical aspects, 23; epistemological status, 157; ethical questions, 3; immeasurable and incomprehensible, 30; in the Scripture, 3; in the works of the Fathers, 3; its (im)mutability, 212-214; its necessity compared to that of a necessary cause, 206; metaphysical assumptions, 2; modes of, 32, 34; most dominant lines of thought, 22; received view in the late Middle Ages, 3; relation to God's will and his power of creation, 2; theological dimension, 236; three major opposing views on, 2, 246; understanding of d., 2; d. vs. human knowledge, 32, 37, 80; first and second object, 252; medieval interpretation of Aristotle and Averroes, 252; provability, 243, 244, 251.

divine omnicausality, 201, 203.

divine omnipotence, 129.

divine omniscience, 198, 201; as religious conviction, 4; as self evident starting-point of reflection, 4; in Antiquity, 4.

divine perfection, 35, 72, 217, 240; coincides with God's essence, 57.

divine persons, 225.

divine powers, 252.

divine will, 237, 249; double evaluation of d., 201, 227, 249.

divini nominis invocatio, 4.

doctores moderni, 78, 207, 225; *nostri*, 223.

educere, 93.
electio, 154.
emanation, 40, 67, 71.
ens rationis, 50, 134.
entitas, 111.
enuntiabilia, 196, 214; *falsa impossibilia*,

104; *falsa possibilia*, 104; *futura*, 196, 201, 204; truth value, 214; *vera*, 104.
epicurei nominales, epicuri litterales, 11.
Erfurt, 10-11.
esse cognitum, 130, 132; *commune*, 74; *deminutum*, 130, 133; *esse in*, 51, 55; *intelligibile*, 80, 82-83; *secundum quid et diminutum*, 89.
essentia, 125, 128-129, 131, 155.
essential predication, 173-174.
eternity, 167, 169-170; as defined by Boethius, 164; compared to eternal duration, 167, 177.
evil, 112; has no idea in God, 113.
exemplar, 89, 122-123, 136-137, 154-155; *e. producendi*, 153.
experience, 92-93, 221.

facere, 209-211, 231-232, 251; *f. aliquid ad quod sequitur Deum ab aeterno praescire*, 232; two senses of f., 233.
fallacies, 244.
figmentum, 131.
final causality in creation, 28.
first principle, and order of reality, 236; is immaterial, 38.
foreknowledge and providence, 2.
form, two senses of, 122.
forma, 127; *f. cognoscendi*, 154.
formal distinction, 39-40, 42-43, 45, 49, 55, 241, 242, 249, 251; and divine attributes, 43, 49, 56, 59; and God's infinity, 44; and the Trinity, 49; as formal non-identity, 42-43; between divine ideas, 155; between perfections, 44; implies real distinction, 50, 56, 58-59; f. vs. God's unity, 46, 48; f. vs. real and rational distinction, 39.
formal non-identity, 58; implies real non-identity, 47.
formalitates, 43, 58.
formalizantes, 58.
free will, 157, 167-168, 200, 220-221; cannot be proved by means of arguments, 221; is known by experience, 221.
freedom human, 5-6.
Freiburg, 10.
fundamentum proximum, 37, 54.
future things, division of, 196.

genera, 123, 125, 129, 134; and species, 68; as qualities of the human soul, 138.

God as *principium universale per imitationem*, 145; as pure act, 35, 37; as pure perfection, 66; as universal principle, 145; can always produce an effect that is greater than the one produced, 120, 253; can create an infinite magnitude, 101, 111, 119; can create matter and form independently, 128-129, 134, 138; can only know his essence, 90; cannot be perfected by creation, 77; cannot be surpassed, 26, 30; cannot have complete knowledge of creation through his causality, 76; cannot know an infinite set of things, 86; cannot know matter, 67.
God cannot know through something else, 65; cause of contingency in creation, 227, 249; cause of everything, 252; cause of singular things, 156; co-operates with all created causes, 29, 223, 145; compared to an artist, 75; contains all being eminently, 74, 85, 87; contains all things before they exist, 145; creator, 121; eternal and immutable, 216; has divine ideas of all perfections, 127; has evident knowledge of all necessary and contingents truths, 185; has immediate knowledge of individual things, 123-124; has intuitive knowledge of his essence, 155; has knowledge of all individuals through his essence, 142; has knowledge of all things, 217; has no knowledge of creation, 65, 73, 90, 101, 108; has no knowledge of existence through divine ideas, 128; has no knowledge of future contingents, 162, 195, 197; his essence contains all creatures in the most perfect way, 142; immediate cause of creation, 200, 226, 249; independent of creation, 134; is not the cause of sin, 187; is omniscient and perfect, 158; keeps the world necessarily in existence, 18; knower and known are one, 38; knows all parts of the continuum, 101; knows all things through his essence, 168; knows all true propositions, 203; knows an infinite magnitude, 100; knows evil and sin *privative*, 113; knows future contingents as present in his eternity, 107, 168-171, 175-176, 179-180, 185, 197, 203, 207; knows future contingents as present in his eternity, two interpretations, 169, 180; knows future contingents because of his immensity, 224, 253; knows future contingents by his causality,

168, 171, 175, 177-180, 203; knows future contingents by his causality, two interpretations, 177, 199; knows future contingents by knowing their causes, 168, 176; knows future contingents by means of ideas, 169-171, 175-176, 186, 198, knows future contingents in their own being, 168, 170-171; knows his essence only as a unity, 45; knows his essence perfectly, 109, 111; knows individual things because his essence contains different rationes, 79; knows individual things directly, 80, 82; knows individual things through differences in the acts of knowledge, 79; knows individuals only through ideas, 123; knows infinitely many numbers, 100; knows only the being of his essence, 240; knows singular things only universally, 67-68; knows the contingent in a necessary manner, 5; knows the differences between the attributes through knowledge of the human intellect, 45; knows the mutable immutably, 164, 178; 229; knows the the *malum poenae* through his causality, 112; most perfect being, 64, 137; needs ideas to be productive in an intellectual manner, 96; pure act, 70; takes infinite delight in himself, 33; the object of his knowledge is not the proposition, 33; three basic properties of G., 145.

God's care for man, 236.

God's caring relation to creation, 3-4.

God's causality, 28, 64, 70, 74-75, 95, 111, 167-168; as root of contingency, 220; concerning celestial bodies and separate substances, 93; medieval interpretations of Aristotle and Averroes, 17, 108; provability, 92-93, 110; warrants contingency, 162.

God's creatorship, 35.

God's dependence upon creation, two interpretations, 117.

God's essence, as equivocal principle, 81, 111; as *ratio intelligendi*, 40; as *ratio volendi*, 40; as univocal principle, 81, 111; coincides with his delight, 60; coincides with his knowledge, 35, 38; contains all perfections, 80, 89, 111; is being qua being, 72; is itself the knowledge of all things, 96; is one intuitive act of knowledge, 185; its spiritual quantity is infinite, 226; represents everything as necessary, 179; vigor of G., 112.

God's essential perfection, its infinite intrinsic power can be proved, 116.

God's eternity, 161, 165, 168, 171, 182, 203.

God's existence, provability, 93.

God's finality, 110.

God's foreknowledge, conceptual stages, 177, 186-187; 199; definition *quid nominis*, 216; has the necessity of the past, 161; is *certitudinaliter et evidenter*, 184; is contingent, 161, 172; its (im)mutability, 228; its certainty, 162; its immensity compared the future fact, 210; its modality, 228; its object, 217; man's influence on, 208-211, 231-232, 251; man's influence on, two possibilities, 232; metaphysical arguments compared to logico-semantic arguments, 203, 245, 251; semantic aspects, 172, 193.

God's infinity, 37, 44-45, 60, 88, 90, 114, 249; G. vs. finiteness of creatures, 45.

God's intellect, as Son, 40; as measure, 88; compared to the human intellect, 81; is an infinitely multiple representation of all different things, 111; is infinite, 82; is perfect, 75; produces the known as *esse intelligibile*, 97.

God's intellectual and eternal eye, 202.

God's intellectuality, 3.

God's knowledge of creation, 238-242, arguments, 63, 75; is by knowing himself as its cause, 66, 72-72, 76-77; is by knowing his essence, 77, 107; criticism of the argument from causality, 76; is directly, 78, 85, 96, 107; is individually, 75; is intuitively, 107, 198; is by means of rational relations, 86; is neither singular nor universal, 72; is only partially, 65; is only universally, 69, 75; is through self-knowledge, 66, 70, 72-74; is without a medium, 199; is without distinction, 74; provability, 89, 107, 109.

God's knowledge of evil, 112-113, 252.

God's knowledge of future contingents, 157, is certain and infallible, 218, 224; is contingent, 181, 189; is incomprehensible, 185, 201-202, 216, 227; is necessary, 204, 248; its (im)mutability, 190; its modality follows the modality of the known, 181, 190, 217, 228, 249; rules concerning its (im)mutability, 192; the act of knowledge compared to the relation of the future contingent to this act, 181, 190, 213, 228.

God's knowledge, 35, 243, plurality of secondary objects, 81-85; primary and secondary object, 63, 81-82, 85-88, 97-98, 117, 198; produces the known as *esse intelligibile*, 88; provability, 31; the known is really and formal identical with God, 88; two modes of G. 217.

God's knowledge, abstracts from time, 197; and discursiveness, 70, 178; argument from infinity, 99, 118; can increase and decrease, 191; cannot be a priori demonstrated, 75; cannot be derived from other things, 66; cannot be perfected, 226; coincides with his essence, 32, 135; compared to his essence, 33; different conceptional stages, 82, 84, 85, 97, 111; distinction of different objects (Gregory of Rimini), 102; does not depend upon the known, 163; is certain and infallible, 32, 164; is eternal and immutable, 32, 158, 161, 164, 173-174; is infinite, 33, 226; is intuitive, 33, 44; is most splendid, 33; is necessary, 173, 184; is neither discursive nor astractive, 32; is not directed towards creation, 98-99; is not of a plurality, 87; is not of individual things, 86; is of the singular, 71; its capacity remains always the same, 229; its intuitiveness, 178; its modality, 106, 189; its necessity, 172; neither universal nor singular, 109; no distinction between primary and secondary objects, 99; of a multiplicity of objects, 73; of contingents, 236; of contraries, 86.

God's knowledge, of his essence is not distinct from knowledge of creation, 87; of individual things vs. his unity, 78, 81; of judgement, 105-106; of the infinite, 119; of the singular, 71.

God's omnipotence, 120.

God's perfection, 30, 32, 73, 82, 95, 98; coincides with his essence, 51.

God's practical knowledge, 122.

God's productivity, needs an intellect, 95.

God's self-knowledge, 41; compared to his knowledge of creation, 63, 76.

God's simplicity, 70, 73, 77, 87, 163.

God's timelessness, 7.

God's unity, 32, 38-39, 41, 43, 50-51, 56-57, 59, 82, 88, 107, 145; compared to God's perfections, 123.

God's will, 35, 40; as cause of creation, 177; cannot be intervened, 196; cannot determine God's knowledge, 186; cause of all things, 200; cause of sin, 200; determines the truth of contingent propositions, 201; determines the truth of contingents, 186; does not determine God's knowledge, 201; followed of necessity by man, 209; its capacity remains always the same, 229; its immutability, 178; root of contingency, 182.

God's, freedom, 29; imitability, 79; immateriality, 3, 25, 37-38, 40, 63, 67; immensity, 224; immutability, 35, 191; independence, 76, 80, 82, 87-88; infinite efficacy, 114; infinite perfection, 116; infinite power, 114-115, 119.

God, as causa of evil, 196, 215; as cause of matter, 70; as cause of sin, 222-223, 249; as cause of the act of the will not of its swerve from the good, 223; as Creator, 3; as efficient causa, 17, 31, 32, 94, 76, 145-146, 149; as efficient cause, provability, 94; as final causa, 17, 32, 63, 76, 94, 145-146, 149; as final cause, provability, 94; as first principle, 35, 37, 79; as formal cause, 76, 145-146, 149; as material cause, 76; as necessary being, 66.

goodness, 43, 53, 56, 56.

grace, 11.

gratia exercitii, 222.

Great Schism, 9.

Heidelberg, 8-10, 16, 18-21, 30, 236.

heresy, 52-53.

hermetical writings, 252.

homo inquantum homo, 147.

homo mortuus, 131.

human freedom, 158-159, 161-162, 165, 186-187, 199-200, 209-210, 215; as root of contingency, 163, 220.

human knowledge, based on non-complex sensory knowledge, 110; h. of God, 36, 55, 60; h. of God is drawn from creation, 44; h. of God is univocal, 44.

human mind, 237.

immateriality and the possession of knowledge, 25.

immensitas, 224-225, 232; i. quantitatis spiritualis, 225.

immensum iudicium, 202.

in esse volito, 180.
in potestate Petri, 209.
in scholis, 223.
infinite effective power as defined by Marsilius, 114.
infinite magnitude, 119.
infinite spiritual magnitude, 114.
infinitum in extensione, 119.
infinity, does not contradict magnitude, 100; *per similitudinem*, 116.
instantia naturae, 84; *i. originis*, 84
intellectio, 82.
intellectuality and order, 236.
intellectum est perfectio intelligentis, 65.
intellectum primum, 63; *i. secundum*, 63.
intellectus agens, 37.
intelligences, depend upon God, 32.
intelligibile species, 37, 63, 67, 171.
intelligibility and being, 27.
intentio sanctorum et philosophorum, 139.
intentiones, 43.
intuitio incomprehensibilis, 202.
Irrtumslisten, 140.
Isny, 11.

knowledge, abstractive, 33 91, 107; depends upon what is known, 109; does not depend on its object, 91; evident, 185, 216; human k. compared to divine k., 226; intellectual k. is of the universal and immutable, 77; intuitive, 33, 91, 107, 155, 186, 202, 252; its modes depend on the subject not on the object, 172; non-complex k. of the one does not yield non-complex k. of the other, 76, 92, 110; object of, 33; of non-existens, 91, through selfknowledge, 66.
Krakau, 10-11, 17.

language vs. reality, 12.
Leipzig, 11.
Liber de causis, 25, 145, 226, 249.
Liber propugnatorius, 46-47, 84-85, 184, 187, 196, 200, 243.
Liber XXIV philosophorum, 20, 30.
library of Marsilius, 20, 30, 152, 223.
libri naturales, 64, 239.
literature on the fallacies, 165.
logic and semantics, 242.
logica communis, 208.
logico-semantic approach, 15, 20, 23, 195, 202, 204, 227, 235, 238-239, 244-246, 251.
λόγος, 5.
London, 244.
Louvain, 11.
Low Countries, 7.
lumen naturale, 18; *supernaturale*, 18; *theologicum*, 17.

malum culpae, 112; *poenae*, 112.
man, loved by the gods, 108.
measure, 80, 149.
modal operator, 213, 230.
moderni, 14-15, 35, 52, 120, 172, 207, 224, 233, 247, 253.
modi reales, 250.
modus platonicus, 143, 148.
modus, 231.
Montpellier, 8.
mover of the heaven, 91, 115.
mundus intelligibilis, 147.

natio anglicana, 8.
natura, 125, 131.
natural causality, 185.
natural reason, 17-18, 34, 60, 92, 94, 107-109, 114, 116, 185, 187; 215; 244, 251.
necessitas condicionalis, 206; *consequentiae*, 165, 183; *consequentis*, 165; *ex suppositione*, 206; *naturaliter praecedens*, 219, 165; *sequens*, 165, 183; *simplex*, 206.
necessity, 5, 157-160, 162-163, 167, 173, 175, 176, 183, 187, 189, 203, 205-206, 208-209, 215, 217-220, 221, 224; and immutability, 183, 188-189; and immutability 249; conditional 206; *ex suppositione*, 106; logical, 165; of the past, 161, 165, 172, 182, 188, 229; of the present, 182, 188, 207; two forms of, 164; unconditional and conditional, 164.
Neoplatonism, 145-147, 163, 241, 252.
nihil, 132, 138.
Nijmegen, 7, 9.
νόησις νοήσεως, 38, 65-66; interpretations of n., 65.
nomen connotativum, 138.
nominales, 13.
nominalism, 1, 10-14; logico-semantic outlook, 13; Parisian prohibition of 1474, 13.
notitia iudiciaria, 105.
νοῦς, 38, 65.

obiectum primum, 81, 85, 117; *secundarium*, 117.
oculus intellectualis aeternusque, 202.
omne quod est quando est necesse est esse, 183.
omnis, semantic analysis of o., 118.
ontological status of the known in God, 130-132.
opinio, famosa, 58; *quorundam valentium*, 151; *valentis*, 154.
opus naturae est opus intelligentiae, 28, 31; its different meanings, 28.
Oxford, 184, 209, 241, 242-244.

Paris, 8-9, 16, 18-19, 42, 58, 195, 210, 214, 231, 235-236, 238-243, 246, 251-252.
partes actu vel potentia divisa, 100.
particular, emphasis on the p., 28.
Pavia, 9, 18.
per se causa mali, 222.
perfect being as defined by Aristotle, 26.
perfectio, 57; *essentialis*, 116.
perfection, coincides with being (Marsilius), 30; pure p., 43, 51, 55; pure p. as defined by Anselm, 26; the p. of an entity is proportionally to its being, 111; created, 45; has an irreducible quiddity, 43; has perfect existence in God, 44; in creation, 36, 41, 64.
perspicacitas, 215.
philosophi moderniores, 209.
platonici, 148.
plurality of substantial forms, 129.
possibile intellect, 85.
potestas, 211.
praesens, 180.
praesentialitas, 207; *p. cogniti*, compared to *praesentialitas rei*, 170; its ambiguity, 207.
Prague, 10, 21.
predestination, 19.
prima radix contingentiae, 182.
principale significatum, 181.
principalis actor mali, 222.
principia to the Sentences, 9-11, 19, 22, 29-30, 143-146, 148-149, 151, 247.
principium universale per imitationem, 145.
principle, of bivalence, 160, 189; of identity and non-contradiction, 165; of the excluded middle, 160; self evident, 92-93.
privatio, 112.
probabiliter, 89.

proportio, 115.
propositio composita/divisa, 230-231; compared to *sensus compositus/sensus divisus*, 230.
proposition, and the structure of reality, 53-54; as token, 191; as type, 192, 194; cause of its truth, 43, 133; conditional p. 173, 206-208, 212, 227; its syntax compared to its meaning, 214; modality, 172; necessary p., 206; p. as object of human knowledge, 33; requirements for truth, 54; the number of true p. is always the same, 190, 192; truth condition, 159; truth value, 3, 160, 172, 185, 189-193, 197-199, 206, 211, 214, 224, 232, 245; p. has truth value only derivatively, 104; ambiguities in meaning, 244; its logical and formal status, 245.
proprietas sermonis, 205.
proprietates terminorum, 244.
providence, 163; connection with universal causality, 5, levels of, 5; structering effect of, 5.
providentia compared to *praevidentia*, 217.
puncta, 100.

quantity, 225; aspects of, 225; corporeal q. compared to spiritual q., 225; immense spiritual q. 225.
quidam doctor, 117, *modernus*, 223, 228.
quiddity, 89; irreducible, 27.
quiditas, 125, 127; *singularium*, 147.

ratio, 57, 137; *definitiva non ab anima fabricata*, 42.
rationabiliter, 95.
rational distinction, 49; definition (Ockham), 50; *ex parte ratiocinantis*, 37; *ex proprietate ipsius rei*, 37; in God, 36-37; *rationalitas*, 45.
rationalization of theology and philosophy, 242.
rationes, 43, 48, 60, 43, 79, 86, 89, 122, 139; *cognoscendi*, 135, 153, 186; *efficaces*, 221; *essentiales*, 155; *formales*, 43, 84; *ideales*, 123, 250; in God, 42; *reales*, 43.
real distinction, 39, 44, 49; between attributes, 52, 55, 56.
reales, 13.
realism, 12, 13, 147.
reality, its intelligibility, 236.

relatio, 79; *idealis*, 79, 82; *tertio modo*, 80-81.
relation, between accidents and subject, 124; its being follows that of the *relata*, 48, 137; knowledge of the r. dependens on knowledge of the *relata*, 81; only two types of, viz., rational and real, 79; rational, 79, 86, 96; real, 79.
relucentia, 153; relucere, 85, 153.
res, 122, 196, 213, 223; *contingens*, 157; *futura*, 196, 203.
respectus ideales, 132.
ruminatio communis modernorum, 120.

sacrament of the altar, 124.
Salamanca, 11, 12.
sancti antiqui, 52; *sancti doctores*, 60.
schola nominalistarum, 13.
scholastic texts, two distinct aspects of s., 237.
science, reflection on the status of s., 242.
scientia, approbationis, 113; *simplicis intelligentiae*, 113, 174; *simplicis notitiae*, 105, 106, 213, 217; *visionis*, 105, 106, 113, 174, 213, 217.
scire, 190.
Scotists, 42, 58, 84, 249-251.
semantic analysis, 118.
sensus compositus/sensus divisus, 165, 175, 183, 213-214, 230, 238, 244; and the syntactical structure of the proposition, 213.
separate substances, 92, 93.
sequaces, 58, 205, 253.
signa, 212, *naturae*, 84; *originis*, 84.
significare, 105; *significans*, 232; *significatum*, 37, 54, 232.
signum, 82.
similitudines, 135.
simplex apprehensio, 214.
simpliciter necessario, 206.
sin, 158, 196, 204, 221-222, 228, 232; distinction between the act and the sin self, 112.
singular things, are known by the senses, 78; cannot be known, 72; knowledge of s., 67;

two kinds of s., 67.
singularity, 70.
solar eclipse, 67-68, 157.
sophismata, 244.
Stoics, 5, 162, 219.
sufficient proof as defined by Ockham, 92.
sufficienter, 89.
superstitio logicalis, 215.
suppositio materialis, 55; *simplex*, 55.
syllogism, 242.
syntactic approach, 214.

terminative, 99.
terminus ampliativus, 153.
θελήματα, 155.
theologia anglicana, 210.
Thomists, 42.
Tivoli, 8.
transcendentals, 44.
treatises on the fallacies, 159.
Trinity, 39-40, 49, 54, 59, 84, 97, 225.

undoing the past, 161.
unity vs. plurality, 40, 41, 97, 239, 241-242.
universale, abstractum a singularibus, 147; *in essendo*, 147-148.
universalitas, ante rem, 145; *cum re*, 145.
universals, 12, 253.

velle/voluit, 229.
Venice, 18.
veritas determinata, 97, 187-188.
via, 84, 221-222; *antiquorum*, 13; *marsiliana*, 1, 10; *moderna*, 10, 12-13, 15; *modernorum*, 13.
viae of pseudo-Dionysius, 25.
vigor, 111, 114, 116.
virtus sermonis, 51, 139, 213.
visio, 105.
voces, 55.
voluntates, 154-155.

Wegestreit, 12-13, 253.
wisdom, 43, 53, 55-57, 59.

Studies in the History of Christian Thought

EDITED BY HEIKO A. OBERMAN

1. McNEILL, J. J. *The Blondelian Synthesis.* 1966. Out of print
2. GOERTZ, H.-J. *Innere und äussere Ordnung in der Theologie Thomas Müntzers.* 1967
3. BAUMAN, Cl. *Gewaltlosigkeit im Täufertum.* 1968
4. ROLDANUS, J. *Le Christ et l'Homme dans la Théologie d'Athanase d'Alexandrie.* 2nd ed. 1977
5. MILNER, Jr., B. Ch. *Calvin's Doctrine of the Church.* 1970. Out of print
6. TIERNEY, B. *Origins of Papal Infallibility, 1150-1350.* 2nd ed. 1988
7. OLDFIELD, J. J. *Tolerance in the Writings of Félicité Lamennais 1809-1831.* 1973
8. OBERMAN, H. A. (ed.) *Luther and the Dawn of the Modern Era.* 1974. Out of print
9. HOLECZEK, H. *Humanistische Bibelphilologie bei Erasmus, Thomas More und William Tyndale.* 1975
10. FARR, W. *John Wyclif as Legal Reformer.* 1974
11. PURCELL, M. *Papal Crusading Policy 1244-1291.* 1975
12. BALL, B. W. *A Great Expectation.* Eschatological Thought in English Protestantism. 1975
13. STIEBER, J. W. *Pope Eugenius IV, the Council of Basel, and the Empire.* 1978. Out of print
14. PARTEE, Ch. *Calvin and Classical Philosophy.* 1977
15. MISNER, P. *Papacy and Development.* Newman and the Primacy of the Pope. 1976
16. TAVARD, G. H. *The Seventeenth-Century Tradition.* A Study in Recusant Thought. 1978
17. QUINN, A. *The Confidence of British Philosophers.* An Essay in Historical Narrative. 1977
18. BECK, J. *Le Concil de Basle (1434).* 1979
19. CHURCH, F. F. and GEORGE, T. (ed.) *Continuity and Discontinuity in Church History.* 1979
20. GRAY, P. T. R. *The Defense of Chalcedon in the East (451-553).* 1979
21. NIJENHUIS, W. *Adrianus Saravia (c. 1532-1613).* Dutch Calvinist. 1980
22. PARKER, T. H. L. (ed.) *Iohannis Calvini Commentarius in Epistolam Pauli ad Romanos.* 1981
23. ELLIS, I. *Seven Against Christ.* A Study of 'Essays and Reviews'. 1980
24. BRANN, N. L. *The Abbot Trithemius (1462-1516).* 1981
25. LOCHER, G. W. *Zwingli's Thought.* New Perspectives. 1981
26. GOGAN, B. *The Common Corps of Christendom.* Ecclesiological Themes in Thomas More. 1982
27. STOCK, U. *Die Bedeutung der Sakramente in Luthers Sermonen von 1519.* 1982
28. YARDENI, M. (ed.) *Modernité et nonconformisme en France à travers les âges.* 1983
29. PLATT, J. *Reformed Thought and Scholasticism.* 1982
30. WATTS, P. M. *Nicolaus Cusanus.* A Fifteenth-Century Vision of Man. 1982
31. SPRUNGER, K. L. *Dutch Puritanism.* 1982
32. MEIJERING, E. P. *Melanchthon and Patristic Thought.* 1983
33. STROUP, J. *The Struggle for Identity in the Clerical Estate.* 1984
34. 35. COLISH, M. L. *The Stoic Tradition from Antiquity to the Early Middle Ages.* 1.2. 2nd ed. 1990
36. GUY, B. *Domestic Correspondence of Dominique-Marie Varlet, Bishop of Babylon, 1678-1742.* 1986
37. 38. CLARK, F. *The Pseudo-Gregorian Dialogues.* I. II. 1987
39. PARENTE, Jr., J. A. *Religious Drama and the Humanist Tradition.* 1987
40. POSTHUMUS MEYJES, G. H. M. *Hugo Grotius, Meletius.* 1988
41. FELD, H. *Der Ikonoklasmus des Westens.* 1990
42. REEVE, A. and SCREECH, M.A. (eds.) *Erasmus' Annotations on the New Testament.* 1990
43. KIRBY, W.J.T. *Richard Hooker's Doctrine of the Royal Supremacy.* 1990
44. GERSTNER, J.N. *The Thousand Generation Covenant.* Reformed Covenant Theology. 1990
45. CHRISTIANSON, G. and IZBICKI, T.M. (eds.) *Nicholas of Cusa.* 1991
46. GARSTEIN, O. *Rome and the Counter-Reformation in Scandinavia.* 1553-1622. 1992
47. GARSTEIN, O. *Rome and the Counter-Reformation in Scandinavia.* 1622-1656. 1992
48. PERRONE COMPAGNI, V. (ed.) *Cornelius Agrippa, De occulta philosophia Libri tres.* 1992
49. MARTIN, D.D. *Fifteenth-Century Carthusian Reform.* The World of Nicholas Kempf. 1992
50. HOENEN, M.J.F.M. *Marsilius of Inghen.* Divine Knowledge in Late Medieval Thought. 1993

Prospectus available on request

E. J. BRILL — P.O.B. 9000 — 2300 PA LEIDEN — THE NETHERLANDS

DATE DUE

HIGHSMITH 45-220